ADVANCE PR

"Someone needed to finally [...] Joe Biden threw away the most secure border in modern [...] and left America increasingly open and vulnerable to a vast and complex set of threats from outside its borders. The U.S. media has abdicated its solemn duty to acknowledge, let alone report, the devastating truth behind the worst border crisis in our lifetime. But thankfully, Todd Bensman finally brings people right into the heart of what happened and is still happening. I know Bensman's border reporting. The nation needs to know it too so that the next generation of elected leaders has a roadmap to end the destruction."

–**Mark Morgan**, former Acting Commissioner of U.S. Immigration and Customs Enforcement July 2019–January 2021

"When we look back at this time during the history of immigration in America, Todd's work reporting, researching, observing, and chronicling what is actually happening on America's southern border will go down as the gold standard. While others work on hyperbole and political opinion, Todd is reporting what is taking place at major border crossings, why the border is experiencing border swells, and how immigration patterns change based on U.S. policy. Everyone interested in border security should read his book."

–**Kristina Tanasichuk**, Executive Editor of *Homeland Security Today*

"The U.S.–Mexico border is an opaque landscape populated with human traffickers, international terror suspects, migrant children and American law enforcement agents. No one truly understands how it all intersects: from the marbled corridors of power to the arid smuggling routes of the desert. Bensman is as close as it gets. With boots on the ground, Bensman paints a portrait that is as thrilling as it is outrageous. Written with a sharp pen, this is a must-read for anyone trying to understand one of the most important issues of our time."

–**Charlie LeDuff**, Pulitzer Prize–winning former *New York Times* reporter and host of the *No BS News Hour* podcast

"I have been involved in immigration enforcement and border security since 1984 and have closely followed Todd Bensman's work.... He tells the truth about illegal immigration and how it is not a victimless crime. With immigration issues being front and center for the American people now, his book is an absolute must read."

-**Thomas Homan**, former Acting Director of U.S. Immigration and Customs Enforcement January 2017–August 2018

"Todd Bensman presents the astonishing story of how the administration of President Joe Biden has allowed pragmatic policy to be canceled by ideological forces of the open-borders left that now dominate the Democratic Party. Bensman takes his readers into the world of the migrants who are being drawn—hundreds of thousands every month—to the southern border of the U.S. by what some glowingly call Biden's 'invocation.' His book is a public service for every American who wants border policies that are based in an understanding of the difference between generosity and recklessness, between reasonable limits and chaos in the name of boundless compassion."

-**Jerry Kammer**, Pulitzer Prize-winning reporter and author of the book *Losing Control: How a Left-Right Coalition Blocked Immigration Reform and Provoked the Backlash That Elected Trump*

"Todd Bensman is one of the only journalists in America who has been willing to spend significant time on both sides of the border, chronicle and analyze events with an unflinching eye, and tell the truth about what's happening. His reportage on the historic and ongoing border crisis is essential right now, not just because so few media outlets will cover it, but because if the American people aren't told the truth, we won't be able to stop it."

-**John Daniel Davidson**, Senior Editor of *The Federalist*

ALSO BY TODD BENSMAN

America's Covert Border War: The Untold Story of the Nation's Battle to Prevent Jihadist Indiltration

OVERRUN

HOW JOE BIDEN UNLEASHED
THE GREATEST BORDER CRISIS
IN U.S. HISTORY

TODD BENSMAN

BOMBARDIER
BOOKS

Published by Bombardier Books
An Imprint of Post Hill Press
ISBN: 978-1-63758-570-2
ISBN (eBook): 978-1-63758-571-9

Overrun:
How Joe Biden Unleashed the Greatest Border Crisis in U.S.
History
© 2023 by Todd Bensman
All Rights Reserved

Cover Design by Cody Corcoran

Cover Photo by Auden Cabello

Photography by Ciudad Acuna Mexico

Interior Design by Yoni Limor

Post Hill Press
New York • Nashville
posthillpress.com

Published in the United States of America
1 2 3 4 5 6 7 8 9 10

TABLE OF CONTENTS

PART III
OVERRUN

PART IV
SCHIZOPHRENIA

I dedicate this book to Bessie "Bubbe" Galsky,
my great-grandmother who immigrated to America.
May her memory be a blessing.

INTRODUCTION

"LA INVITACIÓN"

> *"Immigration is tough. It always has been because, on the one hand, I think we are naturally a people that wants to help others. And we see tragedy and hardship and families that are desperately trying to get here so that their kids are safe.... At the same time, we're a nation state. We have borders. The idea that we can just have open borders is something that is, as a practical matter, unsustainable."*
>
> —Barack Obama, September 28, 2021, interview, *Good Morning America*[1]

I first spotted twenty-three-year-old Jose Antonio listening to mariachi music on a truck stereo and drinking from cans of beer with a group in the deep shade beneath the four-lane international bridge connecting the Mexican town of Ojinaga to Presidio in wild West Texas.

Tall and narrow-shouldered, he spoke through crooked discolored teeth, offering me, after some time, the two women who were with him—who I'd already guessed were hookers—and, then, some of the small, brilliant white block of cocaine they were snorting. Just down an embankment from where we

11

stood, the blue-green Rio Grande burbled pleasantly around enormous white pillars that supported both sides of the split bridge. Vehicles clunk-clunked as they passed overhead on their way to either city. The shade offered cool respite from the sweaty afternoon sun that April 2021.

I'd come to Ojinaga because the flood of immigrants launching from the region around it and into West Texas was booming to historic heights, in numbers far beyond all living memory for that area. I had stumbled across Jose and his group while looking for people who might be able to illuminate what was happening. He was exactly the right guy for that.

Aside from its place in Chihuahua State's storied, generational drug-smuggling trade, Ojinaga was famed because Pancho Villa fought a battle here in 1914 that a Hollywood movie studio actually filmed in real time.[2] More than one hundred years later, I was there to report about this new smuggling product for my Washington, DC, employer, the Center for Immigration Studies and its Beltway audience. Noting his smiles, I figured that Jose and I must have hit it off. This sparked a tightening of panic under my breastbone given that my translator had just informed me he was a foot guide, or *guia*, for the ultra-violent La Linea cartel. I began calculating how to say no thanks to both the women and the coke, without risking suspicion that I was police, which might lead to a wrong outcome. Was he armed? I couldn't tell. I spied a wood-handled shovel amid the trash in the bed of his pickup. Could I grab it?

This impromptu meeting broke one of my top personal security codes: Avoid Cartel People at All Costs. I felt torn between staying and running. I'd developed that rule during my years as a Texas-based newspaper reporter covering cartel drug wars and gun smuggling along the border and from all I'd learned from my subsequent near-decade working the border for the Texas Department of Public Safety's Intelligence and Counterterrorism Division.

I knew all too well that every cartel member must be considered mortally dangerous. Even low-level foot guides like Jose had cell phones or radios to instantly report to bosses. Once a call went out about a gringo claiming to be interested in cartel business affairs, vehicles could quickly screech up to block your way, with gunmen ordering you out of yours and into theirs. Among them might well be the unpredictable, impulsive, and probably coked-up killer types known for going postal without orders.

I'd traveled into cartel country with a rough-hewn garrulous fifty-something fellow gringo named Chris Leland, who served as interpreter and guide. Chris was the perfect choice for this duty as a lifelong back-and-forth border denizen who'd grown up as a hunter and Rio Grande running guide. I'd asked him to help me find immigrants who could tell me firsthand why their numbers had more than tripled of late. Border Patrol, which typically caught 3,000 to 4,000 crossing there in any given quarter, had caught a whopping 14,091 in the first quarter of 2021. But I couldn't find any to interview. Despite their ubiquity on the streets of other Mexican cities farther south, here they were under the control of La Linea. The syndicate kept them hidden in local stash houses and motels until "go" time.

Over in Texas, big columns of them, fifty or a hundred at a time, were getting caught during their ten-day clandestine backpacking treks through the desert wilderness. I later learned that most of the migrants were young, fit Central American men who'd mustered La Linea's price tag of $10,000 or $12,000 each for the run.

That day, hours of hunting interviewees yielded nothing; one group of seven we spotted on the street from their telltale backpacks first agreed to be interviewed and then suddenly sprinted away. A bit later, we discovered Jose and his tailgate party under the bridge and approached. Fortunately, one of the men with Jose recognized Chris as a regular customer at a mechanic's shop in town and enthusiastically greeted him. Both men spoke in Spanish over the truck stereo music, with Chris pausing to translate, telling me that Jose was a guia just back from a trek guiding migrants on foot through the desert.

Suddenly, Jose was on his cell phone with someone. A chill swept over me. Under my breath, I told Chris that we could get out of this quickly if we simply got in the vehicle and drove straight onto the bridge, ten feet overhead. Atop the bridge, I'd just seen a parked U.S. Customs and Border Patrol vehicle with blue uniformed American officers standing by it. But from where we stood below, they'd be of no help whatsoever. On Mexican turf, ten feet may as well be a thousand miles.

Jose hung up and said something to Chris, who turned to me and relayed, "Jose is willing for you to interview him. That was him on with his boss, and they said, 'Sure, go ahead.'"

So we stayed. Despite the risks, getting to interview a cartel human smuggler about business was rare. Jose began telling me about the enormous economic windfall the immigrants were creating for La Linea in just the past few months and how he was about to buy a brand-new truck.

"What do you owe all this to—the money and all the new business?" I asked him.

He looked at me and shrugged, turning both palms up:

"La invitación."

La invitación.

"What's that?" I asked.

He explained that la invitación is what he and his cartel buddies were calling the newly elected President Joe Biden's welcome to immigrants to cross the border illegally and stay. He then offered, unsolicited, that one of Biden's early moves had proven especially inviting: the new president ended interior deportations so that ICE officers would leave his clients alone once they'd gotten into American cities to live and work in peace.

News had spread quickly around the world that Biden's follow-through on his "deportation moratorium" promise during the campaign had indeed defanged and grounded ICE officers at their desks. In response to that extraordinary development, Jose explained, people were coming in droves and paying fortunes for his services.

He had never seen anything like it. Business in Mexico's Chihuahua State was *"como nunca!"*—like never before—Jose said. He and his crew in the cartel couldn't keep up. Every house in the region was packed with smuggled human beings.

"They come in from all over Central America, Haiti, Africa, Indonesia, and from all over South America," Jose explained, leaning into a snort from the flattened head of a sixteen-penny nail, smiling at his new good fortune.

"They just keep coming and keep coming and keep coming."

Blame

Within a very short span of time, before and right after Biden's November 2020 election, *"La Invitación"* set off the greatest mass immigration border crisis in American history. The aim of this book is to provide a first account of it, a building block to document, clarify, and provide reverse-engineered insight about what happened. The crisis is still unfolding, a history in the making.

At the same time, strangely, the causes of the events at the heart of this book are in dispute. The political smoke around them is so thick that many Americans are left unsure that anything out of the ordinary happened at all. When they acknowledged on rare occasions that something unusual *was* happening along America's long southern border, Democratic politicians, "immigration experts," and media punditry often blamed "root causes" like a "broken immigration system," gang violence in Guatemala, a presidential assassination in Haiti, hurricanes in Honduras, or regular seasonal changes. More often, media reporters and politicians denied anything unusual was happening.

For example, on March 25, 2021, just days before I interviewed Jose, the *Washington Post* reported on the 221,000 illegal immigrants who poured over the border that month, breaking all previous national records, by claiming there was "no clear evidence that the overall increase in border crossings in 2021 can be attributed to Biden administration policies." [3] Rather, the story found, "the current increase fits a pattern of seasonal changes in undocumented immigration...."

My reporting, based on immigrant testimony, repudiates all of this. It shows that only Biden's messaging about warm welcomes and good treatment, and then the follow-through policies, were la invitación that sparked off a mass migration that quickly broke every U.S. record and still goes on amid widespread denial. The "root causes" of poverty, bad governance, and crime in home countries that Democrats invoke to explain why immigrants feel pushed to jump the border are certainly real. But those factors—and U.S. employer hiring—do not change quickly enough to explain the monthly, quarterly, and yearly ebbs and flows of mass rushes and retreats. Policy changes in Washington or the American courts do that, as I will prove through the interviews of those it impacts most: the immigrants.

Jose's story jibed with what U.S.-bound immigrants already had been telling me for months before the American election, that they felt any Democrat president would invite them to come. So they did, even before the November 2020 election.

I first discovered and reported the phenomenon during a trip to deep southern Mexico and Guatemala—nine months before America's national election, in late January 2020. At the time, Trump had mixed up an unusual cocktail of deportation and asylum-restriction policies that had reduced apprehension numbers to low, manageable levels. In fact, I'd gone to the migrant trail waystation of Tapachula in the state of Chiapas to observe the extent to which one of those deterrence policies was responsible for sharply reduced immigrant flows: the Mexican national guard deployment of 6,000 soldiers at fifty roadblocks leading from the Guatemalan border. Mexico's troops were pulling migrants from buses and trucks, sending them back to Central America, blocking northward advances. Apprehension tallies at the U.S. border were way down.

I expected to find hardly any U.S.-bound immigrants crossing in from Guatemala. But instead of the expected sleepy Tapachula streets, I found crowds of hope-filled Central American women and children, Cubans, Pakistanis, and Haitians pouring into town, socializing and hustling in the city's downtown central plaza. They were waiting in government lines, filling cheap restaurants, and occupying every room at down-at-the-heel roach motels.

To find out why, I waded into a large immigrant crowd of hundreds concentrated outside a government detention facility, waiting for their turn before a bureaucrat behind a sliding window. All were holding temporary visa permission slips that the Trump administration pushed the Mexican government to require them to issue under pain of bus deportation by the national guard and Mexican immigration officers. They were there to get a weekly renewal stamp to prove they were still in town waiting for final Mexican asylum claim decisions. Once asylum grants came a few months later, they'd be free to pass through the roadblocks and keep going north.

A young, well-dressed and -groomed Honduran woman holding an infant in the line provided the first surprising explanation. Katherine Cabrera said she had decided to suffer through the endless bureaucracy because, once she got her Mexican asylum months from now, she'd be in place in northern Mexico for when a Democrat prevailed in the American election like all the polls were saying would happen.

"Wait, what?" I asked somewhat surprised to hear such a sophisticated calculation.

"I want Trump out. I'll wait for that because it would make things easier to get in," she said simply, explaining the reasoning behind the gambit.

Her logic struck me instantly. Of course! For the last couple of months, a dozen Democratic primary contenders were on televised debate stages promising all illegal border crossers red carpet welcomes, citizenship, an end to deportation, free health care, no detention…

Even if many Americans had tuned out the debates, the rest of the world had listened to every word of them. Most polls said Trump was definitely going to lose.

I spent the next week posing the same question to dozens of other immigrants sweating their way through Mexico's months-long bureaucratic requirements. Almost to a person, they provided the same Trump-defeat calculus, like Honduran

Wilson Valladaras. The plan, he told me, was to get a Mexican asylum claim approved, use the papers to move to Tijuana "until Trump leaves," then cross over the border when any one of those Democrats undid his policies because "right now, the Americans will throw you back" to Mexico.

Even that early, before Biden emerged to win the nomination, immigrants were hearing "la invitación."[4] They'd seen every candidate raise their hand—Biden and Kamala Harris among them—when asked if they'd give free health care to illegal immigrants and decriminalize border crossing. Recalling those debate stage moments, I asked five migrant women from Central America to raise a hand if they came to wait in Mexico this early to be in place for when Trump suffered defeat at the ballot box. All five raised a hand without hesitation.

"A lot of people in El Salvador believe he [Trump] is the reason all this is happening, that he is selfish and cruel and doing everything he can to make us suffer," El Salvadoran Brenda Ramos told me. "But once Trump is defeated and the Democrats take over, things are going to get better."

In cutting through the fog, this book relies on primary interviews with hundreds of immigrants like them who were on their way or just arrived, Border Patrol agents, law enforcement, migrant advocate statements, Mexican officials, current and former American officials, and the few other journalists with thousands of hours in the field. It draws on the experiences of people who lived these events on both sides of the border horizontally from Matamoros and Brownsville to Tijuana and San Diego, and laterally to Mexico's southern border, Guatemala, Costa Rica, and Nicaragua. When it makes sense, I present what I personally witnessed, photographed, videotaped, and recorded as audio from the field. But for anyone to understand the larger event in context, I offer some buttressing policy history and explanatory analysis. Bear with me on that. It'll be worth it.

If my on-the-ground narratives sometimes come off as complicated and confusing, that's because I endeavored to mirror the mixed fiats spilling out of the White House and courts into the borderlands. The end result is what matters: millions of foreign nationals saw it all as opportunity and joined Club America in the Biden administration's first two fiscal years alone. They were still coming in increasingly large swells after the November 2022 midterm elections, when voters in states where Republican candidates campaigned hard to end the border crisis won their offices but not in most other states. Polls leading up to that election did show the under-covered border catastrophe had finally begun to register with the American people, who ranked it among the top three problems of highest concern behind inflation and the economy. But the aftermath of that election did not cut the Democratic Party very deeply, not enough to prompt a change in border policy trajectory.

Asked by an *Associated Press* reporter after the election what he might change, Biden replied: "Nothing. Because they're just finding out what we're doing. The more they find out what we're doing, the more support there is."

And so the crisis was poised to continue and worsen for at least the final two years of the Biden term. My hope is that, as millions more are admitted at the border ahead of the 2024 national presidential election, this book maps out the roads that America traveled into the crisis, resolves disputes about what really happened, and clears the window fog. May this book serve as a comprehensive reference guide should Americans and their leaders decide to debate whether to reverse course— or even stay on it—as the new millions enter the nation.

Bubbe and the Refuseniks

Readers who want to learn about issues highly disputed along partisan lines deserve to know at least something of the qualifications, worldview, and biases of those claiming the credentials to teach. I started working on the border during a twenty-year career as a newspaper reporter. From 2006 through 2009, I published long-form investigative stories about Mexico's civil drug war, which claimed about 200,000

Mexican lives and quite a few American ones. Two multi-part series won National Press Club awards, one about cartel gun-smuggling and another about international smuggling networks that were bringing over Iraqis and other Middle Easterners. After that, the Texas Department of Public Safety recruited me to work in the Intelligence & Counterterrorism Division. I was there for the next decade as an analyst and manager of analysts. Then, I went to work as an analyst for the Center for Immigration Studies. Among all those jobs, I met and interviewed thousands of immigrants. I have teased out their stories in ICE detention centers for law enforcement purposes. I have sat with them all night at their fires. I have broken bread with them. I have followed them on jungle trails, bought them meals, found them shelter, lent them my cell phone, and given them rides. Most importantly, I have listened to their life stories, hopes, dreams, truths and lies.

No human being, including a somewhat jaundiced, cynical reporter like me, can possibly help but empathize with their plights.

I understand in more than one way. My family's own story, my chapter at least and those of the few generations above me, is defined by the lure of leaving one's home for better lands.

I enjoyed an upper middle class Jewish upbringing in Houston until I was thirteen and then in Phoenix when my family moved there. My great-grandmother, Bessie Galsky, lived in our family home for five years in both border states as I was growing up through middle school. We called her "Bubbe," Yiddish for grandmother. All my great-grandparents legally emigrated from the Pale of Settlement, an area covering today's Ukraine and many former Soviet countries that unleashed soldiers and militias to frequently attack them. Few other countries in the world would take Jews in, and Israel had not yet come into being. As a young girl, Bubbe traveled with her father, a rabbi, through Ellis Island to America. Despite my own entreaties as a kid, she never would talk about the Czarist persecutions—the notorious pogroms—that spurred the families to flee and which we all well knew from movies like *Fiddler on the Roof*.

She kept a black-and-white photo of her father on the wall, an unsmiling, long-bearded, narrow man wearing a broadcloth suit who could have played a Talmudic scholar in *Fiddler*. For a classroom assignment in grade school, we were to record a grandparent recalling childhood memories. But when I placed the tape recorder microphone in front of Bubbe, she said nothing. This is a phenomenon common in many immigrant Jewish families. She insisted she couldn't remember, even though she was old enough to speak Russian and Yiddish when her family emigrated. I believe she knew all too well what happened but simply could not bear to remember.

To this day, I'm disappointed that conversation never happened.

We always knew we lived in America because of Bubbe and all my other great-grandparents who left the Pale of Settlement. We got here because of the American open-door policy in the early 1900s that, legally, allowed millions of persecuted Jews from the Pale with nowhere else to go to immigrate here. In the mid-1970s, my parents were part of an organization that helped resettle "Refuseniks," Jewish families the Soviet Union harassed, fired from jobs, and imprisoned for seeking exit visas to Israel and the United States. In our family home, after international pressure forced the Soviet government to release some, Refuseniks were part of the fabric of holidays and gatherings. Bubbe enjoyed using her Russian language with them.

Most of the migrants at the heart of this book, however, are *not* like Bubbe and the Refuseniks actually fleeing real and imminent persecutions, who came in with U.S. government permission on authorized ships and planes. New arrivals at our southern border are crossing a guarded perimeter uninvited, without permission. They are not fleeing their continent's version of Cossack raids and communist apparatchiks eager to imprison them and with no other sanctuary.

Instead, most are fleeing poverty, local crime, and poor governance, which unfortunately describes the common conditions of billions of people throughout the world that the United States simply cannot take in. I see the difference between legal invitation and illegal unauthorized entry as significant distinctions that require separate outlooks and redress. And, in fact, so does prevailing law. Intending border-crossers cannot be cast in monolithic terms as their many liberal champions always seem to do in stateside media and in the parlors of Washington. The stereotype overlooks that some are aggressive, criminal, and dishonest to the core. A great many are just regular people born in a poor country and willing to bend a few rules, maybe tell a few white lies, to live in a rich one. So-called "immigration experts" who have spent far less time with their subjects like to cast all of them as fleeing certain death like Bubbe's family, thereby invoking a pressing moral duty to call them "asylum seekers" and improperly admit them. That narrative is mostly wrong. This book will detail at length how they and their advocates widely use it to defraud and abuse America's asylum system, the one set up for the Refuseniks of the world, on a massive scale. By hook or by crook, the vast majority of the people I've met were grabbing for more material wealth, free education, and the famed indulgent American lifestyle.

To a limited point, I empathize with these immigrants as somewhat similar to the determined peoples who hit the wilderness trails during California's Gold Rush in the 1850s, traveled in westward-bound wagon trains, or trudged up the Yukon's glacial Klondike Trail in the late 1890s to reach the new gold fields. Those early adventurers and settlers were not fleeing certain death back in Tennessee or Pennsylvania when they outfitted a wagon or mule. Instead, they risked it all going *toward* more prosperity. It's a pattern that has been repeated throughout history, from early Spanish to French explorers of the New World, who dreamed of Incan gold or fountains of youth. People have always gambled life for just the possibility of better fortunes; that gamble is hardly flight from unbearable persecutions. Like economic immigrants trudging through the Darien Gap of Panama today, the early American settlers who took to the wagon trails braved death by harsh elements, hostile attack by Native Americans, drowning, robbery, wild animal attack, and illness.

Had I been born in Haiti, Honduras, Cuba, or Ghana facing a joyless life of impoverished sameness with no hope of upside or chance to realize personal potential, I might be neck and neck with them on the trail heading for an American border crossing. But therein lies the line of tension in my own point of reference: my compassion for anyone motivated to better themselves and my respect for rule of law. I part company with them over what they intend for their very first acts of joining America, which is to break the 1996 law against illegal entry, lie to defraud U.S. asylum laws, and then live illegally for years. This should strike anyone as disqualifying first impressions.

Unlike my great-grandparents and the Refuseniks, their dishonorable intention is to foist themselves on unwilling hosts who did not invite them, break American law, and personally profit in spite of the legislated will of United States citizens. For their own reasons, which this book will examine extensively in chapter four, political partisans on the American left dishonestly gloss over the distinctions between legal and illegal, conflating them into something just called "immigration." America is, they want their audience to believe, one big amorphous "nation of immigrants," the Honduran and my Bubbe one and the same. But they are not. America should only be a nation of *legal* immigrants who were invited and stamped for approval under the laws and practices of our times.

This brings us to how my nine-year homeland security intelligence career for Texas DPS informs my views, which start with an abiding belief that America occupies moral high ground as a "nation of law." The country is diminished when duly approved laws reflecting the will of Americans are not followed. Also my homeland security career informs a hyperawareness of national security risk created when millions of people from around the world enter as complete strangers, often without even identification.

My daily job for many long years required that I detect, manage, think deeply about, and predict national security threats that had not yet materialized. By training and practice, I see public safety and national security dangers when millions of total strangers of unknowable repute cross the southern border and start living in the country from 150 different nations, as the greatest number are now. I'll explain why in chapters eleven, twelve, and thirteen why risk to national interests rise when so many origin countries are rife with terrorist organizations, tribal warlords, atrocity-committing militias, organized crime gangs, and adversarial spies.

Because of these influencing experiences, I also wonder how a country of 330 million wants to regulate its gates if hundreds of millions more decide on their own volitions to enter? Behind the current overwhelming flood of immigrants, that's how many are watching our response. As many as three-quarters of a billion people that America simply cannot practically absorb—many of whom are also paying attention to headlines and gauging political winds—would want to line up down-trail to follow the success they observe of those up-trail. At least 700 million people around the world live in extreme poverty at any given time.[5] The United Nations' 2021 Global Multidimensional Poverty Index reports that 1.3 billion people are "multidimensionally poor," a measure of nine main indicators of health, education, and standards of living.[6]

I get how difficult it can be to look desirous people in the eye and say, "No, you have to leave." A Haitian man in northern Mexico coming in the current mass migration asked me if I thought the Americans would let him stay when he crossed. When I told him there was a good chance he'd find himself on a flight back to Haiti, he looked away and wept. I felt the lump form in my throat. But that difficult duty must be done, like other unpleasant government duties required for civilizational stability such as warfare, eviction, eminent domain, animal shelter euthanasia, and sentencing the convicted to prison.

No nation's citizens can cede their inalienable nationhood right to say how many get to come simply because immigrants demand it and especially, when refused entry, they *seize* it in disrespect for American laws and rules. Nations have rights, among them to decide who gets to join them. Why should America be the only nation that has ever existed to open its borders wide to anyone?

I lay most fault for this historic crisis more so on enablers in the Biden White House and the present Democratic Party iteration than on the immigrants of squishy personal integrity, who rationally respond to unlocked doors left open on purpose. One of this book's central theses is that today's Democratic Party has taken a wholesale leave of its senses. It has abandoned its own long-held commitment to oppose, impede, and end mass migrations with strong border security measures as a duty of national sovereignty. Only a short time ago, Democrats in practice shared many ideals with the Republicans about controlling illegal immigration as a routine matter of national security and sovereignty. But in 2020, a radical faction of the party took it and the nation on a wild ride into a most bizarre political experiment. Chapter four is dedicated to how these "new theologians" of an extreme political religion gained power over border policy and neutralized all the nation's immigration laws for the first time ever.

In dismantling these protections, Democrats—wittingly or unwittingly—loosed literally millions of the world's neediest over those borders in a stratospheric and ongoing cavalcade like nothing that I or the most grizzled veteran Border Patrol agents have ever witnessed. This story is not over. But what the Democrats did has already yielded enough lessons for Americans to write its final chapters in the coming years.

PART I

SOWING SEEDS OF CHAOS

"It makes sense that no great nation can be in a position where they can't control their borders. It matters how you control your borders...not just for immigration, but for drugs, terror, a whole range of other things."

—Senator Joe Biden, August 12, 2007,
campaign stop in Winterset, Iowa[7]

CHAPTER ONE

MEET THE NEW PAGE IN U.S. HISTORY

On a late spring night on the Rio Grande, beyond the lights of the nearby historic Spanish colonial town of Roma on the Texas side, I witnessed what could only be best described as a Normandy-like D-Day invasion, which had turned the order of the natural world on its head. It was May 2021, and I had hiked downhill by flashlight about a mile to the river along a white-sand road to see one of many South Texas epicenters of immigrant landings.

Through the last tree line, I heard the river and spotted beams of law enforcement flashlights darting over water and rocky shoreline. I headed for them and saw, exposed, an astonishing scene. Mexican cartel-piloted rafts were moving three, four, and five abreast toward American officers and soldiers standing on the Texas shoreline where they would land. Mostly women and children, many wearing masks and even life vests, weighted down each boat as shirtless cartel pilots in shorts furiously paddled. The rafts had been arriving wave after wave like this from the first day that a new U.S. president had taken office, night after night for five months now. The scene was strikingly different than anything I had ever seen before. The raft formations hit the boulder-strewn Texas waterline feet from American law enforcement officers and soldiers, who stood passively as the migrants poured out in front of them. The cartel paddlers, all business, would nod or exchange a few words with the uniformed Americans, then push back out into the water to clear the beach for incoming rafts.

The raft landings encountered no Normandy-like opposition on the Texas beaches. Badged, uniformed Border Patrol agents, National Guard soldiers, and often local law enforcement officers, all side arms holstered, acted as a welcoming committee. The officers chatted amiably with their former cartel adversaries and accepted the immigrant handoffs like relay racers accepting a baton from teammates with a first-name collegiality that comes with routine and time. They helpfully shined powerful flashlights at the rocky riverbank, lest one of the surrendering migrant women or children trip over something and get hurt.

"How many more ya got over there?" a Border Patrol agent at the water's edge asked a cartel member who was paddling his raft back to the Mexican side.

"Cinco o seis, mi amigo," the pilot called back. Five or six.

Always in the past, raft pilots had to duck, hide, pick less convenient camouflaged crossing spots, find just the right moments, consult by radio with scouts, then cross and drop loads only when no cops were around. The migrants weren't running and evading capture, either. They delivered themselves compliantly to the arrayed Americans, who had been ordered from above to abdicate normal instinct to pursue and capture. Down here, gravity itself may just as well have been turned off. I was witnessing an organized machine unlike anything that any of them, or I, had ever experienced on the border. Here, criminal cartels were in a consummated partnership with federal law enforcement officers in an organized smuggling enterprise that was still earning the cartels billions of dollars.

After one boat unloaded, I ambled over to some Texas National Guard soldiers loitering in the blackness of the night at a Humvee outpost twenty yards behind me, a camouflage drape overhead. They carried semiautomatic rifles and wore flak jackets.

"So, what's going to happen now?" I asked after one of the nearby boats emptied everyone out in the dark.

"Just what you saw," one answered. "I mean, I can't do anything about it."

"Well," I replied, "why don't you guys just tackle the smugglers or something?"

"You would think, right? We're just here to count—all night."

On the other side, mothers, fathers, and children made no attempt to conceal their presence as they would have before 2021. Families and children noisily waited in a line that stretched up the Mexican riverbank and disappeared into a blackness slashed by flashlight beams at every angle. Moms chattered. Children cried, screamed, and laughed. I and every officer around could hear air pumps inflate plastic rafts. These squeaked and squawked as the immigrants boarded. That same night but at a different river crossing spot downstream, a Border Patrol agent busily processing immigrants asked a nearby Texas Department of Public Safety officer to escort several raft-loads about to disembark onto American soil.

"Don't make an arrest," the federal agent, a supervisor, advised the state police officer about the raft pilot. "We aren't doing that. Just leave him be."

I'd overheard it. Why such a request from a U.S. Border Patrol field supervisor, I asked the DPS officer that May 2021 night as we walked to the spot where the raft would land, right to where a National Guard Humvee was parked and its crew stood at ease. That's how the new White House wanted it, the state officer explained. All the federal agents on the river were operating under this arrest stand-down nowadays because President Biden's Department of Homeland Security had decided to let in immigrant families and children, rather than block, detain, prosecute, or deport them as was always at least the goal under past presidents.

"They know [federal prosecutors] won't prosecute; they'll let them go and they'll just be right back," the officer said of the cartel raft pilots. "The Border Patrol agents stop them because they have no backing, none whatsoever. So, there's no use."

The nonbelligerence arrangement struck me as troubling in another way. The immigrants were arriving with in-your-face evidence that it was fabulously enriching Mexico's drug smuggling cartels.

Every migrant exiting a raft wore a numbered, colored wrist band, like what water parks provide, but these bore symbols of a dark purpose. So many migrants were coming that the cartels had been forced to devise an inventory control system to make sure they all paid. They had to buy these wrist bands to prove $2,500–$9,000 smuggling ticket purchases. Even infants had bands tied around tiny ankles. Many tore them off once in Texas, and these littered the waterfront and dirt trails leading up to Roma. It could not have been more obvious to the American greeters what they were abetting and who their new partners were: ticket-punching final delivery in an illegal service enriching murdering thugs on the other side. The American officers could barely stand the knowledge and humiliation.

For them, the orders went from bad on the river to worse just beyond it. Whereas immigration law requires all illegally crossing immigrants to be kept for as long as necessary in ICE detention centers until they can be deported, the Border Patrol agents were manning field processing stations set up just a bit inland, prepping the new arrivals to skip detention entirely for quick releases instead to all four corners of America. The stations might consist of some plastic tables and chairs in a field, sometimes just an open tail gate of a Border Patrol vehicle. At about 2 a.m., I hiked up to one of these in a vacant Roma neighborhood lot. At least 400 migrants in mostly families sat or reclined in groups while a dozen or so Border Patrol agents supplied water, food, diapers, and powdered milk.

"We'll go until the sun comes up," one of the agents told me. "And this isn't even a hot spot."

Once Border Patrol checked them in, they bused the migrants to a brick-and-mortar station, expanded under vast soft-side tents. Inside, they'd all get medical aid, Covid-19 tests, and finally documents authorizing them to go anywhere they wanted in America within a couple of days. Many idled away their time editing and broadcasting the great news with selfies sent from cell phones to home villages.

All this was happening in one spot and on one day. But the very same scene was unfolding for many miles up and down the Rio Grande, for hundreds of miles downriver to Brownsville and upriver to Laredo. Thousands every day, fifty thousand every month, hundreds of thousands every quarter.

With my iPhone camera rolling, I asked groups of these migrants if they were coming now with children because Biden had said they would be let in. In one typical clip, all the women, some holding infants nodded vigorously, saying, *"Si!," "Si!," "Si!"* as I panned down the line.[8]

They had all responded to *"la invitación" and had not been disappointed.*

History by the Nonpartisan Number

I describe this human conveyor belt so that regular Americans who live far away and can't readily go to see it will still know what American leaders responsible for managing the border, by determined choice, also decided never to see. The president, his staff, party, and Democratic media figures denied for months that anything was amiss at the border and refused to go. President Biden still had not as of November 2022. When asked at a March 25, 2021, press conference about sky-high border apprehensions, the president insisted it was a seasonal thing.

"Nothing has changed. It happens every single year," Biden said, then blamed the seasonable blip on "earthquakes, floods…lack of food." "It's because of gang violence and because of a whole range of things."[9]

Official White House communications policy held that no one will call what was happening a "crisis," even if the numbers were shattering records by the week. DHS Secretary Alejandro Mayorkas took to calling it a "management challenge" for a while and blamed Trump. After millions had entered, the DHS secretary went to extremes. He began to claim that "the border is secure." When President Biden assigned his vice president the job of managing immigration, Kamala Harris begrudgingly went after relentless conservative media pressure but not anywhere near nightly unfolding scenes like in Roma. She too stuck to script even after millions of apprehensions: the border is secure.

But all these assertions are objectively untrue. Border Patrol processed more illegal border crossers than any one year stretching back to when the Eisenhower administration decided to start counting in 1960. America was overrun fast after Inauguration Day, and millions more are going to pour in before it's all over. I write this book because what has happened is so mammoth and transformational that it already has made American history, and historical events must be documented. The fact is, since the 2020 presidential election, the Biden administration wittingly facilitated a biblical Noah's flood of humanity to that border.

It is the most monolithic one ever, by every metric. Those who have refused to cast eyes upon it in person could at least see the nonpartisan numbers on a home computer if they wanted. These statistics smashed every U.S. immigration record and just kept going.

Until Biden, the highest number of Border Patrol apprehensions ever recorded was 1.6 million in fiscal year 2000. Apprehensions are the number of times agents lay hands on and process an illegal immigrant. No year came close to that 1.6 million in 2000 for two decades. Between 2010 and 2016, apprehensions never exceeded 500,000, and never topped 400,000 in 2011, 2012, and 2015.

Then for fiscal year 2021, 1.659 million rang the bell as the new most ever. It was 400 percent more than fiscal year 2020, which came in at 400,651. The 2021 record didn't last long. It lay shattered in fiscal year 2022 when the numbers reached 2.37 million. None of this counts "got-aways," which I'll get to shortly. But Border Patrol catches alone in just those two fiscal years exceeded a stunning 4 million and then continued on with monthly averages of 200,000.

As an immigration news story, this was on a par with the moon landing or humanity's mastery of intercontinental flight.

Regardless of how many were returned to Mexico under Title 42 or admitted into the country, 4 million handlings in so short a time constitutes a crushing and unprecedented work load on the 17,000-strong Border Patrol that caused a variety of secondary and third-order consequences. That's four years of work jammed into one year, and Border Patrol some weeks found itself so overrun that agents simply had to just give up and let everyone through to wander around towns. Not a single agent was around; DHS begged other federal agencies for bodies to come help, pulled agents off roadblocks, grabbed airport customs agents from all over America, and redeployed federal agents from the northern border.

There's a better context for contemplating just how big this thing is. Let's go back to March 29, 2019. On that day, former DHS Secretary Jeh Johnson, who served under President Obama, told MSNBC that a genuine mass migration event was unfolding under Trump. Any number of immigrant apprehensions below 1,000 per day "was a relatively good number," he said.[10] But if the number was higher than 1,000 a day, Johnson recalled, "it was a relatively bad number, and I was gonna be in a bad mood the whole day."

A thousand a day "overwhelms the system," Johnson told MSNBC, which was asking because 4,000 had crossed just the day before under Trump's watch.

"I cannot begin to imagine what 4,000 a day looks like, so we are truly in a crisis," he judged.

Working overtime to wheel up deterrence strategies, Trump gifted to Biden a border with manageably low human traffic crossing in the range of 800 to 1,500 per day.

If more than 1,000 apprehensions a day put Jeh Johnson in a bad mood and overwhelmed the system he was running in 2016, he well might not have even survived the coming black nightmare under Biden.

Biden's government carried over Trump's Title 42 pandemic expulsion policy. But on the first day in office, as I'll show, Biden's DHS carved out huge exemptions for families with young children, unaccompanied teens, and women in advanced stages of pregnancy. It was a steroid shot that set the raging monster off. Apprehensions rose from 69,169 the month Biden won the election to 173,699 in April 2021, then 200,658 in July, an all-time national first.

That was an unheard of 6,000 per day. And kept going. All through 2022, the daily Border Patrol apprehensions hovered in the 7,000 and 7,500 per day range, more than six times what former Secretary Johnson thought would "overwhelm the system" in 2019.

If statistics are hard to visualize, think Super Bowl Sunday 2022, when 70,000 roaring sports fans packed into Inglewood, California's SoFi Stadium. Anyone should be able to call up the memory or video of that stadium's packed masses.

Imagine more than three of those—221,303 people. That's how many hit Border Patrol agents in just the four weeks of the month following the big game, in March 2022. Three full Super Bowl stadiums overran Border Patrol again in April, and so on every month afterward.

The numbers far exceed the populations of major American cities on a par with, say, Charleston, Syracuse, Savannah, or Kansas City crashing the border every four weeks—for years. Maybe not all of them got to stay inside the United States because many were pushed back to Mexico for the Title 42 pandemic-control measure, albeit always in steadily diminishing numbers. But that almost didn't matter because just processing numbers like that left hundreds of miles of border undefended as agents were reassigned to off-line administrative work. This added other species of chaos to the whole.

In the beginning, his DHS was expelling some 60 percent back to Mexico under Title 42 (compared to Trump's 87 percent), and often the same people over and over again. A chunky percentage of the totals were repeat crossers who made the numbers appear worse that they were. But by fall 2022, Biden's DHS had flipped the numbers around, and was only expelling 35 percent, a minority.

But the ones he let through on temporary parole documents—the exempted families, solo teenagers, and pregnant women—ran into the millions. They were more than enough to create crisis conditions that then collapsed other parts of the border management levy.

The result was a border wholly overrun, the condition that is this book's namesake.

Inward Bound

The administration went to extraordinary lengths to mask from the public how many it was letting inside the country and how many got in on their own through the undefended border gaps left when the agents were off doing paperwork and babysitting duty.

But thanks to monthly DHS status reports a federal judge ordered as part of a Texas and Missouri court case against one of the administration's policies, we have a good idea of those numbers.[11]

The administration released just under 1.5 million mainly family and solo children border crossers into America from inauguration day through June 2022, the status reports say.[12]

That is not even close to the full picture. To that 1.5 million family members and unaccompanied minors can be added another 900,000 "got-aways" who through June 2022 ran, hid, and successfully evaded Border Patrol capture and Title 42 expulsion, the DHS court-ordered reports show (got-aways are notoriously undercounted, so that number is probably substantially higher).

That means America's legal and illegal population grew by *at least* 2.4 million in an eighteen-month span. The reports dried up in June 2022 when the lawsuit resolved but provided a crucial baseline from which to project. It is probable that, assuming all factors remain steady, that the number reaching interior America from Inauguration Day to the end of Biden's term will exceed six million and reach higher than *seven million*, accounting for got-aways and the narcotic additional allure of the final lifting of Title 42, the pandemic-era rapid expulsion policy that had deterred some.

From the vantage point of November 2022, the trajectory path only went higher. Sometime during the remainder of the

Biden term, the administration will have lifted what was left of the Trump Title 42 expulsion measure, the last impediment to unbridled entry-and-stay illegal immigration. In spring 2022, the intelligence community estimated that between 12,000 and 18,000 a day will come then, although it was never clear for how long.[13]

Assuming Title 42 is lifted with a half year left of the Biden administration and other variables remain unchanged, a reasonable projection is seven million total admittances from inauguration to January 2025 term completion and more if the measure is lifted earlier. That is a megacity on the order of Los Angeles and Chicago combined, of mostly unskilled, uneducated, uninsured people speaking a Babylon of languages and in need of public welfare assistance and medical care for which many will never pay. Only time knows if the number reaches seven million by end-of-term.

Seven. Million. That constitutes transformative changes to the nation in terms of fiscal burden on those who already live here, on public education, health care, social welfare, and criminal justice systems. Now imagine, for a moment, what would happen if another Democrat is elected in 2024 and continues these policies for an additional four years. You get the drift for what's at stake.

For the benefit of holdouts who would cling to the position that what Biden has wrought at the border is not a historic national moment, consider the case of Ellis Island, the terminals through which America legally admitted millions through New York. Ellis Island holds *the* moniker of top immigration history moments, its place in the nation's museums and public school textbooks long secure. School children and researchers worldwide study the phenomenon of Ellis Island. Two million tourists visit the old island grounds every year to ponder what happened there as not just a remarkable moment in American history but in human history.

Biden's border entrance rate is poised to join Ellis Island on its pedestal if not topple it.

The number of illegal immigrants crossing the border under the Biden government has by far outpaced the highest rates by which immigrants came in legally on ships through the Ellis Island port at New York City. In all, the U.S. government admitted more than 12 million immigrants through Ellis Island over a sixty-two-year span between 1892 and 1954. Granted, the U.S. population was smaller then; therefore the impacts of those numbers were felt to a greater degree.

The 2.4 million who were admitted or slipped into America under Biden in his first eighteen months—averaging about 139,000 per month—compares to the 84,000 processed per month of Ellis Island's 1907 grand peak, what History.com's webpage reported as "a whopping" 1,004,756.[14] Most years at Ellis saw an average of a couple hundred thousand in a year. That is typical of *any single month* of the Biden crisis.

Should Democrats win the White House in 2024 and continue these policies, the numbers of border admittances and got-aways would easily hit in eight years the 12 million who came through Ellis Island in sixty-two.

Will these Biden border years earn their page at History.com?

Shattering Firsts

There are other broken records of note.

Never have so many immigrants died trying to reach the border, at it, or just beyond it in the United States.

"The most dangerous border in the world" is what the United Nations anointed it in a July 2022 special report on the matter. More than 1,200 died, according to the United Nations.

Never have more unaccompanied minors crossed, 295,000 in the administration's first twenty months through the end of fiscal 2022.

Never has such a large proportion come from so many of the world's nations other than the long familiar big senders of Mexico and northern Central America, nearly 43 percent of everyone arriving at the border, hailing from some 150 countries by the end of fiscal 2022. I have met U.S.-bound travelers from most nations of Africa, South Asia, and the Middle East. Within that flow, never have more foreign nationals on the

FBI's terrorist watch list crossed the southern border than in the Biden border's first twenty months: 121 between January 2021 and November 2022, according to CBP website statistics, a national security threat gathering at an historic pace as border defenses are down. Demand for shelter grew so much during this crisis that one U.S. non-profit organization opened a 6,000-square-ffoot shelter in Tijuana that catered only to Muslim immigrants, where I met Chechens, Uzbeks, Tajiks, Afghans, Yemenis, and people who refused to name their home countries.

Never has the number of interior deportations across the board fallen so far, so fast, leaving hard-bitten criminals inside America along with noncriminal illegals whom judges had lawfully ordered deported. That should be no surprise since the president announced that he did not consider felony drunken driving convictions sufficient for deportation, and since Secretary Mayorkas announced that simply being present in the country without legal permission "should not alone be the basis for detention and deportation."[15]

The number of aliens ordered deported by a judge but who instead got to stay more than tripled from about 76,000 in 2020 to 260,000 by May 2022, the highest since the government began keeping records on these, according to Syracuse University's Transactional Records Access System.[16] Deportations of noncriminal illegally present people fell from 267,258 in 2019, the last full year of Trump's policies without pandemic restrictions, to 59,011 in 2021.[17] The odds that an alien would be ordered deported fell to the lowest low on record, from the usual 70 percentile range since 1998 to 22 percent in the twelve months through February 2022, an analysis of FOIA'ed government records by the Center for Immigration Studies' Jessica Vaughan showed.[18]

Perhaps the most bizarre and disturbing is that those with hard-core criminal convictions for terrible crimes got the hall pass right along with the noncriminal ones.

Biden's DHS sandbagged a traditional annual ICE deportations report that would have shown how many criminal aliens it deported.[19] The reason became clear when ICE insiders leaked the data and when federal records requests showed what had befallen the country. Deportations of convicted criminal aliens and aggravated felons sharply plummeted. Under Biden, ICE arrested 48 percent fewer convicted criminals, deported 63 percent fewer criminals, and issued 46 percent fewer requests to other law enforcement agencies to detain criminals for them, according to a *Washington Times* report based on the leaked data.[20] In her separate analysis, Vaughan reported that ICE deportations of convicted criminals and aggravated felons nosedived from 85,958 in 2019 to 31,557 through 2021. Left in the country were killers, slavers, child molesters, rapists, armed robbers, and drunk drivers who killed, Vaughan's analysis of FOIA'd records showed. With a fresher batch of FOIA'd ICE criminal alien deportation records, Vaughan found that, of the fifty U.S. counties that typically have the most criminal alien removals, fourteen experienced extreme declines (greater than 80 percent) under Biden policies. There were fifty other counties, parishes, or territories with a minimal baseline volume of enforcement where the number of criminal removals dropped by 90 percent or more." In one representative county, Howard County, Texas, under Biden policies just half the number of criminals convicted of homicides were removed than before, and there also were steep drops in removals of criminals convicted of assault, burglary, drugs, larceny, and sex offenses.[21]

Never have Mexico's ruthless crime syndicates and their paramilitary forces earned so much money from their control of the crossings and from smuggling. For the first time in memory, the cartel proceeds from human smuggling are said to have surpassed those from drug smuggling.[22] Estimates vary widely but all indicate historic revenue.[23]

ICE's Acting Deputy Director Patrick Lechleitner told Congress the human smuggling industry was generating somewhere in the neighborhood of $500 million a year for the cartels prior to 2018. But ICE intelligence estimated the revenue was $13 billion through the end of 2021[24] Another estimate in 2021 from John Condon, acting assistant director of international operations at ICE's Homeland Security and

Investigations, came in lower but no less historic: "between $2 billion and 6 billion per year," Condon told the House Homeland Security Committee's oversight subcommittee.[25]

Even assuming the lesser of the two estimates is truer, the Biden border policies have showered these brutal criminal organizations with many times more than their former annual revenues. They will use the vast wealth to counter Mexican state power with the purchase of weapons, ammunition, vehicles, housing, and government influence for later when the boom ends, if it ever does. Packed with more and better weaponry, Mexico's criminal trafficking syndicates can be expected to lessen the core ability of Mexico to act against them when the United States asks. The American ability to deter the cartels from crossing red lines into core U.S. interests, like assassinating DEA agents or mounting armed attacks on U.S. soil, is intertwined with Mexico's ability to punish them upon request. Mexico, after all, is the key U.S. proxy keeping the cartels from going too far. So the less Mexico feels free to check them, the more impunity the cartels will feel to cross American red lines to include, say, assassinating American law enforcement, conducting cross-border incursions, and maybe even interrupting vital oil and auto parts exports from Mexico to force releases of extradited drug lords.

Meanwhile, for the first time, an American presidency defaulted to a position in polar opposition to rafts of federal law. Instead of the conventional "block, detain, deport and deter of all previous Democratic Party presidents," the Biden presidency has taken the formal stated position that southern border traffic should be made "safe, humane and orderly" into the nation's interior.[26] Never has an American president decided, as a matter of national policy, that the executive branch of federal government would abdicate from enforcing immigration statutes, to *not* work against a flooding torrent of humanity crossing its southern border, and to *not* try to plug the dike.

Biden's position is historic in the annals of American presidencies and homeland security leadership in that it endeavored *not* to block, deter, and slow illegal immigration as required in well-established federal laws. His was first among presidencies to so drastically reduce deportations of the illegally present and of foreign national criminals who prey on Americans. For the first time since federal immigration laws were passed in 1903, a president effectively ended deportation of every kind in America as it has been known for many decades and left in its place a first-ever sanctuary nation.

During the May 1, 2022, edition of Fox News Sunday, in just one of many such instances, anchor Bret Baier asked Secretary Mayorkas if the administration's objective was to "sharply reduce the total number of illegal immigrants coming across the southern border."[27]

But Mayorkas would not say that the Biden administration's objective was to reduce the numbers coming across the border. It was, rather, to grant all comers access to the nation's asylum system at the border, which as I will show guarantees quick interior admittance to the majority of those who ask for it who will never leave no matter what the outcome.

"It is the objective of the Biden administration to make sure that we have safe, legal and orderly pathways for individuals to be able to access our legal system," Mayorkas responded.

Asked to identify legislation that Congress could enact "to help you deport more illegal immigrants," Mayorkas reiterated that deportation was not a priority.

"What we are talking about when we talk about legislation is building the orderly legal pathways for people to obtain relief under our laws," Mayorkas said.

Understanding the real physics that drove so many to come so quickly and with such reverberating impact on American society is key to knowing how to stop them. To build that comprehension, it is necessary to tune out politicians, migrant advocates, media pundits, and "immigration experts," and to listen to the immigrants.

CHAPTER TWO

FROM TRUMP EFFECT TO BIDEN EFFECT, THE SCIENCE OF ODDS

Shortly after Donald Trump's upset 2016 victory and January inauguration, official State of Texas business brought me to two ICE immigration detention centers in South Texas. It was part of my routine then to help the feds interview apprehended aliens from Pakistan, Syria, Somalia, and Afghanistan to collect intelligence about potential Islamic terrorism. The South Texas Processing Center in Pearsall, Texas, some one hundred miles from the Mexican border, was always filled to the brink with detainees. But to my surprise, for the first time, it was as empty as a football stadium in baseball season. So was ICE's larger, ever-packed-to-capacity Port Isabel center near Brownsville, Texas.

"Where is everyone?" I asked the ICE intelligence officers, separately at both facilities. The same surprising answer went something like this: people throughout Latin America heard Trump campaign vows to crack down on illegal immigration and decided to stay home, the intelligence officers explained. Most of these people who did try were here, in their ICE detention cells, all the money in smuggling fees they'd spent to get over the border, gone with nothing to show for it. The ones back in home countries didn't want to risk the money with Trump promising to deport them, so they stopped coming, they explained.

It was the first time I'd heard such a thing, although it seemed so obvious. Before people gambled thousands of dollars in smuggling fees, they wanted reasonable assurance that the money would pay off with successful entries and long-term stays working and earning back many multiples of the investment. If they thought the odds were too low of that happening, they stayed home. That easy, uncomplicated calculus now had some evidence behind it. Huge, empty detention centers and short cafeteria lines in ICE detention facilities for me and the intelligence officers put a fine point on it. But more importantly, immigrants they were catching and interviewing attested to it, the intelligence officers told me, and some of it was even in the media.

"Right now, nobody wants to go" to the United States, Honduran national Victoria Cordova told Reuters in March 2017 for a story about the impact of Trump's border crackdown talk. "If in the future the situation looks better, well, I imagine then people will be more willing to travel."[28]

Of course! Some media outlets heard about empty detention centers and low apprehension numbers and called it "the Trump Effect."[29]

Much later, scores of immigrants would confirm the same calculus to me in interviews.

It was all about whether the smuggling money was going to pay off in a kind of gamble. Those contemplating laying that cash on the felt table were incentivized to start watching the news and listening to relatives and friends who were already in the United States and also watching the news. Both in Latin America and in the United States, audiences were tuned in to everything Trump and Hillary Clinton were saying during his campaign, thanks to Spanish-language media. Relatives in the United States would immerse themselves and tell relatives back home if now was a good time to stay or come.

In mid-2015, Spanish-language news programs that served Latin American and U.S. audiences focused intently on Trump's immigration ideas, drawing 80 percent of all mentions in Spanish-language outlets, the *New York Times* reported.[30] Telemundo anchor José Díaz-Balart said his viewership had delved deeply into the specifics of Trump's plans with a sense of "urgency."

"Our audience is very well versed, very knowledgeable, very well educated on the issue of immigration," Díaz-Balart told the paper. Viewers were eager to hear what Trump was "realistically proposing and planning to do on the issues that are so important to the community."

CNN International's CNN en Español, reaching 40 million households in Latin America and 22 million more in the United States, made sure they re-served every morsel of what Trump dished.[31] A July 2016 story by *The Atlantic*, marveling at the intensity of Spanish-language media coverage, wondered almost hopefully whether Univision might single-handedly tip the election to Clinton.[32]

Remember that, in the run-up to the 2016 election, pollsters were all predicting a Clinton win. With her, the odds were looking great for the gambling smuggling money on a border jump.

Clinton's rhetoric and promises were the opposite of everything Trump was promising.

"Stop the raids, stop the round-ups, stop the deporting of people who are living here doing their lives, doing their jobs, and that's my priority," Clinton said during a March 2016 televised debate, appealing to an ascendant liberal progressive wing of the party.[33]

This and much more were pleasing to foreign ears and stateside relatives listening for cues.

Immigrants thinking about jumping the border perceived high odds that their smuggling money would pay off. With all eyes on the polling in news, some immigrants started voting with their feet. The apprehension norms from 2012 to mid-2016 averaged between 30,000 and 40,000 monthly. All of a sudden in about the summer of 2016, the numbers more than doubled in anticipation of the Clinton victory, to 66,708 by the end of October just ahead of the election. Thousands were gambling their smuggling money before the election.

But as we now all know, Trump pulled off an upset victory.

The number of Border Patrol apprehensions dive-bombed from 63,361 that November to 23,555 by February 2017. By April 2017, they hit a rock-bottom 15,766—one of the lowest numbers in decades.

ICE detention center cafeteria lines disappeared.

In 2021, a National Bureau of Economic Research study concluded that Trump's rhetoric and policies "led to a dramatic...reduction in illegal immigration of Central Americans to the United States" for at least seven months before ticking back up to preelection norms.[34] Researchers Mark Hoekstra and Sandra Orozco-Aleman tapped one of my own favorite datasets to make the discovery: real migrants intending to cross the border. The researchers used the Mexican government's regular "Surveys of Migration across Mexican Borders," which are randomized interviews by government workers of first-time intending border crossers, as well as those recently deported by the Americans.

"We would argue this was one of the more important changes in the U.S. immigration policy space in recent years," they wrote of their confirming discovery that the political communication of American politicians influence immigrant decisions. Hoekstra and Orozco-Aleman reported that Trump's rhetoric dampened reentry plans among the deported. These "fell dramatically" by 10 to 15 percent for many months after the election as compared to the increasing levels before the election.

My 2017 Trump Effect lesson felt a bit revelatory at that time, but later it became a predominant staple in my understanding of immigration dynamics as I started teasing from immigrants in long, in-depth interviews the details of their internal decision-making processes. American policy pronouncements, political communication, and follow-through action on the ground were usually all that ever mattered to them (although court decisions can matter just as much). These are the factors that increase or decrease the odds that smuggling investments will get them in to earn money for a long time.

Take the story of twenty-eight-year-old Haitian named Alexandre, whom I met and interviewed at great length in downtown Tapachula one night in January 2022. Like the vast majority of Haitians heading to the American border that January, his family had not come directly from Haiti. He and his wife left Haiti for a presumed Hillary Clinton border but woke up to the rude discovery that Trump had won instead. They and hundreds of thousands of other Haitians began pooling up in Chile or Brazil to wait out the tough Trump environment.

They knew, for instance, that Trump had just made it very hard to lodge the political persecution asylum claim that everyone was counting on to get them coveted quick releases into the American interior. The plan-ruining program Alexandre described sounded like an early Trump effort called "metering," which required intending immigrants to wait in Mexico until the Americans called a few at a time over for asylum processing.[35] This was a predecessor to the later "Remain in Mexico" policy that denied claimants the highly craved immediate entry. Since most Haitians are rejected for American asylum, those who applied under the metering system found themselves rejected and stuck in Mexico, rather than free to go on the run inside America, now with nothing to show for the cash fortunes they spent on smugglers.

"Under President Trump, his policy was to make us stay outside the country and seek asylum from there. That was bad," Alexandre explained. "A lot of us, we think we got tricked."

I asked Alexandre if he and his wife decided to wait in Chile rather than to gamble their $7,000 that they'd get over the new Trump border and not end up stuck in Mexico.

"Si, si, si, si, si!" he answered in the Spanish he'd learned during his Chile years. "That money, in order to come to the United States...I worked hard for that money. I wouldn't have spent that money when Trump was president."

The couple was suffering no economic hardship in Chile working for tourist hotels and in food service; they had a son who became a Chilean citizen. They saved more money for their smuggling fund and watched the 2020 election campaign carefully.

"The United States…it's a great country. There are a lot of opportunities, and my plan was always to go to the United States."

After Biden defeated Trump, they watched closely what would happen when the first Haitians tried the new border. They were all let in if they came with a child. Alexandre and his wife had one! So they did what tens of thousands of other Haitians did after Trump's election.

"We talked it over with the family, and we decided to make the trip. Under this president, it seemed like things are different."

In November 2021, he gambled the money when he saw others getting in ahead of him and confirmed that his odds of winning could not possibly be greater.[36]

The Biden Effect

That a presidential candidate on the stump and in office could affect the internal calculation of odds among immigrants thousands of miles away may seem like rudimentary conventional wisdom to any thinking person, perhaps too obvious to even mention in a book. But the lesson of the Trump Effect on immigrant decisions clearly never took hold.

During the 2020 campaign, lots of Democratic Party talk about opening the border soon enough produced the same increased anticipatory traffic toward the border as had Clinton's open-doors talk four years earlier.

As I described in the introduction, immigrants started pooling up in Mexico as early as January and February 2020 just on the basis of hearing all dozen Democratic primary candidates promise paths to citizenship and to end deportation and detention, abolish ICE, and offer amnesty to everyone who could cross the border. With the nomination in hand, what were Biden and Harris saying to the same global audiences that had been listening to them and Trump?

All the things that would increase the odds that a smuggling fee gamble would pay off. After the election, for example, the president-elect signaled that his administration would never return an unaccompanied child migrant who "ends up" at the border (as though by no one's illicit doing) to Mexico to "starve to death." Candidate Biden said he would work with faith-based groups to move them to safe locations "as quickly as possible."[37]

Before long, it produced what I called at the time a "Biden Effect" of a massive onslaught on the border. This was the equal and opposite of the Trump Effect's empty ICE detention centers.

To this day, even the most obvious truisms about what really causes or ends mass migrations elude Democratic precincts and influential quarters of the American political, media, and public policy establishments. Nobody seems to *get* that this basic immigrant calculus matters so much. And so the mistake is repeated continuously. Heads of families who earned, begged, or borrowed $10,000 in smuggling fees only to end up blocked at the border drive "don't go" choices for others down trail. Even if entry is successful, high odds of deportation afterward still devastate the smuggling money piggy bank and lead to "no go" decisions. Aspiring border-jumpers need to feel confident of both outcomes, that the fortune they've risked paying smugglers buys both a successful entry *and* a long stay inside working and earning many times more than their smuggling fee investment.

Tilting at Root Causes Windmills

Instead of saying and doing the things that impact emigrant decisions to stay home, Democrats during the 2020 election cycle rallied around an old European idea dating to the 1980s that became newly popular in liberal European political parlors during that continent's mass migration crisis of 2014–2015. It was the notion that if European governments invested in eliminating "root causes" like poverty, high crime, government corruption, and subpar education systems in poor migrant-sending countries, fewer people living in them would want to emigrate.[38] At the heart of progressive appreciation for this plausible-sounding strategy was that it would serve not as a complement to deportation, detention, and deterrence but as their total replacement.

For the 2020 election cycle, liberal American Democrats took up Europe's "root causes" banner as the way out of deporting, detaining, and deterring border jumpers. The Biden White House's strategy called for American taxpayers and big business to create jobs in three top sending countries—Guatemala, Honduras, and El Salvador—so that their people eventually will not want to leave. While the American government was busy with this nation-building project, of course, the migrants could be free to pour in over the southern border.

Biden and Vice President Harris have regularly blamed "root causes" for the vast influx that began right after they took office. Immigration was all so very "complex," Harris explained during a state visit to Central America to get the strategy up and running.

"We are looking at extensive storm damage because of extreme climate. We're looking at drought in an area in a region where agriculture is one of the most traditionally important bases for their economy," Harris said. "We're looking at what's happening in terms of food scarcity as a result of that and in fact, incredible food insecurity, which we used to call hunger food insecurity."[39]

The administration pledged a $4 billion down payment over four years, including $860.6 million in fiscal year 2022 and $986 million in fiscal year 2023.[40]

The Biden government has never offered even basic particulars, such as how much it would spend, on what sectors of those countries, and how long it would take to see big reductions at the southern border. Neither media nor academia seems to have demanded those details nor critically examined whether Europe's expensive nation-building propositions worked.

But even the most cursory glance at Europe's experience addressing "root causes" from the earliest 1980s pilot programs on shows the strategy never worked. For example, the European Union–funded policy think tank MIGNEX reviewed some ten studies spanning more than a decade where development aid was invested to reduce Europe-bound emigration from poor countries.

"In its current form, development aid does not seem to be big enough to create the underlying changes that effect migration decisions," the MIGNEX report concluded, in part. "In cases where we do see a deterrent effect of aid on migration, a noticeable impact would require an unrealistic increase in aid."[41]

Writing for the International Institute of Social Studies in 2007, social scientist Hein de Haas concluded, "Besides the limited scope and credibility of such policies, empirical and theoretical evidence strongly suggests that economic and human development increases people's capabilities and aspirations and therefore tends to coincide with an increase rather than a decrease in emigration."[42]

After tilting at the "root causes" windmills, some European nations along the collective's exterior have turned to what works on migrant decision-making, albeit against constant legal challenges by those who oppose detention, deportation, and deterrence. Since 2015, some 800 miles of border walls have gone up in a half a dozen countries, including Austria, Slovenia, Slovakia, the Czech Republic, and Poland—and diverted some mass migrations through their territories.[43] The collective uses air repatriation flights, and other deterrence-based projects that change immigrant minds. But none are universally deployed, so hundreds of thousands of illegal immigrants per year still breach the EU's common external borders since the 2014–2015 crisis.

Yet, the Biden administration would have the American people accept the European root causes model as a replacing alternative—never in addition—to deportation, detention, and deterrence that the Trump Effect and immigrant interviews show makes them want to stay home.

To be sure, no one can deny that people *always* want to leave poverty and poor governance. But sorrowfully, these steady-state conditions do not change quickly. Maybe an American effort to rebuild the national economies and governments of three Central American nations would, in due time, work out better than did Europe's effort. The problem with "due time" is that the European experiment proves that just testing the theory is an extended long-term proposition, and the discovery at the end will likely be that it didn't work. To find out, the purveyors of a Western Hemisphere version may also require decades and cost untold billions of dollars to the national treasury, *while* people pour across a border left unimpeded. In this model, the root causes stratagem seems a less serious strategy than a misdirecting cover for letting millions of people in over the border.

Other factors would seem to gum up the whole idea. For instance, root causes proponents of rebuilding Guatemala, Honduras, and El Salvador do not take into account that more than 40 percent of everyone reaching the southern border during this crisis are not from those countries or Mexico but from one hundred-plus *other* wrecked countries like Venezuela, Haiti, Cuba, and the Democratic Republic of Congo.

Are Americans expected to eliminate the root causes of *those* nations too or any new poor nation whose citizens decide to come next? Proponents look away from this question. Even if the Democrats expanded the umbrella over every poor nation on Earth, the project does not account for the fact that America is as terrible at nation-building as Europe. Its endeavors failing even after trillions of dollars in expenditures and deployment of American troops. One need only study the examples of Afghanistan, Iraq, and Vietnam. The post–World War II Marshall Plan to rebuild war-wrecked Europe may have been the last success, generations ago. Plans to rebuild Central America do not seem to bake into the cake the terrible failure rate since then.

As much as the beauty queen contestant in all of us would like to see world hunger alleviated, it is unfortunately here to stay for a long time. Fixing the three countries is, at best, a social engineering experiment with a time horizon that is generational. It is not a quantity proven that can change the trajectory of monthly or yearly border-crossing flow rates. It may be worthwhile for the United States to slowly hack away at rebuilding poor countries but not as immigration policy. Certainly not as the "either-or," all-or-nothing replacement for the one strategy that works wonders most of the time: lowering border-jump success odds.

Lowering the odds of smuggling fee payoff is a lever that American leadership can move at will to open and close doors, to start and stop mass migration immediately. It is *the* regulating influence in the most kinetic sense—if those who wield it understand how it works.

Charitably speaking, the Biden administration did not take into account the physics of immigrant-smuggling money fortunes. In ignorance, the administration sprayed enticement around the world, then followed with action that helped millions get their money's worth. If one side of the Trump Effect coin frightened border jumpers away, then the "Biden Effect" side invited them back.

Border flow rates, as reflected by Border Patrol apprehensions, advanced when immigrants thought Clinton would win and retreated when Trump did. Those changes took place absent any sudden violent crime reduction in Tegucigalpa, sudden climate change improvements in Guatemala's western highlands, or outbreaks of integrity among government officials. Rarely were new hurricanes or earthquakes in proximity to advance-retreat decisions as when American leaders or courts acted.

Flows retreated when intending border-crossers perceived elevated risk that they would end up back at the starting line, having lost the smuggling kitty and in debt, possibly to unsavory lenders. My analysis of monthly and annual U.S. Border Patrol apprehension data and interviews with the migrants planning border jumps corresponds tightly with what American leaders say out loud and then, only, if they follow through. Telegraphed intentions and political communication followed by concrete action launch the thousand ships, or return them to port. The Trump Effect wouldn't last, in part because, as a November 2019 *Forbes* article pointed out, "No president has been sued over his immigration policies as much as Donald Trump."[44] Court challenges stymied Trump's immigration agenda, which added to evidence that aspiring border jumpers pay close attention to factors that raise or lower their odds of smuggling money return on investment. Lawsuits that stalled

Trump's plans raised their odds of entry-and-stay success, so immigrants started coming again. Until he won the lawsuits, put plans in effect, and they stopped coming. The calculus can work for any leader, including Democrats like President Obama in 2014.

Obama's pre-Trump Card

In a March 2017 report for Reuters, Mexico City reporter Gabriel Stargardter showed he understood the odds calculus in migrant decision-making when he correctly predicted that President Trump's words alone would not suppress the migrant tide for long. The lull would only last if "he follows through with his hardline vows, past experience shows."[45] What past experience? The one that happened under President Barack Obama in 2014, Stargardter wrote.

The Obama episode is worth recalling because, when a crisis of unaccompanied minors from Central America spun out of control under his watch, he immediately wrestled it back by reducing the odds that anyone else would successfully cross and stay.

In 2014, 70,000 unaccompanied minors from Central American countries flooded over the Texas border in just a few months, a 77 percent increase over the prior year. Nothing jarringly new with "root causes" happened in climate change, gang violence, poverty, or government persecutions.

What caused the border rush were the usual causes: media coverage, radio advertisements, and word spread by "religious organizations" that the Americans were granting kids *"permisos"* that got them in and got them in to stay, the *Washington Post* reported.[46] The newspaper cited corroborating migrant interviews conducted by Democratic Senator Dianne Feinstein's staff and, separately, a confidential internal Border Patrol intelligence report. Both sources concluded that the main reason unaccompanied minors began crossing into the United States that year was "to take advantage of the 'new U.S. law that grants a free pass or permit.'

"The subjects also indicated that 'everyone' in their home countries is aware that 'permisos' are being issued to family units in South Texas" and that "the news of these 'permisos' is spread by word of mouth and international and local media," the Border Patrol document was cited as saying.

It was never precisely clear which new "laws," but several proposals to welcome immigrant minors were getting a lot of public play at the time. One was President Obama's proposed executive action to expand the Deferred Action for Childhood Arrivals, which stayed deportation and provided work authorization (permisos) to those whose parents crossed them illegally over the border as children.[47] Parents in Latin America misunderstood that DACA would give permisos to new arrivals when it really only meant those brought in *before* 2007. Perhaps parents sent their kids anyway (or sent *for* them) thinking the Americans would extend it to the newer arrivals.

In any case, DHS Secretary Johnson regarded the misinformation about DACA as such a powerful tractor beam that he acted to turn it off with a January 2015 open letter to Central American families. In it, Johnson pleaded that they not come because DACA "does not apply to a child who crosses the U.S. border illegally today, tomorrow or yesterday."[48]

The likelier spur was that smuggling groups belatedly spread old news about an obscure 2008 anti–sex trafficking law known as the William Wilberforce Trafficking Victims Protection Reauthorization Act (TVPRA).[49] The law required that DHS stay deportations for child border crossers from noncontiguous countries and get them into the asylum system with access to lawyers and, while waiting for that, reunite them with family already in the United States at government expense.[50]

The TVPRA legally enshrined rapid catch-and-release for unaccompanied minors. When word of it finally spread years after its passage, big numbers of those it would benefit naturally put their smuggling fee money down on the felt table and came running for it.

The "broader discovery of this law years after its inauspicious bipartisan passage in 2008 became the root of the potentially calamitous flow of unaccompanied minors to the nation's southern border," the *New York Times* reported.

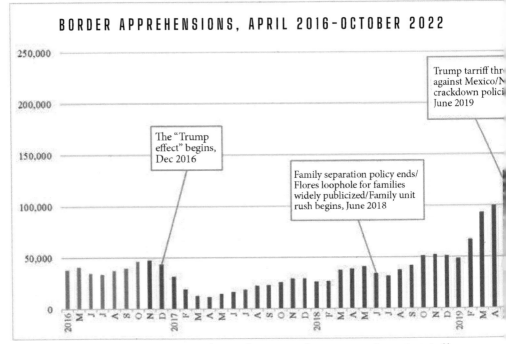

BORDER APPREHENSIONS, APRIL 2016–OCTOBER 2022

The "Trump effect" begins, Dec 2016

Family separation policy ends/ Flores loophole for families widely publicized/Family unit rush begins, June 2018

Trump tarriff thr against Mexico/N crackdown polici June 2019

Like Biden-Harris, the Obama administration initially blamed systemic poverty, gang violence, and government persecution in Central America—"root causes." But when it came time to really fix the problem, Obama defaulted straight to reducing entry-and-stay odds that threatened smuggling money fortunes.

The Obama administration took out radio, television, and internet advertisements warning families not to send children because they would be deported. DHS Secretary Johnson's Spanish-language letter to Central American parents warned that "it is now more likely that if you come here illegally, you will be apprehended, detained, and turned back in accordance with our laws." Obama himself threatened to deport the children home.

"Children who do not have proper claims will at some point be subject to repatriation to their home countries," he told leaders of El Salvador, Guatemala, and Honduras in July 2014.[51]

Most importantly, the administration followed up with action. Obama ordered deportation flights filled with children. On home-country airport tarmacs, they sent sorrowful text

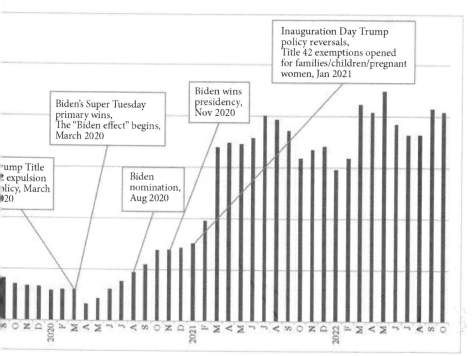

Inauguration Day Trump policy reversals, Title 42 exemptions opened for families/children/pregnant women, Jan 2021

Biden's Super Tuesday primary wins, The "Biden effect" begins, March 2020

Biden wins presidency, Nov 2020

ump Title expulsion licy, March 20

Biden nomination, Aug 2020

messages about their terrible fates to home villages.[52] The administration also pressured the Mexican government to interdict at its southern border with Guatemala any kid trying to return.

With these simple measures, the Obama administration drove down the odds of successful entry and stay. The crisis ended quickly. Apprehensions fell from 68,804 in May 2014 to 34,003 in September. It was all over.

For this operation, Obama had not bothered himself about fixing "complex" root causes of gang violence, climate change, or bad economies in Central America. Through the policy of air deportation flights and political communication, Obama's administration lowered the entry-and-stay odds right away. Apprehension numbers fell precipitously, and his border crisis soon ended. It was just in time for the 2016 presidential election cycle.

Gold Rush Loopholes

Sometimes the courts and legislature move the odds needle high well outside any president's power to pull the lever. Congress's

TPVRA, with its mandatory fast-release guard against deportation, created a powerful enticement for young migrants as Obama discovered. But one single court case from 1997, and especially the amendment to it in 2015, would prove an even more powerful catalyst for southern border mass migration events after 2015. From this point forward, I will refer to this double-barreled set of legal rulings as "the Flores loophole." When it too was widely discovered long after its birth, the Flores Settlement loophole ended the seven-month Trump Effect and sent that president scrambling to end a very large mass migration event in 2018–2019. He was successful.

But the Flores loophole was and is the problem. Anyone who has ever wondered why women and children became so ubiquitous in the crises since 2015 need only look to the Flores Settlement loophole for the answer. An understanding of it is essential to comprehend the current catastrophic crisis, a central characteristic of which are families and children, and why the loophole will foment future gold rushes until it is, once and for all, put down.

Bear with me as I explain this because it is important.

The story of the loophole begins in 1997, when a liberal U.S. District Judge in California named Dolly M. Gee decided a lawsuit over the care and treatment of immigrant children who were caught crossing and detained without parents or guardians. Judge Gee brokered a settlement that limited how long the government could detain unaccompanied migrant children to under twenty-one days. That meant the government had a few weeks to deport kids to home countries. That was usually too short a time to get that done, guaranteeing that almost all of them got released into the nation, usually to relatives, where they could permanently join the massive illegal immigrant population.[53] That was the ultimate payoff for smuggling money investments.

For a long time, much of the migrating world did not know about the Flores Settlement; back then, so few families or children illegally jumped the border that DHS would not even start keeping statistics on them until 2013.

But in July 2015, Judge Gee, who had maintained an oversight role, issued a game-changing amendment. She essentially expanded the Flores Settlement so that parents and guardians who crossed with children could be released with them within the twenty-one days too.[54] Because of various circumstances, now whole families that got picked up crossing the border together got the twenty-one-day release treatment and could evade deportation if they also claimed asylum. The American asylum law became complicit in the scam as I will elaborately report in chapter five, "Insane Asylum."

Think about it: families across Latin America and the world realized that if they crossed and claimed without having to provide evidence to be politically persecuted refugees, the Americans would free them within twenty-one days to work illegally, whether they abandoned the claim or lost it. Asylum became an inseparable first cousin to the Flores Settlement loophole.

Still, it took a couple of years for word of this guaranteed smuggling fee payoff to spread. Once it did starting in about 2016, no one with kids could resist. They were coming in increasing numbers by the time Trump took office. That was when he moved to shut down the Flores traffic. Ironically, what Trump did to shut it down only spread awareness of it farther and wider and quicker. It was the controversy sparked by Trump's so-called "family separation policy" that brought true international renown to the twinned Flores-asylum loopholes.

Today, the tale of how court rulings and media coverage of Trump's family separation policy controversy pushed the enter-and-stay odds needle to high and Trump returned it to low stands as yet another important testament to the truism that immigrants pay attention to all information that might inform whether a smuggling fee investment will pay.

Bullhorn

By April 2018, litigation had bogged down most of the president's immigration initiatives. Increasing numbers of migrants saw that and poured in for the Flores and asylum catch-and-release loopholes. The Trump administration was looking for innovative new ideas to tamp down the gathering crisis.

It turned to an old Bush-era "zero tolerance" deterrence program called Operation Streamline, which federally prosecuted mostly single adult immigrants coming through parts of Texas for illegal entry. Convictions of the federal misdemeanor came with a six-month prison sentence for first-time offenses and more time for subsequent ones.[55] It proved a powerful deterrent in the areas where it was used, so much so that Obama retained and expanded it to all of Texas, New Mexico, and California. But Operation Streamline pretty much exempted families with children under both Bush and Obama.[56]

Why? For one thing, children obviously cannot go with their arrested parents into mixed-adult lockup facilities for safety reasons. DHS would have had to take care of them, creating a child-care burden no one really wanted.[57] Its architects no doubt considered that separating children from their federally incarcerated parents, as would be required, could become a political liability.

In May 2018, Trump's administration decided to start prosecuting parents coming in with children anyway.

"Today we are here to send a message to the world: we are not going to let this country be overwhelmed," former United States Attorney General Jeff Sessions said during a speech in San Diego. "I have put in place a zero tolerance policy for illegal entry on our Southwest border. If you cross this border unlawfully, then we will prosecute you. It's that simple. If you are smuggling a child, then we will prosecute you, and that child will be separated from you as required by law."

Because obviously the kids could not go with their parents into federal lockup facilities, they were separated and delivered to the U.S. Department of Health and Human Services (HHS) for safekeeping, which included deportations back to relatives in their homelands while their parents were still in prosecution.

International outrage broke out. Democratic politicians and media outlets pounced on this irresistible story of ostensible Trump heartlessness and, especially so, its underdeveloped plans for keeping track of everyone so that they could eventually be reunited with convicted parents.

Middle America on both sides of the partisan divide saw the policy as unpalatable, to say the least.[58] Three months of controversy later, in June 2018, Trump saw the political damage this was doing to his agenda and ended the policy.

HHS had taken custody of children from several thousand parents. One of this episode's unintended consequences was that the entire world learned of its original purpose, to dull the Flores loophole's glittering allure. Once Trump relented on prosecutions, the path to the Flores loophole goldfield was wide open. They piled through the border to get at it.

CBP apprehensions of family group immigrants averaged 9,400 each of the three months of the family separation policy. The numbers exploded the minute Trump ended it in June 2018—12,760 in August 2018, 16,658 that September, a quadrupling to 53,204 by March 2019, then to 84,486 in May 2019. Whereas Border Patrol apprehended 77,674 family group immigrants for the entirety of fiscal 2016, and about the same in 2017, they took in an astonishing 473,682 family members in 2019.

A much-overlooked November 2019 report by the bipartisan Homeland Security Advisory Council ruled out crime, gang activity, or poverty as causes for this mass family immigration event because none of those metrics had changed.[59] The *Families and Children Care Panel Final Report* saw only a "single motivating factor for migration of families" as the Flores Settlement that Judge Dolly Gee expanded in 2015.

"Once it became clear the migrants with minor children would have to be released after 20 days of detention, or often even less, and could lawfully stay in the U.S. for years, the rush of [Family Migrant Units] overwhelmed CBP Border Patrol's capacity," the panel concluded, in part. "For as long as *Flores* remains unaddressed, the risk of large-scale family migration remains."

The panel understood how asylum system abuse worked in conjunction with the loophole's twenty-one-day maximum detention, writing in part, "It is clear that a twenty-day limit on detention makes it impossible for DHS to conduct any meaningful evaluation of asylum claims." It went on elsewhere: "Until our asylum system is reformed and the restrictions of *Flores* relating to family detention, which led to the widespread catch and release of [Family Migrant Units] are removed, the pull factor of bringing a child will remain."

The Trump border spun out of control as families down-trail saw on social media and television thousands up-trail get ushered right into America through this Flores loophole and with a simple asylum claim.

So powerful was the loophole that it spawned a new tactic designed to get the most people possible into it: caravans. Like social media flash mobs in Brooklyn, unknown organizers in Honduras would set a date and place on social media, and people would form in Honduras to get at Flores. Thousands would drive through police roadblocks, walking and hitching rides on trucks toward the American border.

The new tactic had great appeal. Caravans didn't charge thousands in smuggling fees. People who threw in with a caravan could travel across two or three national borders for free until they had to pay cartels for a final crossing, much cheaper. And caravans provided some safety in numbers for vulnerable women and children along the way. They barreled violently right over police, so no bribes became unnecessary too.

In October 2018, 1,600 mostly Honduran families gathered in a public park in San Pedro Sula to head for the Flores loophole. It began its long hitchhike north. It was the first caravan of unending ones to come. I spent time with two of them. Most Americans who saw what happened to that first one and to many others that formed afterward might think these all ended in catastrophic failures. All of them actually ended in fantastic success, given that the only goal was that everyone got into America to stay. That part always happened after the cameras departed and explains why caravans keep forming.

Come Now the Caravans

In the morning hours of November 25, 2018, the first elements of a 6,000-strong migrant caravan that had formed in Honduras a few weeks earlier charged straight at one last Mexican police blockade. Counting on the reluctance of Mexican police to use force against them, the hundreds of men, women, and children overwhelmed the first skirmish line. They stormed the international border crossing connecting Tijuana to San Diego at three separate spots, looking for the soft one.[60] It seemed that nothing now stood between them and, at long last, the Flores loophole.[61]

This moment of truth had been weeks in the making. Unknown organizers had conjured up the caravan like a flash mob during the heat of the American midterm election campaign. After the caravan nucleus of 1,600 formed in San Pedro Sula, Honduras, it moved northward, collecting families with children like a snowball rolling downhill until thousands were marching, hitchhiking, singing, and young single men up front were smashing their way through roadblocks.

When the battered, outnumbered police yielded the road, all would sprint gleefully through, whooping and howling in victory toward America.

But the greatest game of chicken lay ahead, with Trump. Everyone knew of Trump's seeming impotence in the face of court-ruled loopholes like Flores and the asylum system. For months, television and cell phone video had been showing hundreds of thousands of families and solo children walk right into the country. The president hadn't then been able to disable Flores.

When the caravan arrived in Tijuana, a place where walling between the two nations is double-layered for miles, Trump had his riot battalions readied behind it.

The Trump administration, correctly, understood that if it allowed a first caravan through, all of Central America would form one single, long, continuous one and follow them through the open breach to the loopholes. So, he made stopping the first one a signature stance. As it left Honduras, then Vice President Mike Pence showed he understood it mostly consisted of families when he urged the presidents of Honduras, El Salvador, and Guatemala to persuade their citizens to stay home.

"Tell your people: don't put your families at risk by taking the dangerous journey north to attempt to enter the United States illegally."[62]

The caravan's violent young men easily smashed their way through a tepid Mexican police cordon while others flanked right around it. Over the next two hours, hundreds of caravanners charged. Trump's CBP agents responded. Over an area of about one kilometer, they fired volleys of tear gas in and around hundreds of immigrants, who fell back and came again.

Some immigrants hurled rocks and projectiles at the agents. Others who tried to climb the wall fell back in the face of the gas. Other groups rushed a railway bridge but were forced back there as well. The agents fired rubber bullets.[63] Still others tried crossing a dry Tijuana River bed, but federal agents drove them away.

Almost as though following the caravan strategic play-book, the *New York Times* published a photo that went viral, showing an anguished mother with two older, diapered children running back as a tear gas canister fumed behind them.

Soon, it was all over, but it was also just starting. On January 1, 2019, Trump's riot-control officers of the CBP fired tear gas and made arrests during a second wild caravan melee at the Tijuana border.[64]

Caravans became a ubiquitous element of mass migration because almost everyone eventually got over for the Flores loophole treatment later anyway, so they had proved useful as a way to cut out the smugglers and still cover long distances in the relative safety of numbers.

Trump deployed troops to the border in Operation Faithful Patriot, which busied itself stringing barbed wire along miles of borderland as a deterrent to further caravan-sized incursion attempts. This proved unnecessary because caravanners switched to a better tactic that drew less attention.

Mexico's Duplicitous "Ant Operations"

Mexico had no interest either in expensive deportations of these thousands of people or in having them linger on Mexican turf. So, Mexico quietly embarked on a thinly veiled ruse. It began handing out humanitarian visas and freeing their bearers on their own recognizance after the empty tear gas canisters were cleaned up and the TV cameras were gone.[65]

At least 2,500 of that first Tijuana caravan got into America that way, and Mexico issued the coveted visas to 2,900 others, the Associated Press later figured out, meaning they all probably crossed in.[66] Just about everyone in a caravan that looked like it was militarily defeated on the battlefield got right to the Flores loophole's twenty-one-day quick release.

Not long after Mexico issued those thousands of visas, groups of 100–300 suddenly began turning up at border zones unaccustomed to such traffic, such as the desolate Antelope Wells area of New Mexico seventy-five miles west of El Paso.[67] This went on for weeks, overrunning DHS. Everyone got in. Everyone stayed in.

"Although some applicants say they may consider remaining in Mexico, many acknowledge that their ultimate aim is to enter the United States and apply for political asylum," a January 2019 *Los Angeles Times* report about the work visas said.[68] Mexico gave 10,000 work visas to Central American immigrants in those months, even though government officials acknowledged that "the vast majority of the migrants want to head to the United States," the *Washington Post* said.[69]

Some years later, a newspaper publisher I interviewed in Tapachula described one of these migrations that had recently happened as an "ant operation." It's usually a tactic favored by criminal organizations to move contraband in small lines of people or vehicles that draw little notice.

When caravans came after those first American uses of tear gas in November 2018, the Mexicans turned to ant operations to move them out of their own territory. Sure, the Mexicans would make a big public show of breaking up the caravans, but that was all part of the operation. Once the cameras were gone, Mexico would quietly issue the humanitarian work visas and release them in small, diffused groups. No one in the United States noticed that everyone got in.

The first time I witnessed an ant operation was in February 2019. Half of a fresh caravan of 6,000 had barreled its way into the northern Mexican city of Piedras Negras, right across from Eagle Pass, Texas. Mexican troops had made a big public show of rounding them all up under a demand from Trump and forced at least 2,500 of them into an abandoned ceramics *maquiladora* factory, well out of the media limelight.[70] The reporters gave up and went home. But a good friend who was years-long buddies with the camp's manager arranged for me to cross in through layers of soldiers and riot police.

There I was suddenly, the only reporter inside with all the women and children, mothers, fathers, soldiers, and immigration officers. The Mexican government was in full-bore ant operation mode. As one small measure of the caliber of some people in the caravans, most of the single young men had just rioted inside, attacking the officers and burning mattresses and material in a demand to be set free to the American border just a few last miles to the north. The Mexican forces had forcibly removed twenty-five hardened Honduran gang members, identified in gang databases, for deportation, the shelter manager and Piedras Negras City Councilman Jose Angel Hinojosa told me.

They need only have exercised patience, and they'd have soon entered the United States. In one section of the factory, hundreds of caravanners lined up to apply for their work visas at plastic folding tables, a year's duration each. Elsewhere in the camp, migrants who already had their freshly minted visas waited for Mexican immigration officials to call their names. They would board idling buses that would then lumber out of the factory grounds to many different convenient Mexican cities in the north.

Handwritten signs taped on front windows read "Monterrey" and "Hermosillo." Mexican officials in the camp, as well as the immigrants taking part, acknowledged they were all heading straight to the American border from their assigned cities.

"The process portends precisely the outcome sought by everyone in this caravan and in any future ones," I reported after leaving the Mexican factory. "Under the auspices of a special visa program, Mexico is essentially dispersing the migrants around northern Mexico where they will be free to try their luck crossing other parts of the American southern border and to then access the much-prized American catch-and-release loophole they have always sought, though in smaller, less visible groups."

Within a week, the ceramics factory was abandoned again, the media all gone, and no one the wiser as to what just happened: caravan success. This is why caravans still form to this day.

CHAPTER THREE

AN IMPERFECT MIRACLE CRACKDOWN

In January 2019, hundreds of thousands of families had so overrun all systems that the Flores loophole almost didn't even matter. Immigrants were being released in places without papers or processing of any kind into the streets, often without papers. So many migrant children had flooded the loophole zone that the government was running out of space to house them. DHS was going to open up civic convention centers and military bases across the country. The president used the occasion of his first Oval Office address to call on congressional Democrats to close the loopholes and provide some emergency funding for the kids.

"Close border security loopholes," Trump beseeched Congress so that "illegal immigrant children can be safely and humanely returned home." Trump warned that without more money to increase HSS bed space, the system was going to collapse.

But no one would believe Trump's talk of loopholes.

Instead, Trump's opponents widely pilloried the speech as racist. The president's characterization of the loopholes was "a dark vision" with no basis in truth, one columnist for the liberal National Public Radio said.[71] David A. Graham of *The Atlantic* wondered why Trump was misdirecting from "the underlying causes, especially violence in Central America's Northern Triangle."[72]

As these proponents provided political cover, the families poured into America in a drowning tide until the system actually collapsed as Trump predicted. Trump's opponents seemed to revel seeing *him*, of all people, struggle with a mass migration crisis. Schadenfreude kept the loopholes open.

The bipartisan Homeland Security Advisory Council's *Families and Children Care Panel Final Report*, mentioned earlier, laid blame for the "extraordinary and unprecedented" crisis squarely on the Flores loophole. But it also laid blame on the Democratic-controlled Congress's "purposeful delay" in providing Trump's requested HHS money to handle all the kids. These actions "caused the system to collapse," the bipartisan panel concluded. The system of handling family groups "completely broke down…the system, already on the verge of collapse, collapsed."[73]

What did that look like? The HSS Office of Refugee Resettlement, responsible for the care and custody of migrant children, had to send new child arrivals to Border Patrol facilities never built nor suited for them. They were packed in for lack of anywhere else to put them. Trump's many political enemies delighted in framing the outcome as "kids in cages."

Eventually, the space shortages became so severe that DHS had to release the families into local border communities "to fend for themselves," the advisory panel reported.[74]

Congress eventually coughed up the money to take care of the kids. But Trump realized that if he was going to end the crisis, he was on his own, surrounded by rabid political denialism about why this was happening and legal obstructionism of every measure he would try.

During his Oval Office speech, Trump said he'd given Congress "a detailed proposal to secure the border and stop the criminal gangs, drug smugglers and human traffickers."[75] It was a combination of innovative policy and diplomatic power ball that no president in modern history had ever tried.

Trump's cocktail of strategies for the 2019 Flores loophole crisis worked, judging by apprehension numbers and interviews with the targeted immigrants. In fact, this unique compilation of policies worked so well that, in retrospect, it should be viewed as a laboratory-worthy experiment in illegal immigration control warranting thoughtful study for future application. Among the most impactful—and therefore embattled—was Trump's "Migrant Protection Protocols," known as Remain in Mexico.

Striking the Decision-Making Primer

In July 2019, I crossed the international bridge from El Paso to the sprawling Mexican border city of Juárez to gauge the effects of Trump's Remain in Mexico policy. His government had designed it to remove the central incentive of the American asylum system, which was that anyone who claimed it could wait inside the United States for years until their hearing came up in the long backlogged line.

Instead, they had to "Remain in Mexico" for their hearings. This outcome played deviously—or ingeniously—on the core incentive of asylum, which was and is always to simply Get In. The architects of the policy understood that the Great Mexican Dream never anyone's goal.

At the time, courts had finally ruled in Trump's favor to implement the policy, and DHS had expelled some 20,000 of an eventual 75,000. I traveled to Juárez to see how the policy was playing on the psychological core of immigrant decision-making.

I made my way by taxi to a couple of migrant shelters in town. Fresh Remain in Mexico expellees filled them to capacity. I found dozens in a Juárez church shelter high up on a rise in the dangerous neighborhood of Anapra, within eyesight of Mexico's side of the American wall and the outskirts of El Paso beyond. I was soon interviewing recent expellee Veronica Janeth Tejeda of Yoro in northwestern Honduras as she played with one of her two children in an outdoor yard area between small residential buildings.

The single mother of two told me that she decided to journey over the American border with her fourteen-year-old daughter and nine-year-old son because she "heard on the news that mothers and fathers who had kids were crossing in to the United States. I was told the people from immigration control were going to find us and take care of us, that they were going to take our information and just let me go into the United States."

That was a reasonable decision perfectly in line with immigration cost-benefit physics. Veronica laid down several thousand dollars for smugglers to guide them through the southern part of Mexico and then over the Rio Grande. But she got caught in the new Americans policy. She and her kids were bounced with a Remain in Mexico document that bore a first court hearing date two months hence.

With no guarantee now that she would get inside the United States to work, American asylum suddenly held no interest for Veronica. She said she planned to toss the court papers in the trash and return to the supposed death trap of Honduras with the kids.

"If I knew before that things were going to be like this, I never would have left the country," she said.

I had to ask the obvious question, since she had come ostensibly to claim asylum from persecution back home. "Didn't you have to flee Honduras with your children or die?" I asked.

Not at all, she answered, a puzzled expression forming on her face. "I just want to go home and find a job in Honduras," she said.

What I learned from many other expellees on that Juárez trip was that Trump's Remain in Mexico policy was having its intended psychological impact on decision-making. The policy struck at the basic calculus underlying decision-making. They did not see the American asylum system as anything other than a mechanism that would get them inside the country to work, not as protection from places that immigration advocates always characterized as house-on-fire death traps.

Take Gaixania Reyes, a twenty-two-year-old Honduran woman in the same shelter. When I met this young woman, she was dissolute over her Remain in Mexico deportation two days earlier because her paper's hearing date was five months hence. Gaixania said she reached her decision to head for the Texas border to achieve "the American dream" after seeing half her town's families get in through the border on asylum claims.

"Thousands left my town. The schools were empty. No kids. No parents. Everybody was saying I can cross with kids," she said. "I really thought I would make it in because so many people crossed and got a better life."

Gaixania was single without the child golden ticket in. But she heard even Hondurans without children were getting pass-through treatment on asylum claims (maybe because detention centers had run out of space by this time). She ran nose-first into Remain in Mexico instead. Gaixania was still pissed off recalling it.

"I didn't expect this!" she spat, waving her documents. "I think these papers are a joke! They played with our sentiments, and all they did was gave us these papers? When I came here and saw this, I realized they just want to run us off!"

Unless this asylum process was going to get her into the United States, Gaixania had no use for it. She said she would leave Mexico "as soon as possible."

"I've suffered enough, and I don't want to suffer more for a waste of time."

I couldn't help following up: Wasn't Honduras supposed to be a government killing machine and rape trap, forcing young women like her to flee for their lives and honor? Gaixania said she didn't see home like that at all. The only other place she wanted to live was the United States because of all the financial opportunities there.

At a different migrant shelter across town, Honduran expellee Jose Luis Funes told me he and most of the 700 migrants at the shelter with him were going home instead of waiting out some American asylum claim that didn't get them into America.

That decision was based on the (correct) knowledge that U.S. immigration judges almost never grant Hondurans asylum so, "I'm going back."

In fact, so many expellees were returning to their ostensibly intolerable dangerous hometowns that the United

Nations International Office of Migration (IOM) was filling free chartered buses to drive them all the way.[76] Although impossible to tally, other aspiring border-crossers no doubt stayed home in droves.

But Remain in Mexico was only one of other Trump policies that worked because they too took bites out of the immigrant decision-making calculus—particularly the incentivizing properties of American asylum in conjunction with Flores—as to whether to leave or stay home.

Trump hit the asylum nail in two other ways that drove it deeper.

Trump's DHS backed it all up with a huge deportation airlift of migrants back to Central America, Obama-like, so that those arriving on the tarmacs became living proof to the home village that smuggling investments weren't going to pay off.

Dusting off the Big Stick

By cutting off millions in aid to them, the president forced Guatemala, Honduras, and Mexico to sign "Safe Third Country" agreements. The gist of these was that any migrant who passed through one of these countries without first applying for asylum would be ineligible to apply for U.S. asylum and could be returned home. Trump's DHS thereafter would deny Salvadorans who had crossed through Honduras access to the American asylum process, and to Hondurans who crossed through Guatemala, and to Guatemalans who crossed through Mexico.

An underlying predicate was that authentically desperate political abuse refugees don't ask asylum of only the richest country around; they'd seek refuge in the very first safe country they came to. But that wasn't what any of these northward treks were ever about. Safe Third Country was just another way to block their releases into the United States, removing the smuggling fee payoff that first drew them in to claim asylum.

A third important innovation was Trump's demand that Mexico block off its southern border and make entries there hurt in various ways. To do this, Trump had to threaten Mexico with debilitating progressive trade tariffs unless it cordoned off its southern border with Guatemala, historically a migrant superhighway with no speed bumps or speed limits. It worked, for as long as the Mexicans were pressured to focus. Mexico deployed 25,000 militarized police and national guard on its southern and northern borders. The troops set up dozens of roadblocks throughout the southern provinces and bottled up the migrants while requiring them to apply for Mexican visas and asylum on pain of deportation. The Mexican troops were also to confront new caravans coming up through Guatemala. For so long as U.S. pressure was on, the Mexicans would beat hundreds into submission and force them onto deportation buses back to Central American countries.

To achieve these policies and make them work, Trump created national interests where none existed for these four countries. Not in an asking mood with his border being overrun, Trump dusted off Theodore Roosevelt's big stick. He threatened to pull millions in security assistance from the Central American countries if they didn't play in his sandbox and vowed that he would destroy Mexico's economy with progressive trade tariffs against all Mexican products. Now, these countries had a national interest in stopping the flow. He demanded those countries break up the caravans, take American expulsions under Safe Third Country and Remain in Mexico, and secure their own southern borders to shut the spigot as close to off as possible.

No single one of these measures would probably have lowered the enter-and-stay odds without the other layers. Short of permanent legislative fixes that would never come from a divided Congress, together these worked like an imperfect miracle.

Apprehensions of family units plummeted from the May 2019 peak of 84,486 to 15,824 by September 2019. They stayed down for all of the months leading to the Covid-19 pandemic in early 2020, when Trump ordered that every border-crossing migrant be expelled, and then the numbers fell even further.

Trump's cocktail of policies—Remain in Mexico, Safe Third Country, big stick diplomacy, air deportations, and more—began to turn back the tide, just as did President Obama's in 2014. And the reason was that each component was machine-engineered to squarely hit at the real root cause of mass migrations, the ones inside immigrant minds and bank accounts.

If Trump's tough actions-backed communication about cracking down on illegal immigration caused a Trump Effect, it follows that what Joe Biden and Kamala Harris were saying on the campaign trail caused an equal and opposite Biden Effect of spiking illegal immigration.

Indeed, the Democratic Party and every one of its mainstream presidential contenders, to include Biden and Harris, began messaging as their own the most fringe ideas about immigration and the border ever heard on the main American public square:

- Abolish ICE.
- End all deportation.
- End detention.
- Extend U.S. asylum access to all comers.
- Grant mass citizenship.
- Free health care to all.
- Stop the wall.

No Democratic Party in modern history had ever taken such unconventional positions about illegal immigration. The universe of aspiring migrants was listening and, reasonably, sprinted toward the border as fast as possible the moment that those issuing these promises came to power and followed through. But who were these people?

CHAPTER FOUR

THE NEW THEOLOGIANS

> *"We simply cannot allow people to pour into the United States, undetected, undocumented, unchecked and circumventing the line of people who are waiting patiently, diligently, and lawfully to become immigrants in this country."*
>
> —Senator Barack Obama (D-IL), 2005 press conference[77]

> *"There is a limit to how many migrants any society can take without severe disruption and assistance,"*
>
> —President Bill Clinton, September 2022 CNN interview[78]

When the American people elected Donald Trump on November 8, 2016, my job suddenly changed. Overnight, I was required to fear, prepare for, and prevent the assassination of Texas Governor Greg Abbott and a coming bloodbath in downtown Austin.

The threats emanated from a new front about which I knew almost nothing: the ultra-violent "anti-fascist action" movement most commonly known today by its contraction, "antifa."

I was already six years into a second career as a civilian intelligence officer for the Texas Department of Public Safety's Intelligence and Counterterrorism Division. I'd been recruited to join Texas DPS from a twenty-three-year career as a newspaper reporter, much of it in Texas writing about national security affairs. By the time Trump was elected, I managed a team of analysts in my agency's sprawling headquarters and Highway Patrol cadet training campus a few miles north of downtown Austin. We did all the state's counterterrorism work inside a nondescript four-story building on campus that also housed the Texas Rangers command staff. As this unit's manager, I was also responsible for the intelligence to secure the state's huge capitol complex in downtown Austin, a fifty-building region that included the handsome Red Sunset granite state capitol building that housed the legislature and the iconic 1856 plantation-style governor's mansion nearby.

Broadly speaking, we helped detect and eliminate threats from violent Islamists and also politically motivated domestic extremists of all kinds. This was, after all, Texas, a state with probably an outsized national share of kooks and killers. Antifa followers fit that bill. It's a decentralized leadership movement composed of groups that include "extreme actors" who engage in "violence or vandalism at rallies and events," an Anti-Defamation League (ADL) description reads.[79] Its adherents come from the anarchist movement or from the far left to oppose fascism, although the ADL's page on antifa explains that since the 2016 presidential election, antifa's expanded definition of fascism included "many conservatives and supporters of former President Trump."

Now, suddenly, followers of this antifa movement—some masked and armed with AR-15s, others brandishing handmade weaponry like *Mad Max* movie characters—were attacking at my capitol. This was especially problematic because, the year before I joined DPS, on June 8, 2008, someone burned the mansion to the ground with a hurled Molotov cocktail during a $10 million restoration project. Governor Rick Perry and his family were away. No one was caught by the ten-year statute of limitations, so whoever tossed the Molotov got away with it. But throughout my tenure, the mansion attack remained an embarrassing unsolved crime that everyone in my world understood could not happen again. So, there was that. But also after Trump took office, antifa groups launched an "Occupy ICE" campaign that involved semi-permanent camps whose inhabitants would try to disrupt ICE operations. That ramped up in Texas too.

I recount my DPS experience with antifa and leftist anti-Trump militants here because this is how, when President Biden later took office a couple of years after I let state service, I immediately recognized the origins of the ideas his administration adopted for the border.

The antifa street fighters and ideological cousins throughout the leftist Occupy ICE fringe were always clear about their goals for immigration after Trump was gone: tear down the entire U.S. immigration system of laws and enforcement, especially its scaffolding of detention and deportation, and not replace them. They wanted to "reimagine" the border as open to all who would like to cross it, maybe leave a rump infrastructure to regulate imports or exports of goods. The entire Democratic Party's immigration policy agenda seemed as though it were lifted straight from the antifa street signs and graffiti we'd studied.

Long before Trump won, we started to receive FBI and DHS intelligence reports warning that an "anarchist extremist" constellation of groups under the antifa banner was emerging as a significant national domestic terrorism threat. These "anarchist extremists," as the DHS and FBI called them in early 2016, were attacking peaceable Trump campaign rallies across the country with organized premeditation, long before he even won a primary, and ramping up as he advanced.

The activists began striking at the Austin capitol complex and elsewhere in the state when Trump took office. For my last eighteen months with DPS, antifa occupied my team to protect the capitol and ICE agents, who had by then come under ubiquitous death threats.

To better understand the origins of the Biden mass illegal immigration crises, know that Biden entered office implementing versions of the ideas we observed in the placards, website slogans, protest chants, and graffiti of violent extremists and their supporters. The administration's keynote policy of ending detention and closing detention centers, for instance, was simpatico even with a manifesto left behind by one of them, Willem van Spronsen, after he died in his armed attack on an ICE facility in Washington State.

What other of their ideas made it into the White House, and who were the people carrying them to America's riots? I can write now about what the feds were telling us then because *Politico* reporter Josh Meyer published a story about the leaked Obama-era FBI and DHS intelligence reports that we were receiving.[80]

Antifa militants began showing up outside Trump campaign stop venues as early as February and March of 2016 among demonstrators keenly focused on the candidate's immigration rhetoric and policy vows, Meyer's reporting and isolated local media accounts show. The militant protesters followed Trump on the road all through March, April, and May 2016 in California, Utah, Chicago, Ohio, New York, Texas, and elsewhere through that summer. The attacks left a trail of property damage, wounded police officers, jailed militants, and bloodied Trump supporters who'd come to listen. Long before actual white supremacists marched on Charlottesville and finally reacted with clashed against leftist activists, Obama's DHS and FBI regarded the anarchist extremists of antifa as the *"primary instigators* [author's emphasis]*"* of antifa's long preelection attacks campaign, Meyer reported. The FBI viewed the attacks as "domestic terrorist violence."[81]

One April 2016 DHS-FBI assessment said the groups had become so aggressive that national intelligence community launched a global investigation to "determine whether the U.S.-based anarchists might start committing terrorist bombings like their counterpart groups in Greece, Italy and Mexico, possibly at the upcoming American political conventions."

Although political convention bombings never materialized, photos in the intelligence assessments show the assortment of deadly handmade weapons antifa adherents were using, such as ax handles and shields with industrial-length bolts attached as bayonets. A September 2016 DHS intelligence report stated that the militant attacks showed a "proficiency in pre-operational planning, to include organizing carpools to travel from different locations, raising bail money in preparation for arrests, counter-surveilling law enforcement using three-man scout teams, using handheld radios for communication, and coordinating the event via social media."

One thing we noticed was that immigration as an issue was preeminent in and around all of this antifa violence. The issue clearly inflamed opponents and motivated attacks on Trump events once he became the presumptive Republican nominee. Immigration had clearly emerged as a catalyzing cause in the broader leftist protest community that cocooned antifa. Typical was the April 2016 riot in California's Orange County city of Costa Mesa. Like most, this one left Trump supporters bloodied and more than twenty mostly antifa rioters in jail after the speeches. Throughout the violence, demonstrators waved Mexican flags "in apparent opposition to Trump's call for a border wall," the *Washington Post* reported in one line.[82]

That same month, antifa activists attacked Trump supporters leaving an indoor rally in San Jose, California. Protesters punched passive rally participants bloody, pelted them with eggs, and snatched Make America Great Again hats off heads and lit them on fire.[83] Front and center in all this were the Mexican flags waving from vehicles nearby. In Albuquerque a week earlier, energetic protestors chanted and held signs criticizing Trump's immigration positions while antifa militants launched a violent assault on 1,000 peaceful protestors at a Trump rally. The event suddenly "morphed into madness…when mostly young, raucous rioters joined the ranks, hurling burning T-shirts, rocks and bottles toward the police and police horses trying to contain them," the *Washington Post* reported.[84] Immigration again was a central stated issue.

Texas saw action too. On June 19, 2016, antifa militants tried to start trouble at a Trump rally in Dallas, attacking some of the Trump rally attendees before Dallas police horse patrols separated them.[85] Dallas police arrested one. Another Trump supporter hit by a hurled rock was hospitalized. Demonstrators lay in wait for Trump near Houston the next day, though police kept the two sides under control there.

We in Austin certainly paid attention to these events and to the federal intelligence reports about these hopscotching antifa attacks following the Trump campaign. But I did not reorder our priorities that summer of 2016, for several reasons. We were too focused on the devastating July 8, 2016, lone offender sniper ambush of five Dallas police officers and another one later that month in next-door Louisiana. Leftist black nationalists carried out the carnage in both attacks. A black nationalist extremist named Micah Johnson, acting alone, emerged from an otherwise peaceable Black Lives Matter demonstration in downtown Dallas to shoot fourteen white police officers, killing five before a police robot carrying explosives to Johnson killed him.[86] It was the worst massacre of police officers in national history and racially motivated.

Two weeks later, another lone black nationalist and military veteran from Missouri named Gavin Long killed three more white police officers in Baton Rouge, Louisiana, in the midst of violent demonstrations over the recent police killing of Alton Sterling.[87] Long left behind a handwritten manifesto filled with BLM talking points about the need to "create substantial change within America's police forces and judicial system."[88] We also set antifa aside at that moment, despite the federal intelligence reporting, because its street violence didn't promise longevity; polling at the time was predicting that Trump would shortly lose.

Except that he did not. Trump's surprise victory set off a nationwide orgy of violence and property destruction in cities across America that went on for weeks, then months. From election day forward to Inauguration Day 2017 and beyond, antifa groups launched a relentless series of attacks— on police, on university campuses where conservative figures were scheduled to speak, and on demonstrators, anyone they viewed as fitting their expanding definition of "fascist."[89] They roamed the country setting arson fires and destroying property along the way. We had no choice but to make room for antifa alongside left-wing black nationalist cop killers, who evidently mixed in the same stewpot at the demonstrations anyway. The federal intelligence assessments that had been landing on our desks for eight months warned of significant "intelligence gaps" about antifa, the groups that were forming and the individuals joining up. Filling those gaps also became especially urgent because Republican Greg Abbott won the Texas governorship, partly on calls to spurn the resettlement of Syrian war refugees, and because he was planning an Inauguration Day parade through downtown the same day as Trump's in Washington. I directed the team to learn everything possible about the movement's ideology and groups in Texas as they related to violence and threats of violence. We were worried about the Micah Johnsons, Gavin Longs, and whatever violent activity antifa groups planned to bring for the capitol parade and beyond now that Trump and Abbott were going to be around.

It didn't take long for the antifa violence to hit Austin's capitol complex. On November 19, 2016, antifa militants showed up among hundreds of demonstrators who came to oppose a small group of two dozen peaceful, albeit demonstrably racist, white supremacist demonstrators at the capitol complex calling themselves "White Lives Matter." Wild melees ensued when the black-clad antifa activists attacked them and beat DPS troopers who tried to intervene.[90] Our agency had deployed a protective cordon around the White Lives Matter group but had to send in more riot troopers as reinforcements. We arrested eight of the antifa attackers.

This was only the beginning.

Considering the level of organizing and threatening language we were seeing on social media, I recommended at one brainstorm meeting that Governor Abbott cancel his inauguration parade. The Trump-Abbott inaugurations seemed like a double-barreled provocation. We feared someone also inflamed by one, the other, or both inaugurations would try something horrific, like an assassination of the governor. While it was our job to think that way, the governor proceeded with his parade.

The Washington inauguration of Trump spawned widespread antifa riots beyond the security perimeter. Rioters burned cars, smashed store windows, took control of street blocks, and attacked officers trying to stop it. The melee went on for hours. Police pounded the rioters with stun grenades, tear gas, and bean bag projectiles. Six officers were injured. As Trump walked along part of the parade route toward a group of black-clad demonstrators, the Secret Service hustled him back into his armored vehicle. It took riot police hours to regain the streets with brute force, arresting more than 200.

Back in Austin, Abbott's parade was a white-knuckled, nerve-racking affair for us, but the massive security we put out in coordination with Austin Police Department worked. Although demonstrators tried to blockade streets to disrupt it, our perimeter held without serious incident.

What we had seen in Austin up to that point was a small taste of more to come. As I've mentioned, a searing animus about the candidate's immigration agenda, in chants, waving Mexican flags, and some of the placards, fueled the violence against the earliest Trump rallies. After the election, that catalyzing energy went into the "Occupy ICE" national protest campaign. Militants set up tent camps near ICE properties throughout Texas and set about trying to disrupt the detentions and deportations of illegal immigrants. At the same time a fiery propaganda campaign began to demonize ICE agents. Credible threats to their lives led to an immigration-related phase of our intelligence work, which continued for me until I left government service in August 2018.

Traditional Democrats Cut from Trumpian Cloth

It wasn't always this way. In fact, these positions had never spread as far and fast on the far left as they did during this time. The contemporary Democratic Party has always loathed illegal immigration, its leading voices the greatest standard bearers of border and immigration policies that would qualify as outright Trumpian.

Consider the Democratic Party labor leader hero Cesar Chavez of United Farm Workers (UFW) union fame, whose legacy is so cherished among the party elite that President Biden positioned a bronze bust of Chavez on his Oval Office desk alongside family photos. Surprisingly, the renowned champion of agricultural laborers was furiously anti-immigrant. In fact, he mounted his famous boycotts of grapes and lettuce to counteract the federal government's refusal to stop illegal immigration. Powerful agricultural interests wanted the cheap labor of illegal workers. But Chavez saw that they drove down wages and undermined his strikes on behalf of legal workers. Chavez went even further by opposing *legal* immigration through the 1942–1964 Bracero Program, the World War II–era worker permit initiative used to keep agriculture production going while American men fought overseas.

Chavez reserved special ire for illegal Mexican migrant workers, whom he routinely called by the charged, derogatory term "wetbacks." In 1974, Chavez went so far as to dispatch 300 thugs to establish a "wet line" near Yuma, Arizona. The vigilantes organized into patrols to intercept migrant workers and "persuade them to turn back." But the patrols quickly turned violent.[91] They beat at least thirty-seven migrants as they crossed the border to discourage others from breaking a lemon-pickers strike that year.[92] The UFW also bribed Mexican officials in San Luis to stop border crossers on their side.

In the 1970s, the man whose bronze bust made it into Biden's Oval Office conducted the "Illegals Campaign" that ultimately reported 2,200 illegal workers to immigration authorities, "an effort he deemed second in importance only to the boycott," his biographer Miriam Pawel wrote in her book *The Crusades of Cesar Chavez*.[93]

"There's an awful lot of illegals coming in," Chavez said in a 1974 interview. "They're coming in by the thousands. It's just unbelievable. It's a vicious attack on the local worker. The workers themselves, even though a lot of them are Mexican descendants...are very upset and very worried and very mad about the illegals coming to break their strike. It takes away their jobs and livelihood and so on."[94]

Other leftist icons took similar hard lines. In 1990, Martin Luther King's widow, Coretta Scott King, joined civil rights leaders to stop a congressional attempt with the pro-illegal immigration National Council of La Raza to legalize hiring illegal immigrants.[95] It worked. In the mid-1990s, the iconic civil rights trailblazer Barbara Jordan, the first black woman elected to Congress from the South, headed a presidential commission that called for strict enforcement of immigration laws and a reduction in legal immigration.[96] Jordan later proved tireless in arguing for tight border controls as a means to end illegal immigration.

Even the progressive Democratic icon Bernie Sanders, the most recent hero of hard-left America, mirrored the 1970s sentiments of Chavez up until 2015. It's almost striking today to note that no meaningful distinction exists between what Sanders believed, circa 2015, and Trump's "America First" notions about protecting working-class people from illegal immigrants. No one ever called the Jewish socialist a racist for his belief that unskilled illegal immigrants drove down the wages of working-class Americans. In a July 2015 interview with Vox's Ezra Klein, Sanders characterized "open borders" policies as "a right-wing proposal" championed by corporations hooked on cheap foreign labor.[97]

Like me and former President Obama, Sanders also saw illegal immigration as threatening American sovereignty.

"You're doing away with the concept of a nation state, and I don't think there's any country in the world that believes in that," Sanders told Klein when asked if he supported open borders immigration. "If you believe in a nation state or in a country called the United States or UK or Denmark or any other country, you have an obligation, in my view, to do everything we can to help poor people."[98]

To get anywhere politically in the 2016 and 2020 campaigns for the Democratic nomination, Sanders had to ditch those long-held positions, as we'll see.

The last two Democratic presidents, Barack Obama (2009–2016) and Bill Clinton (1992–2001), both lawyers, would never have countenanced dismantling the basics of immigration enforcement. Both presidents not only defaulted to existing laws and policies that required detention of illegal immigrants until deportation but signed some new ones. Clinton supported and signed the Illegal Immigration Reform and Immigrant Responsibility Act of 1996, which increased the number of Border Patrol agents and beefed-up criminal penalties for alien smuggling and immigration fraud. It also required proof of claims made in asylum applications.[99]

Clinton was downright proud of border crackdowns and attitudes that would have turned future President Trump green with envy. He went farther in his 1995 State of the Union speech than even Trump would during his presidency:

> All Americans, not only in the states most heavily affected, but in every place in this country, are rightly disturbed by the large numbers of illegal aliens entering our country. The jobs they hold might otherwise be held by our citizens or legal immigrants. The public services they use impose burdens on our taxpayers. That's why our administration has moved aggressively to secure our borders more by hiring a record number of new border guards, by deporting twice as many criminal aliens as ever before, by cracking down on illegal hiring, by barring welfare benefits to illegal aliens. In the budget I presented to you, we will try to do more to speed the deportations of illegal aliens who are arrested for crimes, to better identify illegal aliens who are in the work-place. We are a nation of immigrants. But ulti-mately, we are a nation of laws. It is wrong and ultimately self-defeating for a nation of immi-grants to permit the kind of abuse of our immi-gration laws we have seen in recent years, and we must do more to stop them.[100]

In fact, when Biden was a senator (also a lawyer), he and then-Senator Obama were among sixty-four Democratic lawmakers who voted in favor of the Secure Fence Act of 2006, which significantly expanded the construction of walls and barriers along the southwest border.[101] During Obama's second term and after he left, party liberals pinned the derisive "deporter-in-chief" nickname on him for presiding over some four million removals, with Biden as his vice president, on grounds that he had to follow the law.[102]

During a 2013 San Francisco speech on immigration, a South Korean heckler in the United States illegally complained that deportations were separating families, shouting, "You have the power to stop all deportations!"[103] In response, Obama shot back: "Actually, I don't. If in fact I could solve all these problems without passing laws in Congress, I would do so. But we are also a nation of laws. The easy way out is to yell and pretend like I can do something by violating our laws."

When a Univision reporter asked Obama that same year if he would consider a "moratorium on deportations of non-criminals," Obama the lawyer stayed the course:

> I think it is important to remind everybody that, as I said I think previously, I'm not a king. I am head of the executive branch of government. I'm required to follow the law. And that's what we've done.[104]

Yet in 2019 and 2020, in a stunning turn, every Democratic presidential candidate came off like Occupy ICE activists living in tents. All fifteen of them tried to one-up each other as to who was *most* willing to end the *most* deportations and be the *quickest* to shut down detention centers, who would go the *hardest* to curtail ICE, and who would *most enthusiastically* expand the abuse of asylum laws, who would deny with the most vigor that most border-jumpers were coming for jobs and not fleeing murderous government persecution. Suddenly, extreme ideas long rejected by the Democratic Party mainstream were center stage orthodoxy.

So, what the hell happened? What were these ideas and their wellspring? And how did they become the putative new law of the land?

Signposts on the road to the White House

Early on the morning of July 13, 2019, a self-employed carpenter and social justice warrior named Willem van Spronsen drove away from his home on Vashon Island in Washington State for one last battle. A sixty-eight-year-old recovering alcoholic who as a boy had immigrated to the U.S. legally from the Netherlands, van Spronsen took with him an AR-15 semiautomatic rifle with six full magazines, a satchel full of flares, and Molotov cocktails. He mailed farewell letters to his closest friends, timed to arrive afterward.[105] He wrote a manifesto to be found later too.

His friends and family—and local police—knew van Spronsen as a committed anarchist and social justice warrior.[106] One of his heroines was the late nineteenth-century anarchist radical Emma Goldman, once convicted of inciting a riot and also implicated, though never convicted, in the 1894 botched assassination of an industrialist and in the 1901 assassination of President William McKinley.[107]

Trump's victory had energized van Spronsen and thousands of other leftist activists like him.[108] He was the first to join a local antifa group that believed its members should all be armed for self-defense, the Puget Sound John Brown Gun Club, and he built its membership as an early recruiter.[109] The group's namesake, John Brown, was a nineteenth-century abolitionist who helped runaway slaves evade slave catchers. He led guerrilla raids on proslavery towns until locals caught and hung him. The John Brown Gun Club provided firearms training to members who carried their weapons at pro-Trump rallies to contest ostensible fascist control of the streets.[110] It claimed to be a "public facing, above ground, armed community defense group," although members never had to fire weapons in defense or anger.[111]

Starting in early 2018, Occupy ICE militants were moving into tents near federal facilities for weeks and months and fought with authorities. As the main DHS agency responsible for carrying out American immigration laws, ICE arrests, detains, and deports those for whom lawful deportation orders are issued, at the border or from interior American cities. The agency runs government detention facilities and also oversees private ones built to alleviate bed space shortages at greater cost-saving speed and efficiency.

Van Spronsen jumped into the Occupy ICE campaign in his area that summer of 2018, squatting with other militant activists in a parking lot area of the privately owned Northwest Detention Center on the Tacoma Tideflats, one of the nation's biggest.[112]

Antifa groups and now a growing army of thousands of progressive liberals in other group types descended on the nation's detention centers for often stormy daily protests during which many tried to disrupt operations by blocking roads, doors, and fighting with security.[113]

Van Spronsen threw himself into this work with vigor. During one of many melees, Tacoma police arrested him when he lunged at one officer to free a fellow protester. Officers found a baton and knife on van Spronsen, and he pleaded guilty to obstructing a law enforcement officer.

Still, after a year of social justice action, in the summer of 2019, ICE was not only still standing, it was readying one of its routine annual nationwide roundups of criminal aliens with outstanding deportation orders on them.[114] Apoplectic with rage over this news, the Occupy ICE groups vowed more action to stop the coming raids.[115] But van Spronsen saw a need for more productive tactics.

At 4 a.m. the day before the raids were to start, he pulled into the Northwest Detention Center parking lot determined to *really* make a difference.

"Detention camps are an abomination," van Spronsen wrote in his farewell manifesto. "I'm not standing by."

He set flares under a 500-pound propane tank. In an apparent effort to prevent immigrants from being taken to their doom, he hurled Molotov cocktails at ICE buildings and transport buses, hoping to disable transport of victims.

One building caught fire. He'd turned his own vehicle into a swirling ball of flames fifteen feet high, a video shows. He still had the AR-15 when four Tacoma Police officers showed up on the flaming, smoking scene and ordered him to drop it. He pointed it at them instead.[116] It malfunctioned. He went down in a hail of gunfire.

Today, government homeland security personnel regard van Spronsen as a radicalized left-wing domestic terrorist in the classic legal sense, in that he chose deadly force to coerce social or political change.[117] His story is not recounted here because of that inglorious status. Rather, his story helps illuminate the unlikely journey of a largely rejected belief system from the fringe precincts of violent leftist hooligans and onto the main debate stages of Democratic presidential candidates, into the White House, and then on to become national immigration policy.

Collectively, the ideology that animated van Spronsen and his antifa cohorts traces to late nineteenth-century anarchist protests against industrialization and the abusive power of monopolistic corporations run by capitalist robber barons.[118] In those days, activists who rallied around the idea of reigning in capitalist abuses were known as "left liberals," or "progressive liberals." [119] In the late 1930s, the Spanish civil war energized the left liberals, as well as their newer cousins, communists and socialists, to armed opposition against the fascist dictator Francisco Franco in a civil war for control of the country. The fascist Spanish nationalist Franco ultimately prevailed with the help of Nazi Germany and ruled from 1939 to 1975. For the progressive liberals and socialists who fought them, the defeat cemented "fascism" as a long-lived enemy that had to be suppressed by force lest it ever again become unassailable.

Thirty years later, in the 1960s, the so-called "New Left" movement picked up the baton. Yes, the enemy was still the old robber-baron capitalism but also, now, disempowered peoples viewed as vulnerable to unjust oppression in the interest of corporate capitalism: blacks, women, gay people, and Vietnamese, though not yet immigrants.

Willem van Spronsen and his generation of militant leftist activists is better understood if seen in the framework of social psychologist Jonathan Haidt. His book, *The Righteous Mind: Why Good People Are Divided by Politics and Religion*, explains that modern communications technology and media now grow modern leftist movements. With instant communication, people of "righteous minds" coalesce into "tribal moral communities" that next coalesce around "victim groups" they then "sacralize."[120]

"If you sacralize these groups, it binds you together to fight for them," Haidt wrote, adding a dark warning about this. "Once you sacralize something, you become blind to evidence. Morality binds and blinds. Everyone goes blind when talking about their sacred objects."

Once tribal moral communities are established, they build "grand narratives" around the defense of their sacralized victim groups and perceived persecutors. In this way, modern activist leaders are most like twelfth-century theologians who would defend and expand their religion with state military forces. Any group that disagrees with grand narratives around the tribal community's chosen sacralized victim groups is then demonized, which can lead to "moralistic killing, and many religions are well suited to that task," Haidt said.

I raise the Haidt theoretical model because probably nothing like the arrival of Donald Trump did more to forge new "tribal moral communities" on the American left since the 1960s. Trump's vows to hermetically seal the southern border and to deport the millions of illegal immigrants living inside the United States turned heightened alarm into hysteria on the left. He'd won office by promising to build a "big beautiful" border wall, enforce immigration laws, and remove the asylum system loophole enticements that kept drawing foreign nationals north.

In all of this and more, Trump proved more galvanizing than when the Great Recession of 2009 drove people like van Spronsen to mount the Occupy Wall Street civil disobedience movement in 2011 and 2012 against corporate excess.[121] That first year, van Spronsen built tarp structures for Occupy ICE encampments.[122] In terms of longevity, Trump was far more galvanizing than the World Trade Organization's 1999 annual meeting in Seattle that drew tens of thousands of anarchist and leftist anti-capitalist activists to riot for more than a week and seize several blocks of the city's downtown. Trump proved the most galvanizing for antifa and other groups ideologically aligned with them on the far left.

More than thirty years of aggressive New York media coverage of the celebrity real estate developer somehow missed that he was a white supremacist Nazi. But his opponents on the far left created a brand-new "grand narrative" that conjured Trump and his voters as the spearhead of a rising new white nationalist fascism.

"Trump changed the world," explained Thomas Cartwright, a volunteer social justice activist for the pro-immigration group Witness at the Border in an interview with me. "When you have something so extreme on one side…the reaction becomes extreme. And so I think people who are driven to say, 'we can't stomach that and so, therefore we're going to go all the way over here,' there's no question that happened, me being in the middle of that fight.

"Even if people want to moderate a bit, there's no willingness to step back to a more moderate position," Cartwright told me. "Nobody's going to move on the left. It's like this standoff."

In van Spronsen's manifesto, we can see the inflammatory grand narratives that were spinning about the ICE infrastructure for detention and deportation once Trump was in office. One particularly influential narrative found comparison of ICE enforcement of immigration laws approved by Congress to Nazi brown-shirt thugs throwing Jews into "concentration camps."[123] By this propagandistic construct, Trump and his ICE thugs, for instance, loaded their abused political detainees onto "death flights," as Witness at the Border has termed ICE Air deportations, that delivered them to home countries where they faced absolutely certain brutalization. (Cartwright points out that he does not support use of the "death flights" term.)[124]

In his farewell manifesto, van Spronsen wrote that as a child in postwar Holland and France in the 1950s, he heard the terrible stories of Nazi fascism and struck a bargain with himself: "I would not be one of those who stands by as neighbors are torn from their homes and imprisoned for somehow being perceived as lesser."[125]

"Evil says concentration camps for folks deemed lesser are necessary," he wrote. "The handmaid of evil says the concentration camps should be more humane."

And now, he wrote, that day has come to strike at them.

"Here it is," he wrote, "in these corporate for profit [sic] concentration camps."

"Here it is, in brown and non conforming [sic] folks afraid to show their faces for fear of the police…."

Along with Holocaust metaphors came the demonization of ICE officers as subhuman and the new rallying cry of "Abolish ICE!"[126] This new, new American progressive left idealized itself as antebellum abolitionists; hence the name of van Spronsen's antifa group, the John Brown Gun Club. It considered the immigrants as sacred, desperate puritan neighbors at risk of annihilation. The framing presumed a "human right to migrate" with no distinction between invited and uninvited.[127] They would find an out-group to demonize: ICE agents.

The dehumanization language and sense of violence were already in the air about police in general, at riotous BLM demonstrations that had started in Ferguson, Missouri, over the police killing of teenager Michael Brown (later ruled justified). The table was well set for the militant protest groups to add ICE agents to the growing anti-police movement in those political precincts. It was catching.

In the fall of 2018, ICE arrested Occupy ICE activist Sergio "Mapache" Salazar at a San Antonio protest camp following a lengthy FBI terrorism investigation. The FBI zeroed in on the eighteen-year-old illegal immigrant, brought over as a young child, for posting threats to bomb ICE agents and pointing the way to instructional videos to build explosive devices.[128] ICE ended up deporting Salazar to Mexico as a national security concern. Later in an antifa-affiliated *It's Going Down* podcast interview from Mexico, Salazar betrayed how he viewed ICE and FBI agents.[129]

"I could tell anybody first-hand, anybody who works for ICE looks like the most miserable piece of shit on Earth," Salazar said. "They look like demons. I don't know what it's like to work for ICE, but they don't look like humans anymore."

In August 2018, the FBI arrested Cambridge, Massachusetts, activist Brandon Ziobrowski for using Twitter to offer at least his 448 followers $500 to "anyone who kills an ICE agent… seriously, who else can pledge…get in on this…let's make this work." He tweeted in response to an ICE field office director's tweet that agents risk their lives to arrest criminal aliens. Ziobrowski replied: "Thank you ICE for putting your lives on the line and hopefully dying, I guess so there's less of you."

A jury later acquitted Ziobrowski on a free-speech defense. "He was only joking, a jury ruled," read part of the *Washington Post* headline.[130]

ICE animus like this had grown so phosphorescent during 2018 that activists scraped the social media platform LinkedIn for personal information leading to home addresses of some 9,000 agents. DHS Deputy Secretary Claire Grady issued a memo to all agents warning of "specific and credible threats levied against certain DHS employees and a sharp increase in the overall number of general threats against DHS employees."[131] It was in this atmosphere that van Spronsen conducted his suicide terror attack.

It should not surprise anyone that van Spronsen, embedded as he was inside the moral community of leftist militant activism, would imbibe its radical ideas about shuttering detention centers and grand narratives about illegal immigrants as a civil rights victim group.

What was a big surprise, however, was that California Senator Kamala Harris, Joe Biden, and a long who's who list of mainstream Democratic politicians adopted all of it as their own—the new encoded language, the ideology, and the policy ideas. That included every serious Democratic Party primary candidate for president.

Hardly anyone noticed that tectonic plates had shifted on immigration.

A Border Erasure by Many Other Names

Just one week after police killed Willem van Spronsen and found his manifesto decrying corporate profiteering from private detention centers, Senator Harris, who was running in the Democratic primaries at the time, tweeted: "Let's be clear: private prisons are making money off the incarceration and suffering of human beings. One of my first acts of business as president will be to begin phasing out detention centers and private prisons."

"Certain communities" saw ICE as comparable to the Ku Klux Klan for "administering its power in a way that is causing fear and intimidation, particularly among immigrants and specifically among immigrants coming from Mexico and Central America," Harris said earlier, during a Senate confirmation hearing of Trump's nominee to lead ICE (Ronald Vitiello).

Harris was just one of many Democratic officeholders repeating the Far Left dogmas on immigration wafting around with the smoke of anti-police BLM arson, antifa attacks on Trump supporters, and Occupy ICE campfires.

As can be understood from antifa and other radical group website writings, news accounts, placards, protest chants, and public statements, what the rioting Left was demanding throughout the Trump years was that leaders tear down the U.S. immigration system, which successive Congresses and presidents—both Democrats and Republicans—built over the years by the consent of their voters.

Remember that the Immigration and Nationality Act *requires* the American government to detain every border jumper, put them into deportation proceedings, and keep them detained throughout those proceedings. There are loopholes and exits. But no Democratic Party–led government had ever seriously considered ignoring or dismantling those laws.

This newly energized species of progressive leftists suddenly demanded, and virtually every mainstream Democratic Party candidate promised, policies that could only result in unimpeded immigration over the border with no resistance, negative consequence, or limit. Under this new design, anyone from anywhere in the world who wanted to come could get in and stay forever and with no fear of deportation. Boiled down, this new political leftist bloc was finding significant political purchase for the following demands, which I have somewhat generalized for easier comprehension:

- Decriminalize illegal border entry, which Bill Clinton's 1996 reform law regarded as a federal misdemeanor carrying up to six months in prison and progressively more for subsequent offenses.
- End deportations of every stripe, minus terrorism or the most extreme criminality, not only for new border-crossers but also for the estimated eleven million foreign nationals living illegally inside the United States.
- Build no physical barriers like walls that might impede pedestrian foot traffic over the border and demilitarize law enforcement surveillance of the frontier.
- Abolish ICE by reformatting it for some other duty not involving deportation.
- Close the ICE detention facilities and cancel government contracts for the network of private ones enabling detention and deportation, since these will no longer be needed.
- End permission requirements for new arrivals to work and otherwise fully participate in the economy and public welfare systems.
- Provide legal pathways to citizenship for those who illegally entered and remained illegally in the country.
- Solve the root causes of immigration by rebuilding origin countries in Central America.

Senator Harris was now telling the MSNBC cable news network the United States should "probably think about starting from scratch" on enforcing immigration laws, while a spokesperson for Harris said the senator was weighing "a complete overhaul of the agency, mission, culture, operations."[132]

In a 2019 interview with National Public Radio, candidate Harris expressed a seeming willingness to declare all illegal border crossers refugees from definite political violence, even if that meant breaking the law.

"I disagree with any policy that would turn America's back on people who are fleeing harm. I frankly believe that it is contrary to everything that we have symbolically and actually said we stand for," she said.[133] "And so, *I would not enforce a law* [author's emphasis] that would reject people and turn them away without giving them a fair and due process to determine if we should give them asylum and refuge."

Joining Harris in demands far beyond Democratic Party immigration policy convention were Senators Kirsten Gillibrand of New York and Elizabeth Warren of Massachusetts, along with House Representatives Pramila Jayapal of Seattle, Washington; Mark Pocan of Madison, Wisconsin; Alexandria Ocasio-Cortez of New York City; Jim McGovern of Worcester, Massachusetts; and other prominent officeholders such as New York Mayor Bill de Blasio.[134]

"It has become a deportation force, and I think you should separate criminal justice from immigration issues," Gillibrand told CNN in July 2018 about ICE. "You should get rid of it, start over, reimagine it, and build something that actually works."[135]

Until this strange moment in time, the only groups that would have countenanced such extreme notions were Mexican cartel smugglers, illegal immigrants themselves, immigrant resettlement organizations, and wacky Libertarians pushing for unhindered global economic activity.

It almost seemed as though van Spronsen had not died in vain. Democratic pollsters and strategists were repackaging antifa and BLM street graffiti, placard slogans, mob chant lines, and dark world visions for the Democratic Party debate stage, televised globally. They also filled a dozen presidential campaign websites, appeared on all the Sunday news shows, and informed the party's official 2020 platform.

"ICE is a terrorist organization, and its egomaniacal leader is Donald Trump," Cynthia Nixon, the *Sex and the City* television show actress who ran for governor of New York, tweeted during her campaign.[136]

Democratic primary candidate Joe Biden was no exception by 2019. It's hard to overstate what a stark departure Biden's new views represented from his very recent views on the subject. While he would not say anything so radical as "abolish ICE" out loud, he dog-whistled it.

During the debates, he telegraphed that he saw no need for detention centers and indicated he would do whatever was necessary to open the one-way superhighway to the asylum system and add some lanes.

"Look, we should not be locking people up," Biden the candidate said during a June 27, 2019, internationally televised debate. Those who come seeking asylum…we should immediately have the capacity to absorb them, and keep them safe until they can be heard."[137]

The campaign website went farther into previous forbidden zones, claiming that Biden "will make clear that the federal government should not use private facilities for any detention, including detention of undocumented immigrants."[138] He promised an unheard-of, potentially renewable one hundred–day moratorium on all interior deportations pending a review of what he'd do later—and that meant *every* deportation.

A moderator in the January 2020 debate asked Biden what changes he would make to ICE. He would fire any ICE agent who tried to deport an immigrant who had not committed a felony, Biden answered, adding a foretelling caveat that he would pare back deportation of even some felons.

"You only arrest for the purpose of dealing with a felony that's committed, and I don't count drunk driving as a felony," he said at the debate.

And the new Joe Biden now thought the old 2006 Joe Biden wrong on building walls since now all of a sudden "a wall is not a serious deterrent."[139]

Other candidates defaulted to the pretense that every foreigner crossing the border authentically needed asylum because they were definitely fleeing violence. The candidates also expressed outraged disdain for private detention centers, detention, deportation, and ICE. Democratic El Paso Congressman Robert Francis "Beto" O'Rourke vowed that, if elected, he would order the defunding of private, for-profit prison operators on day one.[140] In the shadow of El Paso's steel border wall, he went so far as to say, in response to a television reporter's question, that he would gladly tear it down.

Obama's former Housing and Urban Development chief, Julian Castro, a Latino politician from San Antonio, was first to propose decriminalizing illegal entry; then everyone else played catch-up. At a June 27, 2019, debate, nine of ten candidates raised hands when asked if they supported decriminalizing border crossings. [141]

Castro then upped the ante with a companion measure: to "put all undocumented immigrants—as long as they have not committed a serious crime—on a pathway to citizenship."[142] Most of the other candidates promised the same.

Candidate Elizabeth Warren threw logs on the blaze of inflammatory, ICE-abuse propaganda that subsequent investigation rarely bore out.[143] One Warren proposal would abolish ICE but did not call it that.

"I'll reshape CBP and ICE from top to bottom, focusing their efforts on homeland security efforts like screening cargo, identifying counterfeit goods and preventing smuggling and trafficking," Warren's campaign website said in July 2019, notably omitting the agency's core deportation and detention duties.

What was the source of newly empowered ideas to totally dismantle U.S. border sovereignty, and how could they have traveled such an improbable journey to the bright lights of this main stage?

A New American Civil Rights Campaign—
for Foreign Nationals—Is Born

The central package of demands from the hard-leftist corner of the activist community had been in circulation for years before Trump, perhaps waiting for his spark to set it alight.

On the conservative side of the aisle, many speculated that some organized cadre of billionaire leftists must have schemed to import future Democratic Party immigrant voters to monopolize power, the presumption being that these immigrants would increase the population counted by the census and create new congressional seats or Democrats. Maybe so.

But almost certainly, another influential culprit for an agenda to end immigration enforcement is the gratification that comes with seeing ideology made real, and a dash of profit motivation. A major force for proposals like ending detention and deportation was the hundreds of small and large nonprofit organizations that specialize in migrant assistance and resettlement, which earn government money by the head. Others that don't get government contracts raise private donations by claiming urgent needs associated with swamping numbers. Bottom line: the more immigrants coursing over the border, the merrier all the organizations become financially.

Most of these rejected ideas that led to a borderless America emerged from this constellation of progressive left immigrant advocacy organizations.

They really began pressing to end detention and deportation in 1996, as a reaction to congressional Democrats and President Clinton signing the statute that first criminalized border crossings and also denied social assistance to those who did. This leftist progressive wing of the party began building the current theology about immigration then. Among the ideas was that America's borders were anachronistic and threatened "universal human rights." Of course, that kind of crazy talk went nowhere fast in the halls of Democratic Party power. The argument that enforceable borders should be dismantled piece by piece to protect the supposed inalienable human rights of foreign nationals to cross the American borders at *their* will and leisure was always a tough sell in the United States on both sides of the aisle. Its purveyors had to get creative.

For the first time, in the late 1990s, the focus of those opposed to immigration restrictions moved away from classic economic arguments about immigrants' contribution to the gross domestic product—to something with a proven track record. These groups recast federal immigration enforcement as a threat to "civil rights," of the kinds sought and won by American citizens of color, women, and gay people.

Non-U.S. citizens and illegal immigrants under lawful deportation orders now got pushed under the rubric of "human rights" tied to "American values," according to *Journal of Ethnic and Migration Studies* researchers in a 2019 paper about how these groups recast their arguments for retail political sale.[144] That sell had to overcome a unique hurdle, the researchers wrote, because, unlike victim groups of the 1960s, illegal immigrants had no obvious claim to the same extra legal protection of U.S. citizens in matters of voting, working, and living their sexual preferences.

"Appeals to citizenship, and the rights of citizens, have served as important rallying cries, from Martin Luther King Jr.'s appeal to the 'promissory note' of the U.S. Constitution to gays and lesbians' call for the right to marriage equality," the *Journal of Ethnic and Migration Studies* concluded. "But how does one make claims on behalf of foreign residents who cannot even evoke second-class 'citizenship'?"

Pretty easily. By repackaging the messaging. Social movement leaders created a new "rights language…of empathy and commonality" by which to frame their anti-deportation campaigns for retail political sale, the authors wrote. This gave rise to a refurbishment of vocabulary from the 1960s civil rights movement that may sound familiar to readers today, for instance that "immigrant rights are civil rights" and "no human is illegal."

The Encrypted New Language

The failure of a massive immigration reform bill in 2007 gave new theology and its moral tribal community a fresh boost.

One of the more notable new marketing ideas was to mortar over the Grand Canyon–sized space that demarcated illegal from legal immigration. It was all now "immigration." In the language of the new advertising campaign, the leftist ideologues zapped the divide out of existence. They started using foretelling slogans like, "No Human Is Illegal."[145] Left-leaning political candidates then began using the alt-language to signal hard-left voters that they would jettison border enforcement, without alienating mainstream voters unfamiliar with the new linguistics.

New encrypted synonyms described radical ideas to eliminate detention and deportation; "humane," "fair," "dignified," and "compassionate treatment" meant free flow over borders. Conversely, "cruel," "inhumane," and "racist" became synonyms for any immigration law enforcement and deterrence policy at all. With the new double entendre words, candidates could dog-whistle to far-left constituencies in the tribal moral community that they sympathized with the new ideas at little to no risk of causing regular voters to recoil in alarm.

The Democratic Party's official 2020 platform wrapped its proposals in the new packaging.[146] One proposal to establish deportation sanctuaries across the country, preventing ICE officers from carrying out the removal orders of judges came out sounding like this:

> We will ensure that enforcement mechanisms are *humane* [author's italics] and consistent with our values and international *humanitarian* obligations. That's why we will end workplace and community raids. We will protect sensitive locations like our schools, houses of worship, health care facilities, benefits offices and Departments of Motor Vehicles from immigration enforcement actions....

The platform made it clear to its progressive wing—obliquely, tangentially—that detention and deportation were on the chopping block.

"We believe detention should be a last resort, not the default," the position paper said. "Democrats will prioritize investments in more effective and cost-efficient community-based alternatives to detention," all of which would free immigrants. Throughout the Biden administration's term, all senior leaders, policy directives, and executive orders used the same familiar descriptor of "humane, safe and orderly" when discussing policies that resulted in the admission of huge volumes of illegal alien border jumpers into America. When Border Patrol agents heard words like these, they knew they'd soon be putting in overtime to process the illegal alien border jumpers.

Foundations and nonprofit organizations poured hundreds of millions of dollars into marketing the new American "civil rights" campaign. Among them were the Carnegie Foundation, George Soros's Open Society Foundations, and the Ford Foundation, according to the Pulitzer Prize–winning author Jerry Kammer in his 2020 book *Losing Control: How a Left-Right Coalition Blocked Immigration Reform and Provoked the Backlash That Elected Trump.*[147]

Kammer estimated that between 2002 and 2020, foundations invested more than $400 million in public education messaging, lobbying and pestering big media companies to start using the language and promoting the idea that normal immigration enforcement offended the civil rights of all humanity. The money went into public policy think tanks like the Immigration Policy Center, social policy litigators like the Mexican American Defense and Education Fund, and the National Council of La Raza (now UnidosUS), which campaigned relentlessly to get the new language into mainstream newspapers like the *New York Times*. Other organizations joined in the campaigns, including the American Civil Liberties Union and environmental groups like the Sierra Club, which had once opposed illegal immigration on grounds that it put population pressure on natural habitats.

The table was well set for when Trump entered the public stage with his rather traditional policy ideas, albeit couched in off-putting barroom rhetoric. By 2017, hard leftist groups reacting against Donald Trump were gobbling it all up and so did, eventually, mainstream politicians who knew they needed these voters to put them in office or keep them there.

The reaction against Trump is how these extreme ideas breached the mainstream Democratic Party before the 2020 election cycle and remained there for years. Every Democratic candidate now felt they had to signal alignment with the moral tribal community and its new "grand narrative"—that U.S. civil rights extended to the entire world and that immigration laws were as anachronistic as Jim Crow laws, to be ignored until legislated out of existence.

I've answered the *what, who*, and *why* this fringe theology so soundly entered the mainstream of Democratic Party thinking and then the White House. I'll now turn to the *how*. The unlikely short answer is the socialist senator from Vermont, Bernie Sanders.

The Socialist Army of Bernie Sanders Ascends to Power

Writing for *The Atlantic* in September 2017, Peter Beinart was probably among the first to observe that Trump's rise bred "wider sympathy" throughout "the mainstream left" for antifa's cause, violence, and political ideas.[148]

"Since antifa is heavily composed of anarchists, its activists place little faith in the state, which they consider complicit in fascism and racism," Beinart wrote. "They prefer direct action: They pressure venues to deny white supremacists space to meet. They pressure employers to fire them and landlords to evict them. And when people they deem racists and fascists manage to assemble, antifa's partisans try to break up their gatherings, including by force.

"Such tactics," Beinart concluded, "have elicited substantial support from the mainstream left."

Beinart didn't provide details, but by "mainstream left" he was almost certainly referring to a liberal progressive wing of the party coalition that, during the 2016 election, taught the 2020 generation of Democratic candidates to fear Vermont Senator Bernie Sanders, the self-described "Democratic Socialist" that wing adored.

To reiterate, the real origins of the mass migration crisis that began in 2021 can be most properly laid at the feet of Donald Trump's presidency because it pumped high voltage into the liberal progressive political movement that Sanders built and wielded. In turn, all the candidates that year had to kneel and bow to a Sanders movement because of its surprising new influence.

Consider:

During the 2016 campaign, Sanders showed he could rally millions of under-thirties, liberal progressive supporters, and left-leaning independents and to threaten so-called centrist, establishmentarian candidates like Clinton. As an old-school workers' union socialist calling for "political revolution," Sanders himself was not regarded as a serious threat to a mainline Republican candidate for the presidency. His aim of reordering the known world from capitalism to a European-styled social-welfare system fell too far outside the rails of American politics.

But Sanders's unique charisma succeeded in selling his retro ideas to the Democratic polity's mostly white, young, liberal progressive wing moved by Trump to political activism in expanding numbers. His natural base didn't care yet about immigration until after Trump's election. The Democratic Party constituency that was thought to care most about immigration in 2015–2016 were Latinos, the so-called "Latino vote."

As I mentioned, Sanders's previous positioning on immigration resembled that of Cesar Chavez and Donald Trump's America First agenda, calling for the protection of working-class American citizens from illegal immigrants who would work for much less. But Sanders doubled back in 2016 to put him more in lockstep with the "Latino vote" and also with some of his own young people who were hating Trump and Trump's immigration rhetoric.[149] Clinton bested him, as we know.[150]

What matters more in the next cycle's immigration context is that Sanders showed he could raise threatening amounts of money, draw huge boisterous crowds at rallies, win state primaries, and—significantly—knock out rivals. Sanders became the party's ultimate power spoiler. In a field of six major Democratic primary candidates in 2016, Sanders ended with 46 percent of the pledged delegates, not that far behind Clinton's 54 percent. It was not bad for an old avowed socialist.

The party's elite white-knuckled its way through moments of existential dread of a Sanders victory. While the party nominated Clinton, Sanders "has still left an outsize mark on its future," Vox News' Jeff Stein wrote after the bruising campaign.[151] For starters, Sanders forced a string of policy concessions on the Democratic Party platform, pulling the entire party farther to the left than ever before. Party officials after that election described the new party platform as "the most progressive" in the party's history, "a characterization that's hard to dispute," Stein reported.

Four years later, that meant every candidate had to act strategically when Sanders entered the 2020 Democratic Party primary. Much had changed since 2016. This time, Sanders's white, young, progressive base, souped-up on Trump hatred, had exploded in size and energy. Unlike in 2016, this bigger progressive base focused avidly on immigration, since that was how they saw Trump channeling his inner Nazi.

This was the new army Bernie Sanders commanded going into the 2020 election.

Democratic voters in the largest numbers ever now held "progressive" views on immigration, more so than did all prior Democratic Party leaders like former President Obama, wrote Alex Samuels, an analyst with the statistical analysis site FiveThirtyEight.[152] In 2015, FiveThirtyEight polling showed that 65 percent of Democrats thought "immigrants strengthened our country." By 2020, that number had climbed to nearly 90 percent, which Samuels described as a "seismic move to the left on immigration."

Samuels reported what they wanted:

Many want to abolish or dramatically restructure U.S. Immigration and Customs Enforcement—a rallying cry that became popular among some Democrats amid some of Trump's most stringent immigration policies. And they want the federal government to stop deporting immigrants. They also want to broaden immigrants' access to social safety net programs.

The Latino electorate was much less a factor this presidential election cycle. If anything, it largely abdicated to Trump. A post-2016 election *New York Times* analysis of 28,000 precincts in twenty cities showed every precinct with a majority Latino population shifted from "heavily Democratic" to Trump, "including ones with tens of thousands of residents of Mexican descent."[153] Trump won 45 percent more votes in these areas than four years earlier, the newspaper reported. (This trend would continue four years later, during the 2020 election cycle, when Mexican-Americans in traditionally blue districts along the southern border voted Republican red.)

Given the significant movement of Latino votes to Trump, it was mainly the progressive wing that propelled open borders ideas onto the main stage. A Pew Research Center survey reported that two of the party's most liberal sectors had expanded to about a quarter of the party by November 2021.[154] They were the insurgent, infuriated "Progressive Left" segment, which accounted for 12 percent and a close cousin Pew called the "Outsider Left," of an additional 16 percent. This latter segment's "liberalism is particularly evident when it comes to race, immigration and environmental issues," Pew reported.

Overwhelming majorities of progressive liberals—86 percent—now favored "immigration," pushing Bernie Sanders supporters to as much as 30 percent of Democrats, the study found.

The progressive left faction of young, politically active, and highly educated whites were going to vote, and hard. Every Sanders competitor wanted them. None dared alienate them. As their commander in chief, Sanders was a powerhouse in so crowded a Democratic field. No centrist Democratic primary candidate could expect to survive without siphoning off some from the Sanders movement or at least not lose supporters to it. So, with slight deviations here and there, candidate immigration agendas all bore remarkable similarities to the one Sanders rolled out, copied right off the Occupy ICE placards.[155]

"The fact that Democratic presidential candidates were discussing decriminalizing border crossings represented a significant break" with the past, noted Samuels of FiveThirtyEight. "Over the years, Democrats have moved to the left on immigration, and Democratic voters now hold more progressive views on immigration than both their Republican equivalents and one-time Democratic Party leaders."

Sanders did not need to win nomination for these measures to become part of the Democratic Party policy fabric.

Eventually, after Sanders gave up, he turned his progressive bloc over to Biden in his bid against Trump. Their support pushed Biden over the hump and into the White House. In return, Biden owed umbrage to the Bernie Sanders bloc. He gave them immigration.

All the President's Radical Men and Women

By the January 2020 inauguration, the Biden transition team had selected policy advisors to carry out the progressive agenda on immigration. Biden's campaign had repeatedly vowed that as president, he would kill Trump's immigration policies. Between the November election and inauguration, about a half dozen advisers, give or take some who came and exited quickly, went to work. In an April 2022 account, the *New York Times* explained those early days this way, dutifully parroting the encrypted code words on open borders:

> Mr. Biden came into office with high hopes, saying he wanted a system that would allow the United States to determine, in a more compassionate way, which migrants should be allowed

to stay in the country. He recruited a team of immigration advocates and others eager to put in place the humane system they had envisioned for years.[156]

And who were these immigration advocates?

Few of the new Biden immigration aides and advisers came from the usual policy think tanks from which new presidents typically draw advisors and political appointees. Most hailed from advocacy organizations that openly favored policies to dismantle the American immigration enforcement system and open the border to the world. Collectively, the advisors who entered the White House comprised a who's who of Haidt's "tribal moral community."

They had spent professional lives advocating for prescriptions that could only lead to mass migration over the border. They subscribed to building the grand narrative of illegal immigrants as the new victim group worthy of civil rights campaigning. They were as pious about their beliefs as any theologian. They presumed all economic migrants to be endangered political refugees and asylum seekers. They believed the United States had no right to refuse entry to people crossing its border. They believed that foreign nationals who crossed a border illegally were no different from legal migrants who'd cleared required hoops and paid their dues. They believed immigration enforcement to be cruel and therefore ignorable. All insisted on entirely trading enforcement for the disproven experiment of rebuilding troubled nations so their citizens would want to stay home.

At the top of the organizational chart as head of the Department of Homeland Security and all of the nation's immigration enforcement arms was Alejandro "Ali" Mayorkas. He was the son of Jewish-Cuban refugees who fled the 1959 communist revolution. Previously, from 2009 to 2013, Mayorkas headed USCIS during the Obama administration.

Mayorkas's oversight of USCIS during the Obama years was controversial.[157] A 2010 investigation into employee complaints by Senator Chuck Grassley (R-IA) found that Mayorkas once ordered underlings in California to stop prioritizing asylum fraud investigations.[158] He ordered the California USCIS office to abandon an anti-fraud measure that checked for high-risk applicants on a government database, and for fraud specialists to stop investigating such applications.

"Why would you be focusing on that [detecting fraud] instead of approvals?" he reputedly demanded. "A witness said 'his message was offensive to a lot of officers who are trained to detect fraud.'"

Infamously, at a management conference, Mayorkas directed his top officials to "get to YES" regarding "customer" immigrants filing visa applications. He told his subordinates that approvals were the main means to an end goal of "zero complaints" against the agency, which immigrant applicants would file when declined. At a conference in Lansdowne, Virginia, Mayorkas said some managers who wouldn't approve benefits had "black spots on their hearts." Mayorkas had said he was "dealing" with them and subordinates "too close" to them with involuntary reassignments.

Illegal immigration advocacy groups trilled over Biden's pick.[159] Mayorkas was one of *them*. After the Obama admin- istration, Mayorkas associated with pro-illegal immigration groups like the American Immigration Lawyers Association. He served as a board member for the refugee resettlement agency HIAS, which advocates for the most liberal possible application of asylum regulations and opposes any kind of detention. HIAS President and CEO Mark Hetfield described "Ali" as "an empathetic leader who "knows the heart of the stranger" and that "America is at its greatest when we build bridges, not walls."

Janet Murguía, president of UnidosUS (originally the National Council of La Raza), which opposes what it termed "indiscriminate" immigration enforcement, told the *New York Times* that "after four long, dark years" of the Trump administration and "a general contempt for Latinos from the highest office in the land, Mayorkas's nomination signaled a new day for the Department of Homeland Security and for all our country."

The conservative Daily Signal found that five officials "who now run the Biden administration's immigration policy" all hailed from far-left "farm teams" bankrolled by liberal billionaires such as George Soros and Facebook founder Mark Zuckerberg.[160] The so-called farm teams like FWD.us and America's Voice advocated "pathways to citizenship" for illegally present foreign nationals and the other extreme ideas recounted here.

"When activists hold outsized sway, that's the policy you can expect from an administration that opposes a border wall and border security," Hayden Ludwig, senior investigative researcher at the Capital Research Center, told the Signal.

The Zuckerberg-funded FWD.us, for instance, did hold unconventional positions to end deportation and grant amnesty to the nation's eleven million illegally present people.[161] The FWD.us lobbying group also advocates those hundreds of thousands of foreign nationals granted Temporary Protected Status (TPS) decades after hurricanes, earthquakes, and wars be made permanent residents. America's Voice called for an end to ICE arrests at places of employment, legalization for all illegally present foreign nationals, and an end to the pandemic rapid expulsion policy for its return to "due process for asylum seekers."[162]

There was, for instance, Tyler Moran, Biden's senior advisor for migration on the Domestic Policy Council. Prior to joining the Biden immigration team, Moran served in the Obama administration and worked for Nevada Senator Harry Reid. Moran would drive many of the new administration's opening salvos such as a deportation moratorium and opening the asylum system to ineligible economic migrants. When hundreds of thousands of migrants responded to "la invitación" by stampeding to the border, Moran urged them forward.

"So we think asylum is legal, and *we don't want to have a closed border* [author's italics]," Moran told MSNBC in May 2021. "We want to have a system where people can apply for asylum in a fair, in an orderly, and in an efficient way."[163]

Moran also boasted of having processed those border-jumping immigrants "in an orderly means through the border...to ensure that people got to their destination. So these are all learning experiences that we are going to use as we sort of rebuild that muscle memory so we have a system in place that reflects American values."

Anyone familiar with the migrant advocacy complex's worldview would find nothing surprising about Moran's ideas and double entendre language choices. She worked as policy director for the National Immigration Law Center, which seeks "long-term transformational change" by challenging "unjust laws and policies that marginalize low-income and other vulnerable immigrant communities...." Moran's former employer also aimed to "engage in narrative and culture change to shift the public debate toward the notion that—no matter where a person is born and how much money they have—everyone has a stake and constructive role to play in shaping the country's future."[164]

Moran also was the cofounder of Immigration Hub, another immigration advocacy group of former congressional staff and executive branch officials that erases distinctions between illegal and legal immigrants and citizens.

"We believe in an inclusive society...where America recognizes immigrants as intrinsic to our national identity and heritage," the Immigration Hub website explained in an obvious reference to illegal immigrants.[165]

Esther Olavarria, another senior immigration advisor who worked with Moran at the Immigration Hub, became deputy director for immigration of the White House's Domestic Policy Council.

The Cuban-born Olavarria's Washington credentials date to her work for Senator Edward "Ted" Kennedy, as immigration counsel on the Senate Judiciary Committee in 1998. She practiced immigration law in Miami for three nonprofit immigration groups and worked on immigration policy for the Obama administration.[166] She worked too for the Center for American Progress (CAP), a Democratic Washington, DC, think tank with strong ties to Clinton and Obama.

The CAP has taken millions in support from philanthropist George Soros's Open Society Foundations and Foundations to Promote Open Society, which give hundreds of millions to groups that push open borders agendas.[167]

In her role at the White House, Olavarria tirelessly promoted ways to expand access to the abused asylum system and a variety of permanent protections—read, amnesties—for millions of illegal immigrants inside the United States.[168]

Lucas Guttentag, a civil rights litigator who took on the job of senior counselor for Immigration Policy in the Department of Justice, came from the same ideological ether. His mission was to dismantle Trump's immigration policies, of which he was a frequent and vociferous critic.[169] He'd previously served the Obama administration as a senior adviser on immigration policy (2014–2016) after a long stint running the ACLU's Immigrants' Rights Project. The project litigated against immigration enforcement in dedication to "advancing the constitutional and civil rights of immigrants," an ACL biography said.[170] In an April 22, 2019, Q&A blog at Stanford Law School, Guttentag betrayed a familiarity with the new encrypted language of open border advocacy.

"The system is mired in the past and treats migrants as threats who should be jailed and deterred rather than as refugees seeking protection whose claims must be heard and fairly adjudicated," Guttentag said when asked about changes at the border. "Responding to the current situation with inhumane measures that violate our legal obligations is a moral and management failure."[171]

In explaining that people immigrate for safety and opportunity, he also asserted that "laws and punishment won't change that fundamental human imperative" and that this imperative can "only" be addressed by changing the conditions in countries of origin.

Amy Pope, a lawyer and former Obama advisor who joined the Biden White House temporarily, had worked as fellow for the London-based Chatham House think tank. She often harshly criticized Trump's wall and especially Trump's policies that kept economic immigrants from accessing the asylum system.

Pope routinely inveighed against enforcement, deterrence, and wall-building that intending border-crossers always told me kept them home.[172] Instead, she wanted to usher them into the United States while rebuilding foreign nations.

Over the next year, some or all of the president's immigration men and women would play some part in 296 executive actions on immigration before political pragmatists inside the White House, seeing political liability in the massive onslaught their policies wrought at the border, begin to reign them in.[173]

Handing over border security to the most fervent theologians of a fringe political religion immediately led to lasting, severe consequences for the nation. What they wanted and fought for with the greatest fervor was a return of the American asylum system set at its widest possible aperture. Why? Because they well knew that the American asylum system is the main ingredient for mass migration.

CHAPTER FIVE

INSANE ASYLUM

> *"Individuals apprehended by DHS and placed into expedited immigration proceedings are to be removed from the country without a hearing in immigration court unless they express an intention to apply for asylum, or a fear of persecution, torture, or return to their country."*

> —General Accountability Office report, February 2020[174]

> *"Asylum fraud occurs when an asylum seeker knowingly misrepresents information as part of their application for protection."*

> —National Immigration Forum fact sheet, October 8, 2021[175]

On Christmas Eve 2018, an eight-year-old Guatemalan Mayan immigrant boy named Felipe Alonzo Gomez lay gasping for breath, deathly ill with severe flu-like symptoms in an Alamogordo, New Mexico, hospital. He'd come over the border about a week earlier near El Paso with his farm worker father,

Agustin Gomez Perez, who now stood vigil at his bedside. Border Patrol agents waited outside for the verdict from doctors.[176]

"Father, I can no longer stand it; I think I'm going to die," the little boy told his father in their Mayan dialect.[177]

Father and son had come a long, much-trammeled route from their small indigenous village of Yalambojoch in Guatemala's rural western highlands in a district known as Huehuetenango where, months later, I would travel. Agustin and Felipe were part of a vast human exodus that had half-emptied the highlands by December 2018 to the southern border, more than 300,000, by far the largest number of all Guatemalans who made the trek during the mass migration emergency during Trump's term.[178]

Felipe's farmer father may have been poor and not well-educated, living in the traditional subsistence level, but Agustin was not stupid. Word had spread that migrants traveling with a child were making it into the United States.[179] Augustin discerned the new great odds that a smuggling investment would likely pay off, so he borrowed $6,500 to pay smugglers for himself and Felipe. He gambled that they too would win fast release into America for years to earn back many multiples of the loan.[180]

He may not have understood the exactitudes of why the Americans under Trump were admitting Guatemalan families, but neighbors were calling home with the good news that asylum claims would get them in to stay. Recently, smugglers started spreading word that immigration officials would release families within twenty-one days under a court ruling and then all they had to do to avoid deportation was utter the magic: "I need asylum" words and tell a story.

All they had to do was get themselves over the border, and they'd be released "to await a deportation hearing as the smugglers had promised," the *Washington Post* reported.[181] When a reporter later asked the boy's stepsister in Yalambojoch why Agustin took Felipe to the border, she answered, "We heard rumors that they could pass into the United States" with a child. Agustin thought he would take advantage of "the opportunity" to better provide for his family, she said.[182] For the father and son, however, it was a tragic gamble.

Felipe died of influenza in the hospital that December 24 night shortly before their loophole release.

I recount the story—and my own subsequent reporting trip to the Guatemala western highlands village they left—because it helps illustrate the centrality of the American asylum system's lavish return-on-smuggling-investment rewards in begetting or ending mass migrations. There can be little doubt that Felipe would be alive today at home had they not seen the beckoning allure of the asylum system in the northern distance. It indisputably lured Felipe and many others to their deaths from illness, drowning, and murder.

The broader story that must be told here is how millions of immigrants and their champions game, defraud, and unfairly exploit this law on a vast scale and why it is what draws millions more. For the low cost of a few lies, the asylum system has offered an easy evasion of required deportation and a highway straight into the American heartland for years. At the political level, that one central prize has elevated asylum to a ruthless partisan war for control of it.

The system's earliest foundations were laid in the 1950s and 1960s with Jews fleeing Nazis fresh in the minds of lawmakers. Over time, Congress updated it with others in mind, such as Vietnamese boat people fleeing communist "reeducation" camps. It lets almost anyone in who claims to have been persecuted on grounds of race, religion, nationality, political opinion, or membership in a social group,

It is rarely used now for those lofty purposes. Asylum has come to act like a narcotic draw on the world's millions of people who are not so much persecuted by Hitlers and Ho Chi Minhs as they are merely poor.[183] Vast majorities who use it are less interested in the system's intended sanctuary from government persecution as in its ability to get them inside to earn money.

The migrant advocacy industry shoehorned Felipe's death into a political narrative that all who use asylum face definite torture and political imprisonment back home. In the ensuing international media coverage of Felipe's death, they framed the tragedy for retail political sale (as well as that of another child migrant who had died in government custody a few weeks earlier) as proof that Guatemalans would die to escape "extreme widespread violence," rampant government persecution of indigenous populations, torture, organized gang violence, spousal abuse, anti-gay sentiment, and police abuse, the United Nations and left-leaning media outlets insisted.[184] The only solution? End all border enforcement so they can live.

"Families are escaping extreme violence and poverty at home and are fleeing for their lives," the United States Conference of Catholic Bishops declared, for instance, in a March 2019 statement condemning Trump's Remain in Mexico policy.[185]

"New asylum restrictions a death sentence for Central Americans fleeing violence," a June 12, 2018, Doctors Without Borders report fairly screamed.[186]

"As long as CBP continues to deny access to asylum seekers, drive people further underground, and treat people seeking safety as though they are criminals, people will die," Michelle Brane, director of Migrant Rights and Justice at the Women's Refugee Commission, told The Daily Beast in one typical assertion about Felipe's death."[187]

Reporters who traveled with Felipe's body to his village in Guatemala's western highlands reported grinding poverty amid broader regional persecutions and dangers that made life barely tenuous.[188]

But I would find a very different reality on the ground in Yalambojoch.

Root Cause in Guatemala's Western Highlands: House Envy

It took my Guatemalan interpreter and me all day to drive my rental from the southern Mexican city of Tapachula to Yalambojoch. Once we ascended into the highlands toward evening, I started to see the first clues that persecution and misery weren't as pervasive as the world was led to believe, although I could not know it in the moment. Passing through mountainous villages, we saw huge multihued concrete homes jutting up like mushrooms from the jungle canopy. They were yellow, orange, gray, or blue concrete homes.

Yalambojoch is one of many hundreds of villages. It is twenty miles off a winding, pot-holed track in a lush green valley surrounded by verdant hills. As I pulled into town, undulating along the muddy road, I saw that these same structures dotted Yalambojoch too. I made a note to self to find out what the big concrete houses in various states of completion were all about.

After spending the night in the town's one hostel, I was talking to the owner of two new ones going up. Phillippe Marcos Domingo, fifty, a subsistence corn and bean farmer, had raised his family of five children on a plot of land near the center of town. Phillippe explained that the houses realized a plan he and his wife devised ten years earlier, when their sons and daughters were too small to understand what it portended for them.

Inspiration came from a neighbor. The neighbor had built a canary yellow three-story, eight-bedroom home. More than a home, it was an ornate mansion. Money from that neighbor's son in the United States funded its construction, with gleaming tile floors, faux-gold-rimmed windows, and especially the indoor plumbing.

The incomplete and unpainted homes of Phillippe Marcos Domingo in Yalambojoch going up on his children's remittance money from the United States. Author photo January 2020.

It was the first such house in the village. As I regarded the Miami Beach–style monstrosity—for that's what it called to mind—it seemed out of time and place here in the mountainous jungle. Typically, most homes here were constructed of wood and mud brick, with tin roofs and hardpack dirt floors. But that first giant concrete house changed everything. It filled Phillippe and the other townspeople with envy.

"I saw that—the big house—and I wanted the same thing," Phillippe told me, pointing at it next door. "I wanted a big house for *my* family."

From that moment forward, Phillippe and his wife planned to send those sons and daughters, when they grew big enough, to work in the United States and send money back so that he too could build a giant house like that.

When I visited in January 2020, his American-Guatemalan dream was rising nicely on his children's $2,000 monthly remittance money. In fact, he was building not one but *two* double-story concrete houses of eight and nine rooms each. Amid the sounds of workers pounding nails and sloshing wet concrete around in wheelbarrows, Phillippe told me his extended children and grandchildren will move into them when they return per the plan.

A typical traditional dwelling in Yalambojoch.

Return?! The word stuck in my craw. Asylum seekers fleeing deadly persecutions did not plan to return because they would die if they did. Asylum-seekers from Guatemala swear to American adjudicators, under pain of perjury, that they faced death, destruction, and torture if returned. Guatemala, they swore on pain of perjury, was a no-go zone, a land of no-return.

I pressed Phillippe for more.

To the contrary, he said, people from Yalambojoch like his children weren't running from anything, he said. He had sent them north upon learning the Americans were quickly releasing any parent traveling with a child to live inside the United States. On the strength of experience reported by his neighbors, he borrowed thousands of dollars in smuggling money so that three of his children, with two of his grandchildren, and a teen-aged nephew, could join the exodus in late 2018.

Astonishingly, of Yalambojoch's 1,500 residents, only an estimated 300 remained in town, local leaders told me later.

From Phillippe's house, I walked over and introduced myself to Angelina and Francisco Santizo as they busied them-selves about their truly massive new-construction house. It was only an exterior gray concrete husk at this point, but with three stories up so far and concrete stairwells on the exterior at various points for climbing to certain entrances at the higher stories, my best guess was that it must have measured 10,000 square feet. Chickens pecked around in one of the rooms, its doorway blocked off. Bags of corn, some of it spilling out, filled a second room.

The couple was still living in the original family home-stead a few feet away, a tiny wood and tin-roof affair, while the new house slowly went up. It would be torn down once the new house was finished.

Francisco told me they sent a twenty-year-old son to the United States on the new migration wave.

"Why?" I asked.

"A lot of people started to see a lot of people going to the U.S. starting to build big houses," answered Francisco, a subsistence bean and corn farmer like Phillippe and his ances-tors. "And we wanted the same."

In the case of his son, Francisco told me he traveled alone, without a child. The Americans still let him in to legally claim asylum. Francisco said he didn't know what his son might have told the Americans about life back home. Whatever it was, the Americans still let him in to legally pursue it. Not provided for in current American asylum law is the apparent motivation his father described:

"When my son was growing up, we saw that everyone was building houses and when my son grew up, he said to us, 'I'm going to go to the U.S. now so I can send you money to build a house too.'"

For several generations, the Santizo family has lived on a plot of land in the standard wood and mud-brick dwelling. He was looking forward to moving into the new home one day.

Window treatments on one of the new Yalambojoch houses.

"I feel happy and calm now because I have a big house. I'm really glad to have this—and proud," Francisco said.

I encountered roughly the same story from two other families building new concrete homes. They all believed their children will return in a few years to live in their new houses with them and raise families, while continuing to work as subsistence farmers.

Not a single person I met said their loved ones and neighbors had felt compelled to escape persecution, gang violence, or even poverty or hunger.

All this was at sharp odds with frenzied American depictions of Guatemala as a death trap where torture chambers abound.

Consider Consuelo Jorge Domingo, a young mother of two whose husband left with one of her family's kids for America. I found her working the counter behind a tiny grocery store in Yalambojoch. A big, ornate concrete home going up just across the rutted dirt road. It was hers, and her in-laws, who were doing the construction. She did not pretend that there was some *other* reason her husband took one of their children from a village so safe and sustaining that they were willing to invest in its long-term future and then return, as was the plan.

Her husband and child applied for U.S. asylum like everyone else and got in, Consuelo told me. That told me he would have had to attest that he and the child could not possibly return lest they be harmed. That was obviously a lie.

Consuelo said he was not escaping anything terrible in the village. He wanted to get one of those big houses everyone else has.

I nodded when Consuelo asked if I wanted to take a tour of it. Blue tiles and window and gold-colored ornamentation adorned the doors and windows of the massive two-story house. The doors inside were not like the wood used in traditional dwellings up and down the mud track road; they were made of gleaming polished dark wood and opened with gold-colored metal handles. Wires extruded from unfinished electrical boxes. A gleaming clean mirror hung in a downstairs bathroom. As money comes home, the family puts on the finishing touches, little by little. Consuelo said she felt sad she and her eight-year-old daughter must live without her husband for so long, but the loss was offset by the sweeping house and the belief that they would all soon live in it.

"We wanted a big house for our family like everyone else is building," she explained of their departure. "It will be finished soon, and then he will come home and live in it with us."

None of this squared with any U.S. reporting I had read about Guatemalan immigrants. Certainly not Nina Strochlic's *National Geographic* piece, which teased out a variety of reasons for flight from a region she seemed pained to describe without explanation as "relatively" peaceful. She did quote the local director of an empty school explaining that everyone left "fueled by rumors that asylum claims were easier with a child." But rather than exploring the newsworthy discovery of this dramatic new catalyzing pull from a U.S. court case, she let the director ruminate about how highlands people were "running from" hunger, a drop in coffee prices, lack of economic opportunity, and income inequality.

Strochlic mentioned local political tensions over a government hydroelectric dam project that local "environmentalists" opposed and how the government's deployment of soldiers to secure the project against sabotage reminded people of military brutality thirty years ago.

"In places like Yalambojoch," Strochlic ended up concluding, "the only way to escape poverty is to go north."

A March 2022 UN-sponsored study of the very large emigration from these highlands found that what had driven so many from the western highlands were factors that would not qualify for U.S. asylum.[189] Emigration from Huehuetenango "is overwhelmingly driven by poverty and...has become an important strategy for families to improve their livelihoods," the researchers concluded.

But poverty is not an eligibility or American asylum. U.S. immigration judges overwhelmingly reject poverty, hunger, low coffee prices—and especially coveting a neighbor's house—as qualifying persecutions. So Yalambojoch's sons and daughters must have offered imagined or coached stories of "well-founded persecution" at the U.S. border to get in through the credible fear interview. That means they made up persecution stories.

And as an aside, one life lesson I picked up from traveling around the world a bit is that "poverty" too often is in the eye of outside Western beholders judging through rather parochial worldview prisms. I wondered if American press, human rights activists, and Western academics unfairly besmirch traditional subsistence villages like Yalambojoch as impoverished, backward, and somehow lesser. I find that assessment not only unfair, paternalistic, and condescending but also just factually wrong. Where American political narrators saw "grinding poverty," I saw a proud, traditional indigenous community where generations lived sustainably from the land as had their ancestors. Many residents speak the Chuj language, enjoy a rich religious culture, and farm their needs from small plots of land.

To understand the threats bearing down on this way of life, I noted a singular feature in the center of the town that looked like trouble to me. It was a tall cell phone and internet antenna tower. Had they imported Western advertising about dollar-based prosperity in other countries? Had they planted images in the minds of people like the Domingos and the Santizos of faux gold-trimmed windows that indigenous ancestors would never have envisioned?

Still, given the press about widespread persecution, I couldn't help doubt whether or not something as prosaic as house envy really could be driving the region's mass exodus. Was I missing something? I went to the village leaders to find out.

Yalambojoch Mayor Francisco Pais and Vice Mayor Pedro Garcia met me in the village lodge. They asserted that violent crime in Yalambojoch simply did not exist, excluding gang violence. An informal local civil patrol handled the petty crime issues and disputes that cropped up, they said. If that were true, there were no local cops to persecute anyone for their ethnicity or political opinions.

"This is a really quiet and calm place," Mayor Pais said. "The problems of gangs and criminals don't happen here."

"Well, doesn't the government discriminate against indigenous tribes like many people in America believe?" I asked. They shook their heads no in unison. Government persecution for that hasn't been a problem since the civil war that ended thirty years ago in the 1990s.

"People in this town tend to die of old age in bed," the vice mayor quipped. I asked if maybe his people left because they couldn't take the terrible poverty and food insecurity due to climate change or something else.

"No, not at all," they answered. Everyone always had plenty to eat. The mayor then offered up, with no prompting from me, the main reason why he thought so many of his constituents had deserted Yalambojoch.

"People see other people building the pretty houses, so they want to go too. They work for four or five years, and then they come back and live in them."

The Build-and-Return Root Cause

It's not known exactly what Felipe's father initially claimed to forestall their deportations. But all this left me thinking that if he or even a portion of the hundreds of thousands who left these highlands claimed deportation would kill them, an extraordinary amount of perjury-based asylum fraud was happening on the southern border. And if the U.S. media had fouled up *this* story so terribly, the American public was in the dark.

It's true that Guatemala's big cities have their share of real gang violence, abusive cops, high murder rates, and government neglect in duty to protect. But most Guatemalans traveling the American border were coming from these peaceful, rural western highlands, which were largely free of those afflictions.

Government statistics point to widespread abuse of the system by all nationalities. According to Department of Justice statistics between fiscal 2008 and 2019, fewer than 17 percent won asylum, and 32.5 percent were declined and ordered removed. The rest, half, abandoned their claims.[190] But Guatemalans were among the most abusive.

Since 2014, Guatemalans have been among the top foreign nationals claiming credible fear, according to Government Accountability Office reporting.[191] Asylum officers interviewed more Guatemalans for credible fear than the next three ranking nationalities in 2018, even before Trump's mass migration crisis, which would be significantly fueled by Guatemalans.[192]

But immigration judges don't believe Guatemalans' stories of persecution and turn them down in huge percentages, so, naturally, most never bother to lodge one or follow through because, after all, they're already inside the country. Judges granted asylum to just 5 percent of Guatemalans who followed through. In 2019, 77 percent abandoned the process.[193] Guatemalans topped the list of nationalities in deportation proceedings, some 313,836 in February 2022.[194] But great numbers evaded deportation. By the end of 2017, more than 1.4 million Guatemalans were living illegally inside the United States, according to Pew Research Center, and almost certainly far more following subsequent surges in 2019 and after Biden was elected.[195]

The statistics show a similar pattern for other Central Americans, Haitians, Cubans, and many other nationalities, indicating the vastness of asylum fraud.

Back in the United States in February 2020, I called some academic experts in Latin America migration to get their take on what I'd seen in Guatemala.

Sarah Lynn Lopez worked as an associate professor of architecture at the University of Texas-Austin, not far from where I live. She had studied remittance house building for fifteen years and authored *The Remittance Landscape: Spaces of Migration in Rural Mexico and Urban USA*.[196]

She said her research and that of a small number of other academics clearly show that thirst for large houses is a primary impetus for immigration to the United States, especially in Mexico but also in Guatemala.

"It is definitely one of the findings, that it [housing] is an impetus for migration. It absolutely is one," Lopez said. "That is definitely something that people would completely agree on, and there's evidence to back it up."

But she was also puzzled that this immigration push factor "hasn't reached popular discourse yet."

"I've been researching for fifteen years, and it's always kind of amazed me that I didn't start seeing articles that even referred to it—even a little bit—until the last two years."

Professor Néstor P. Rodriguez, an immigration studies expert also at UT-Austin who has traveled extensively through Central America for research, said, "Your observation is correct, that building homes is a big status symbol." Not only is the quest for big-house status an important motivation for immigration in Guatemala and Mexico, he said, but researchers also have found evidence of it in Vietnam and China.

Rodriguez said he believed the absence of public discussion about this cause from the Northern Triangle countries of Guatemala, Honduras, and El Salvador is because it has never been systematically studied from that angle.

"It's not part of the debate because research hasn't told us yet how prominent this home construction is as a motivation," he said. "We have yet to measure this."

However widespread the build-and-return root cause turns out to be, should anyone ever study it, there is at least strong anecdotal evidence that it is not limited to Guatemala or China, whose citizens have crossed the southern border by the thousands for well over a decade.[197]

In June 2019, a terrible photo taken by journalist Julia Le Duc and published by the Mexican newspaper *La Jornada* went viral. It showed the drowned bodies of twenty-five-year-old Salvadoran national Óscar Alberto Martínez Ramírez clutching his almost two-year-old daughter, Angie Valeria. The Salvadoran father and daughter died in the Rio Grande, their bodies grounded on a sand bar. The image became another pawn in liberal calls to widen access to the asylum even more and to stop enforcement.

"These families seeking asylum are often fleeing extreme violence. And what happens when they arrive? Trump says,

'Go back to where you came from.' That is inhumane. Children are dying. This is a stain on our moral conscience," Kamala Harris, then running for president, tweeted.

Another candidate, Senator Cory Booker (D-NJ), tweeted to urge Americans to not look away: "These are the consequences of Donald Trump's inhumane and immoral immigration policy. This is being done in our name."

The ostensibly fact-neutral Associated Press uncritically described the context of the "searing photograph" as highlighting that Central American migrants hoping for asylum in the United States were "fleeing violence and poverty."

But two-thirds down in an Associated Press story, Óscar's mother, Rosa Ramírez, explained the root cause that drove Óscar to take his kid to the southwest border:

"I begged them not to go, but he wanted to scrape together money to build a home," she said. "They hoped to be there a few years and save up for a house."[198]

Neither the writer nor editor of this story let that passing revelation break prevailing narrative. The dead boy's grandmother just said he'd only left El Salvador to earn money for a house to which he evidently planned to return and live in. Lured by the knowledge that American asylum would get them in, they too died. Despite this admission, the AP still ended its piece with mike-dropping moral-of-the-story quote from Cris Ramón, senior immigration policy analyst at the Bipartisan Policy Center think tank. Ramón did not invoke the narcotic allure of a door-opening asylum system that drew father and daughter to their deaths. Instead, against all evidence to the contrary, he blamed the death on Trump's attempts to get rid of the asylum system's siren call.

"With greater crackdowns and restrictions, we could see more desperate measures by people trying to enter Mexico or the U.S.," he said.

Clearly, he hadn't listened to Rosa Ramírez, who knew the asylum system had called her child Óscar and grandchild Valeria to their deaths so that they could build a big house back home.

From Noble Sanctuary to Ignoble Narcotic

The American asylum law was never envisioned as a salve for the world's regular poor people, like Felipe and his dad, and Oscar and Valeria, who lived under merely bad governance in high-crime neighborhoods or where farming can't afford the big houses they see on the internet.

But for many years, the system allowed millions of economic migrants to use it just as though they were gulag escapees or stateless Rohingya Muslims fleeing ethnic cleansing by former Burma's military junta. The system allows life-changing rewards on the strength of their initial word that persecution awaits them too. How true to their word are Central Americans, Haitians, and other peoples fleeing mere poverty and looking for better economic prospects, by and large? U.S. judges don't believe most of what they're hearing, but by then it doesn't matter. Those who merely claimed it are *in* and not leaving.

Here's why:

Amended from earlier laws and international agreements that contemplated World War II–era refugee flows, the current asylum system comes from the post–Vietnam War era Refugee Act of 1980. Its intent is that America "respond to the urgent needs of persons subject to persecution in their homelands…" and avoid deporting "refugees of special humanitarian concern" back to dangers and persecution. The legal term for this prospect is "non-refoulment."[199] The kind of people this amendment's late seventies architects had in mind to save were Vietnamese boat people fleeing communist "reeducation camps" aboard rickety sea craft after the 1975 fall of Saigon, or North Korean defectors facing summary execution.

What the laws' authors never anticipated was that economic migrants looking for jobs would so easily use it too. The law was written to prevent deportation of people who reach U.S. soil and credibly claim "a well-founded fear of persecution" by governments or groups the governments tolerate or can't control, based on one or more of five criteria:

- Race
- Religion
- Nationality
- Membership in a particular social group
- Political opinion

From the perspective of poor economic immigrants who want to work and their champions, the system as it stands could not be more perfectly designed.

In times of normal, routine flows, an immigrant crosses, is detained at an ICE facility, and put into deportation proceedings in accordance with the law. The immigrant triggers the first delay in deportation proceedings by simply declaring they intend to claim asylum. Enter asylum officers of the U.S. Citizenship and Immigration Service (USCIS). Soon, one of these officers will come around and conduct an interview of about a half hour to check out the proffered persecution story. This is called a "credible fear of return" screening. If the immigrant passes the credible fear screening, the YES check in the box puts the immigrant into the court-hearing backlog.[200]

Getting into the backlog is the ultimate end goal for most. More than 70 percent of the time from 2014 through 2019, asylum officers check that YES box because the bar is laughably low—the USCIS officers need only judge a 10 percent likelihood that the petitioner faces potential persecution—and no verification of persecution stories is required, the Supreme Court has ruled.[201] "The applicant need not show that he or she *is in fact eligible* for asylum" at the initial credible fear screening stage, the Supreme Court in 2020 noted in *DHS v. Thuraissigiam*.[202]

It is little wonder that from 2014 through the first two quarters of 2019, asylum officers approved 71.4 percent of all screenings and declined only 14.2 percent (the remaining 14.4 percent were administratively closed for abandonment).[203]

A check in the NO box for credible fear can lead to deportation but is appealable for years.[204] Although the law requires both yesses and no's to remain in lockup, they never are. Deep court backlogs and refusals by Congress to fund more beds made the lockup requirement untenable. So Republican and Democratic administrations let claimants make bond and live freely in the years-long backlog. In fact, the early credible screening part of the asylum system is the main prize of any expensive smuggling trip. (In June 2022, the U.S. Supreme Court ruled 6–3 that the government doesn't have to offer the bonds and can keep immigrants in long-term custody as the law prescribes.[205])

Losing and abandonment of cases is winning because immigrants wind up in a backlog of court hearings for just an initial ruling that averaged 4.5 years in 2022.[206] Asylum claimants can ramp up the number of hearings to as many as four, extending their stays for up to eight years. Appeals and legal ping-pong can extend final rulings for even longer. Those who merely claim they'll apply get to live and work for a decade to get a final judgment and appeal for more years. And then, if denied asylum, they can just disappear into the illegal population of eleven million and confidently bet that ICE never shows up at their doors.

So, a Honduran yam farmer fleeing a failed crop who claims government persecution on one or more of the five criteria is highly likely to lose the claim but still win the same long-term reprieve from mandatory deportation as would a North Korean gulag escapee.

Now, anyone who knows all this can start to see why leftist champions of eliminating national borders fight like banshees for the widest possible aperture for economic migrants to access the asylum system exactly as it stands. And when these immigrant champions demand, as though unaware of the abuse-based outcomes, that asylum law be made available to all foreigners crossing the southern border, they exploit a broad ignorance in the American public and media that almost everyone who uses it will enter and stay indefinitely.

But while most of America remains in the dark, the rest of the world basks in the light of knowledge that a secret passageway in exists for the low, low price of a few simple words.

The Great Haitian Asylum Scam

A common narrative about Haitian immigrants permeated American thinking when 17,000 mostly Haitian border-jumpers suddenly formed a massive camp under the international bridge at Del Rio, Texas, in September 2021. Haitians began pouring over the Rio Grande from the first day of the Biden government, mostly unremarked upon. But the encampment became an instant international media sensation, spawning an open public discussion about what to do with them.

Those demanding that every Haitian be admitted hewed to a narrative: all Haitians deserve immediate American asylum because they were fleeing widespread, inescapable gang and government persecution at home, plagues of hurricanes and earthquakes—as well as the July 2021 assassination of Haiti Prime Minister Jovenel Moïse. The island nation was a death trap.

Because the assassination left Haiti "reeling from extreme political unrest," the Biden administration must end using the pandemic-related Title 42 instant expulsion policy as a "tool to justify mass deportations of people seeking asylum," Jonathan Blazer, American Civil Liberties Union (ACLU) director of border strategies, demanded in a September 2021 letter to the administration.[207]

But the narrative was patently untrue.

Almost none of those thousands of Haitians had lived in their homeland in years. To get a credible fear YES that they could not be returned to Haiti, every one of these Haitians was going to have to lie about where they'd been living for years since they left home.

What I learned from my interviews with the Haitians on their way to the southern border—in southern and northern Mexico, in Nicaragua, and Costa Rica—was that most had found safe, secure asylum already in Chile or Brazil in 2016, 2017, and 2018 to wait out the Trump administration. Every Haitian I met had sheltered in those two countries to wait out Trump's Remain in Mexico and expulsion measures to preserve their smuggling money. They learned Spanish, made good livings at jobs, and had children who became Chilean or Brazilian citizens. Chile, the long Spanish-speaking nation hugging hundreds of miles of South America's Pacific Coastline, boasted the continent's strongest economy, which acted as a magnet on regional economic migrants like Haitians or Venezuelans seeking economic opportunity, according to the *CIA's World Fact Book*.[208]

The ones I interviewed all enjoyed Western lifestyles with buying power and educational opportunities for themselves and children. One boy's Polo shirt bore the patch of a private Santiago Christian school choir.

USCIS credible fear officers would check the NO box if they knew the real reasons why Haitians were coming and that they had been safe and sound in Chile and Brazil, which had kindly granted them work authorizations and residency.

One twenty-four-year-old Haitian man I met relaxing at a hostel full of his countrymen in the far northwestern Costa Rica town of La Cruz explained to me what his future U.S. immigration lawyers would never let him say aloud.

He and his brother had arrived in Santiago, Chile, four years earlier, in late 2016 as Trump was campaigning about deporting all illegal immigrants, he told me. While waiting out Trump, the young man found work as a baker and Uber Eats driver. He and the brother made good money and built their smuggling savings fund. The brother had already crossed a couple of months earlier, with his requisite wife and young child. I wondered aloud if something bad in Chile pushed him to escape north.

"Did the government of Chile ever threaten you?" I asked.

"No, that never happened there."

"So, you were never afraid?

"No, never."

The Haitian pulled out his iPhone and showed me videos of beautiful Chilean beaches he'd enjoyed and others depicting warm memories of urban Santiago nightlife. He said he always found enough work to support himself and a lifestyle allowing him to buy his favorite fashion clothing brands on the internet.

"It's a nice country," he said of Chile.

The brothers only decided to abandon that nice life because the Biden win "makes it easier to get into the States."

"It's the reason," he added.

Asked how he would compare his Santiago life to the one he left in Haiti, the probable future U.S. asylum claimant promptly answered: "A thousand times better."

"Then why come to the United States border now, when his life in Chile was so peaceful and non-threatening?" I asked.

"Because," he said, chuckling with a kind of glaze in his eyes that I came to recognize in almost every migrant I spoke with about America, "life in the United States will be a *million* times better."

All the ones I interviewed over a year described circumstances that made them patently ineligible for the U.S. asylum.

Thousands of migrants like Tomas Hubian, a twenty-six-year-old father of nine-year-old and three-year old boys, uprooted their families and headed north for the fabled economic and lifestyle upgrade. I met Tomas in the far northeastern Costa Rica town of Los Chiles in June 2021 as he was preparing his family for a local smuggler to take them over the Nicaragua border.

He was shopping in a small, shabby convenience store at the bus station, hoping to buy some flip-flops for the three-year-old, a Chilean-born citizen. I picked up the tab for those and some snacks, and we deposited ourselves on a patch of nearby grass for an interview.

Tomas said he'd been living in Santiago for the past four years, sitting on a stack of smuggling money he figured would go to waste if he tried going up against President Trump's border enforcement policies.

"When he [Trump] was in, it took luck to cross the border successfully," he explained for his calculus. "We would have been put back in Mexico and lost our money."

They settled in to wait out Trump. Tomas never lacked for work to support his family in Chile. He told me he always felt safe, secure, never once threatened by the government.

As soon as Biden took office, Tomas said, word arrived from the U.S. border that Haitian parents with children and pregnant women were receiving fast-pass legal authorization to go anywhere in the United States.

"If we have kids, my friends said, we have a high chance of getting through."

Maybe the Haitians of Chile and Brazil had not gotten rich like they undoubtedly hoped they could in America. But I noticed that many Haitians coming from Chile or Brazil dressed fashionably, wore jewelry, and sported the latest iPhones and accoutrements. Most of the Haitians I met would qualify as fairly well-to-do, just seizing the opportunity to move up a few notches from good to great in an American lifestyle.

I met Ronald Polydor, twenty-five, at the Los Chiles bus station. He'd arrived with fifteen other Haitians by bus for an overnight stay in a bare-bones hostel with his wife and six-year-old son. In the morning, they would all be moving with smugglers through Nicaragua.

Ronald told me he'd been supporting his family as a mechanic in Chile for four years and even found opportunity there to obtain advanced certifications in his field. Chile provided legal residency and plenty of work. Never did the government there persecute Ronald or any Haitian he knew over all the years he lived there.

"No. No. No. No," he answered quickly when asked that question.

But Ronald complained that the U.S. government twice turned him down for nonimmigrant visas, first as a tourist and later as a student, for no apparent reason. (The U.S. probably rejected him because Haitians are at high risk of overstaying those visas to live illegally in the country.)

Now, he laughed, the illegal way to enter is…legal, he told me, laughing. He got on the road as soon as he could raise a bit more smuggling money, he added, because he can earn in a month in the United States as a mechanic what he could earn in an entire year in South America.

"I prefer the legal ways but now, it's up to God," he said, chuckling at his good timing.

All of this is, of course, a nonstarter at the credible fear opening stage of the asylum process. The Haitians would have to cover up their time in South America and assert they were coming directly from Haiti.

"The vast majority will be denied," said former immigration Judge D. Anthony Rogers, who held court in Dallas, Texas, for eighteen years. "The fact that they've resided somewhere else is a negative factor in front of a judge about whether they actually have a fear of return to Haiti."

Even citing fear of returning to Haiti itself can stretch the credulity of immigration judges because political unrest there might affect a fractional few. By and large, most Haitians are fleeing the island's infamous poverty and crime. While these are horrors, to be sure, they do not form a legitimate basis for asylum, Rogers said. Neither is reaching from a good economic situation to a great one.

Indeed, only about 7 percent of Haitian asylum claims were granted in 2020, accounting for an abandonment or withdrawal rate of 42 percent and a denial rate of 51 percent, according to statistics compiled by the Executive Office for Immigration Review, the federal agency overseeing immigration judges. This means the immigration judges don't believe Haitian claims.

"Asylum is for people who don't have anywhere else to go," said Art Arthur, the CIS fellow who previously served as an immigration judge in Pennsylvania. "These people actually have somewhere to go where their lives are not in danger. They were already settled. They'll lose. They're all going to lose.

"A drowning man will reach for the point of a sword; that's the idea behind the asylum system," Arthur continued. "But these people aren't drowning. They're sitting on a beach."

In the Rio Grande Mud: Evidence of Haitian Asylum Fraud

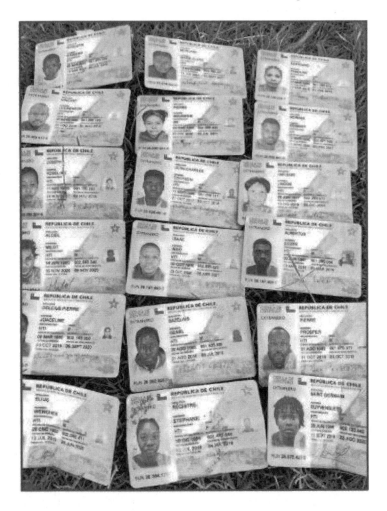

During the Del Rio Haitian migrant camp crisis, I discovered evidence of the mass fraud afoot in the dirt and boulders along the Rio Grande. I was on the Mexican side, in the city of Acuña, at a highly trammeled crossing to Texas.

All along the river bank, I found hundreds of Chilean and Brazilian identity cards and passports, discarded by their bearers at their last step from Mexico and their first step into Texas. The identity cards all bore the names and faces of Haitian men, women, and children. There were hundreds of them lying around. I also found Chilean and Brazilian passports bearing the faces of Haitian children born there. Their owners had torn and twisted them, ripped out photos, or tried to burn them at the last minute.

The Rio Grande undoubtedly washed a great many Chilean identity cards into the Gulf of Mexico.

Why would all these Haitians toss their identity cards here? The only plausible answer is that someone familiar with the system told them their cards were evidence of asylum ineligibility that would keep them from a credible fear YES check; if they were already had residency in a safe, secure land like Chile, they'd get the NO check instead. As a hard-bitten world traveler myself and friend to many other international travelers, I know that no honest person—and, I mean nobody, ever—throws away their official government identity documents or the passports of their children while in a foreign country traveling to another. The only reason large groups of international travelers of the same nationality would purposefully discard such documents is that they needed to appear as something they were not. They were up to no good.

In this case, the Haitians were going to lie to the Americans that they were coming directly from Haiti.

How widespread? As of 2020, between 185,000 and 237,000 Haitians were living and working in Chile.[209]

Estimates of how many Haitians lived in Brazil vary widely. Brazilian agencies reported in 2019 that 128,968 Haitians entered Brazil between 2010 (the year of a devastating earthquake) and 2018 and were given a total of 90,607 work permits, including 8,560 in the first six months of 2019.[210] For all of that decade, Haitians made up the largest immigrant nationality in the formal labor market in Brazil, which ranks as the world's eighth-largest economy and was strongly rebounding from the pandemic by 2021.[211]

For most of 2019 and 2020, Border Patrol apprehensions of Haitians each month was in the low- to upper-hundreds. That election year, Border Patrol picked up a total of 4,116 Haitians, including just 97 in November 2020. By March 2021, though, Border Patrol had caught 3,084. By August, the number ballooned to 7,569 and then to 17,638 in September, much of it at the Del Rio camp.

It was no accident that many I saw were pregnant women, always about seven months into their terms. [212] Haitian national Peter Thesaus, twenty-five, who was traveling with a wife and Brazilian-born child to join a relative in Florida, said his sister, who was six months pregnant, was behind him to the south but making the same journey north from Brazil. He and his extended family had been living and working comfortably and securely for six years in Brazil, at his job with a local hospital. Biden's election prompted his departure.

He admitted that his pregnant sister's trip was carefully timed, after his own, so that the child would be born an American and qualify the whole family for public assistance.

The Fine Art of Persecution Fiction: Recovering "Repressed Memories"

But what to tell American asylum adjudicators? If a Haitian unschooled in the tall tales of what USCIS officers need to hear for the YES box check, all is lost. They need just the right plausible narrative. Fortunately, plenty of those who have gone before them and got the YES box checked pass the information down trail to those still coming up, in online chat rooms and telephone calls. Sometimes, criminal smugglers know the right stories to tell and coach their clients on what to say as part of the service, at extra cost.

Sometimes, nonprofit migrant advocacy groups and sympathetic lawyers offer classroom coaching in transit countries.

In January 2022, I discovered the United Nations was funding fake persecution stories in Mexico. I was reporting again in Tapachula in Mexico's farthest southern state of Chiapas on the border with Guatemala. The city is a stepping stone on the international migration routes from South America. At the time, Mexico was requiring foreign travelers to apply for asylum and refugee status to get the residency cards necessary to legally travel on to cross the American border. The Mexican system is similar to the American one with eligibility requirements being persecution and certain hardship.

But as in the United States, job-hunting and poverty don't qualify either, and Mexico was rejecting and deporting scores of hapless applicants who never got the email about how important asylum story interviews are.

I found that at least two UN-funded nonprofits in Mexico's south had come up with an artful solution to rescue them and teach thousands of others not to make the same mistake. Stables of clinical psychologists were helping rejected migrants recover "repressed memories" of more eligible government persecutions.

Enrique Vidal, coordinator for the Fray Matias de Cordoba human rights center, laid it all out for me in a recorded interview.

"The most common mistake migrants make during interviews...is that they are saying they are suffering economic hardship. It's not one of the criteria for refugee status," Vidal explained. "That may cover up one of the true reasons why they are coming. They need psychological help so they can remember the situation they experienced.

"That's the most important part of the process," he continued. "That's when the Mexican authorities listen to the motives of why the left their country. And those motives have to be according to international conventions."

Decades of controversy have dogged so-called "recovered memory therapy" in the United States, with some in academia concluding that it amounts to debunked science that too often implanted false memories.[213]

I asked if the main purpose of memory recovery was to reverse negative interview outcomes.

"Yes, through the psychological help we give them," he responded. "For example, if they have an economic need, that's not necessarily one of the requirements. However, once we do our interview with them we find out they did suffer some type of violence or persecution or anything that qualifies as refugees, we tell them to emphasize those."

Vidal said the nonprofit organization's clinical psychologists have helped untold thousands of such immigrants get their verdicts reversed with the unearthed stories. Mexican immigration adjudicators conduct no verification investigations of these stories, he said, just like American ones.

Outside a different UN-funded migrant advocacy nonprofit in Tapachula named Servicio Jesuita a Refugiados, which is the organization Vidal told me was offering the same "legal and psychological services," I briefly spoke with a Honduran mother with a young child waiting at the front door for her turn inside. At this point, I didn't know the purpose of those services. A worker was arranging appointments at the door with a security guard, some dozen migrants waiting their turn in the line outside. I asked her why she was there.

"Mexican immigration rejected me for asylum," she answered, saying that this place would help fix the problem. Asked why she'd been turned down for Mexican asylum, the woman responded that she told them she was going to the United States to work and make money. That's a red light.

Vidal said his organization holds seminars to ensure green lights. Lawyers in Mexico and volunteers from a variety of nations, including from the United States, explain to thousands more what Mexican asylum interviewers need to hear. Their migrant students learn which testimonies to emphasize and which not to emphasize, Vidal told me. Almost everyone who goes through his organization's programs wins Mexican status and the prized Mexican residency cards that enable unfettered travel to the American border.

I have found hundreds of freshly minted Mexican residency cards, bearing the faces and names of foreigners from all over the world, strewn along the Rio Grande banks at popular crossing points, obviously no longer needed but also showing that their bearers had safe legal haven in another country but just wanted the better American lifestyle.

I asked Vidal how he might respond were his group to be accused of running unethical coaching and asylum fraud mills that enable tens of thousands of migrants to reach the U.S. southern border.

"If the majority of people were lying, we wouldn't be successful. The Mexican authorities would not recognize them as refugees," he replied. "If we have a high percentage of success, it's because we have truth. With migrants, it's harder to lie. The authorities would find out about it."

I returned home to Texas wondering if the persecution stories unearthed by Mexican psychologists were getting recycled at the American border. It was certainly happening there according to some pretty credible reporting.

For example, Indians from the relatively prosperous Punjab region had a conveyor belt rolling to the southern border for years, greased with fake persecution stories, NPR reported in June 2019. Punjabis by then made up one of the fastest-growing illegal populations in the United States, with 500,000 inside the country as of 2014.[214]

At least 32,000 Indians had crossed the southern border between 2009 and 2019, including 8,997 in 2018 and another 7,675 in 2019, CBP apprehension data shows.[215] For a long time, India was one of the "recalcitrant" nations refusing to take back deportees because of the value of the remittance cash they sent home.

President Trump had threatened India and other recalcitrant nations with visa sanctions if they did not take back deportees.[216] NPR's Lauren Frayer revealed that thousands of Indian border crossers had practiced posing as government-persecuted torture victims to game their way into the American interior.[217]

Smugglers moving the Indians had charged tens of thousands of dollars per person to route them through as many as a dozen safe countries to the U.S. border and "often supply the migrants with fake backstories to help them try to win asylum," she found.

"According to NPR interviews with U.S. and Indian government officials, police, licensed immigration agents, lawyers and Indian deportees, most of the would-be migrants face no credible threats to their safety or livelihood," she reported. "They're simply leaving India for better job opportunities abroad and to reunite with relatives who've already emigrated."

One Sikh migrant recalled how, along the migration trail, "fellow Sikhs would rehearse fake backstories about Sikh separatism and persecutions," she found. "The stories were untrue for the individuals telling them but were fashioned out of quite real decades-old strife."

It's worth noting that these immigrants hailed from one of India's wealthiest states, Punjab, where spiking land prices allowed many to afford the $20,000 and up smuggling fees, not that poverty qualified as persecution anyway.

Satish Bhargava, director of Crown Immigration Consultancy Services, a licensed immigration agency in India, explained the only motivation he ever saw: "They are desperate to go to foreign countries due to [their perception of] good lifestyles. They just keep thinking like that."

While prior administrations ignored this well-known fraud by Indians, the Trump administration ordered new India-specific training for asylum officers responsible for the credible fear interviews in April 2019, according to Frayer. In the six months prior to that training, credible fear was found in 89 percent of Indian nationals evaluated by asylum officers. After the new training, the rate dropped to 17 percent through February 2020, probably too high even at that.

One reason these offenses persist is that the asylum system is not geared to detect common fraud, and U.S. prosecutors aren't very interested in prosecuting, according to General Accountability Office (GAO) reporting in recent years. Sometimes they do when the offenses are too big and bad to ignore. One April 2021 federal indictment charged Elvis Harold Reyes of Tampa, Florida, with filing bogus asylum applications for 230 illegal immigrants from South and Central America.[218] At the time, they had to show that they had cleared credible fear and actually filed federal asylum claims to secure temporary Florida driver licenses and work authorization.

Falsely presenting himself as a pastor, lawyer, and former FBI agent, Reyes charged $5,000 for driver licenses needed to build lives after illegal border entries. He did this the time-honored way: by making up phony persecution stories and getting in the backlogged line for years.

Reyes filed hundreds of "fabricated representations about threats, persecution, and fear of returning to the applicants' native countries due to drug-cartel related crime, political corruption, gang-related violence, other organized crime, and government-sponsored torture," the indictment said. Reyes pleaded guilty and went to prison for twenty years.[219] But the government case under Biden's Department of Justice painted the immigrants as duped victims. Only six of Reyes's 230 clients ever got deported, a *Washington Post* story said.[220]

Mostly, though, the government doesn't police this kind of asylum fraud despite fifteen years of persistent government reports pointing to a general inability or interest in detecting asylum fraud in the nation's eight United States Citizenship and Immigration Services division field offices.

Enter the Rubber-Stamp Asylum System

Early in the Biden border crisis, the normal working of the asylum system as I have described it above collapsed. The administration went ad hoc, nixing the whole credible fear interview process, skipping all mandatory detentions and bond hearings, and simply releasing illegal entrants into the interior with pinky finger promises to report to ICE sometime over the next year. Border jumpers did not even have to declare asylum at the border; strikingly, DHS decided to *presume* all who crossed would report in and apply, a stunning departure from orthodoxy and, according to some, lawful action.

They did it by abusing a 1952 executive branch authority called "humanitarian parole." Originally, the parole power was limited to one-off emergencies, like if an alien was injured or dying. Think of humanitarian parole as like a presidential commutation of sentence for a terminally ill inmate.[221]

In fairness, many prior presidents have misused the discretionary parole power to manage surges or various refugee crises in "illegitimate and extra-constitutional" ways, George Fishman, former deputy general counsel for the Trump administration, wrote in an aptly titled February 2022 paper titled "The Pernicious Perversion of Parole."[222]

But the Biden DHS went farther than any predecessor, Fishman wrote. It started rubber-stamping paroles to hundreds of thousands of illegal aliens on the honor system that they would report to immigration within a year. Many who received these hall passes are unlikely to ever check in or finish an asylum process can work for years anyway as part of the nation's roughly twelve million illegal immigrants until the highly unlikely moment when an ICE officer catches up to them.

The incentive to cross illegally and claim asylum under these circumstances would strike any reasonable person who really knew the working details as clownish. Yet the Biden administration constantly shot the system full of incentive steroids so that the most economic migrants possible would want to exploit it, counting on the fact that most Americans know little of how the scam really works.

One of the most remarkable incentives the administration added, if measured by destructive brashness, was to virtually end almost every kind of interior deportation, which created a highly alluring sanctuary America. Ending deportation inside the country now meant that no ICE officer was going to come after anyone who lost or abandoned an asylum claim. The spigot opened to full and then some.

Furthermore, Democratic political leaders have frequently promised and delivered general amnesties or endlessly renewable temporary protections for illegally present foreign nationals like Hondurans, Haitians, and Liberians. So, the narcotic draw on illegal aliens to ignore deportation orders until one of those rescues materializes was simply irresistible too.

No amount of actual or prognosticated flooding seemed to prick the consciences of illegal immigration proponents who opposed the idea of borders. For example, by the fall of 2022, the Biden administration was preparing to dismantle the Title 42 pandemic expulsions policy still denying some 40 percent of economic migrant border-crossers access to the asylum system. In late March 2022, American intelligence agencies began warning that restoring broad access to the asylum system would generate yet another high: up to 18,000 per day, or 540,000 a month (compared to recent apprehension numbers in the 170,000 and 210,000 monthly range).[223]

But the party's far left *wanted* the deluge of claims that size, pressed relentlessly for Title 42's lifting, and never raised a concern about those incredible projected numbers. They hated Title 42 because, as one communique accurately complained, it was designed to "deter as many people from entering the United States as possible."[224]

When a federal judge temporarily delayed Title 42's end in May 2022, one advocacy group howled that this was tantamount to murder![225] Never mind the big houses immigrants wanted to live in one day back home or that Haitians enjoyed the good life in Chile but just wanted a little more.

In perhaps the most remarkable capitulation to the progressive wing of all, Biden's DHS implemented the most radical change in asylum processing since the laws were established in 1980. The new scheme removed immigration judges and adversarial ICE lawyers from the adjudication process entirely and handed the awesome duty of granting or declining asylum to USCIS officers with five weeks' training and who answered directly to political appointees in Washington. The scheme was advertised as a way to reduce the backlog of cases, but the reality was that it raised the specter that political appointees could order the rubber-stamping of asylum approvals within weeks of immigrant illegal crossings, with no checks, balances, or chance for the American people to appeal them.

A pilot program showed that, of ninety-nine such adjudications by low-level asylum officers in the spring of 2022, twenty-four were approved, an 8 percent increase from the average. The rest were declined; however, rather than deport those who were declined, they got to get in the four-to-eight-year immigration court backlog for the old process, the *New York Times* reported.[226] It's a safe bet that none will ever be deported.

From now on, low-level frontline USCIS asylum officers who answered to DHS political masters in Washington would decide who gets asylum or not. They were to be given total authority to rubber-stamp all asylum claims, right at the border, or much sooner after entries than ever before.[227]

Border security hawks howled that the new proposed asylum system amounted to a recipe for rubber-stamping approvals.[228] Under the headline "Biden Administration Prepares Sweeping Change to Asylum Process," a March 24, 2022, *New York Times* story reported that critics predicted the new system "will draw even more hopeful migrants to the border."[229]

It is only human nature, of course, for them to feel so drawn and to lie up a storm. Economic migrants will lie for life-changing profit and never tell the truth when deportation is the outcome. The U.S. asylum system is structured to facilitate lying and to discourage truth-telling. And that's why champions of illegal immigration love it so much.

PART II

PANDEMONIUM

CHAPTER SIX

ADRENALINE RUSH

On New Year's Eve 2020, President-elect Joe Biden and future First Lady Jill Biden appeared live from their home on ABC's *Dick Clark's New Year Rockin' Eve with Ryan Seacrest*, who conducted the interview from New York City's eerily empty Times Square. The first couple had the Covid-19 pandemic on their minds.

Seacrest asked what the president-elect hoped for most of 2021, when he would be leading.

"Look, there's never been a single thing America's not been able to overcome, no matter how drastic it's been, when we've done it together. Never. Never. Never," Biden said. "America can do anything, and I am absolutely confident we're going to come back and come back even stronger than where we were before."

The day before, far to the south and the west, 400 Cubans in Juarez, feeling intensely optimistic about America too, stormed the international to El Paso, Texas. They swept past Mexican border guards, leapt pell-mell the wrong way over Mexican pay turnstiles, and sprinted for America in a criss-crossing bonzai stamped over the bridge lanes. They were going to blast right into Biden's new America. Except that it was still Trump's America for a few more weeks.

And while Trump was preparing for a lavish black-tie New Year's Eve bash at Mar-a-Lago, his officers of the U.S. Customs and Border Protection Mobile Field Force were already suited up in riot gear and waiting behind heavy concrete blocks tipped by concertina wire, blocking the bridge lanes. [230]

They stopped the migrant charge cold.[231] The American agents broadcast a recorded bilingual message over loudspeakers warning that any further trouble would be met by force and prosecution. Bunched up, frustrated, the foiled mob loosed a telling chant about how they were seeing 2021 for themselves.

"Bi-den! Bi-den! Bi-den! Bi-den! Bi-den!"[232]

A smaller group of twenty-five or thirty immigrants staged a similar bonsai rush that night on the international bridge connecting Acuña, Mexico, to Del Rio, Texas, hundreds of miles downriver.

Although no one could know at that moment, this was the leading edge of the coming storm, a foreshock of the coming earthquake. Until dawn, the Juarez crowd demanded that Biden now keep his promises, betting that the American border guard would turn on Trump and let them by.

"We are calling out to Mexico and the U.S. and to Biden, the new U.S. president, to remind him of the presidential campaign promises he made. To make him aware we are here," one of them, Raul Pino Gonzalez of Havana, told a Cuban news reporter.

"There is expectation, there is hope and there is enthusiasm in those who believe that, with the change of administration, will come new measures and that they will immediately enter and there will be new conditions that will allow them to request asylum," explained Enrique Valenzuela, head of the Chihuahua State Council for Population and Migration.[233]

Both bridge incidents seemed to have escaped the notice of an America preoccupied with New Year's Eve and a contested national election. But they were strong harbingers of the crisis boiling across Latin America during the transition period between election and inauguration. All along the migrant routes from Mexico to South America and beyond, citizens of 150 nations were stuck behind Covid border closures. [234]

Biden's nomination—and then his election, even with its disputes—had hit the global migrant bloodstream like a dose of adrenaline. The whole world stood mesmerized by his neon welcome sign at the border, flashing the promises of eventual citizenship for all, an end to deportation, and fast reentry into America of everyone Trump had kicked out.

Governments may have closed the migrant routes and militarized them for the pandemic, but the closed-for-business trails came alive after the election.[235] Unable to wait a moment longer, they began battling police, even if to advance by one country. At a Panamanian government camp in the remote village of La Penita, 1,500 Haitian, Cuban, Indian, Nepalese, and Bangladeshi citizens rioted. So urgent was their desire to get to the American border in time for its opening that they burned down a local building, set their own tents alight, and attacked local police trying to quell them.[236]

In late November 2020, Cubans backed up in Suriname by pandemic border closures formed the 500-migrant "Por la Libertad" (Freedom Caravan) because, a Cuban newspaper reported, "Joe Biden won the U.S. presidential elections and many Cubans thought about chasing the American Dream."[237]

As Por la Libertad participants chanted, "Let us pass! Let us pass!" they tried to violently force their way past border guards into Guyana. They seized a government building and set fires before riot police rounded them up and sent them back to Suriname for the time being.

Once the election was done and won, the barometric pressure gauge spun up new caravans too. One caravan formed in Honduras right after the election in November. But a vengeful cash-withholding Trump was still presiding, and Honduran police violently broke up that first one. In early December, police in Guatemala broke up a second bigger one, thousands strong.[238]

The pressure building inside the cooker was obvious to a few, but their voices went unheeded.

"The elements of a new crisis are gathering," the *Washington Post* reported in early December 2020 as part of a story that acknowledged migrants were bridling against the coordinated border closures.[239] At the Texas and Arizona border, the number of foreign job seekers attempting illegal entries began "swelling," the *New York Times* reported on December 13, 2020, in what appeared to be the "leading edge of a much more substantial surge."

The increase was "shaping up as the first significant challenge to President-elect Joseph R. Biden Jr.'s pledge to adopt a more compassionate policy along America's 1,100-mile border with Mexico," the *Times* reported. The reporter went on to blame hurricanes in Central America, of course, but still grudgingly allowed that "expectations of a more lenient U.S. border policy drive ever-larger numbers toward the United States."[240]

For their part, some incoming Biden transition team advisors did heed the warning signs and took action to disappear the immigrant movements that might draw media attention and trouble.[241] Reuters cited six anonymous U.S. and foreign officials in reporting that the Biden administration had secretively promised billions in aid if Central American and Mexican governments would use their militarized police forces to break up the caravans.[242]

The blood of immigrants would soon soak these diplomatic understandings and continue to do so throughout 2021 and 2022 as military police in Mexico, Honduras, and Guatemala regularly beat the caravans into oblivion.[243]

But then the administration, either in hapless or willful ignorance, spurred the gathering crisis to fruition—and guaranteed bloody clashes—with promises to the anxious crowds on the trail.

In addition to everything else Biden promised aspiring border-crossers, his transition team in late December announced it was considering granting "Temporary Protected Status" to more than a million Hondurans and Guatemalans illegally residing inside the United States to prevent their deportations to hurricane zones from Eta and Iota a month earlier.[244] Hondurans and Guatemalans realized TPS would cover them if they could just get over the border in time—and pressed forward.

Then, on December 21, the president-elect called a press conference in Delaware and told the world he would need "probably the next six months" to dismantle the Trump system and install his more humane one for the waiting throngs.[245]

"It will get done," the president-elect beckoned. "And it will get done quickly but it's not going to be able to be done on Day 1."

With the TPS coming for Hondurans and Guatemalans and the new humane system chumming the blocked migrant trails, it was little wonder that a vast new third migrant caravan organized in Honduras with the stated intention of forcibly busting pandemic border closures and being at the American border just in time for Biden to unlock the gates.

The Associated Press acknowledged a driving motivating factor for this caravan, albeit in the last sentence of a report: "Migrants have been hoping for a warmer welcome at the US border with the administration of President-elect Joe Biden, who takes office on January 20."[246]

That late-December caravan set out January 15 from San Pedro Sula, Honduras, on a journey timed for it to reach the American border on or about Inauguration Day, January 20. Its 5,000–6,000 participants hiked along highways and hopped aboard trucks while Guatemalan soldiers further north set up militarized roadblocks, ostensibly to enforce its pandemic border closure.

During this period, American news media let leftist advocates of a borderless United States continually insist without challenge that hurricanes and global warming were motivating all this, not Biden's policy promises. But foreign media put the lie to the gaslighting.

In a January 8 opinion column for the *New York Times* titled "With Biden, more immigrants will come (and that's fine)," the open borders proponent Univision anchor Jorge Ramos attributed the fierce new determination to emigrate now to the hurricanes.[247]

"It's no surprise that the end of the racist, anti-immigrant Trump administration would once again make the United States an attractive destination for migrants, particularly the challenges many face at home," Ramos wrote.

As the human mass was about to start out, the French media outlet AFP ran a Spanish-language story about the earlier caravans that police broke up in October and November. Under the headline "Honduran hopes Biden will let him into the United States," the story quoted Honduran citizen Emerson Lopez, eighteen, hoping aloud that the transition from Trump to Biden "will benefit us." He wasn't going with this caravan but would wait to see if Biden let it in because "if they arrive well, most of us here are going to make the decision to leave later."[248] A neighbor of Lopez's, fifty-one-year-old Martha Saldivar, told AFP how Biden's election mattered in her life-planning choices.

"It has been heard that Biden is going to remove the wall and we will have to fight to get there" with the caravans, she said.

In El Salvador too, hope sprang eternal with the Biden victory and message that rescue was coming.

"With Biden, the immigration laws in the United States will change and become more humane," California resident Cecilia Aralavo, who was visiting relatives in San Salvador, told AFP. Cristian Panameno, a forty-two-year-old Salvadoran mechanic living about fifteen miles south of San Salvador who had already been deported once from the United States, would not have dared spend time and money trying again under Trump. But now? He had saved up enough to go a second time to make money in America.

"I think that with this new president, things will change for a migrant who arrives without papers, because with Trump, we are screwed."

On January 17, the 6,000-strong third migrant caravan tried to violently smash its way through a thick cordon of Guatemalan police along a highway in southern Guatemala. Video from above shows an epic melee. The young men attacking at the caravan's spear tip almost broke through at the middle point in the police skirmish line. But Biden's transition team had promised billions in aid to Guatemala's government, and the police line held strong. In response, police flanks peeled away to reinforce the middle in just the nick of time and prevailed with a hail of beating sticks.[249]

Inexorable Forward March

In early January 2021, with inauguration day in sight, I traveled to heavily walled El Paso and crossed over the bridge to Juarez, Mexico, where the bonzai charge had happened, to take the pulse. Nothing and everything had changed.

The migrants pushed back months earlier under Trump's Remain in Mexico policy were still there behind multiple layers of wall extending east and west for many miles. They were mightily pissed off that they hadn't been let in. But that fact hadn't prevented waves of newcomers from appearing in the huge Mexican city thinking they were going to get through soon. In this, Mexico's southern border with Guatemala played an important role. I have often called this frontier "America's OTHER southern border" because what happens there provides a predictive mirror as to what will soon happen at the U.S. border.

Increasing numbers of migrants were punching through all the borders from Brazil and Chile and, significantly, through southern Mexico's national guard deployment. They were reaching Mexican cities and towns across from Texas, New Mexico, Arizona, and California. Juarez was typical.

In northern Mexican cities and towns, the criminal cartels were gearing up for the bonanza too. Almost no one was going to avoid paying big again. Ruthless crime syndicates controlled almost every crossing into the United States on pain of death. About a half dozen militarized Mexican cartels smuggled America's drugs over these crossing regions, also known locally as *"plazas,"* but ran human-smuggling subsidiaries too. The cartels were going to cash in on this bonanza with the kind of lethal force they were infamous for using.

In all these places, the hopeful border jumpers would wait for Trump's departure and for the new Biden people to flick the red light to green. Some wouldn't wait. They'd pay cartel guides to get them past the Title 42 expulsion threat to the hundred-mile mark, the outer reaches of Border Patrol jurisdiction, and wait for the deportation moratorium to take root. It seemed like people were constantly prodding and poking and testing the American lines, looking for any give in U.S. government resolve.

At the halfway point of the Paso del Norte International Bridge, I got to see what that looked like. I took up a position next to two CBP inspections officers manning a barbed wire cement barricade in the middle of the span, presumably the same equipment used to block the Cuban New Year's Eve dash. The officers told me more than a hundred Central Americans had just trudged up the bridge's pedestrian walkway with a few personal belongings and children, expecting to be let in. They were all turned away.

As I stood with the agents at the international line, a Central American mother and father showed up at the barricade, each holding a sleeping child. The CBP officer implacably told them they couldn't pass the international line just underfoot without documents and can't have asylum either because of Title 42. But the parents just stood there anyway for another half hour, swaying back and forth with the sleeping children. Tears welled up in the father's eyes.

But Trump's policy hadn't yet changed.

"They can do whatever they want to do on the Mexican side," the officer under orders told me. "They can stand there all day. They're not coming in."

Some were finding gaps in the wall and slipping through them.

Late one night on the Texas side, I made my way to the short, notorious Anapra Gap just west of El Paso, right where an older steel wall ends and an unfenced Mount Cristo Rey rises. This gap on the mountain is actually in Sunland Park, New Mexico, overlooking El Paso. It had been left open years ago when some wall got built with 2006 Secure Fence Act money under the George W. Bush administration. Difficult topography and opposition from local Catholics who considered the mountain and its 1930s cross monument on top sacred had kept the steel wall off Mount Cristo Rey.[250]

But the Trump plan had it down for eventual walling. That wouldn't happen now. On the Texas side, Border Patrol agents cruised a spot right at the gap called "the bowl" because of a sweeping bowl-shaped indentation of white desert sand where migrants often make their dashes after stepping over a knee-high cement barrier between the steel wall edge and open mountain. That night was really dark. Many more runners than usual were sprinting through.

Standing guard just on the Mexican side of the short cement barrier was a Mexican immigration officer by his parked truck, its headlights on. Up the blackened mountainside, fires burned at intervals, warming members of the Mexican national guard who were still on duty. The Mexican officer explained that nothing had changed on the Mexican side; their orders were to prevent passage. But things had gotten very busy lately, the Mexican officer said. His orders had not changed to block that little gap and not let any migrants through.

While he was explaining this, a squad of Mexican national guard carrying M16 rifles emerged out of the dark and into the headlights. They had just filed down the mountain herding a group of six migrants they'd caught somewhere. The Mexicans lined them up against their side of the American border wall, took photos, then piled them into a vehicle to be dropped off somewhere else in Juarez.

On the Texas side, Border Patrol agents chased down "runners" and finding trucks, U-Haul trailers, and stash houses crammed with illegal Cubans, Haitians, Mexicans, and Central Americans looking forward to the new Biden way. When the agents would round them up and try to put them in transport trucks for the Title 42 expulsion, the Cubans especially became aggressive, as though suddenly realizing they'd been victimized in some kind of cruel bait-and-switch scheme that wasn't supposed to be happening anymore. The Cubans often assaulted the agents, taking swings, shoving hard, and trying to run from a Title 42 expulsion, three different agents told me. The Haitians had built a reputation for nastiness to get out of Title 42, often spewing venom at the agents when they too weren't throwing punches.

Back on the Juarez side the next morning, I found Cuban Victor Manuel hawking Spanish-language newspapers on a curbside kiosk at the bridge, a street cube his office chair. He told me of a social media–driven plot where some 1,300 of his countrymen were going to charge over the river again all at once—an immigrant flash mob—if they didn't get what they wanted after January 21.

"If it turns out that there is no hope of crossing it [a mass charge] will happen again," Victor told me. "They don't want to do anything wrong, but they are tired of being in Mexico."

At one of the city's migrant shelters, I found Brazilian Gislaine Aparecida da Silva Batista, pushed back under Remain in Mexico a year earlier with her ten-year-old daughter. She said her asylum hearing was still on for the next month as far as she knew but was waiting to find out when Biden would let them in to wait in America instead.

"I suspect everything changed with the new president. There's a new president! There are new rules. There's a new law!" she told me, a bit premature for accuracy.

While much confusion reigned initially in the borderlands about what rules were new and which ones were retiring and which applied to whom, there was no confusion about one thing: the border was going to open under Biden sooner or later, and crowds were pushing their way toward the party.

They would get it soon.

CHAPTER SEVEN

MEXICO TRIGGERS NOAH'S FLOOD

"Mexican authorities in some areas of the border stopped taking back families returned by the United States... after barely a week of Biden's presidency...citing a new law that went into effect last month requiring children to go to family-appropriate shelters."

—*Washington Post*, February 7, 2021[251]

"I really hit the roof on this. No one told me it was on the agenda. I remember thinking this is really going to screw us on some of these issues."

—Christopher Landau, ambassador to Mexico under Donald Trump, recalling Mexican legislation that sent hundreds of thousands of migrant families to the U.S. border on Joe Biden's Inauguration Day

About ten days after inauguration, a friend in Del Rio called with a tip. The Biden administration had ordered the local Border Patrol in the Del Rio sector to suspend the Title 42 pandemic instant expulsions of every migrant caught coming through, the tipster said, and now they were freeing and transporting at least hundreds of them to resettle inside the United States. If true, this would be the first evidence that the Trump's levy was breaking under the brand-new Biden administration. I was expecting it after just returning from the border in West Texas.

If catch-and-release was back already—so soon after Biden took office—that was major news as a sign of system-breaking numbers.

The tipster said most of those now being released into the United States were Haitian and Cuban migrant family groups. They were coming in so hot and heavy they couldn't be detained, and USCIS asylum officers could not even conduct credible fear interviews. After processing the migrants at a local facility for a day or two, Border Patrol was releasing them on their own recognizance to a local nonprofit advocacy organization in Del Rio called the Val Verde Border Humanitarian Coalition. The volunteers were arranging buses and flights into the American interior to cities of the immigrants' choice.[252]

All the way up until Trump left office, Border Patrol had been pushing all migrants back to Mexico under the pandemic expulsion measure; the border was arguably under the best control in modern memory. But I also under-stood that if there was any truth to what this tipster was saying, it was on. Why would I think that? Because I knew that those caught and released would send home news of it down trail and to hometowns around the world, which begets ever more just like a gold rush following discovery of a first nugget.

Soon, I had Shon Young on the horn. He was director of the Val Verde Border Humanitarian Coalition, the nonprofit volunteer organization in Del Rio said to be accepting the Border Patrol handoff deliveries. I asked him if it was true that Border Patrol was handing off immigrants to his group for release and transportation into the interior.

It sure was, Young confirmed. The same thing was happening in towns far downriver from Del Rio. Without me even asking, he volunteered an important time stamp.

"For some reason, *the day after inauguration* [author emphasis]," Young explained, "we had a big influx of people. So we fired up the coalition at full speed."

He elaborated. Before the inauguration, Border Patrol typically might bring three or four released immigrants a day to the coalition building, situated about a mile from the international bridge to Acuña. But on the very first day *after* the inauguration, "for some reason," Border Patrol started dropping off sixty to a hundred, Young reiterated.

Young said his organization was arranging Greyhound buses and even, for those with money (usually the Haitians who'd been earning well in Chile for years), local flights out of Del Rio International Airport to whichever cities they picked for resettlement. Border Patrol was dropping off so many at the nonprofit's campus, they had to move out the old fast to make way for the new, Young said. To do so, they were mainly using buses.

The way it worked, Young explained in my first February 2 phone interview with him—and this would soon become normalized on an industrial scale—was that the families would cross the river and turn themselves in to any federal agent they could find or wait by a roadside until the agents found *them*. The agents, who were used to doing most of the chasing around there—not the other way around—would transport them to a limited-capacity Border Patrol station just north of Del Rio and find it filled.

Since most ICE detention facilities were closed for Covid-19 and the Border Patrol stations were unsuited for high-volume, long-term family care, Border Patrol was quickly releasing them to Young's group with legal papers called "Notice to Appear," or NTAs, and Notices to Report, NTRs. I later learned NTAs and NTRs were part of the new "honor system" that provided temporary legal residency for their bearers to remain inside the United States on a promise that they self-report to an ICE office in destination cities, presumably to initiate an asylum claim.

It was a conveyor belt system. From Rio Grande water to city took all of about two days. There were signs that this was going on all along the Texas border south of Del Rio. Young said the same ad hoc quick-release system was already happening on a similar scale fifty-five miles downstream in Eagle Pass with a sister nonprofit organization, across from the Mexican city of Piedras Negras. One of the van drivers said it was happening in Laredo and in McAllen.

Later, I interviewed Tiffany Burrow, operations director of the Del Rio nonprofit coalition about what had happened. Like Young, Burrow traced the surge in family unit releases through her organization directly to "the switch of administrations."

"We saw an immediate surge," from the normal 25 or so a month during the Trump administration's final year to 100 to 150 every day, Burrow told me. Her organization was arranging their transportation to other American cities as fast as her group could organize buses and planes out.

A Border Patrol agent in the area confirmed all this, and so did a third federal official in the Del Rio area.

"We are releasing hundreds from many different countries of origin simply because we don't have enough room to hold them all," the agent told me. "We can't hold them because they are crossing all day long in groups of 20 to 40...men, women, children."

"They're filling bus after bus after bus" with temporarily legalized migrants heading to interior American cities, the federal official told me.

With just those calls on a single day, February 2, I learned that it was *on*, at least from Del Rio, Eagle Pass, and Laredo. No U.S. media had picked up the story. I checked Mexican media in the State of Coahuila across from Del Rio and Eagle Pass. Some Mexican press reported that army and national guard units had mobilized to manage unusually high numbers of migrants who were causing problems.[253]

I wrote what I knew for the Center for Immigration Studies, which published my February 3 blog post titled "'Catch and Release' Resumes on Texas Border in the Face of Rising Migrant Numbers."[254] Citing "federal sources and the head of a migrant-assistance agency," I reported that unknown numbers of border-crossing Haitian and Cuban families with young children were "enjoying the first return to 'catch-and-release' policies since President Donald Trump's administration all but eliminated them." To my knowledge, it remains the first public report of the mass migration. A bit later, I would learn that it was widespread.

If Young, Burrow, and the others I interviewed by phone that day were correct, that all these families abruptly rushed the border on Inauguration Day, what the hell happened? The answer is that Mexico mounted a diplomatic maneuver so mendacious and bizarre that it defies belief, too weird to possibly have succeeded against the new administration. But it is true, and, worse, it worked like a charm with the incoming Biden administration.

Mexico's Duplicitous Play

For quite some time, I did not know precisely what triggered the flow of immigrant families on that particular day, and neither did anyone else. To the time of this writing, twenty months and millions of apprehensions later, the U.S. news establishment has let the mystery fester uninvestigated, and the Biden administration has never volunteered answers. All I knew at the time, with certainty, is that no new hurricane had destroyed South America, Haiti, or Cuba the day before or after Inauguration Day, one that only victimized families with young children. Gang violence in Honduras did not severely worsen from the day prior to the inauguration to the day following it and beset only families. Guatemala's government did not suddenly begin mass political incarcerations of just families, either.

In time, I discovered that the first catalyst for the crisis was a stealth maneuver by the Mexican National Congress and the state government of Tamaulipas, with—at least—later witting complicity of the new Biden administration. Mexico's play remains a largely untold story of diplomatic cunning and manipulation supported by American duplicity afterward but possibly even beforehand. The complete story of what happened may never be told, so hermetic was the secret intrigue surrounding it.

But first, it is important to know first that Trump's Remain in Mexico and pandemic instant expulsion policies were no picnic for Mexico. The country, facing threats of debilitating trade tariffs from Trump, had been forced to take on the extreme burdens of housing, feeding, and caring for hundreds of thousands of migrant family groups either expelled by Trump or unable to proceed over the border. Many could not be easily deported to Africa, Cuba, Haiti, or one hundred other countries. Caring for them was a highly expensive, complex, and long-lived chore for which Mexico had been ill-prepared because it had never before had to do it.

Once Trump's expulsion policies took full effect, as the *Texas Tribune* put it once, Mexico was quickly "overwhelmed by the number of migrants in its border cities."[255] Women with very young children that Trump expelled soon became a migraine headache for Mexico, which under other Mexican laws had to care for them somewhere, somehow. So they filled Mexico's fifty-eight detention centers to capacity. And when those centers filled up, problematic squalid camps that drew undesirable media attention began to form in parks or in the central squares of northern Mexican cities like Nuevo Laredo, Piedras Negras, Juarez, Acuña, and especially so in Tamaulipas State across from South Texas in the cities of Reynosa and Matamoros, long the most heavily trammeled border-crossing areas into the United States. Managing Covid-19 burdened the Mexicans too. The government had to build Covid-containment shelters to house and manage infected migrants.

So Mexico began closely eyeing the American election, undoubtedly looking for the soonest possible relief from these terrible burdens should Joe Biden win. Mexico was clearly prepared for that.

Immediately after the American election, the Mexican congress secretively passed a new and unusual law that had already been pre-written and a pathway for its quick approval cleared. On November 6, 2020—within seventy-two hours of Joe Biden's election—the "Various Articles of the Migration Law and the Law on Refugees are Reformed, Complementary Protection and Political Asylum in the Matter of Migrant Children" was on President Andrés Manuel López Obrador's desk for signing. On November 11, 2020, President Obrador put pen to paper with no formal announcement or press coverage.[256]

The law's execution was carefully timed to coincide with Trump's departure and Biden's seating as president. A timer in the legislation was set for it to implement sixty days later, on January 11, ten days before Trump would leave office so he could do nothing about it. So what did this law do?

Boiled down, it was a Mexican version of the American Flores loophole. It prohibited federal detentions of migrant families with minor children—with or without parents—in all fifty-eight Mexican detention facilities nationwide. To remain in compliance with Mexico's other laws requiring the feeding and sheltering of migrant children, the new law required the government to merely refer them to voluntary-stay shelters. This meant that after January 11, 2021, Mexico could start emptying its detention centers, and thousands of families with their young children could travel freely inside the country, which everyone knows means the U.S. border.

But what to do about Title 42 expulsions once they tried to cross? The law had that baked into the cake. It gave individual Mexican states authority to refuse U.S. Title 42 expulsions—if the states deemed the private shelters as too full or to be closed for Covid. The State of Tamaulipas, the most heavily trafficked by migrants, did just that. It refused to take Biden's family expellees—on Biden's Inauguration Day—saying it had no shelter space.

The collective effect of the "reforms in favor of migrant children and adolescents, asylum seekers and refugees" was that thousands of migrant families found that they were not only freed from Mexican detention centers, but that, when they crossed the U.S. border, the Americans would have to keep them. A massive breach was thus opened into America through which an unremitting onslaught of migrant families would pour for years.

By the time Mexico implemented the law on January 11, Trump was all but out and embroiled in domestic political controversies about the American election anyway. He'd do nothing to stop the families before Biden took office.

But Joe Biden? Clearly, the Mexicans wagered that he'd take all the families without resistance and threaten nothing like Trump's trade tariffs. Did Biden or anyone on his transition team know in advance this was coming or even help arrange it? No telling at this point. But migrant advocates and human rights groups clearly knew all about it and understood exactly what it would do.

For instance, five Mexico-based United Nations organizations issued a November 11, 2021, Spanish-language press release celebrating the new law. Their laudatory release said that it had finally "regularized" the migratory status of children "in order to avoid their *expeditious return* [author's emphasis] from the United States and thus guarantee that they can see their basic rights fulfilled, including access to international protection," no doubt meaning American asylum.[257] A March 2021 fact sheet about the law published by the Institute for Women in Migration (IWM) explained that "human rights organizations" had for a full decade fruitlessly advocated to end involuntary Mexican detention of foreign immigrant families and that—for reasons the sheet left unexplained—"the reforms were finally passed."[258] It's not clear which "human rights organizations" were behind this.

The Mexicans, human rights, and migrant advocacy groups managed to keep the Trump administration in the dark that a major piece of legislation was in the works for a Biden victory.

News of the law's sudden passage came as a complete surprise to Trump's ambassador to Mexico, Christopher Landau. In an interview with me in May 2022, Landau said he only learned of the law after it was signed, from a staffer in a routine morning meeting shortly before Trump's term expired. Landau, who resigned at noon on Inauguration Day, January 20, recalled feeling angered and betrayed that Mexican diplomatic partners had never informed him that such a momentous policy scheme was in the works.

"I really hit the roof on this," Landau recalled, referring to migration as the most important issue on the bilateral agenda. "And no one told me it was on the agenda. I remember thinking this is really going to screw us on some of these issues, especially if it's implemented with any teeth." Had he known it was coming, he added, "I would have been on this like a fly on honey."

By the time Landau learned of it, no time remained of Trump's rapidly dwindling tenure to react.

Even today, there is almost nothing in the Mexican media about the law, despite its momentous impacts on the Mexican treasury and implications at the border.

"Some Adjustments" and Then: A Human Onslaught

Four days after my own story revealing large-scale catch-and-release was underway, on February 7, 2021, the *Washington Post* joined me. The paper reported a massive catch-and-release operation involving migrant families with children pouring out of Tamaulipas and mainly into Rio Grande Valley border cities in far South Texas. The influx so quickly overran Border

Patrol agents and facilities in the Rio Grande Valley that Biden's DHS had no choice but to free them into the wild, so to speak, around local bus stations and nonprofit shelters.

The newspaper carried this small nugget: "Mexican authorities in some areas of the border stopped taking back families returned by the United States...after barely a week of Biden's presidency...citing a new law that went into effect last month requiring children to go to family-appropriate shelters."[259]

The *Post* requested comment from Mexico about the new law. In a prepared statement, Mexico acknowledged that it had "made some adjustments in recent days" due to the implementation of a new law. It wasn't much, and neither that newspaper nor any other would ever go on to press the matter.

The Mexican moves are understandable because they served its national interests. In decades past, Tamaulipas could always count on most immigrants passing through to become America's wards and problem. All the countries to America's south happily played the hot potato game knowing that the potato landed in the United States' lap every single time. But Trump's policies forced Tamaulipas and Mexico to take the hot potato this time. Mexico successfully conspired to send it back to the Americans.

It is now clear, in retrospect, that this is why the vast majority coming across from Tamaulipas into southern Texas were families and unaccompanied children and that southern Texas became the main epicenter of the crisis. But repercussions would spread far beyond just this one opened channel through Title 42.

In a knock-on effect, single adults began taking advantage of system breakdowns in Texas. Other Mexican states didn't follow Tamaulipas' declaration and were still accepting U.S. expulsions of families. So families that tried to cross in other states—California, New Mexico, and parts of West Texas—still found themselves expelled.

But word spread quickly that the way was clear in southern Texas, creating a suctioning or funneling effect, where families all headed to the Tamaulipas crossings and singles pushed through everywhere as Border Patrol agents struggled to process in the crowds of especially needy people.

In its way, the Mexican law was brilliant. It served Mexico's national interest, at the expense of U.S. national interest, sure, in that Mexico transferred the burdensome population of Trump expellees to the new and accepting Biden land as soon as the "administration switch," as Burrow put it to me. They knew exactly what would happen. IWM noted in its fact sheet that "the families know that they can't be detained, so they leave the shelter." These migrants took off over the border as soon as the Mexicans released them. Everyone knew they wouldn't have to support themselves and bother local populations for longer than a few days with the way the law's implementation was timed. When Biden took office, they simply walked over as Tamaulipas told the Americans they wouldn't take them back.

Mexico would never have tried tossing that hot potato at Trump. As president, Trump had proven willing to economically thrash longstanding allies to achieve a range of wants, from forcing Europeans to pay back balances on the cost of NATO to slapping tariffs on Canadian steel and aluminum imports.[260] The Mexicans saw Trump's threats of imposing debilitating tariffs on Mexican exports as entirely credible. As a result, they accepted his expulsions to avoid economic ruin.

But Joe Biden?

The full story is not known but the Mexicans must have reasoned that Biden was a more docile sort or a very willing victim of the intrigue. I also allow for the possibility that some progressive advisers on Biden's transition staff, having hailed from the same immigration advocacy industry that orchestrated the law in Mexico. If so, I have yet to find evidence of it. In any case, the new administration could have threatened sanctions or offered incentives to force Mexico to reconsider the new law. But the Biden government accepted the new Mexican dictate without blinking or pushing back.

When asked much later about why the administration was allowing swells of foreign immigrant families into the United States after illegal border crossings, DHS Secretary Mayorkas struck exactly the kind of docile note the Mexicans must have calculated.

"With the Rio Grande Valley, there are some families who cannot be expelled in that particular area of the south-west border by reason of capacity constraints in Mexico," he explained to reporters months later in May.[261] None ever followed up.

Ultimately, blame for opening this first breach does not, in my opinion, fall on Mexican shoulders, but rather on American ones for passively accepting Mexico's manipulations and dictates. Complying with Mexican refusals to take expulsions was an affirmative American policy choice—an unnecessary one that came at the expense of U.S. national interests. But make no mistake, that choice is the reason why family groups not just from the south, but from around the world, began pouring in from Tamaulipas once news of the Title 42 breach spread.

The Chosen

"They understood that if they were pregnant by seven months by the time they got to the border, they would be allowed to go through. I was told they would get pregnant just for that reason. Everyone knew that this is the way to do it now. Let's get pregnant and we can get through. That's a free pass to get across. That's common knowledge."

—Nurse practitioner Diane Edrington, twenty-year volunteer health careprovider to U.S.-bound immigrants in Panama and indigenous tribes

The Biden administration did not open the border wide during the first eighteen months because it did not have to. If water metaphors can be used to describe what the administration did, it was to blast some holes through the dike, carve wide breaches in a levy, or punch siphons into the pipeline. It did this only for certain demographics of immigrants at first and in a couple of areas. Meaning, certain demographics of immigrant were anointed for immunity from Title 42 expulsions, free passes to permanent new lives inside America, winning lottery tickets. They were "the chosen."

Who were they? Obviously the families with children seven or younger who chose to cross through Tamaulipas.

Border Patrol apprehensions of family unit individuals, almost all of them in Texas, rocketed from 4,406 in December 2020 to 54,132 by the end of March, a 1,400 percent increase, and kept going. Apprehensions of family units hit 86,631 for August. And kept going at open throttle.

The number of family apprehensions leapt from 70,094 for fiscal year 2020 (October 2019 through September 2020) to 479,000 for fiscal 2021 and another 454,817 through July of fiscal 2022.

The chosen were unaccompanied minors who crossed anywhere.

In fiscal year 2020, they numbered 33,239. Six times that many crossed in fiscal 2021, or 146,925 and 150,000 in fiscal 2022.

A lesser-known chosen group was women in advanced stages of pregnancy, usually seven months who also could cross anywhere. After the first Title 42 passes for family groups, the prevalence of pregnant women in the third trimester became plain to see too. On July 1, 2021, the administration announced a policy that ICE agents could no longer detain pregnant, postpartum, or nursing women or put them in detention centers for deportation.[262] The fathers of their unborn children got in with them, no proof necessary.

The government does not publish statistics reflecting apprehensions of pregnant or postpartum border-crossers, so it's impossible to quantify the extent to which they too rushed the border to take advantage of their chosen status. But all of a sudden after Biden took office they were ubiquitous everywhere along the trails from Colombia to northern Mexico.

Mississippi-based nurse practitioner and medical director for Panama Mission Diane Edrington noticed them in the jungles of Panama where for twenty years she has volunteered to help indigenous tribes and migrants moving through.

Rarely in those two decades did Edrington see families or pregnant women trek the long dangerous jungle routes until Biden took office, she told me. Then, starting suddenly in mid-2021, Edrington noticed they were the majority coming through. The pregnant women always seemed to be about six to eight months.

"I think just the idea of a woman going through there pregnant...I just don't understand it," Edrington told me in a phone interview to Mississippi during a break from Panama. "It's unheard of."

As Edrington and her staff treated the pregnant women, they talked.

"They understood that if they were pregnant by seven months by the time they got to the border, they would be allowed to go through," she said. "I was told they would get pregnant just for that reason. Everyone knew that this is the way to do it now. Let's get pregnant and we can get through. That's a free pass to get across. That's common knowledge."

Supposed migrant advocates conveniently overlook tragic realities when arguing for policies that specifically draw in vulnerable demographics like children and pregnant women.

Pregnant migrant women died en route to the border. On May 26, 2022, a pregnant migrant was among seven killed when their U.S.-bound bus crashed in northern Mexico, read one Associated Press story. A month earlier, in March, a pregnant Nicaraguan woman died of dehydration in Mexico after smugglers abandoned her and dozens of other migrants in an overheated freight truck in northern Mexico.[263] That same month, a pregnant Guatemalan woman fell to her death while trying to climb over the border wall into Texas. [264] But none of that deterred anyone. The border was open to pregnant women and the ostensible fathers and husbands. The incentive for pregnant women to keep coming was as powerful as it was obvious: having U.S. citizen babies qualified the new young families for welfare and blocked future deportation.

In general, the losers were single adults; they remained targets of Title 42 expulsions and became runners who tried again and again. Sometimes, the Biden administration even let them stay too, especially when illegal border crossers simply overwhelmed Border Patrol's ability to even process them. Then the singles got processed into America with the families and pregnant chosen. I have seen hundreds of single adults processed in right alongside the families.

Selfies showing videos of real families flashing the thumbs-up as they boarded their U.S. city-bound charter buses spread like flame burns pure oxygen—and spurred rush after rush behind them, just like the 1848 discovery of gold at Sutter's Mill triggered the California gold rush.

Nothing the president or his people ever said again could overcome the narcotic allure of the selfie evidence showing smiling families holding up their new government Notice to Appear documents. When DHS Secretary Mayorkas went on international TV that March to pronounce that "the border is closed," their cell phones showed thousands of friends, neighbors, and third cousins quickly being released into America in live time. So, the parade went on and on.

When Vice President Harris beseeched migrants a few months later during a June trip to Guatemala that immigrants were being expelled and, "Do not come. Do not come,"[265] the migrants fact-checked their cell phones, saw that her words were untrue, and kept coming.

It did not matter to the immigrants that the border was partially sealed or that many were still being expelled back to Mexico in other areas. They came running. It did not matter that the administration's policy seemed unevenly applied and confusing from one day to the next. They poured in. Everyone knew the administration had torn open huge breaches in Texas across from Tamaulipas for families with young children, older kids if they came in without a parent or guardian, pregnant women, and often enough even single adults. They made up the millions who would come take their shot in Texas over the next two years—and mostly win.

Fake Families

"I'm thinking to myself: Horror. Horror. Horror. Horror."

—Monica Maple, retired assistant special agent in
charge of ICE Homeland Security Investigations
when asked how she felt about Biden administration disinterest in uncovering fake families crossing

Policies that created special rights for people who cross the border with children naturally elevated the value of children among those without special rights. In that environment, children became a rare-earth commodity for barter, sale, rent, or trade. They were visas, permission slips, crossing passes. Any parent with more than one found that they could defray thousands of dollars in smuggling costs to get the whole family in, maybe even cousins, uncles, and relatives but also complete strangers so long as the biological parents didn't mind taking some risk with the kids they'd rent out.

We first saw the advent of "fake families" during the 2018–2019 Trump-era crisis when nearly a million family group members rushed in to exploit the recently discovered Flores loophole's twenty-one-day detention-and-release provision. Among them were adults bringing in children who were not theirs. Quite a few iterations of "kinship fraud," as the government calls it, arose in the new black market for kids-as-visas.

Monica Maple, a retired assistant special in charge of the San Antonio office of ICE Homeland Security Investigations who managed the agency's response, told me about the most common one. Most typically, human smugglers or brokers in home countries would cut package deals with a parent of two or more children. Strangers would pay to take one over, defraying the cost to parents who would keep one child to take over themselves. Parents who agreed to do this could have most or all of their huge smuggling fees waived to bring the whole family over. The fake parents would do all the paying.

Sure there was risk handing a kid over to a nonparent. But the incentive was intoxicating.

The smugglers honed the package to include altered, counterfeit, or fraudulently attained birth certificates—often through corrupt Honduran government officials—that would match children to nonparents smuggling over the border, said Maple, who retired in 2020. Once on the U.S. side later, the parents would recover their kids. Very young children and infants were most valued because they couldn't answer Border Patrol questions and blow everyone's cover, Maple told me. That's why Border Patrol agents often saw the arrival of single men carrying infants without baby formula, bottles, diapers, or any other accoutrements indicating infant caretaking.

Maple said she believed the scam was widespread, based on the constant stream of reports and leads her office took in from Border Patrol during the 2018–2019 crisis. But finding dispersed suspects and connecting all the dots made investigating most of the leads extremely difficult.

The damage to children is tragic because the mothers have often lost track of their children after everyone is in, Maple told me. And if anyone recalls the occasional media stories about babies and young children found alone and wandering abandoned in the corn fields of South Texas, fake family scams were the culprits. Maple went after the cases hard despite strong headwinds.

"It's a new low for humanity that you would give your child away like this to a stranger," she said. "I'd hate to see something happen to that child after the handoff occurs. They are with somebody who is not their parent. What if fake mom or fake dad needed to make medical decisions for the child? It's just not right; the person who is supposed to be protecting them is not there."

One group of emblematic but rare fake family cases actually prosecuted is laid out in the court records. In February 2019, Honduran Belkin Idania Martinez-Parada, a mother of four, agreed to a scheme to rent three of her four children, ages six months to twelve years, to three different Honduran men so they could pass through the Texas border as families, court records show.[266] For risking the three children, Martinez-Parada would earn free passage for herself and all four kids. It was an exceptional deal for the men taking the kids because all had been previously deported more than once and would almost certainly be deported back to Honduras and lose their smuggling fees if they tried it as singles. But if they came in with a child, Border Patrol would let them pass even though they were deportable.

"Those who were detained as a family unit knew they would be released quickly (Flores Settlement) upon identifying their U.S.-based sponsor's address and their subsequent purchase of a transportation ticket to that address," an agent wrote in the criminal complaint, naming the notorious loophole in the document that was causing all this.[267]

Each of the three men received a fraudulently obtained real birth certificate showing that the kids belonged to them. The whole group traveled together with a smuggler up to the border, then split the children up for separate crossings, an agent complaint stated. Martinez-Parada kept the twelve-year-old daughter for herself (remember that older children can be questioned and risk blowing the cover). She gave the valuable six-month-old infant to a stranger who flew with the baby to Florida after entry. She doled out the eight-year-old girl to a second stranger, who took her to Houston after entry. Mom parceled out her six-year-old boy to another man.

It almost all worked. The whole scheme broke down when the man with the six-year-old boy got caught lying at the border and Border Patrol decided to deport him, Maple said, which started the ICE investigation. The fake father confessed everything because he was going to be deported and did not want to take the boy with him.

"It wasn't his kid. He at least had some morals and ethics," Maple said. None of the rest were as saintly, especially not the mom, who was eventually convicted of alien-smuggling charges.

The boy ended up alone in a DHS facility and would not see his mother for at least another month. Her other kids would not see her for a long time either.

That's because Martinez-Parada didn't bother leaving Mexico with the twelve-year-old for another month, abandoning the infant to a strange family in Florida. The fake father who had her eight-year-old daughter, Kevin Cardona-Perdoma, began complaining bitterly to friends and neighbors on Facebook that the mom didn't seem to be in any hurry to get her daughter, so he eventually had to leave the child alone every day so he could work, court records in his separate case show. One day, he came home, and the girl was gone. A neighbor found her wandering in the parking lot of the apartment complex and took her in.

Cardona-Perdoma wrote to friends that he felt so relieved and lucky. But not because the girl was okay. He felt lucky because the neighbor who found the girl wandering alone didn't call the police. Otherwise, he wrote, "I'd be back in Honduras."

Martinez-Parada finally came across because DHS investigators who found her in Mexico pestered her to claim her abandoned son, whom the deported fake father left in detention. They also had to demand that she reclaim the infant in Florida after months of her showing no interest, Maple said.

"She had no intention of going to get that baby again," Maple said, adding a string of pejoratives describing how disgusted she felt about this.

Federal prosecutors in Del Rio convicted her and the two men who were not deported.

The Solution Biden's DHS Will Not Pursue

ICE finally managed to significantly curtail fake family abuse in 2019 by deploying rapid DNA testing to eleven locations across the southern border. These could quickly verify parent-child relationships. Border Patrol would force the families to line up to get their inside cheeks swabbed and have a verification or case of fraud in about ninety minutes, according to a February 2022 DHS Office of Inspector General report.[268] As part of testing the pilot program when it first came out, about 30 percent of everyone tested failed.[269]

"People who were told they were going to go through the machine were just breaking as they were waiting to give their swab," Maple said. "It was, 'Oh yeah, that's not my daughter; it's my niece. It's my cousin or some other story. It could have been a copy machine; they didn't know the difference.'"

That slowed the fake family scam, maybe even ended it, Maple said. But all this is recounted here not because the problem is solved but because of evidence that fake family fraud soared once again in the Biden border crisis, where the numbers of families crossing vastly exceed the numbers seen crossing during the Trump crisis.

As of April 2021, the Biden administration was running few DNA tests on migrant families anymore, maybe a few dozen a month compared to Trump's 250, the *Washington Examiner* reported using leaked government data.[270] The Biden DHS was showing no indication that it would test people before releasing most into the country, the paper reported, and would only test when "absolutely necessary" or when there is "significant suspicion." Toward the end of 2021, CBP was planning to expand Rapid DNA testing from the original eleven locations under Trump to only eighteen.

The reason?

"This administration wants these families and kids released quickly. That is their No. 1 goal, so they are not going to do anything to slow that process down," the newspaper quoted one senior DHS official saying.

The disinterest in deterring fake family crossings using the field-proven rapid DNA tests is likely why a May 8, 2022, *Wall Street Journal* story was able to report that at least several thousand Brazilian children entered the U.S. with an adult who was falsely claiming to be their parent.[271]

It was the same old story. Most of the time, children are brought over by one real parent with one of them tagging along as a fake parent for the split up at the border and crossings. The real parent received $5,000 for allowing it, helping to defray the biological parent's smuggling fee, the paper reported, quoting three high-ranking Brazilian federal police investigators.[272]

"Kids are a guarantee that you can get in here; it's as if they were visas," one woman who did this and was living in Massachusetts with the child told the *Journal*.

"This has been a very common practice among illegal immigrants," Eugenio Ricas, who headed investigations into illegal immigration to the U.S. for the Federal Police between 2018 and 2021, told the newspaper. The paper also quoted a senior U.S. DHS official as having seen "a high instance" of Brazilians falsely posing as families. Smugglers who learned how to profit from the American policy hand out leaflets with detailed instructions advising them on how to fake their way through.

It's not just Brazilian police spilling the beans that fake families resurged in the Biden crisis. In April 2021, Border Patrol in the Yuma sector identified two fraudulent families in one weekend. One involved an eight-year-old girl who came in with a thirty-six-year-old man who claimed to be her father, a government press release recounted.[273] After agents confronted him with discrepancies in their stories, the man admitted to being a "friend" of the child's mother still in Brazil. In another case, agents found that a fourteen-year-old girl and a forty-year-old woman who claimed to be daughter and mother were actually niece and aunt.

I asked Maple, the former ICE Homeland Security Investigations official who crusaded against fake families in 2019, what she makes of reports that thousands of fake families have been crossing the border with no apparent government resistance.

"I'm thinking to myself: Horror. Horror. Horror. Horror."

In the beginning of the Biden border crisis, it was easy for the American public to miss that families with young children and infants were center stage. The families and pregnant women were quickly put on buses and hauled away from visibility to new lives throughout America, lest they be seen in any kind of buildup.

But that was not the case with the massive influx of children crossing in alone. "Unaccompanied minors" became the one most visible aspect of the crisis for a time. That traffic boomed and has never stopped booming.

CHAPTER EIGHT

CHILD ENDANGERMENT

Sometime around 1 a.m. in early May of that first year, I spied the cartel smuggler help them into the small inflatable raft on the Miguel Alemán, Mexico, side of the Rio Grande. I could see them on the Mexican beach of the Rio Grande, two small forms that could not be adults. They crawled into the inflatable by themselves, the shirtless pilot obviously a criminal cartel operative authorized to work here the only adult around.

He lay on his stomach hanging over the front of the raft and began paddling them over with only his hands. They were just enough downstream from the Roma–Miguel Alemán International bridge high over my own head to catch a sparse bit of its lights.

That particular morning was quiet in the deeply troubled cartel town of Miguel Alemán across from Roma, tranquil enough for the now very big business of human smuggling. Several times a month for years, furious often mortal gun battles raged over there between the Cartel del Golfo (CDG) and Cartel del Noreste (Los Zetas). From the high bluffs upon which the old Spanish colonial settlement of Roma was built, observers could watch the weekly firefights between gunmen shooting shoulder-fired rocket grenades, .50-caliber rifles, and belt-fed fully automatic machine guns. There was some risk to viewing these macabre shows; stray rounds sometimes whizzed by to hit downtown Roma's riverfront historic district buildings.

The two children described by the author.

I never managed to be in town when a battle erupted, but many a video shot from the Roma bluffs shows the orange and red tracer rounds flying when two rival cartels battle for control of this lucrative crossing. That early morning I'd been hanging around under the bridge watching rafts come in full of migrant families who would land and turn themselves in to Border Patrol and National Guard soldiers who manned this point and processed them into America.

From my vantage point, I watched the incoming raft carrying the two children disappear into a dark patch of reeds on our side. I walked toward it for about seventy-five yards, my flashlight on and got there just in time to see the rafter on his stomach hand-paddle away in his empty purple craft, looking back at me as I shined my light on him. I knew those kids were in the brush somewhere. My light landed on them a minute later. They were squatting together on their haunches in a patch of tall reeds.

"Buenas noches," I offered. No reply. One was a Hispanic boy, probably twelve or thirteen. The other was a Hispanic girl about fourteen or fifteen. The girl wore jeans and a Calvin Klein sweatshirt, wet in spots, her black hair tied up

in a bun on top. The boy wore a light purple Nike T-shirt, his hair tightly cropped and groomed. Their sneakers were in good shape. Neither carried any personal possessions that I could see.

The kids just stared at me from their spot, not moving, I guessed preferring a uniformed authority figure. I suggested *"Vamanos, mi amigos, to la policia,"* waving them out of the brush to follow me back toward the bridge. *"Por favor. Por favor, andale."*

By that time, a uniformed Texas DPS officer had reached us who could speak Spanish and explained to them that we were going over to Border Patrol under the bridge. On the slow walk over, the state officer translated a series of my questions to the kids.

"Are you brother and sister?"

"No."

"Where are your parents?"

They didn't respond.

"Where are you going?"

No answer again.

"What's your plan?"

Silence.

"You were just in a dangerous town with very dangerous people." (This was true. Miguel Alemán was one of the few Mexican border towns I have resolved never to visit because of its prevalence of cartel gunmen, intelligence networks, and frequent sudden eruptions of violence.) "Did you have any problems over there? Did they treat you well?"

No answer.

"What are your names?"

No answer.

"Where are you from?"

"Honduras."

By this time, we had delivered them to some Border Patrol agents, and I was not allowed to speak with them anymore.

I departed with a familiar impression from past encounters with unaccompanied teenagers. They always seemed highly coached about what to say or not to say. I could tell. They might readily answer some innocuous question but look down or away in silence if asked for details like with whom they had traveled and where their parents were right now.

The Wandering Orphan Waif Myth

Advocates of limitless immigration over the border would have America believe that somehow all these young immigrants are orphans whose parents were murdered or imprisoned in political gulags and have no choice but to save their lives by passing through five other countries to reach the U.S. border. But over time, I came to believe many of these kids and their families were coached to say nothing at this delicate moment of gaming the American system.

Why would I think such a cynical thing?

Remember that families with children under seven years old were an anointed "chosen" population. They got a free ride in immediately. So did minors up to age eighteen if they showed up without parents. But what about families who came with kids between the ages of seven and eighteen?

They tended to get expelled under Title 42.

Older sons, daughters, and siblings were an expulsion ticket. Conversely, their own families were an expulsion ticket to the teenagers. They couldn't get through together.

But they could get in if they split up. And that is the root of the unaccompanied minor crisis.

The older kids would cross alone and ring the "unaccompanied minor" bell. The parent or parents with the younger kids could then cross and ring the "family" bell. Everybody could meet up later inside America.

One important piece of evidence for this scheme comes by way of a May 2022 CBS News investigative story. Previously unpublished government statistics showed that 12,212 supposedly "unaccompanied" minors were not really unaccompanied at all. Because they were older, their whole family had been expelled back to Mexico during 2021, CBS reported.

Back on the Mexico side, they "self-separated." The 12,212 teenagers came back over alone and declared themselves to Border Patrol as "unaccompanied minors," CBS reported.[274]

They got right in. Those were just the ones DHS were able to learn about, so the practice is undoubtedly far more widespread. This scheme would explain the uncomfortable silences to questions about where their parents were and how they came to be crossing alone, exactly, with fresh haircuts, well-fed and appropriately dressed, and able to pay cartels thousands of dollars.

The boy and girl I interviewed who came across in a raft that night were almost certainly not just wandering abandoned waifs fleeing government persecutions in home villages, as migrant advocacy groups and the president usually portrayed them with no evidence. I knew they could not possibly have reached a cartel-controlled town like Miguel Alemán, the scene of often nightly full-scale warfare and one of the few border towns so truly dangerous that I won't set foot in it, unless an adult paid thousands of dollars for the raft I witnessed carry them over from it. The cartel in that city was not running a charity and let no one through who hadn't paid at least $2,500 each. These two young teens had accompaniment all the way to the point at which they boarded their raft. A great many do actually travel with groups, friends, relatives, and smuggling guides, sent *for* by family in the United States or sent by a parent *from* a home village.

But the wandering desperate orphan waif is the stuff of political mythology. It was only logical for them to scheme the opening Biden's government created when he promised none would be left behind in Mexico or ever expelled. Yet administration officials and their supporters seemed confounded when the predictable result was chaos, mayhem, and massive taxpayer expense to manage the fomented crisis. Many children died answering the president's siren call.

How and why did Biden's people do this to them and us?

The Teen Immigrant Crisis: Ready, Set...Inauguration

The Biden administration exempted "unaccompanied minors" from Title 42 on its very first day, when Mexico decided under its new law not to take them back. BuzzFeed News reporter Hamed Aleaziz probably filed the earliest known report of it on February 2.[275] Aleaziz reported that the Biden administration had, the week before, stopped using Title 42 to expel unaccompanied minor migrants back to Mexico. In response to a direct inquiry from Aleaziz, a White House spokesperson confirmed the policy for the first time. The spokesperson told Aleaziz the new administration's policy "is not to expel unaccompanied children who arrive at our borders.

"The president's approach is to deal with immigration comprehensively, fairly and humanely," the spokesperson said, using the encrypted code words. "The Border Patrol will continue to transfer unaccompanied children to the HHS Office of Refugee Resettlement so they may be properly cared for in appropriate shelters, consistent with their best interest."

The Biden administration had returned to a system of powerful gravitational incentives that proved irresistible. Not only would "unaccompanied" minors of any age under eighteen now become exempt from Covid-19 expulsion going forward but would be released as quickly as possible to custodians in the American interior at government expense.

How did the first trickle become a swell and then a historic flood? The quick, perhaps flip, answer is: selfies.

Remember that just about the entire universe of aspiring border crossers had been waiting with white-knuckled suspense and bated breath since the November election for any first sign that post-Trump America was letting in their kind. Any confirming peep that the Biden border was finally open for business would trigger an advance forward.

If knowledge is power and a picture is worth a thousand words, none could compete with video selfies loosed from cell phones. In all my travels among the immigrants, I don't think I ever met a northbound foreign national older than fifteen without a modern cell phone fully connected to the internet and social media. Migrant chatrooms by nationality and language were ubiquitous. Many an immigrant showed them to me. I have been invited into several different ones, including a Senegalese WhatsApp room where I could imbibe the constant live-time intelligence about border crossings and what the Mexican or American governments were up to today.

When Biden opened the border to families, pregnant women, and unaccompanied minors, selfies of them boarding buses and airplanes in Texas reverberated around the world like the alluring songs of sirens in Greek mythology.[276]

CBS News followed the BuzzFeed story a day later, helping spread the word worldwide that Biden was letting all unaccompanied minors stay.

From there, the Biden administration energized and confirmed the news at every turn, the connection between word and migrant decisions to journey always eluding leadership. When it came to unaccompanied minors, the Biden government went many steps beyond passive naiveté. They drove the historic wave of underage illegal border crossings that cost lives and billions of dollars.

Offering a Nirvana of Rewards

Senior officials, including President Biden himself, used words and deeds to tell migrants to come, revealing a stupefying ignorance of how migrants reach decisions. For example, as the unaccompanied child migrant crisis was breaking monthly first-ever records, Mayorkas told CBS News that parents should not send their kids to cross the border because the trip was dangerous but then said America would accept them in if they did.

"Some loving parent might send their child to traverse Mexico alone to reach the southern border—our southern border—I hope they do not make that perilous journey, but if they do, we will not expel them," Mayorkas told the national news organization.[277]

Loving parents around the world were not just listening, they were also viewing the video of happy child reunions with relatives inside the United States.

Parents throughout the world responded by sending their children alone over the border. It kept going like that. After one early March reporting excursion to the southern border, I pulled over for lunch in Uvalde, Texas, and to watch a presidential news conference on the diner TV. I dropped my chicken-fried-steak-filled fork to slap my forehead upon hearing Biden defiantly declare that, unlike that cruel Trump, he would leave no child behind to starve to death in Mexico. I texted a Border Patrol agent in the Rio Grande Valley, "Get ready *mi amigo*, the kids are about to flood your zone like nothing you've ever seen. Just saw the president invite in every kid in the world. OMG."

In a one-on-one interview March 16 with ABC News' George Stephanopoulos, Biden said he'd heard it said that the migrants were coming "because they heard I'm a nice guy…"[278]

Stephanopoulos agreed: "They're saying this!"

Biden: "Yeah, well here's the deal. They're not! The adults are being sent back. That's number one." The vast majority were teenagers, Biden marveled.

Stephanopoulos followed up with an invitation that Biden tell the teen migrants not to come. "Yes, I can say quite clearly, don't come over!"

But then in the same breath, Biden advised the world's parents with older-than-seven kids to just delay their journeys a bit, until his administration got everything ready for them, such as expanding the capacity to manage their asylum claims and rebuilding Central American economies to alleviate root causes.

"And so in the meantime, we need to be making sure we provide beds for these children," he told the parents of the world before going on to describe the alluring nirvana that awaited them. He explained that HHS was at that very moment expanding its ability to provide shelter, food, medical attention for all border-crossing kids and to reunite them with family in the United States.

"And that's what we're in the process of doing now. We will have, I believe in the next month, enough of those beds to take care of these children who have no place to go but they need to be taken care of."

Parents already inside the United States, who heard that and were pining for children they left behind in home villages, now sent for them since the gate to this incredible nirvana was open. And why wouldn't they? The president had just promised provisions of room, board, and transport to caregivers inside the United States at full government expense! Parents who happened to still be with their older children in home villages now borrowed the smuggling money and sent them forth to presidentially guaranteed American futures.

The rewards package for unaccompanied minors to enter was so wildly generous that it set forth an unparalleled gully washer of them into America. In November and December 2020, before Biden announced no child would be left behind in Mexico, agents took into custody 4,591 and 4,965, respectively. In February, the first full month of the Biden administration, the number of apprehended unaccompanied minors doubled to 9,402, then doubled again in March to 18,870. In total, 303,982 single minors crossed since Biden won election and the end of fiscal year 2022, compared to 33,239 during Trump's last year in office.

The wave was so massive that it crashed all systems in a noisy, hugely expensive public collapse that portended secondary and third-order implications for years to come, starting with public schools that would have to take in hundreds of thousands of them.

Whereas families with young kids gained quick release into America, often within three days, releases for unaccompanied minors caught more popular attention because the government had to keep them in a safe facility for as long as it took to find a relative or foster family. Soon, severe over-crowding became a political problem. DHS couldn't resolve their reunifications fast enough to clear the facilities. By April 2021, teenagers had overrun every DHS facility and agency. At first, they overflowed half-closed detention facilities and Border Patrol stations from Texas to California, all the spots where there was no wall.

To further put that in perspective, the so-called "unac-companied minors" crisis that beset President Obama in 2014 reached what was regarded at the time as a historically severe 68,445 over a full year, which Vox News reported had "over-whelmed the systems…to the point where Border Patrol had to keep children in temporary facilities on military bases."[279] During the brief Trump-era crisis of late 2018 through early 2019, some 70,000 unaccompanied kids got in. The wave generated by Biden was more than 100 percent greater in just over eight months and did not lose momentum as time passed until nearly 300,000 had entered the country by fall 2022.

Flooding the Zone

As children, their resettlement inside the United States became the responsibility of the U.S. Department of Health and Human Services Office of Refugee Resettlement (DHH), which, in idyllic times would place them in holding facilities outfitted for children, with medical care, educators, books, movies, and playgrounds.

While waiting in these shelters, again ideally, HHS staff would locate their relatives or caregivers inside the United States, arrange a reunification, and pay for commercial air flights to anywhere in the United States.

But an unprecedented crush of migrant children sapped all time or space for any normal HHS activity in the first months after inauguration. By April, all Border Patrol station holding areas, detention centers, and HHS facilities were bursting at the seams. Children were sleeping on gym mats anywhere spare federal floor space could be found.

This was happening at the same time that family groups were flooding in through the other breach Biden's government had just opened. But unlike when overrun border agencies had no choice but to just release family groups onto public streets and bus stations, HHS could not just loose children into the public unsupervised, for obvious security considerations. They had to be held in safe environments. Because of high volumes, processing soon blew apart the customary three-day wait. In April 2021, HHS was receiving three times more teens and children than the number it was releasing.[280] Costs soared. One estimate early on had the administration spending $60 million a week just to shelter them.[281]

HHS had to undertake measures beyond anything that was necessary during the Obama administration's 2014 crisis and Trump's early 2019 one, when they had to use military bases. This new crisis was larger by magnitudes than either of those.

The Biden government mounted "Operation Artemis" to manage it down. [282] It directed thousands of children out of inadequate Border Patrol holding stations and into convention centers in Dallas (2,270), San Diego (1,450), and San Antonio (2,000).[283] HHS had to go find more "influx sites" for 15,000 kids.[284] The government pulled in two dozen other facilities and military bases again too, at Fort Bliss, Lackland Air Force Base, Fort Lee, and even a NASA site in California, an oil field work camp in Texas, and foster-care providers in New York and Pennsylvania.

The agency had to expand staff to work double-time connecting children to relatives and foster families.[285] So great was the desperation to place the teens quickly that the administration cut deals with illegally present relatives who'd gone underground, granting them a kind of deportation immunity so they would step forward (albeit, most deportations had been halted by then anyway).[286] There was no money for any of this. White House had to redirect more than $5.5 billion by the end of September to finally expand its conveyor belt capacity enough to return convention centers to their cities and bases to regular military duty.[287]

By the summer of 2021, the administration had expanded HHS's capacity to more quickly process unaccompanied children but did nothing to reduce their record high numbers. Case resolved; a new extreme normal was in town. The media drifted away after the government returned military bases, oil field camps, and convention centers to their usual uses and fine-tuned the conveyor belt so that it could efficiently haul hundreds of thousands into America without inconveniencing anyone.[288] The Biden administration never considered closing this breach as an option. The goal was to bring in everyone who wanted in, just in a humane, orderly way.

DHS was able to shorten child stays for most in government shelters with all the expected comforts of American life, with doctors and dentists and teachers and psychologists. The media was absent for the most important part of the story, which was what happened to them next.

Along with medical care, teachers, and Netflix inside detention centers, HHS assigned each kid a kind of travel agent. These travel case agents arranged reunifications of the teens by air to cities across the country. What was odd about these flights wasn't so much that they were happening but that the government devised them to be done as secretly as possible. By at least August 2021, the federal government was flying tens of thousands of the teenagers on charter planes— in the dead of night—to both politically red and blue cities.[289] DHS never issued press releases about the predawn flights nor sent for friendly media to record the deliveries nor offered fact sheets. It sent the flights at off-hours where few could see them and ask questions. Conservative media finally pried confirmation about these from Freedom of Information Act requests.[290]

Later, an anonymous HHS official told the *Washington Post* the government chose to stealthily disperse the children around the nation on aircraft to protect the privacy of underage immigrant minors.[291] That makes some sense; all American criminal justice systems and government agencies do strive to protect the identities of children for which they are responsible in whatever capacity.

But the anger about the secrecy was also justified in the sense that receiving communities would have to pay to absorb them into local school districts and for public assistance. Any community would naturally want to debate the pros and cons of the policy saddling them with the significant new tax burdens. Flying hundreds of thousands of kids into cities in the dead of night avoided all that democracy stuff. It was all fait accompli.

Months of flights would pass before one reporter finally asked White House press secretary Jen Psaki about them, at an October 19, 2021, press conference. [292] Psaki acknowledged the flights were happening "earlier than you might like to take a flight" but dodged any culpability for the administration having directly and irrefutably caused the crisis it now was scrambling badly to manage.

"It is our legal responsibility to safely care for unaccompanied children until they can be swiftly unified with a parent or a vetted sponsor," Psaki responded. "And that's something we take seriously; we have a moral obligation to come to do that and deliver on that. It's no surprise that kids can be seen traveling through states, not just New York. It's something that we're also working to unite children with their family members or vetted sponsors in other parts of the country as well."

After that, fifty-one members of Congress wrote DHS demanding public disclosures about the program, especially where the kids were going and how many so that communities might have an idea of the cost burdens. [293]

A February 2022 *Washington Post* "Fact Checker" analysis framed as having somehow debunked the story ended up confirming it. As evidence that the flights story was untrue, Glenn Kessler noted that "there's been virtually no coverage of this supposed news by mainstream media outlets" but then concluded the story was completely true. "A lot of plane flights were needed" to ship the children to Florida, New York, Maryland, Tennessee, North Carolina, and Virginia, he wrote. [294]

Of course, the immigrant families of the kids always knew everything about the night flights. When they disembarked, they just used flash to light the selfies they would send back home about the government conveyor belt that began at the river and ended with free flights to family reunifications in American cities. And so the teenage immigrants were still storming America without end as of this writing.

American Citizen Endangerment

Many families of teenagers figured out how to exploit, defraud, and abuse the system to get in.

Young-looking single men and women figured out that they could just lie that that they were seventeen so they can get in as unaccompanied minors. A Border Patrol agent once told me how easy that was:

A young man in his early twenties crossed and insisted he was seventeen, knowing the reward he would receive. The Border Patrol agent challenged him and demanded to see his identification. The young alien smirked and said his wallet was stolen with all his identification.

"I'm seventeen, and you have to let me in," the man said.

The agent said that was certainly true—"he was correct, and we both knew it"—and the agent let the man join a line for processing in.

The Biden government bestows all first benefit-of-doubt on the aliens and policy does not require that anyone prove their age or claims. During past, much smaller mass migrations involving teenagers traveling without parents, many scores of Salvadoran MS-13 youth gang members entered the country and went on crime and murder sprees in major cities around the country. [295] That is almost certainly happening in this crisis.

Had a verification process been in place, a U.S. citizen and father of four arguably would be alive. Honduran national Yery Noel Medina Ulloa was twenty-four when he successfully posed as a seventeen-year-old minor to get free passage into the country not long after the election.

DHS paired him with a kindly foster family in Jacksonville, Florida, who took him into their home. The head of the family, father of four Francisco Javier Cuellar, even gave Ulloa a part-time job in the family business, a food store. But there was an altercation in October 2021.

Ulloa brutally stabbed Cuellar at the business and, after he was down, beat him to death with a chair, leaving four children without their father.[296] Police followed a trail of blood and arrested the soaked Ulloa. By the way, the suspected murderer's age lie held up so well that arresting officers initially booked him into a juvenile jail. Only then was Ulloa's true age discovered: twenty-four.

Unaccompanied minors adopted by foster families in haste, for the political purpose of preventing shelter overcrowding that draws unwanted media attention, expose other teens to sexual and labor abuses.

An August 2022 *Washington Times* report by Stephen Dinan showed that under other administrations foster family adults subjected young girls to rape, enslavement, and physical beatings.[297] In April 2022, for example, the foster family sent a twelve-year-old girl to the home of a man who obtained fake documents claiming she was old enough to work and was a legal resident. Then he put her to work outside the home and stole all of her paychecks, the newspaper reported.

"There's a guarantee that this is happening right now," Dinan said in a phone interview about foster family abuse. "Given the numbers we're talking about coming over now and the fewer checks being made by this administration, it's as close to a certainty as you can get to actual proof that it's going on. It takes time. We won't know how bad this stuff is now until the cases start coming out in two or three years."

Child labor abuse is probably already happening on a significant scale too. In July 2022, Reuters reported that a subsidiary for Hyundai, one of the most "powerful and profitable automakers in the world," used illegal immigrant minors to labor in a Montgomery, Alabama, car parts factory.[298] Instead of attending school, dozens of underage Central Americans as young as twelve worked at a metal-stamping plant operated by SMART Alabama LLC, which the company claimed a temporary staffing firm referred. The company denied any wrongdoing and dismissed a number of underage workers when it learned of them. Federal agencies are investigating labor-law violations.

That Reuters report followed an earlier one that temporary staffing firms hired unaccompanied minor immigrants from Guatemala to work long shifts in an Enterprise, Alabama, poultry plant. It followed sixteen-year-old "Amelia" from her hometown to find work in the United States, ending up in a chicken processing factory.[299] No one made her do it. The plan was to send money home.

"School isn't for me. I have debts," Amelia told the news agency.

"Authorities are struggling with long-term follow-up to ensure minors aren't sucked into a vast network of enablers, including labor contractors, who recruit workers for big plants and other employers and at times have steered kids into jobs that are illegal, grueling and meant for adults," the Reuters story said.

In typical fashion, Amelia refused to provide Reuters with any of the details about her travel, which would of course include information about the involvement of parents and smugglers and, most importantly, how Biden administration policy influenced the family's decision to send her.

Based on recent past experience with much smaller migrations of solo teen foreigners, Americans will need to brace for a much broader and long-lived outbreak of violent gang crime, school overcrowding, child sexual abuse, child labor violations, and other social ills. All this would have been avoidable, unnecessary evils were it not for White House policy choices and communication divorced from knowledge about how immigrants think.

CHAPTER NINE

THE DAY THE SOUNDS OF WALL CONSTRUCTION DIED

One week after Inauguration Day, I headed to El Paso, New Mexico, and Juarez to take stock.

On Inauguration Day and in the days that followed, the new government implemented what it described in a White House Fact Sheet as "the first steps in a broad, whole of government effort to finally reform our immigration system."[300] The administration ended all new enrollments in Trump's Remain in Mexico policy.[301] It forwarded to Congress the U.S. Citizenship Act of 2021, a bill proposing to legalize eleven million illegally present aliens as "Lawful Prospective Immigrants" if they were present in the United States on or before January 1, 2021.[302]

And it ordered a work freeze on Trump's $26 billion wall construction, which had put up 450 miles of new or replacement walls thirty feet high but was far from completion.[303] Perhaps no other policy was more laden with symbolism and messaging about whether the border gate would swing from closed to open than the border wall.

Trump had positioned his "big beautiful wall" that Mexico would pay for as the apotheosis of his border security agenda from day one on the campaign trail. He billed the structure as foundational to his other policy ideas to hold back illegal immigrant criminals, terrorists, and drug traffickers.

Of course, his opponents and critics had pilloried it as a terrible message of exclusion to the world, not only contrary to the "nation of immigrants" value but ineffective and easily defeated; build a ten-foot-high wall, the saying went, and there'll be a sales boom in eleven-foot-high ladders. They argued that walls just don't stop illegal immigration.

"Building a wall from sea-to-shining sea is not a serious policy solution—it's a waste of money, and it diverts critical resources away from real threats," candidate Biden's campaign platform asserted in a typical line. "A wall is not a serious deterrent for sophisticated criminal organizations that employ border tunnels, semi-submersible vessels, and aerial technology to overcome physical barriers at the border—or even for individuals with a reciprocating saw."[304]

In Washington, the undoing of Trump's wall became the equal and opposite apotheosis of Biden's agenda. Its opponents demanded that Biden not only halt construction but tear the whole thing down and recycle the steel. The candidate said he wouldn't go that far but did promise in an August 2020 interview with NPR that "There will not be another foot of wall constructed on my administration, No. 1."[305]

Biden set his work-freeze day for January 27, a Wednesday. But after the November election, contractors ramped up work 24/7 to put up as much wall as possible before the inauguration, a literal race against time. By the time Biden shut it down, the government had spent about $15 billion.[306]

Curious to bear witness to the end of construction on that fateful morning, I set out in a rental truck west from El Paso on State Highway 9, which almost hugs the Mexican border only a half mile or a mile inside New Mexico.

This was beautiful, if forbidding, high desert scrub brush country. Enormous brown vistas contrasted hard against blue sky. I'd always loved this stretch of border for its escarpments and burgeoning hills, which struck me as otherworldly, evocative of images delivered to us from the Mars exploration rovers.

The drive west along 9 provided a constant view of the long brown wall always on the left. The plan was easy: drive until I could see where the wall stopped and then go there and report whatever was happening.

I was hoping to meet Border Patrol agents who worked the area before the wall went up and what they would have to contend with after the construction halt. Listening to wall opponents and their arguments over time, I'd come to really appreciate Border Patrol agents as the most reliable experts on border security and especially the walls, since it is they who spend forty hours a week every week for months and years working along them, mingling with immigrants and smugglers, and imbibing intelligence reporting.

I followed the wall on westward until its punctuated end came into view, a widened construction road gashing on past the final panel and up a steep hill and over. I turned due south down a dirt access road that emptied onto the east-west construction road right in the wall's shadow and took a right alongside its towering panels. I was some seventy-five miles west from El Paso, some thirty miles west of the tiny historic New Mexican town of Columbus. The town was infamous as the site of a losing 1915 incursion by Mexican revolutionary and guerrilla Pancho Villa, the only time an armed foreign army invaded the U.S. and killed American citizens. American cavalry troops armed with new belt-fed machine guns drove Pancho Villa's raiders away in a bloody battle. The foundations of destroyed buildings are still visible, and you can still walk up the small rise in the center of town and stand right where American machine-gunners positioned themselves.

For the last couple hundred yards, I passed giant, parked, yellow bulldozers, cranes, and trenching machines facing the other direction, lined up for evacuation. I parked at the wall's final sputtering panel, which had gone up the night before. I got out, stretched, and sauntered over to it. An empty trench maybe twenty feet long and at least seven feet deep had been dug the day before where workers would pour concrete and then set the next panel. This stretch of wall was replacing an old 1990s-era vehicle barrier that ran up the etched distant hill and over. I easily hopped back and forth over it to check out the trench, careful not to fall in.

The death scene of Trump's infamous border wall, one of America's great political controversies, felt decidedly anti-climactic. An evacuation of equipment and workers was underway, sure. There were no security guards, no public affairs officers, and no reporters. There were no news stories the next day or week. Hundreds of millions of dollars' worth of paneling and equipment and contracts would lie fallow from this day on, with no cleanup plan. But no one on either side of the partisan divide cared enough to mark the event or hold a field press conference where reporters might ask obvious questions like: What's the government going to do with all these acres of paid-for steel paneling stacked in the desert? There were no gawkers other than me, and no one cared that I was roaming around open trenches, sharp-edged stacks of rebar, and heavy machinery.

To my right, on a vast scraped acreage, work crews busied themselves amid more giant CAT machines and piles of wall panel, steel bollards, gear of unspecified purpose, and port-a-potties. I walked among them and climbed atop a pile of panels to shoot video. The workers struck me as desultory, maybe a bit depressed, and who could blame them for having lost well-paying jobs?

Occasionally, a driver would hop aboard one of the CAT earth-movers and fire it up. Beeping at intervals, these machines would trundle on their heavy tank-like treads over to the wall road and creak slowly eastward until they were out of sight. A poignant ending scene in a movie drama or children's book, I thought, as I videoed a lonely trench digger slowly shrinking into the distance next to the wall it helped build but was no longer wanted. Ironically, none of the workers I asked to interview could speak English. None wanted to interview with me, anyway, sensing trouble talking to a notebook-toting stranger about a sensitive topic. One guy called someone to report that I was trying to interview him, but I stuck around hoping that whoever came might be willing to be interviewed. No one bothered.

Eventually, a Border Patrol agent rolled up to the final panel and stopped. I sauntered up for a chat at the window. I felt grateful that he was so talkative, especially because he was responsible for this area and had strong opinions. He wasn't happy about the construction stoppage.

All the Democratic presidential candidates, including Biden and Harris, incorporated anti-wall policy and arguments prominently in their campaign platforms. The argument was always that walls just don't work to stop illegal immigration and drug trafficking, and taxpayer money should not be wasted on them. But this agent and a number of others I would interview who work the wall described the same simple, inalterable physics about its impact on regular pedestrian immigrant flows.

Illegal immigrants and their smuggling guides avoid places where there are walls and go to where there are no walls. That is the simple genius of the wall. Were there no gaps, maybe most people wouldn't even bother.

The agent said the plan was that this section of the wall would be built westward until it touched with another segment that was being built eastward, something like the transcontinental railroad, probably minus the golden spike ceremony. The work stoppage had left a beckoning 1.5-mile gap of open ranchland between the two wall ends that he'd have to patrol now. The agent said he wished the gap was a lot shorter. Out here, a mile or two of desert crevices with lots of hills and dales is still a lot of land for one or two agents to patrol.

"What do you think about these experts who say walls are but a useless folly?" I asked.

"You hear TV, and they would say, 'Well the experts say the wall isn't effective,' and I never understood who these experts were," the agent responded. "Because all of *our* data says, you know, 90 percent effective rate…dropping of crossings…increased apprehensions and all of that. And it's like, well who are these experts to say it wasn't effective and what are they basing that on? You know, they never really specify."

"Yeah, well what about the ladders, cutting tools, and rope-climbing they say entirely neutralize wall effectiveness," I asked?

These tactics, he answered, only ever enable a few of the strongest, boldest, youngest physically fit Olympiads at a time to get over this thirty-foot-high wall, he replied. Whereas before it was built, groups of sixty–eighty immigrants would routinely just climb over the chest-high vehicle barrier. That's a big difference for Border Patrol.

"That was always a fallacy, that 'well, they can dig under… they can climb over, or even have those gliders that come over,' and it's like, yeaaahhh nothing's 100 percent," he said. "It [a wall] was always something we wanted. It was always something we wanted more of. Every administration gave it to us. It was always proven effective."

That last part was true. Dating back to the mid-1990s under President Clinton's Operation Gatekeeper, 135 miles of pedestrian border wall went up mainly in the areas of El Paso and San Diego.[307] The Secure Fence Act of 2006, signed by President George W. Bush (and voted for by then-Senators Obama and Biden) provided for about 700 miles of fencing and vehicle barrier. Ultimately about 278 miles of fifteen-to-eighteen-foot pedestrian wall and another 249 miles of the easily defeated "vehicle barriers" of the sort Trump's thirty-foot wall was replacing were constructed. Obama kept the wall building going, putting up another 128 miles.[308]

It is true that drug trafficking cartels and human smugglers don't beat the walls, especially in remote areas where the Border Patrol is thin or most agents were redeployed to South Texas to help process families the Biden administration had decided to admit. But this agent said Olympian drug smugglers are a tiny fractional minority of a wide cross-section of migrants who would come through if the wall weren't there. The means Border Patrol agents have plenty of time to hunt down fewer smugglers with less effort, he said.

Later that day, in a parking lot at the international crossing port to the little Mexican town of Palomas across from Columbus, I asked another Border Patrol agent about the import of the construction halt.

"As much as people like to let their gums flap about things they don't know about…a wall is a great deterrent," he said.

"That whole tall-wall-taller-ladder thing? Hahaha, fine, let them lug a forty-five-foot ladder out there in the middle of the desert. It's a deterrent. It's not a 100 percent guarantee, but it stops most of the people. A lot of people have no interest in risking their lives to climb that high or lug a band-saw and cutting tools out to the middle of nowhere. A lot of people are just deterred by that. And most people are not willing to risk their lives to the extent people think they are."

I know I'd never go thirty feet high up some teetering ladder, I told him, unless maybe I stood to make a ton of drug money taking that risk. Some still do, but their numbers are, in relative terms, minuscule. Statistics published in April 2022 by University of California at San Diego physicians in the journal *JAMA Surgery* tallied 375 falling injuries since the barrier's height was raised along much of the California border in 2019, including sixteen deaths.[309]

Prior to the extended height, people got injured climbing the lower seventeen-foot walls, but falls weren't often fatal. The smugglers tote improvised ladders for their customers to climb the taller Trump walls and maybe ropes or nothing at all for the descent on the American side, which is how the injuries occur. Improvised ladders litter the brush between San Ysidro and Otay Mesa crossings, fashioned from metal rebar or lightweight aluminum with sections that fit together like tent poles.

Videos on social media show "athletic young men" breezily shimmying up and gripping the bollards like fire poles to zip down the other side, an April 2022 *Washington Post* story reported before going on to point out why these athletes are a tiny minority. "But that type of skilled maneuver is beyond the abilities of many migrants...."[310]

Indeed, the few nonathletes who are brave, motivated by drug profits, desperate, or foolhardy enough will give climbing a chance. Everyone else is heading for where there is no wall. The 375 injuries and deaths compare to more than 350,000 Border Patrol apprehensions in California since Trump's wall went up in 2019 and the UC San Diego physicians study.

Mexican smuggling gangs sawed through new segments of the border wall 3,272 times in three years, costing the government $2.6 million in repairs, another *Post* story reported based on CBP records obtained through the Freedom of Information Act.[311] The smuggling gangs were cutting through the steel bollards with cheap saws.

But so what? It is a net good for the country if the presence of tall walls has Border Patrol agents spending their shifts hunting breaches rather than processing 100,000 immigrants who just walked over.

That only a comparative few physically fit Olympiads, drug traffickers, or people of questionable judgment sometimes climb or cut through thirty-foot-high walls inversely reveals much greater numbers of crossers are going elsewhere. As these media accounts and my own interviews with agents show, walls reduce numbers to levels that Border Patrol can comfortably manage, which was always the point of them.

But it is just as true that walls only work when agents are present patrolling their side of them. The Biden administration pulled them from duty, leaving the walls unguarded.

For instance, in the Douglas, Arizona, sector, where the walls are older and only eighteen-feet high, cartel human smugglers realized that almost all the Border Patrol agents were called to help Texas process families far away. Each night for eighteen months and to the day of this writing, cartel "ladder crews" sent hundreds of mostly young, fit male men up the wall and down the other side on ropes. No one is there to catch them as they run into Douglas and disappear because Border Patrol agents are all in Texas.

This breaching activity is far less an argument that walls don't work than that gaps must be filled so that Border Patrol agents need not be away processing in those who pour through them. Similarly, in Naco, Arizona, tens of thousands of immigrants simply poured over and around the walls that did get built there because all the Border Patrol agents were away on family-processing duty in Texas.[312]

"We've had over 60,000 get-aways. These are people that are seen on Border Patrol cameras but have not been captured," Cochise County Sheriff Mark J. Dannels complained to Border Report in May 2021, early in the crisis. "I don't fault Border Patrol on that. I fault Congress and this administration. When you divert Border Patrol into immigration processing, childcare, administrative work, that opens up opportunity for the cartels."

Mind the Gaps

Masses were funneling to and through the gaps left in Trump's wall.

The January 27, 2021, construction freeze left them everywhere, some just a few feet across, others many miles.[313] In some areas, only a few-hundred-yard stretch of wall stands as a kind of monument to American political division over this issue. On a Texas DPS helicopter tour of the wall in South Texas, I noticed miles of walling that resembled the jaw of a shark with every other tooth missing. With some wall up and gaps between panels, a kind of funneling draws people through the missing teeth in ways that actually can be helpful to Border Patrol agents—if any are available—though not as helpful as when there are no gaps.

One Border Patrol agent I met on the much-walled outskirts of El Paso, where thirty-five miles of new steel Trump wall went up, said the construction halt left one glaring gap over the rugged flanks of a large mountain. This agent explained that most smugglers and illegal immigrants preferred to hike along the wall to this gap, rather than risk climbing it or driving dozens of miles to another construction-halt point. So, they funneled to the unwalled mountain gap because...that's how walls work for most. It's literally better than nothing, the agent said, but hardly better than a completed wall with no gaps.

"Honestly, when they started putting this one over there, it's like everything's down. Everything's better. It's a good bit easier," he said. "Everything's moving to other areas where there isn't any wall. Obviously, it's easier for us."

Once upon a time, when he was running for president in 2007, Senator Biden showed he understood the basic physics.

"People can go over and under a fence, but you can't take a hundred kilos of cocaine over and under a fence," he told an audience in Winterset, Iowa. "And what you do when you have limited places where fences are in populated areas is you force these drug dealers and others around and making it easier to apprehend because there's fewer places to come through."[314]

The gaps did not draw in merely a few hundred young Olympiads like those climbing ladders over walls and breaking legs or dying in falls. They sucked in hundreds of thousands of illegal immigrants, not to mention drug traffickers. Another Border Patrol agent I met worked along a four-mile stand-alone section of wall in West Texas built a decade ago. Trump plans called for finally connecting it to wall for many dozens of continuous miles.

"In that area where the wall's at, we never have any problems," the agent explained. "It was a pretty awesome thing because, before that, our guys were getting into gunfights with drug runners who were driving through the river. But where it ends? We've seen things where along the river they bring people down there by the truckload and they drop as many off as they can because they know we can only catch one or two out of ten. They get picked up and go into the interior of the country and go live as illegal immigrants.

"When there was a commitment to building fences and walls," he continued. "there had to be a commitment to finish. Without committing and completing it, it's really just a wall that only sort of makes people go around it. It's really no sweat."

While that funneling can sometimes help Border Patrol, gaps can irresistibly entice overwhelming numbers of economic immigrants of all ages, shapes, sizes, and nationalities who would never dare climb a thirty-foot wall.

One emblematic gap attracted such an unending mass of humanity that Border Patrol has had to throw up its hands in surrender at times, unable even to process them. Eventually, the Biden administration had to do the unthinkable: put up Trump's now-rusty panels.

The spot was on the Yuma, Arizona, border with Mexico and became infamous as "the Yuma Gap." From January 2021 through September 2022, some 421,600 crossed through the Yuma sector, through the wall gaps in it. There immigrants crossed over some local dam infrastructure, climbed up an embankment and were through.

The Trump administration decided to shore up the notorious crossing area years earlier because, as then-DHS Secretary Elaine Duke wrote in an August 2017 column for *USA Today*, it "was besieged by chaos as a nearly unending flood of migrants and drugs poured across our border. Even as agents were arresting on average 800 illegal aliens a day, we were still unable to stop the thousands of trucks filled with drugs and humans that quickly crossed a vanishing point and dispersed into communities all across the country."[315]

As the 2021 mass migration crisis ginned up, the gaps funneled them through all day and night right past the panels lying on the dirt. Apprehensions spiked by thousands of percentage points.[316]

Almost unbelievably, the Biden administration let this torrent flow for a full year and a half, refusing to speak of it or visit it as Republican Arizona politicians and local law enforcement furiously complained. National media largely ignored this incredible story until the Biden administration finally announced in July 2022 that it would close the four Yuma gaps.

"These projects address operational impacts, as well as immediate life and safety risks," the DHS offered in its short statement.[317]

Liberals howled in protest at what they saw as a breach of personal principle while conservatives crowed smugly at what they viewed as a first acquiescence that Trump's wall worked so well that Biden couldn't live without it in Yuma. In the ensuing delay, Arizona Gov. Doug Ducey stepped in with old shipping containers and tightly packed them side-by-side at some of the most heavily trammeled gaps right at the dam.

That seemed to do the trick, as a personal testament to their impacts demonstrates. In November 2022, I visited from the Mexican side with Mexican journalist Oscar "El Blue" Ramirez to see how things were going. We were the only ones anywhere in sight as we hiked gingerly through four inches of water along the bottom of the dam toward the shipping containers visible several hundred yards ahead.

Oscar hung back on the last feet of Mexico while I moved forward to risk stepping onto the American side. A single Border Patrol agent stood vigil up the embankment fifty yards ahead. I shouted up that I was an American, a writer, and, by the way, how busy was it these days now that those shipping containers behind him were in place? He said, not very busy at all any more, at least not right here. The immigrants were now going through other gaps in the area that hadn't been closed, including an Indian reservation not far away that remained unwalled. Now, with time on his hands and not much do, the agent ordered me to return the way I came, or else he would arrest me for improper return outside an official port of entry, a crime that came with a $5,000 fine.

As we hiked back to Oscar's blue jeep, a Border Patrol boat zoomed up and hit its lights and sirens. Back near the jeep, two Mexican cops were waiting, saying the Border Patrol agent had called them in to get rid of us. All of this served as a testament to how Border Patrol is able to capably turn away human traffic when the numbers aren't swamping them.

Much of what Border Patrol agents told me about walls seems so conventionally obvious that I wonder if opponents really could believe their own claims that walls are so ineffective. If in their heart of hearts they authentically believed walls were useless, why say anything at all? Would they not just shrug their shoulders, maybe allow a slight private smirk over the sheer folly of border wall-building, and go about their business? Would not wall opponents take refuge in their private *knowing* that immigrants flow as though nothing new was put in their way?

But that never happens. Instead, opponents battle, file lawsuits, lobby, and demand their candidates halt construction as soon as possible, as would people who know deep in their hearts that walls work really well on most illegal immigrant flow.

Perhaps most telling that walls work far too well is that Mexico's government, which benefits from the $26 billion a year in remittance money its citizens send home, issues the loudest caterwauling. I've come to believe that the louder the oppositional squealing, the greater their inner conviction that border walls wreck the party. If not that, then anti-wall activists are suddenly fiscal conservatives who can't bear the "waste" of $25 billion on a wall that does nothing? Doubtful, given that progressive liberals do not very often seem interested in controlling government spending. It's not their thing.

There is one great flaw with border walls that opponents could mention but don't. Immigrants can always just walk up to one and claim asylum. Most of the wall is built hundreds of yards, even miles, north of the Mexican border, on American territory. Illegal immigrants who know about this can walk up to the Mexico-facing side of a wall on U.S. soil and say through the slats that they want asylum. Border Patrol will have to come around to the other side, retrieve them, and let them into the country anyway. Until the asylum law is reformed, no wall can keep out immigrants who learn they can do this.

A comprehension of basic wall physics is foundational to understanding how they work, their strengths and limitations, which they have, so that future leaders know how to use them.

PART III

OVERRUN

CHAPTER TEN

LAND OF THE DEPORTATION-FREE, HOME OF THE CRIMINAL ALIEN: RUNNERS AND GOT-AWAYS

This chase hit speeds of more than 100 mph, and it went on for fifty miles. Two vehicles roared through the vast, empty former Spanish land grant desert of southern Texas. In one, a Texas state trooper gripped the wheel of his agency-issued Chevrolet Tahoe SUV, its reds and blues up top flashing as he radioed for assistance and issued progress reports, engine and adrenaline raging. Just ahead, the driver of a maroon-colored Dodge Ram pickup filled with people in the crew cab and back bed was gunning it.

This contest started just outside Del Rio maybe thirty-five miles to the south on the Rio Grande that March 15, 2021, morning, when the trooper flashed at the maroon truck for a traffic violation and it sped forward instead.[318] Now, a full thirty minutes later, the two vehicles were still flying north up the twisting two-way ribbon of U.S. Highway 277 that sliced through this huge ranchland country. At those speeds, both vehicles would have caught air on the sometimes uneven, undulating surface, the people in the back holding on for dear life.

But they would lose their precious hold. The fleeing driver, Sebastian Tovar, a twenty-five-year-old born in Toledo, Ohio, and lately living in Austin, crossed the center line and hit a Ford F-150 pickup head-on. The shattered remnant of Tovar's truck flipped into the air and landed on its roof dozens of feet off the pavement. Eight people in the pickup's bed or in the cab flew forward at 100 mph and could not possibly have lived. Seven of the dead were illegal alien men, and the eighth was a woman, all from Mexico between the ages of eighteen and twenty.

It turned out that all had crossed the night before near Eagle Pass, a border town about fifty-five miles downriver from Del Rio, and had paid to be smuggled by road deeper into the country.[319] Saved by airbags, Tovar extricated himself and bolted into the desert rather than aid a father and daughter injured in the other vehicle (and who none-theless survived). When he was caught, Tovar admitted to officers that he worked as a smuggler and had been paid to drive the aliens inland, court records from his federal smuggling conviction showed.

Were it not for the terrible toll in life, this car chase would only have typified a sharply escalating series of similar cinema-worthy dramas that were starting to transform border communities into chaotic fear zones. A level of pandemonium broke out from the Texas Gulf of Mexico to the California shoreline that many living there swore they'd never seen in their lives. While always an occasional feature of border town life, wild car chases that sent townspeople scurrying for their lives or leaving people, houses, and parked cars smashed by car crashes soon became hallmarks of an unpleasant new norm with a curious common denominator: most of the immigrants sneaking in with smugglers were young single adults and convicted criminals Biden was not exempting from Title 42 and who were desperate not to get caught and returned.

Of late, smuggler vehicles were blasting through school zones at high speed with police hot on their tailgates, sirens piercing the air, vehicles peeling around pedestrians in business districts and disappearing out of town. Others crashed and flipped.[320] Schools on the main town roads devised early-warning alert systems that, when principals triggered them, sent students scurrying for shelter several times per week.

The kind of chaos in border communities included the very next thing that happened at the terrible crash site on Highway 277, when police barricaded the road so that authorities could recover the still-warm bodies. One of the first vehicles caught in traffic behind the police roadblock was a tan Ford F-150 that had been traveling with Tovar. When Border Patrol agents approached to tell its driver to turn around and leave, twelve more illegal immigrants leapt out and fled in every direction, single adults with no children. They scattered into the desert, drawing helicopters and police tracking canines, and cops on all-terrain vehicles to round them up while others worked the bloody crash scene investigation. Police call these "bail-outs."

No town in South Texas or even large cities farther inland was immune from the bail-out. When wheels stopped, illegal aliens and smugglers scampered everywhere so that law enforcement could only catch a few or none. If the bail-outs happened in populated areas, immigrants would break into houses, apartments, parked cars, and business to hide, or jump into dumpsters, as local police hunted them down. Residents learned to live with the drama of hiding strangers and cops looking everywhere for them.

Just over the horizon from the Highway 277 crash is the two-light Kinney County ranching town of Brackettville, whose 1,700 residents thirty miles north of the border have endured so many high-wire smuggler car chases that the local school in spring 2021 spent $60,000 to install rock barriers to protect school facilities against smuggling-related crashes. The district also implemented a "hold in place" system where the high school's administrators can warn students over speakers that a high-speed chase is on the way, a weekly occurrence and sometimes more than once a day.[321]

"Unfortunately, we could use that towards our students for their education," school board member Mark Perez told the *Epoch Times*. "But right now we're using it for their safety because of everything that's going on. I think everybody in the community could probably agree that it's uneasy, not knowing when you're going to have a pursuit come down and if the kids are going to be at recess or walking back and forth between classes."

From October 1, 2021 through February 2022, all law enforcement in Kinney County arrested almost 300 smugglers, the *Epoch Times* reported, including dozens who began their flights from police on Highway 90 far outside of town and were pushing 100 mph when they entered, Kinney County Sheriff Brad Coe told the newspaper. One crash left an immigrant occupant a quadriplegic and another a paraplegic. Other crashes in town left immigrant passengers mangled. Still other chases sent citizen pedestrians running for cover. One ended with a collision into an apartment building whose inhabitants were just on the inside. Another ended in an armed standoff between deputies and a teenage smuggler.

"Before this is over, somebody's going to get shot," Coe said. "I just pray it's not one of my guys."

The death of eight migrants was hardly the worst, first, or last crash that would kill single adult immigrants—the ones still subject to Title 42 expulsions—as their drivers hauled them from the borders. A week before the Highway 277 crash, an SUV jammed with twenty-five illegal aliens collided with a semi-truck in California, killing thirteen. Near Tucson, on April 21, 2022, three migrants died when their teenaged smuggler led state highway patrol on a chase and rolled over.[322] Too many other fatalities and mutilations stain this crisis to list here. But a central characteristic of this Biden border crisis is that fear zones sprang up all along the border as an expanding smuggling industry sated spiking new demand among those who did not make the Biden administration's list of "the chosen."

South of the sleepy West Texas town of Sierra Blanca on Interstate 10, convoys of 4 x 4 smuggler vehicles began driving rugged roads and trails up from the border to reach the interstate. Once in early 2021, local law enforcement chased down a five-vehicle convoy packed to the roofs with methamphetamine and eighty-seven illegal aliens.[323] In Presidio County not far away, Sheriff Danny Dominguez was leading a hot pursuit of a smuggler vehicle through Marfa that ended up abandoned at the sheriff's own backyard fence, one of the suspects hopped over it and fled right through the officer's property and was never found.[324]

No central database captures and tallies such incidents. But a prevalence of town media and Border Patrol agent accounts reveal an emergent scourge of single immigrants hiring smugglers and trying to blast through positions whose defenders were ordered to process child migrants elsewhere after Biden took office. Often, only local sheriff's deputies, town cops, or state troopers were around for a chase. While this pandemonium resides out of sight and worry for most Americans, the bliss of ignorance cannot last. The worst criminals in the world are in those vehicles and making it into towns and cities all over America.

What spurred this insane aspect of the Biden border crisis? Part of the answer is that those who were still subject to Title 42—mostly single adults—saw holes in the Border Patrol defenses and went for them. But something else the administration did added the decisive dose of enticement. By July 2022, nearly one million got away into the American interior. Those who got away formed a major, disturbing component of the Biden border crisis that portends a higher permanent level of damage far outside the mere borderlands but throughout the entire country.

Sanctuary America

While the administration was running a conveyor belt into America of pregnant women, families with young kids, and unaccompanied minors, those who got the straight arm treatment were single adults aspiring to earn money.

But another element was in this mix of those who ran and got away: criminals who'd been deported after serving prison or jail sentences in the United States and figured there'd never be a better time to return.

"I would say a lot of them are undesirables," said Border Patrol Agent Ron Boren, who represents the agency's union local 2554 in Southern California. "The criminal aliens who have been convicted in the United States, the guys convicted of rape, theft, multiple DUIs and Lord knows what else. They're the ones coming most often."

The field agents call all illegal immigrants who do not turn themselves in "runners." The runners not caught graduate to become "got-aways." Neither is merely Border Patrol slang. Both terms are official government vernacular.

The term "got-away," for instance, is listed in Title 7 U.S. Code 223 requiring border security metrics and means "an unlawful border crosser who is not directly or indirectly observed making an unlawful entry into the United States, is not apprehended and is not turned back."[325] The government has never released these numbers publicly. But sources in the Border Patrol shared them with me, and a Texas judge presiding over a federal court case required DHS to file got-away "status reports" reflecting January 2020 through June 2022. Enormous numbers of runners were achieving got-away status, close to a million just through June 2022, the status reports showed.

The times couldn't be better for runners from the earliest days of this crisis. Early on, nearly 1,000 got-aways every day, or 30,000 a month, were sneaking into the United States because Border Patrol agents were reassigned to processing duty for the women and children, the *Washington Post* reported, quoting three officials familiar with the data.[326] Later in the data shared with me confidentially, got-aways were hitting 60,000 and 70,000 a month.

Besides the improved odds of evading capture, another often overlooked incentive exerted a powerful pull: the Biden government turned almost the entire United States into a deportation-free sanctuary.

On Biden's first day in office, a pre-prepared memorandum went out declaring a hundred-day "pause" on deportations of "any noncitizen with a final order of removal" except for terrorists, those who wanted to leave, and those who entered the U.S. after November 1, 2020.[327] That quickly died in court for its bold illegality. However, the administration pulled out the backup plan. It issued internal policy memos sharply restricting ICE's arm responsible for interior deportations—the Enforcement and Removal Operations (ERO) Branch's 6,000 officers—which illegal aliens they could arrest and which ones they must leave in peace. As if that were not enough, DHS established a long list of "protected areas." These no-go zones included public grade schools and private universities, health care facilities, houses of worship or religious study, anywhere that children gather, and parades, demonstrations, and rallies.[328]

Compared to normal years past, ERO now could arrest almost nobody, including aggravated felons of every stripe. The curtailments were so broad and ran so deep as to effectively eliminate deportation in America, certainly as the nation has known it in the modern era. Did the street protest demands of "Abolish ICE" come to fruition? Yes, even if not on paper.

ICE's ERO continued to exist. Agents were still getting paid. But rules and limitations shackled them to their desks. The progressive utopia of a Sanctuary America arose where, as they had always hoped, no illegal alien would ever again have to "live in fear," meaning watch their backs for the deportation cop.

Criminal aliens and young adult workers still subject to Title 42 expulsion quickly realized that once in under Biden's America, government deportation officers would leave them alone. The Border Patrol's jurisdiction extended one hundred miles inland from the border. The runners need only get past the hundred miles to be free for at least as long as Biden was in office.

So while average Americans outside the hundred-mile mark may feel they need not concern themselves with the hundred-mile border zone's daily cinematic dramas, from now on they will have to contend with the hard-bitten criminal former deportees running the gauntlet and making way for cities everywhere inside Biden's new nationwide sanctuary zone.

Reasonable people might sympathize with the many reasons why progressive liberals don't like deportation, especially for working illegals who have caused no trouble. But an enduring and deeply troubling mystery is that progressives insist their absolutist umbrella covers murderers, child rapists, drug traffickers, and aggravated felons.

The new DHS rules allowed ICE officers to deport only terrorists, spies, and aggravated felons but only "if they pose a risk to public safety."[329] Terrorists and spies are rare and never easy to find until it's too late, so ICE officers were never going to spend too much time deporting them. But they stopped spending time deporting the aggravated felons no matter how often administration officials would claim otherwise.

Spraying a Protective Deportation Coating on Violent Criminals

That's because administration sprayed a wide protective deportation coating over most criminal aliens, even the aggravated felons.[330] ICE officers were told not to arrest one until after spreading out the files and studying if the target's mental health had anything to do with committing the crime or if they were sick and needed medical treatments. Officers would have to study "the impact of removal on family in the United States, such as loss of provider or caregiver," or if the alien served as a church deacon, and if they or someone in the immediate family had served in the military "or other public service."[331] ICE officers had to call headquarters for permission to arrest or deport any criminal.

If any of those exculpatory boxes got checked, the target went free. ICE ERO supervisors were given bushels of "outs" for deporting the bad guys. The outs were the real reason why so many deportable aggravated felons got to stay in America. The outs were the real reason why so many deported years earlier were now trying to get back in. (A federal judge in Texas threw out these rules in June 2022 on grounds that they had harmed the nation; however, the Biden administration has continued litigating for them as of this writing in November 2022.)

An ICE ERO officer I interviewed in March 2021 on condition of anonymity told me they always had wide discretion to arrest anyone who was illegal or found to have a valid deportation order, on their own volition, never having to ask political appointees at ICE headquarters in Washington.

"We all know the law, and we followed it as our main guidance," the officer told me.

Now, he and all his fellow ERO officers sat in their offices ignoring alerts and reports of dangerous criminal aliens who didn't fit the new approved list of administration priorities or probably would get the NO from headquarters.

"They've told us to stop arresting people, except for aggravated felons, but we have to ask Washington first if even they meet the new criteria," the officer told me. "And they decline some of them."

For this officer and others in the Texas office, it might take days to get an answer. By that time, the trail was cold and the suspects long gone.

"It's really, really weird not being able to do what you're supposed to do," he told me, pausing a moment to add, "Yeah, it's just really weird. It sucks."

The predictable result was that rivers of outbound interior deportees slowed to a trickle while the inbound trickle became flooded rivers of previously deported criminal aliens getting back in.

The administration went out of its way to suppress reporting the results. It refused to publish a traditional annual *ICE Enforcement and Removal Operations* report detailing every kind of ICE deportation statistic. But the data got out in other ways.

It showed ICE left tens of thousands of deportable criminals free to roam in the country, including aliens convicted of homicides, sex assaults, weapons offenses, and offenses involving dangerous drugs, according to data retrieved under Freedom of Information Act requests by the *Washington Times* and Center for Immigration Studies.

ICE's immigration enforcement division recorded major declines in nearly every category of operations in 2021. For instance, "detainers," which are official requests to local police to alert ICE to come pick up deportable criminal aliens getting released from jail, fell from 122,233 in 2020 to 65,940 in 2021.[332] Even deportations of people convicted of human slavery fell from fifty-two under Trump to twenty-eight under Biden, and kidnappers deported under Trump fell from 451 to 288 under Biden in 2021, the FOIA data from ICE showed.[333]

Indicators of a Coming Carnage

"When you start scaring and discouraging officers from doing their jobs, the whole system falls apart very quickly," lamented Jon Feere, who served at ICE as senior advisor to the director and chief of staff from January 2017 to January 2021. "Officers are bringing cases because they don't want to be reprimanded. Their superiors will err on the side of caution. So the memo's out, literally and figuratively, and the message is that officers should ignore most illegal aliens. Officers don't want to waste their time on cases that are going to go nowhere."

Indicators of a coming carnage can be found over on the government site's "Criminal Noncitizen Statistics" page. During fiscal year 2021, 10,769 "criminal noncitizens" convicted of one or more crimes were caught at the border, three times the 2,438 during Donald Trump's last year in 2020 and the most since 2016. The year 2022 through July 2022, Border Patrol had already caught 9,381. Among them were 53 convicted for homicide or manslaughter, another 1,241 for drunk driving, and 283 for sexual offenses.[334]

Scrolling through the seemingly endless CBP press announcements warns us that interior America should worry more about sex offenses against women and children. [335]

Oddly, the press announcement files overflow with cases where sex offenders were caught coming over the border, immigrants who'd been convicted of molesting children inside the United States, deported after serving sentences, but now returning. Here's what comes up in just one recent few-day cluster:

In August 2022, Border Patrol agents caught a Guatemalan national coming over who'd served twenty-two years in a California prison for lewd and lascivious acts with a child under fourteen by force.[336] On the same day, they caught a Salvadoran convicted in 2016 of indecent exposure with a child and deported. Now he was coming back. In the same span, agents caught a Mexican national convicted of rape in Oregon, deported after serving a prison sentence, and heading back in again.[337]

The same night, agents caught another Mexican national convicted of cruelty toward a child and transmission of child pornography in Florida. That busy day of sex abusers wasn't over. Agents arrested yet another Mexican national convicted of sexually assaulting a child under eleven in South Carolina and who served fifteen years in prison.

In one period in the Del Rio area, agents reported ninety-five convicted sex offenders from October 2021 through May 2022.[338] The convictions included forcible sexual assault, sexual assault of a child under fourteen, sexual conduct with a person under thirteen, statutory rape, second-degree sexual assault of a child, and lewd and lascivious acts with a child.

You get the gist, but know that CBP's press releases reporting like this go on for miles.

Not Minding the Gaps

Single adults still subject to Title 42 expulsions also kept coming because there was no limit to the number of times they could try and no consequences racked up as they did in normal flow times. The old saying that "the definition of insanity is doing the same thing over and over again and expecting a different result" did not apply here. Trying over and over again did not trigger prosecution or disadvantageous records. Trying eventually paid off. In Mexico, I found no shortage of single adult immigrants who told me they've tried four, five, six, or more times to get across. Their explanations for doing it struck me as perfectly rational.

In normal times, repeat crossers face prosecution, jail time, and black marks that accrue on a personal record and could trigger years-long bans on the privilege of legal entry. But not with Title 42. They can go as often as they can afford until they graduate to "got-away."

The immigrants always told me why they kept trying.

"Half of us get through and next time, God willing, maybe I will be one of those," one young Nicaraguan man in his early twenties told me in the Mexican city of Piedras Negras across from Eagle Pass, right after he was expelled for the fourth time.

A CBP air and marine helicopter pilot stationed on the Texas border told me why that was the case.

"Sometimes I'll be flying over a ranch and there's people there, five or 10 maybe, and I'll radio, 'hey there they are!" the pilot said. "And the supervisor will come back and say, '1079 that [disregard]; no one's available.' So there're verified people on the ground right in front of you, and you can't do anything about it. And it's all day, every day."

The Sinaloa cartel across from Douglas, Arizona, perfected an outrageous method to exploit the absence of redeployed Border Patrol. By the summer of 2022, all but one or two Border Patrol agents on a shift remained to patrol the eighteen-foot Bush-era wall between Douglas from the Mexican side.

Seeing this unique opportunity, the cartel formed "ladder crews." Right in front of the outnumbered agents on the other side and in clear view through the slats, the crews would calmly lean their ladders and throw down a rope on the American side while two agents readied themselves, hopelessly. Then, hundreds of single adult immigrants let themselves down the ropes to swarm around and past the agents.

Once the two agents caught a few, they were booked up for the night, and the rest were free to leisurely walk into Douglas with impunity. The ladder crews sent 200–700 a night every night for all of the border crisis, according to Ben Bergquam, a conservative activist journalist for Real America's Voice News and founder of Frontline America.

Bergquam, who made a name for himself covering both sides of the border crisis, stood and filmed them running and walking all around him on their way into town. He even caught one on camera himself. Local cops told him almost all of these were previously deported criminals who knew they could finally get back in.

"I had several agents tell me they don't even know how many got-aways they're missing out there because much of the time they don't have the resources to even track them," Bergquam told me by phone from the Douglas wall one night. "It's a constant every day."

Fear, insecurity, violence, pursuits, and chaos are part of life for regular citizens of the borderlands now in no small part due to the "protected areas" the Biden administration established too. The 550-acre campus of Cochise College in the Sonoran Desert south of Tucson, for instance, suddenly found itself a stepping stone for nightly transits of spooky immigrant runners wearing camouflage clothing. The traffic frightened students and faculty to the extent that administrators were forced to beef up security, unable to count on Border Patrol. That's because, you may recall, Biden's DHS had exempted college campuses from all immigration enforcement.[339]

In April 2021, I set out for Texas big sky country, a laboratory case study for the burgeoning national problem of the runners and got-aways, which was pushing toward its first one million by July 2022.

Where Prada Meets Smugglers

A popular faux store artist's sculpture on Highway 90 near Valentine, Texas that has become a nighttime smuggling pickup point. April 2021 photo by Todd Bensman.

After the November 2020 national election, a contemporary new daily drama began to play out throughout a vast sweeping desert valley floor that had seen its share over the centuries, Comanche war parties, Spanish explorers, Mexican soldiers, Texan nationalists, and modern ranchers who have lived, fought, and struggled here.

Now, Border Patrol agents were fighting a losing battle against huge groups of single adult illegal immigrants suddenly coursing through the barren territory, the most anyone had ever seen and only four months into the crisis with no letup through September 2022. They were outmanned and outgunned despite their superior technology.

The valley was just one of several epicenters of the struggle between Border Patrol and smugglers of runners far beyond public sight in West Texas. At the center of it is a working railroad track built through in the 1880s and sixty-mile stretch of Highway 90, which connects the artist colony of Marfa, an aged frontier-era settlement taken over by artists who have famously refashioned old buildings into works of art, to Van Horn at Interstate 10.

This struggle was all about Highway 90. The stretch roughly parallels the Mexican border some fifty to seventy-five miles to the southwest. The smugglers were guiding their groups of 50 to 150 young, fit-enough adults on grueling days-long backpacking treks from the border to reach it. Once in its vicinity, the professional smugglers would have their groups hunker, dodge, and wait for cartel-paid drivers to pick them up in the dead of night, cover the forty miles to Van Horn on I-10, and be gone into America.

While driving Highway 90 one morning that April, I came across several of their iconic green and white SUV patrol vehicles parked on either side of the highway, the empty desert brush cut by rivulets and gullies for as far as they eye could see. Coordinating with in-vehicle radio handsets, agents were hunting what one described to me as a "sizable" group of illegal immigrants a surveillance camera had spotted. The group was out there, sheltering in place.

But even the untrained eye could tell how unassailable was the task, with so much territory. Some agents cruised slowly along Highway 90. Others slowly hiked the arroyo-riveted land or rumbled their vehicles off-road. The strategy called for a driver or agent on foot to flush the group. Drones overhead and a "scope truck" with a retractable high-tech lens tower in the back helped them see more, but there was just too much.

After an hour of this, the supervisor called off the search. The agents all accelerated away in a convoy north up Highway 90, their prey having gotten away again. Unless they were caught somewhere else that day, the agents would log them as "got-aways."

Agent friends had been complaining to me too about a feeling of impotence in the face of an adversary that seemed really well prepared to get their cargo onto I-10. Some told me the smugglers had even established as a pickup waypoint a famous piece of standing art, the faux "Prada boutique" store about twenty-five miles out of Marfa on the highway right outside the dwindling old railroad town of Valentine, population 135. Now a ramshackle collection of windblown abandoned circa 1930s and 1940s buildings, Valentine has long outlived its attempted branding as the Lone Star State's "Most Romantic Town."

The one bright spot for Valentine, though, is the lonely Prada art building sculpture made of biodegradable materials, which appears to hold actual fashion artifacts. Two Berlin-based artists known for criticizing modern consumerism created it in 2005. Their intention was for it to stand as a negative critique of American consumerism as the desert harshness degraded it. But unfortunately for the artists, it became too much of an iconic tourist destination frequently visited by celebrities and used as a backdrop for fashion photographers.

And lately, according to my Border Patrol sources, alien smugglers have pinned it as a landmark pickup spot where immigrants hidden in the deserts behind it in the dead of night rush forth to meet their vehicle driver.

On a first pass by the art during daylight, I saw a photographer shooting a young model posing pertly in front of it.

They ignored me as I reconnoitered the small box-shaped building and hiked a ways behind it looking for tracks. I saw some, though I'm not a great tracker.

I decided to come back late that night from Sierra Blanca, where I was staying. I parked a few blocks down the highway and waited inside my rental with all lights off. It was pitch-black out there. The idea was that maybe I'd get luckier than the Border Patrol, see a truck pull up and immigrants run out of the desert into it. They certainly could have. No one was there to see. I suspected Border Patrol would have hidden cameras somewhere in the vicinity. But if I triggered them, no one came to check me out. Every half hour, a vehicle would blast by, but none stopped to pick up migrants at the Prada store. I departed after a few hours.

Conditions in West Texas greatly favored the smuggling guides and easily shielded their human contraband from sight. These tended to be fit single adults with some smuggling money and *cajones*.

Many agents who normally patrol Big Bend sector's 165,154 rugged square miles and 571 miles along the Rio Grande got redeployed to help southern Texas agents process in the families. The administration redeployed Border Patrol agents from other sectors, including 1,250 along the Canadian border and coastal areas, to process families and teens in the Rio Grande Valley.[340]

That left Big Bend sector exposed. Only three or four agents on a patrol shift were responsible for a fifty-mile band of extremely inhospitable terrain, agents told me that spring of 2021. Only a half dozen agents per shift were available to patrol another 120-mile section of river border, arroyos, canyons, and mountains.

"There's no one watching" on the American side, the La Linea smuggling guide Jose told me a few days earlier.

Texas governor Greg Abbott would send some National Guard and Texas DPS troopers and quite a few choppers, which did begin to catch more drug traffickers and large immigrant groups in inaccessible mountain crags (see chapter sixteen, "Texas Insurgency"). But by all accounts, it did not seem to have appreciably reduced the success odds for runners. They poured over in groups as large as one hundred. I saw photos of them in long single-file lines, shot by Border Patrol motion-detecting game cameras placed on some of the trails.

"They're just bum-rushing the border," one frustrated agent in the Big Bend area lamented to me in a confidential discussion. "Probably three-quarters of them are getting away. It's like each station is only allotted a certain number of agents hired and, even if we had the maximum, it's not enough to stop the groups. They know we're overwhelmed and the word has gotten out. As long as they send a giant amount of people, they'll get through."

Meanwhile, Americans along the border were frustrated by cessation of work on Trump's promise to fill gaps in George W. Bush–era walling.

Ray Whetstone owns the Neely Ranch, which backs up to a standalone 4.5-mile wall segment built when Bush was president. Under Trump plans, it was to be extended for miles eventually to connect with other segments. While Trump was in office, the immediate vicinity of the 4.5-mile wall section near his ranch had quieted things down for years. But now, large groups of single military-aged men were coming through, crossing to its north side and then moving horizontally across the southern part of his property. He told me he'd been sleeping with a gun at the pillow for the first time in his life, "ever since the new president."

"Since the election, there's lots of traffic coming through," Whetstone told me. "A *lot* more."

Shelly Means, a rancher outside of Valentine, told me she was calling Border Patrol like she never had before.

"Maybe in the last four years, we've seen eight illegals," Means said. But since the inauguration, "I think they've probably picked up 200 off of us."

All this illegal stranger traffic—plus a group of migrants showered in a guest house, left the water running, and caused major damage—left her family with an unexpected new sense of insecurity, she said. Members of her family had begun carrying guns at all times.

"We still have a heart, but I don't want them on my place," she said. "If we have some I call the Border Patrol and go out and ask them if they're hungry, infirm, what they need—clothes, shoes, and then I just pray that the Border Patrol gets here quickly."

My driver, friend, and interpreter Chris Leland, who spends most of his waking hours guiding hunters in and around Terlingua, told me Border Patrol was always part of the scenery since the 9/11 attacks, a highway check point opened "pretty much 24/7."

Now?

"Ever since what's-his-name got elected, we do not see 'em down here," Chris told me. "They're getting pulled out of here right and left on babysittin' duty, and we just don't see 'em."

CHAPTER ELEVEN

A UNITED NATIONS OF MASS MIGRATION

"The American border was too tight with Trump. Now, everybody knows the Americans are handing out papers to everyone. That's why they come. That's why everybody is going to the States."

—Human smuggler in northern Costa Rica after negotiating a deal with five Senegalese, June 2021

Felix with two corrupt Nicaraguan soldiers who agreed to take three Haitian immigrants to smugglers inside Nicaragua for money. Photo derived from author video June 2021.

My new best friend Felix, a driver for northern Costa Rica's booming human smuggling industry, finally answered my pestering with a "Yes, okay" in Spanish; he would let me tag along on an immigrant delivery to corrupt soldiers of the Nicaraguan Armed Forces. They were to take possession of the three Haitians at a clandestine border rendezvous in the jungle for $150 each and deliver them to smugglers four miles inside Nicaragua.

"Don't be afraid," assured Felix, a deserter from the Nicaraguan army whose contacts seemed to be paying off these days. "Because nobody's going to fire on us or anything like that."

This day in June 2021, however, was not going to turn out well. Before the day was out, I and my native Costa Rican interpreter, Federico, would have to flee Los Chiles for our lives, a gas-pedal-to-the-floor flight where final destination was unimportant.

I'd traveled that summer of 2021 to the far northern Costa Rica town of Los Chiles in Alajuela province to gain a better understanding of yet another of many firsts in President Biden's historic border crisis. Unlike all previous known mass migration events, multinational immigrants from all points of the planet made up a record-high proportion of all those reaching the American border. A United Nations of mass migration was underway from 150-plus countries.

"There are huge masses of people going through the border now," a Costa Rican border frontier guard commander confirmed for me soon after I landed in the northern city of Liberia that June of 2021 and drove to the border town of La Cruz.

All those moving through the Costa Rica-Nicaragua border had just come through the treacherous Darien Gap passage, an eighty-mile stretch of lawless, roadless jungle that immigrants had to trek on foot for up to ten days to get from Colombia in South America to Panama in Central America. Many suffered injuries and death by wildlife, flooding rivers, armed indigenous bandits, and by just surrendering to exhaustion death.

But once in Panama, the survivors found a most accommodating government policy called "Controlled Flow."[341] Under Controlled Flow, the Panamanian border guard, SENAFRONT, would collect and transport the immigrants to hospitality camps. The immigrants could recover, reequip, receive medical treatment, and wire in some more smuggling money for the next legs. Helpfully, Panama's government arranged for buses to load them up at the hospitality camps and drive them to Costa Rica's southern border. Until the pandemic, Costa Rica participated. It received and processed the travelers through to their own hospitality camps up to where I was at the Nicaragua border. Because Nicaragua didn't participate, Costa Rica's government understood it was delivering the immigrants back to real smugglers in the area I chose to visit.

Northern Costa Rica provided the perfect roost from which to observe the phenomenon underway now. All past years of record-keeping showed that multinationals who reached the U.S. southern border from countries other than Mexico, Honduras, Guatemala, and El Salvador made up single-digit percentage points of totals. The Darien Gap passage was a potent deterrent for anyone who wasn't young, strong, and pretty bold.

But the Biden border crisis was characterized by an unusual phenomenon: a record-breaking 40 percent of all those reaching the southern border were coming from 150 other countries. It was no coincidence that much of this huge new traffic was made up of the chosen demographics that Biden's government would not expel back into Mexico. Suddenly, the bulk of people coming through were families with very young children, pregnant women, and solo teens.

From 2011 to 2020, annual flows through the Darien ranged somewhere between 2,000 and a high of 30,000 in 2016 and about 8,594 at the pandemic nadir of 2020, according to statistics Panama compiles.[342] Then, something dramatic happened starting exactly in January 2021; the numbers moving through the gap rocketed to 134,000.[343] The numbers moving through were on track to exceed 215,000 in 2022, a record 32,500 of them children.[344] Many others found ways to fly over the Darien Gap and land farther up trail in countries like Guatemala and Mexico.

The sea change was obvious at the U.S. border. In the year 2000, the vast majority of 98 percent were Mexicans, according to CBP statistics.[345] Seven years later, in 2007, Mexicans still made up 93 percent of the 858,639 illegal aliens apprehended crossing the border, while Central Americans comprised 6 percent, and a single percent came from the rest of the world, according to my analysis of arrests by citizenship.[346] In 2019, Central Americans and Mexicans together comprised about 92 percent, with a sizable growth to 8 percent from everywhere else.

But Biden's border crisis brought in 40 percent and spiked even higher sometimes. In May 2022, when total apprehensions of all nationalities apprehended at the U.S. border hit a nose-bleed historic peak of 222,656, an astonishing 47.3 percent came from around the world.

For a bit more perspective, Border Patrol apprehensions of immigrants from countries other than Guatemala, Honduras, El Salvador, and Mexico more than sextupled from the nadir year of 53,615 in fiscal 2020 when Trump was in office to 378,043 in fiscal 2021. It then went on to triple to more than a million in fiscal 2022.

The Border Patrol apprehensions website lists nineteen countries it tracks, plus a mysterious "other countries" category. Tens of thousands came from countries like Peru, Venezuela, Colombia, Cuba, Chile, Brazil, Ecuador, Turkey, Ukraine, Russia, and Myanmar. Still thousands more extra-continentals hailed from most of the countries of Africa, and plenty from India, Nepal, and China. The number from Turkey rose from 109 in fiscal 2020 to more than 13,000 in fiscal 2022.

Thousands more fell into the masked "other" category—those known to homeland security professionals as "extra-continentals" from, say, the African continent, or "special interest aliens" who hailed from countries of terrorism concern like Iraq, Syria, Afghanistan, Yemen, Pakistan, and Somalia. Consider that those from "other" countries amounted to 7,047 in 2020 but 94,063 by the close of fiscal 2022.

After Russia invaded Ukraine in February 2022, more than 25,000 Ukrainians flew on tourist visas to Tijuana and knocked on the border wall asking for asylum, CBP data shows, despite offers from twenty-seven much-closer European Nations of three-year residencies with food, housing, and health care subsidies.[347] More than 17,000 Russians also reached the border, many claiming persecution as war protestors.

At one motel where a lot of immigrants were staying for a night or two, the proprietor let me thumb through his registry book. In it were registered guests from Guinea, Burkina Faso, Yemen, Pakistan, Nigeria, Sri Lanka, Bangladesh, Somalia, Ethiopia, Eritrea, and many other troubled nations besides. One customer listed his name merely as "Mohamed" from "Africa." Another named Ahmed Talib also listed his country as "Africa."

Something very new and different was up with this mass migration crisis. What was it?

The immigrants rarely hold back their candor when I ask them before immigration lawyers get to them, or when anyone else asks them.

"They'll say, 'Biden number one! Biden is great! Biden is helping us! Thank you, Biden!" said independent correspondent Michael Yon, who spent six months interviewing immigrants coming and going through the Darien Gap in 2022. "They say it. They say it with their mouths! They say it all the time!"

Progressive social media influencers, liberal media reporters, and UN agency officials have spread blame for their coming on climate change, wars, and fallout from the Covid-19 pandemic.[348]

But it is no coincidence that the demographics of those crossing or flying over the Darien Gap neatly correlate with the "chosen" demographics that Biden's DHS was exempting from Title 42 expulsions and letting in: families with young children, adolescent solo teenagers, and pregnant women became much more prevalent in the gap by all accounts after the administration began letting those particular demographics into America to stay. Others getting the border crossing red carpet treatment filled the Darien trails too. So that's who came. For example, Cubans became ubiquitous in the jungle after January 2021 because they saw the Biden administration was exempting a great many from Title 42 expulsions. In 2020, Border Patrol caught some 13,000 Cubans. By the close of fiscal 2022, they'd caught 194,000.

"The Cubans are coming now because they know Cubans don't get deported," Yon told me.

Only after Biden took office did Diane Edrington, the nurse practitioner who has volunteered in the province for twenty years, start to see huge numbers of women, children, and pregnant immigrants pouring into Panama.

"That's always been going on. They were usually young men who were able to do things like that, travel on their own," Edrington said. "They could take off and do things like that. But there weren't women and children. I've never seen this many. A *lot* of women. A *lot* of children."

Edrington also saw the most pregnant women in her twenty years of Darien Province experience, always in advanced stages, because they knew the Americans were going to let them in.

This new United Nations of illegal immigration matters to America because it carries risks to the country's shore that are much different than the more familiar Honduran MS-13 gang members, Mexican cartel operatives, sex offenders, and drug traffickers. By virtue of conditions in home countries outside this hemisphere, this traffic carries a different complexion of threat: infiltration by Islamic terrorists, African war criminals, Ukrainian mobsters, and foreign intelligence agents of Russia, China, Venezuela, Cuba, and Iran.

Beyond those homeland security threat problems, this flooding river inflicts terrible humanitarian costs on those who were enticed to put themselves in it; immigrant mothers, fathers, children, and pregnant women have died by the scores answering the siren call to Biden's more-open borders. They would be alive today had they never been so irresistibly called.

I wanted to witness this historic migration phenomenon, and Los Chiles was *the* place to see it.

A Smuggling Pirate Town off Every Grid

For nearly a week before Federico and I finally had to flee for our lives, we'd been hanging around two of the town's open-air bus stops among drivers-for-hire like Felix who connected the disembarking immigrants to Nicaragua's smuggling networks. Untouched by either journalism or Costa Rican law enforcement, the smuggling trade here happened in the wide open. Cruising through town at night, we could see groups of Haitians, Brazilians, and Cubans on sidewalks and streets, still hauling backpacks they'd used in the Darien Gap, negotiating with drivers on sidewalks and streets. Negotiators huddled in restaurants and scrummed in hotel lobbies around town.

Business was booming.

I almost stumbled across the main reason why when I approached a local driver negotiating with five Senegalese immigrants late one night on a berm along the main Los Chiles drag. This driver was in his forties, well-groomed and -coifed, wearing slacks, a collared button-down, and loafers. After he closed the deal to drive the Senegalese men the next morning to La Trocha, a town of some sort on the Nicaragua border, he agreed to talk on condition I not identify him by name.

He'd gotten into the business because so many immigrants were coming through Los Chiles that year, he said. "At least 10,000 have come through here. You get people every day traveling through to the States. This has been very commercially profitable for us and our families at this time."

I asked how long he had been doing this.

"Since Trump left," was his reply.

"Really?" I asked. "Tell me more."

The American border, he explained, "was too tight with Trump. Now, everybody knows the Americans are handing out papers to everyone. That's why they come. That's why everybody is going to the States."

One Haitian spending the night in Los Chiles explained that he and his group of families decided to make their move from Brazil, where they'd been comfortably living for four years, to the U.S. border mainly because "Biden is very nice for people. The conditions changed with Biden. When you are with your daughter or son, you can come" to the United States.

The way smuggling generally worked here is that the drivers would congregate at the bus stop. As each bus emptied, they'd hit the immigrants like hungry fish on bait.

One day, a bus pulled in at the main stop in Los Chiles. Five African extra-continentals leapt down the short stairwell and into the parking lot. "Where are you from?" I asked.

"Mauritania," one of them answered. My first Mauritanians. These extra-continentals seemed so exotic to me that I got them to pose for a picture with me. But they only spoke French, so dearly desired interviews were not possible. In any case, I overheard them strike a deal for transport to that same place again, "La Trocha."

There were the usual Haitians and Cubans, of course going to the mysterious La Trocha. I met countless Senegalese for the first time too. I met my first Angolan. I met Nigerians.

For two hundred dollars or less per immigrant, the drivers would take them forty or so miles east—to La Trocha. I finally got some of the smugglers to tell me about the place. It was an illegal smuggler's settlement controlled by two criminal gangs. The town was pure outlaw, its one road actually the border splitting the settlement evenly in half between Costa Rica and Nicaragua. La Trocha showed up on no map or GPS.

Neither country claimed nor recognized it. The smuggling organizations that ran La Trocha would guide the immigrants a few miles in to Nicaragua to the San Juan River and put them in boats toward Honduras, several of the drivers told me. I asked if they'd let me follow a load to La Trocha. But even though the drivers didn't mind talking business at bus stops, accompanying them to their criminal groups seemed to cross a line.

Finally, a young woman who made her living driving immigrants to it—the only female I saw doing business— agreed to let me follow. "Let's go. Follow me," the young woman said after I'd seen her load several Haitians into her small, white four-door car near the bus stop.

That short-lived experience should have served as a warning as to what would happen a few days later when I went in with Felix to his corrupt transaction with Nicaraguan soldiers.

We drove about forty miles on rock-riddled dirt roads, through pineapple plantations, stretches of lush vine-draped jungle, and some small, simple villages. At the crest of a final hill, we began the descent into the pirate settlement. At the bottom, we turned onto the main drag. Jagged rocks sticking up slowed travel to a half mile an hour. This "road" was actually the international border. All along it for several hundred yards, wood-planked structures with tin roofs lined either side. One trash-strewn side was Costa Rica. The other side, twenty feet away, was Nicaragua. I followed her car until she stopped at a wooden house on the Costa Rica side. We got out and stood with the three Haitians.

"You're safe as long as you stay on this side of the street," the woman told me. "And as long as it's daytime."

She led us inside the open-air courtyard of the structure with the Haitians, said she'd be back soon, and disappeared on the Nicaraguan side. Its floor was hardpack mud and rock, but at least it was shaded and faced the rocky road we'd just come up so I could study the activity out there. Our three Haitians sat on plastic chairs, clutching their backpacks, stress plain on their faces. Behind them, a desultory young woman ironed clothing while several elderly women cooked and did chores amid pecking chickens. The place doubled as a motorcycle repair shop, a few of the machines in various states of disassembly. I stepped out onto the road to survey La Trocha. Men on irritatingly loud motorbikes gunned their engines as they zipped past on the rocky border road. Across the street, I spied some makeshift restaurants and housing. *The downtown,* I thought to myself. It looked almost like a normal incorporated village. I saw no immigrants other than the ones we followed in and our three nervous Haitians.

Any hope that I might be able to explore this smuggler's roost proved short-lived. Our smuggling hostess returned alone with a stressed look on her ashen face. She explained that thirty other Haitians were in a house up the road on the

Nicaraguan side. A guide would lead them that night to a handoff to guides a few miles inside Nicaragua who will take them to Honduras.

She explained that the powers that be—meaning the local gangs that ran the town—were unhappy with her for bringing us to La Trocha. Terrible scenarios flashed through my mind, like one where she would pay with her life for granting a favor to me.

"I'm so sorry. I would never want to cause you trouble," I said, sincerely. I asked what she thought they would do to her now.

Oh, she would be okay, she replied. She was far more worried about *us*. At this very moment, she explained, pointing to a tin roof of a building on the Nicaragua side, leaders of the two gangs that run the settlement were in an emergency committee meeting about us.

"Oh, really?" I asked, somewhat alarmed. "What's *that* meeting about?"

"About what to do with you," she responded. "If I were you, I'd leave before they decide."

Within a minute or two, I was trundling back over the rocky track the way I'd driven in, checking my six all forty miles back to Los Chiles for any indication that anyone was following with a meeting decision. Worse was yet to come for me as I'll explain shortly.

But for anyone in the world who wanted to reach the American border through the Darien Gap, the Biden administration did all in its power—unthinkingly—to enrich the facilitating gangs of La Trocha.

Biden Government Opens Migrant Superhighway

Rather than launch urgent, decisive steps to staunch the flow, however, the Biden administration's DHS secretary, Alejandro Mayorkas, and secretary of state, Antony Blinken, apparently orchestrated the opposite. They launched a campaign of secretive shuttle diplomacy in Colombia, Panama, Costa Rica, and Mexico during the first quarter of 2022. It was mostly kept out of American newspapers.

The American diplomatic campaign appears to have been a response to rare but intense coverage in the fall of 2021 of the 130,000 immigrants who went through the Darien Gap. The *New York Times, Los Angeles Times, Houston Chronicle*, and other media outlets ran adventurous print and video pieces that often focused on the misery and death of the women, children, and pregnant women suddenly filling the ten-day Darien Gap trail into Panama.[349] Rarely did any of this coverage connect that these demographics of young families and pregnant women happened to be ones chosen for admission into America, that maybe those policies explained why so many were traveling, suffering, and dying.

In any case, following weeks of administration shuttle diplomacy in Colombia, Panama, Costa Rica, and Mexico during the first quarter of 2022, Panama opened two much shorter, far easier routes that bypassed the worst of the deterring Darien Gap. These reduced the ten-day trek to three or even two days.

One of the new bypass routes had immigrant smuggling boats coming out of Colombia move farther up the Caribbean coastline and then up a river to the Panamanian community of Canaán Membrillo. A separate two-day bypass route allowed immigrant vessels to move up the Pacific side of Panama and then by boat to the community of Jaque.[350]

For these new routes to work, Panamanian SENAFRONT ordered its patrol boats to yield the way to coastline areas they had previously blocked, said Embera Chief Francisco Agapi whose villages on the original route bore the brunt of 2021's rush to the border. Panama's federal government once again was clearing the route to the U.S. border, this time with implicit U.S. State Department and DHS involvement. In place of the ten-day backpacking hike was now a two- or three-day trip mostly by boat.

The Biden administration has never advertised nor taken credit but did stage a press event in April 2022 announcing the signing of a "Bilateral Arrangement on Migration and Protection" agreement with Panama. Mayorkas, Blinken, and Panamanian officials all signed. It was short on specifics other than to say that its purpose was to "improve migration management."[351]

"The Panamanians and the Americans were working together to make that crossing safer," said independent foreign correspondent Chuck Holton, who lives in Panama not far from the gap and has reported extensively on all sides of it.

Crossing into Panama now is probably safer for the short term, Holton told me, "because of pressure by the Americans. SENAFRONT lets them go by now."

But he believes the shorter bypass routes were already encouraging more to come, which will only enrich La Trocha's gangsters.

"It's 'Bring the kids! Bring the old people! Bring everybody!'" Holton said. "They'll double and double again the number of people coming. They're talking about facilitation. They're not talking about deterrence."

The Biden administration had plenty of help easing the international journey to America's southern border.

United Nations Cash Cards

Just before Thanksgiving 2021, I was visiting a nonprofit migrant shelter called "Senda De Vida," or Path of Life, in Reynosa, Mexico, just across from McAllen, Texas. Inside its high-walled, ten-acre compound on the banks of the Rio Grande, more than 1,200 intending U.S. border-crossers sheltered from the storm of the surrounding cartels and Reynosa's immigrant-hostile native Mexican population. A who's who of U.S. and foreign nonprofits had set up shop inside to provide for every kind of immigrant need, including Covid vaccinations and tests that the Americans had just required for legal entry. Long, snaking lines led to various service tables.

I stopped by the front of a long line to one of the service tables and saw, to my astonishment, that the workers behind it were accepting paperwork from the immigrants and then handing them debit cards. I asked a worker what that was all about. He said they were giving money to needy families on behalf of the UN's International Organization for Migration (IOM).

"How much money is on one of these?" I asked.

The answer came back: $400, rechargeable every fifteen days. Not everyone got them, just people determined to be "vulnerable," the worker told me. I took some photos and video of the cash cards and tweeted one out.

It practically went viral. The photo ruffled feathers among several Republican Congress members who follow me. An AFP "Fact Check" article called my assertions and photos a "misleading claim about UN aid for migrants in Mexico," pointing out that the workers were handing out "e-wallet" cards, not actual debit cards, and that the workers were not paid IOM employees but, rather, volunteers who worked with IOM.[352] Fair enough about who was signing the paychecks of the employees I met.

But everything I reported they were doing was true.

Subsequent digging, interviews, and another trip to Mexico showed the debit cards (or e-wallets, whatever you want to call plastic cards that buy things in stores) to be a formal, global program of the United Nations called "Cash-Based Interventions." An online UN document titled "IOM Emergency Manual" (since removed from the internet but not before I screen-shot it) said the program did indeed hand out "debit cards" along with the e-wallets, as well as bank transfers, mobile transfers, paper vouchers, e-vouchers, and, my personal favorite: "cash in envelopes." [353] No details were offered about the cash-stuffed envelopes, but those are never a good look. The money was for "unrestricted...unconditional" use in local country areas.[354]

Still other handouts subsidized the lodging, rent, and utilities of intending border crossers for "safe tenure, to reduce the risk of forced eviction." There was also "movement assistance" in the form of conditional or unrestricted cash transfers. The IOM described this money as providing transportation after, say, a camp closed but also simply "to sites and other situations related to onward movement of population."

CSI was intended to "restore feelings of choice and empowerment to beneficiaries," which could only mean that financial support helped migrants decide to stay on the trail rather than to return home when travel plans were delayed. Some form of CIS had been around for years, I learned, but really ramped up during Trump's migration crisis in 2019.

By the time Biden's crisis had dwarfed any prior one, the UN was planning a massive expansion. UN agencies were handing out cash and other material support to intending illegal border crossers in as many as one hundred shelters it helped build, expand, or support from South America north along the known routes.

I saw the debit cards yet again some months later, this time while in the far southern Mexican city of Tapachula. There, I found the same long lines of multinational clientele outside a UN High Commission on Refugees building applying for their cards. At the time, Mexico was blocking forward travel from Tapachula until migrants could get word on Mexican asylum applications they had to file. That could take months, so the money kept them on the trail.

Down there, a single migrant might get $180 a month. It was cheaper to buy necessities in Tapachula than in Reynosa in the north. Workers wearing UN blue shirts and carrying clipboards worked the long line. They set appointments and answered questions about the benefits.

UNHCR Tapachula did acknowledge the debit card program in responses to my written questions. The bottom line was that the cash reduces the suffering of the most vulnerable people, local spokeswoman Silvia Garduno wrote to me, "who have international protection needs, including those with particular vulnerabilities such as children at risk, single mothers, sexual- and gender-based violence survivors, and people with medical needs."

But if "particular vulnerabilities" of single mothers was the main criteria to qualify for a card, it's unclear how their dire need is ever verified. They clearly did not demand bank statements from a Haitian mother of two teens named Jeudy.

U.S. journalist Chuck Holton met Jeudy in Colombia as she was preparing to cross the Darien Gap to the U.S. border with her teenage daughter and teenage son from Chile.[355] His story about the family's Chile-to-New Jersey journey explains that Jeudy, who watched the U.S. election closely for cues that a Democrat would win, saved much of the $600 per month she earned from three years of working as a maître'd at an upscale restaurant. Once Biden won and opened the border to families, she deposited the savings with a friend who would wire cash to her on the trail as needed.

Despite the hefty savings account, Jeudy still applied for a cash card in Tapachula—and got one! It paid her $200 a month. The adjudicators probably took the unverified word of others who had plenty of means to travel and needed no assistance.

One of the men I met in line at Tapachula, a Haitian named Luis Ponce, said he was waiting to complain to someone that the UN was in arrears. The international agency had not recharged his debit card–linked local bank account with the 3,600 pesos owed (about $180). He showed me the yellow and gray plastic card had a UNHCR/ACNUR insignia in the upper third left corner.

"We don't have money now," he complained.

Others said they were in line to get applications started because, why not? How much the migrants get and for how long is a mystery I was never able to sort out. I did meet one Honduran mother of two in Tapachula who drew $180 a month from the card for three months, and the UN told her that was all they could give. She said she would have returned home with the kids were it not for that.

To some border security proponents, all this looks, feels, and acts like the UN is using American tax dollars to support the collapse of the U.S. southern border and to help needlessly import national security threats from the rest of the world.

Indeed, the State Department provides tens of millions of dollars to UN agencies handing out cash. In turn, the IOM spent more than $60 million in 2019 for activities in the northern part of South America, Central America, and Mexico during the so-called "caravan migrant crisis" earlier that year, its public budget reports. Biden's 2022 budget called for $10 billion in humanitarian assistance "to support vulnerable people abroad." There was no detailed breakout.

However much American money is paying for this, Republican lawmakers reacted with outrage when I reported witnessing the IOM and UNHCR handing out these cards in Reynosa and Tapachula.[356]

"All of this sounds like they're using U.S. tax dollars to encourage this invasion into the nation, and it seems strange to me that we would support an organization that encourages and funds this," Representative Lance Gooden, (R-TX), told me. "It's totally crazy. I am baffled that there's not more outrage, but I think the lack of outrage is due to the lack of knowledge."

Gooden and eleven lawmakers cosponsored the "No Tax Dollars for the United Nations Immigration Invasion Act" bill to prohibit the $3.8 billion contribution the Biden White House was proposing to give the UN in 2022.[357]

Public accounting for this UN program is typically opaque. In 2020, the UN doubled the number of countries where "Cash-based Assistance" is used and increased by 77 percent the number of recipients to 1.6 million worldwide, including somewhere between 10,000 and 100,000 people just in Mexico that year, according to an annual 2020 IOM report.[358] That's not very specific, but in 2021 the IOM was clearly intending a sharp upward trajectory for the cash giveaways in alignment with a fairly recent pact among an international consortium of organizations known as "The Grand Bargain," of which IOM is a signatory.[359] The Grand Bargain pact dates to 2016.

An Inter-Agency Standing Committee Grand Bargain website reports that number three on the objectives list was to "increase the use and coordination of cash-based programming."[360] A November 26, 2021, Grand Bargain caucus on cash coordination had all principals agree to increase the use of cash "beyond current low levels" using more means of delivery.

I'd met far too many international immigrants to know that cash alone, which might help them stay on the road, was not what was drawing them. They always told me they were coming because Biden opened the gates, but the cash almost certainly helps keep thousands on the road.

Death Threat

Among smuggler drivers I'd met around the Los Chiles bus station, I'd gotten along best with Felix, a short, thick-set Nicaraguan, forty-two, with a trimmed goatee and military haircut. He had a wife and daughter back in Managua but rarely got to see them because of the army desertion thing. I may have won over Felix by showing him my older video reports on my cell phone. He flashed interest when I told him I'd put him in my next one if he'd take me out on a border drop.

Finally, one day, Felix fished three tall, young Haitian men off a bus and agreed that we could follow him the next morning but not to La Trocha.

That plan was to hand off the Haitians to some Nicaraguan soldiers Felix knew who would charge them each $150 to escort them to a river boat. Felix assured me that he'd checked with the soldiers by cell phone and they were fine with an American writer coming along. I did wonder how the soldiers might react if some American guy recorded them taking bribes. I was grateful that my interpreter, Federico, made his regular living in executive protection and proved himself when we fled La Trocha.

Unbeknownst to me until much later, Felix took us out there in defiance of bitter opposition from other bus stop drivers who theorized that I was an International Criminal Police Organization (Interpol) agent. They threatened Felix with violent repercussions if he took me out to the transaction.

"I told them to fuck off," Felix laughed later when he told us this on the return trip.

With an associate at the wheel of a white 4x4 jeep of some foreign make, Felix set off with the three Haitians. I followed in my airport rental car for about fifty miles through the same familiar pineapple plantations until we halted at an inauspicious small farm on the Costa Rica side and a small clearing in the jungle on the Nicaragua side. After Felix and the Haitians got out of the jeep, its driver sped away, unexpectedly leaving Felix with us. Felix walked me over to the small jungle clearing on the Nicaragua side and showed me paths leading from it as I videotaped him.

"Here in Nicaragua, the boys from the army should be somewhere around in hiding waiting for the foreigners to cross so that they can get some *coinear* [money]," he explained.

About ten minutes later, two soldiers in camouflage uniforms with AK-47s strapped across their chests pulled up on a motorcycle. The driver, evidently a subordinate, waited for his superior to hop off the back, then put the bike on its kickstand and dismounted. He walked about ten yards to one side and repositioned the weapon to a readier position while Felix spoke to the sergeant about us. Both soldiers eyed me and my interpreter hard across the dirt road by the farm, clearly not liking the view, at all. I tried a disarming smile and wave, then started toward them, assuming Felix prepped them for an interview. But the sergeant waved an outstretched palm for me to stop. "No photography!" Felix said. I'd gotten about fifteen seconds' worth from about my waist.

"Oh, *lo siento, mi amigo*," I apologized, halting. I knew I wasn't going to get my interview.

After exchanging some more words with the sergeant, Felix announced that it was time for everyone but the Haitians to leave right away. As I pulled away with Felix in the back seat he told me that just one of the three $150 payments equaled a full month's salary for privates in the Nicaraguan military.

It had still been a worthwhile outing. But as we were reaching the outskirts of Los Chiles, seemingly out of nowhere, a large, red, jacked-up 4x4 Suburban with oversized tires suddenly roared up to my flank, then up to even with my closed driver's side window. A man was leaning out of the opened passenger side window to his waist with both arms gesticulating as he cut loose a stream of profanity at full lung force. In Spanish, he let fly some invective for maybe fifteen seconds, his face twisted in rage. The only part I really caught was *"tu puto hijo de puta gringo...!!!"* The truck stormed forward and away up the dirt road and disappeared.

"What the hell was that?" I asked Federico, my heart already pounding. I turned to Felix in the back seat. He was visibly shaken, his eyes reflecting fear.

That man leaning out from the truck had just vowed that none of us were going leave Los Chiles alive with the story and that the fucking gringo was going to go first. He and Felix exchanged some words in Spanish and translated. Those were some of the men who had most vociferously warned Felix not to take us. Felix's driver must have gone back and confirmed we'd done it.

"Is this something we really need to worry about?" I asked Federico.

"That right there was a credible death threat," he answered. "We can't even stay the night."

"Felix? Do you have an opinion?" I asked.

"You should not stay in Los Chiles."

Neither, apparently, would Felix. Although we were still a few miles from town, he suddenly asked me to pay the $100 I'd originally pledged to cover his diesel. He bailed out of the car.

Federico donned his executive protection hat. His main concern was that the red truck guys had set up an ambush ahead or, if not, an unpleasant surprise at our hotel in town. Federico directed me into a series of maneuvers, like driving down a side street to see what followed, then reemerging, driving some, then parking to observe the surroundings.

Eventually, we neared our hotel but parked several blocks away so we could watch the area for smuggling drivers. We had some calming beer at a local saloon while we watched the street approaches to the hotel, then did a slow drive-by and came up with an exit strategy.

We parked backward in one of the parking spaces, popped the trunk and walked calmly to our rooms. Inside, I quickly jammed all my belongings into my duffel, walked out, threw it in the open trunk at the same time as Federico. We hopped in and gunned the little rental out of town. There was just one more dragnet, the ride past the bus stop where all the drivers hung out and knew my rental. We white-knuckled it on past and ended up staying in a pleasant eco-resort hotel fifty miles away in a remote national park.

Dinner tasted really good there.

CHAPTER TWELVE

TERRORISTS IN THE WIRE

Having often written of the politically taboo threat of Islamic terrorist border crossings and even a book about it (*America's Covert Border War, The Untold Story of The Nation's Battle to Prevent Jihadist Infiltration*), I have long had to contend with ungenerous big-media "fact-check" articles and columnist claims that no such thing has ever happened, that even saying it out loud constituted a fear-mongering lie. Aggravating the denialism that Islamist terrorists sometimes crossed, the federal government for years showed a disinclination to release information proving these incidents.

So, few other people could have been more surprised than me in April 2022 to find a brand-new addition to the U.S. Customs and Border Protection "Enforcement Statistics" page titled, "Terrorist Screening Database Encounters," which is government terminology for the FBI terror watch list.[361] In other words, Biden's CBP "newsroom" site added a new public page, updated monthly, showing the number of crossings by immigrants whose connections and involvements with terrorism, long before they reached the border, had gotten them nominated and approved to be on the FBI's watch list.

It tells us that a new record-breaking first can be added to the Biden border crisis: Border Patrol apprehended more "non-U.S. citizens" on the FBI's terrorism watch list crossing the southwest border between ports of entry in fiscal year 2022—ninety-eight—some 500 percent more than in the prior five years combined. In all, from the time Biden was elected through August 2022, Border Patrol caught some 114 on the terror watch list sneaking through between ports of entry.

In May 2022 alone, Border Patrol caught fifteen on the terrorism watch list, the same number that was caught in the entire fiscal 2021. Border Patrol caught twelve more in August 2022, then twenty more in September 2022. These numbers compare to three when Trump was last in office in 2020 and had the border tamped down fairly tightly, zero in 2019, six in 2018, and two in 2017, according to the CBP page.

For a sense of proportion, that number may seem minuscule compared to the broader totals tallied in this book. However, the proper way to consider ninety-four watch-listed immigrants illegally crossing the southern border is that it is more than five times the number that carried out the 9/11 attacks, which sent the United States to war in Afghanistan for two decades. People on the terror watch list are not just any economic immigrants; they pose a national security threat portending hugely outsized consequences for the nation.

Numbers tell us some things but not much about who these people are. In November 2022, I visited a non-profit immigrant shelter in Tijuana's Zona Norte built by the Latina Muslim Foundation in San Diego, within eyesight of the border wall. The facility provided halal food, shelter, legal, medical, psychological, dental, and movement assistance to Muslim immigrants hoping to get into the United States. Over a few days, I met and tried to interview immigrants who'd traveled there from Chechnya, Tajikistan, Afghanistan, Kazakhstan, Uzbekistan, Yemen and Somalia.

"If America would let me in to live, I would be the first to repay my new country by defending it against terrorists," one bearded young Chechen told me when I asked if U.S. authorities should worry about his background.

Unlike immigrants I'd interviewed for years who were from all over the rest of the world, none of these ones would be interviewed at length nor photographed.

I couldn't possibly attest to the backgrounds of anyone in the steady stream of immigrants I watched spilling out of taxis in front of the center who were coming from countries of U.S. national security concern.

But some there came from the same countries as the first and second suspected terrorists known to have crossed the quickly deteriorating Biden border in January and March 2021, Border Patrol caught a Yemeni man near Calexico, California, a two-hour drive from Tijuana. He was thirty-three years old. To be sure, many Yemenis would probably like to flee their war-torn and famine-stricken nation and live in the United States instead. Yemen is one of the world's most impoverished nations even in the absence of war. But this man afforded the tens of thousands of dollars I know such a journey would cost. He was not only on the FBI's terrorism watch list, he was also on the higher-threshold no-fly list. Something else about this case was disturbing; Border Patrol agents found that this Yemeni had hidden a cellular phone SIM card underneath the insole of his shoe.[362] What run-of-the-mill economic migrant does *that*?

The same press release boasted of a second apprehension of a Yemeni two months later in March 2021 who also was on the watch list. This one was caught two miles west of the Calexico port of entry. He was twenty-six, and in addition to being on the FBI's terror watch list, he too was on the no-fly list. No one knows if the two were connected. Or if, in turn, they were tied to a twenty-one-year-old supposed Saudi Arabian caught months later that year in Yuma.

The Yuma sector's chief Border Patrol agent, Chris T. Clem, announced the apprehension in a tweet, that the twenty-one-year-old was on the watch list with ties to a terrorist organization.[363] Chief Clem's posting showed a blurred photo of the man and said he had ties to some Yemeni terror suspects but did not say if he meant the ones caught in California.

At least these guys and the other 110 plus got caught. But this record breaks at a terrible time. If ninety-four on the terror watch list were caught in those eighteen months, the fair question is: How many were among the 900,000 runners who got away clean?

There should be no question in anyone's mind that more suspected Islamic terrorists began crossing the southern border as part of the vast increase in multinational immigration from around the globe, probably knowing that policies had crashed normal border defenses.

Some terrorist crossings that I know happened during this time period suggest that normal vetting management systems designed to catch terrorist infiltrators were faltering under the strains of this crisis. My book, *America's Covert Border War*, revealed a longstanding counterterrorism apparatus the American government built after 9/11 to guard the land borders against jihadist infiltration. The programs worked well, catching terrorists, breaking up their long-haul smuggling networks, and preventing attacks on the homeland from the southern flank.

Don't take this just from me. On March 16, 2021, DHS Secretary Mayorkas acknowledged at a U.S. House Homeland Security Committee hearing that terrorists did cross the border but that a "multi-layered security apparatus" neutralized them.[364]

"A known or suspected terrorist—KST is the acronym that we use—individuals who match that profile, have tried to cross the border, the land border...not only this year but last year, the year prior and so on and so forth," Mayorkas testified. The "architecture that we built" after 9/11 did catch border-crossing migrants from countries of terrorism concern, Mayorkas said, and "ensure that they do not remain in the United States."

But evidence began to emerge that that Mayorkas's security apparatus, even though it caught ninety or one hundred on the FBI terror watch list, was crumbling under the weight of the crisis.

"High-Risk" Suspected Terrorist Freed to Protect Him from Covid

Exhibit one is the case of Lebanon-born Venezuelan Issam Bazzi, which first came to my attention when Pulitzer Prize–

winning former *New York Times* writer Charlie LeDuff of Detroit first reported about it in January 2022.[365] Someone in the federal government was angry enough about this case to leak documents about it. I have them.

Bazzi was among a swell of Venezuelans who began crossing the Rio Grande in escalating numbers in the closing months of 2021 on confirmation that the United States was handing them free passes into the interior. Some 25,000 turned themselves in at the border in December 2021 and another 22,000 did in January 2022. According to the leaked DHS documents, Bazzi flew with his wife and daughter to Monterrey, Mexico, in early November, then swam the river into Brownsville.

He flagged on the FBI's terrorism watch list. As is part and parcel of America's covert border war programs for when watch-listed immigrants are caught at the border, FBI agents interrogated him in the ICE detention facility in Pearsall, Texas. The agents found that the intelligence file on the fifty-year-old Bazzi "contains substantial high side derogatory information," the leaked DHS records show. They determined he was a high national security risk but also a flight risk, one of the government documents noted, and strongly recommended that ICE hold him.

In 2019, U.S. authorities denied Bazzi a tourist visa to visit relatives in the Detroit area, citing his FBI terrorism watch list status, the documents show. Back then, at least, those systems worked in keeping a suspected terrorist out of the country. But not during the chaotic swell of the border crisis.

I revealed in *America's Covert Border War* that whenever a watch-listed immigrant is caught, the government deports them after investigations are complete. In fact, the USCIS website notes that "generally, any individual who is a member of a terrorist organization…is inadmissible and is ineligible for most immigration benefits."[366] Even one of the very few categories in Biden's sharply constricted list of deportation-eligible immigrants was terrorists. At the time, the U.S. was completing a deal with Colombia to accept deportations of Venezuelans.[367]

ICE headquarters ordered Bazzi released from ICE custody in defiance of FBI agent recommendations that he remain in custody.

The given reason? Bazzi was overweight and therefore at risk of catching Covid-19, the files show.

What this outrage says to me, and evidently to the angry government professional who leaked records about it, is that a crucial border defense failed in its national security function. Instead of a deportation to Colombia, Bazzi's illegal border crossing had him living free on his own recognizance in Detroit while he pursued an asylum claim.

That's the least of the evidence that Biden's avoidable mass migration crisis has degraded a once-managed national security threat.

Overrun Mexico Freed a Suspected Terrorist from Yemen

That goes for counterterrorism on the Mexican side, which people forget also was overrun with immigrants. Consider the case of Yemeni national Ahmed Mohammed. In April 2021, Mexican immigration caught him in Piedras Negras as he was about to cross into Eagle Pass and notified the FBI legal attaché in Mexico City, according to a leaked state government document I have. Mohammed flagged on the FBI's watch list as a member of a terrorist organization. Eventually, the Mexicans deported Ahmed to Yemen. The deportation didn't take. An American law enforcement intelligence source told me the Mexican intelligence officers prematurely left him at a European transit airport and returned to Mexico. Ahmed abandoned his connecting flight and went right back to Mexico. The Mexicans caught him again in Piedras Negras, in July 2021, preparing to cross to the same area of Texas.

But by then, Mexico was struggling to manage historic numbers of aliens illegally crossing between its own ports of entry, more than 200,000 of them apprehended that terrible month on the American side. But instead of deporting him a second time, Mexico flushed Ahmed out with all the other migrants clogging its detention facilities in November 2021.

On his way to freedom, the Mexicans handed him a "humanitarian visa" and asked him to voluntarily report to Mexican immigration once a week.

Right. Ahmed naturally disappeared.

His release evidently so alarmed the Americans that they sent out a "be on the lookout" (BOLO) bulletin to law enforcement on the Texas side to capture him.

I don't know if Ahmed was ever caught.

Suspected Terrorist Release Triggers Manhunt Inside U.S.

Still more cases point to floundering border counterterrorism defenses.

In May 2022, another record-setting month for apprehensions at 210,946, Fox News's Adam Sabes and Bill Melugin reported from leaked internal law enforcement documents that Border Patrol released Colombian national Isnardo Garcia-Amado along with tens of thousands overrunning the Yuma sector in Arizona through a gap left in Trump's wall.

But Garcia-Amado was not just any border-jumping "asylum-seeker."

Border Patrol would have found him on FBI's terror watch list had they not been too busy to check a database before releasing him.[368] At that time and place, a volcanic eruption of border crossings was underway in Yuma sector, which ended the month with more than 30,000 apprehensions, 10,000 of them Colombians.

Not until three days after Border Patrol released Garcia-Amado into interior America did someone finally run his name and fingerprints in databases and find that he is flagged on the FBI terrorism watch list. The FBI and ICE scrambled for a nationwide manhunt. It took federal agents nearly two weeks to arrest him in Florida. We may never know how close a call this was. But what this case and others prove beyond any doubt is that collapsing border management systems have left America more vulnerable to jihadist attack from the border than at any time since 9/11. And also that foreign terrorists are well aware of it.

Foreign Terrorists Discover Broken Border and Go for It

Confirmation of this came from a May 2022 Ohio terrorism indictment of a self-proclaimed ISIS fighter from Iraq who got inside the United States as a tourist and then claimed asylum. Shihab Ahmed Shihab Shibah allegedly plotted to smuggle up to eight members of a terrorist hit squad over the southern border to kill former President George W. Bush at his Dallas home, the arrest warrant affidavit alleges.[369]

Shihab was a self-proclaimed ISIS fighter who claimed to have killed "many Americans in Iraq between 2003 and 2006" while operating in a hit squad translating to "Thunder."

Despite this history, Shihab flew into America in September 2020, on a tourist visa. When it expired, he applied for asylum and stayed to carry out a plot hatched by an ISIS leader based in Qatar. They plotted to smuggle in his former team members over the southern border, probably because the conspirators figured the men were on Western intelligence radars, thus "dirty."

Plans called for each to pay $40,000 to fly into Brazil on fraudulently obtained visas, then through the Darien Gap and over the U.S.-Mexico border wearing faux Border Patrol uniforms, the charging documents alleged. The FBI got a couple of paid informants inside the plot, thankfully. Worryingly, Shihab boasted to the informants that he'd already smuggled in two Hezbollah operatives. While the FBI informants obviously weren't real, it appears that the Thunder men, the Qatar cleric, and the smuggled Hezbollah operatives were real.

Chief among takeaways from this revelatory case is that we should all presume that other America-hating violent Islamists around the world see the southern border chaos as an opportunity to access the country with lower risk of detection than in normal times—and that they know exactly how to do it.

The fact that several of these case examples came from leaked government documents also suggests that homeland security professionals are so worried or angry about these lapses that they feel compelled to warn us. Career homeland security professionals evidently felt the heat too.

Reward

In October 2021, as the border and all who work on it were drowning in live bodies coming over, the U.S. State Department offered a $2 million reward that was rare for a mere international human smuggler.

It was for information leading to the arrest of Abid Ali Khan. The fugitive Pakistani oversaw an intercontinental network that for years had transported Afghans, Pakistanis, and Middle Easterners through the Darien Gap, Costa Rica, and Nicaragua to the American border.[370]

Prosecutors in Miami had already indicted Khan in absentia for moving men from that part of the world out of Nowshera, Pakistan, which is known as a center of violent Islamic militancy.

In a sign of just how much of a priority Khan became after the American pullout from Afghanistan, the Treasury Department designated Khan and three others in his network as a transnational criminal organization, which puts the network's ability to move money around at risk.[371]

The government's announcements of these moves passed entirely under the American media radar, perhaps because they did not mention terrorism, national security, the fall of Kabul, or the historic Darien Gap surge then underway. But various government announcements about the Khan network did indicate reasons for its new high priority.

The Khan network transported "people with nefarious motivations" into the United States, Anthony Salisbury, special agent in charge of ICE's Homeland Security Investigations, noted in a press release that busy April. He added that his Miami team was committed to prosecuting people like Khan who "pose a threat to national security."[372] Afghans do cross the southern border, not in large numbers, but regularly because a route from there runs through Gulf States like Qatar and Dubai to the Western Hemisphere, then through the Darien Gap. Afghans pose elevated security risks just by virtue of the prevalence of Taliban sympathy and involvements with extremist combatant groups in their country like al-Qaeda and ISIS.

About fifty Afghan evacuees resettled in the United States amid the chaotic U.S. final withdrawal in 2021 turned out to have had derogatory intelligence information in their files flagging them as potential terrorist threats.[373] Those who were spurned for special immigrant visas when the U.S. military withdrew from Afghanistan are already crossing the southern border. Agents down there send me their photos.

The government moves sought to pressure Khan and smugglers like him "who seek to profit from…jeopardizing our national security," Acting Assistant Attorney General Nicholas L. McQuaid of the Justice Department's Criminal Division noted in a Treasury Department statement.

All these moves almost assuredly were related to the crush of humanity then moving through the Darien Gap, and for good reason.

CHAPTER THIRTEEN

OF STRANGERS, WARLORDS, AND SPIES

My collection of disfigured and discarded passports and identity cards of Africans among many other nationalities from around the world should inspire no peace of mind anywhere. I find them on the banks of both sides of the Rio Grande, destroyed just before and after illegal entries. I keep a grocery bag full of these in my home office as a reminder that the multinational traffic pouring over the southern border carries very different kinds of public security menaces.

Immigrants who rip up their identity documents as they cross into America are up to no good. What that may be, no one may know for a while.

I have met people on their way to America who hail from Iran, Syria, Pakistan, Uzbekistan, Russia, and most of the countries of Africa.

A fair question is what's the problem with granting refuge to people fleeing from places as terrible as those?

My answer is informed mostly by a homeland security intelligence career, which points to the fact that many of the countries whose citizens cross the American border are awash in tribal warfare, atrocities, and human rights violations. Even when border flows are relatively low and managed, American homeland security agencies are challenged to ever discern persecuted from persecutor. Others are arriving from adversarial nations, such as Iran, China, Russia, and Venezuela, posing the threat of espionage or terrorism.

All bets are off learning who is what when human swells this large entirely submerge border control management systems as they did starting in January 2021. From the beginning of the Biden border crisis, DHS has too quickly ushered thousands of people of unknown histories from these troubled distant lands to ever properly investigate histories, hearts, and minds.

Cooking and Eating the Hearts of Victims

Stepping through the ruins of America's collapsing southern border infrastructure are thousands of people from some of the most deeply ill nations in Africa teaming with tribal warlords and vicious armed militias that rape, pillage, plunder, and murder. In fairness, many of the Africans and those I've met on the trail from similarly bloodied nations like Sierra Leone and Liberia may very well have been persecuted victims of these militias as they say.

But "Jungle Jabbah" of Liberia was certainly not one of the persecuted. His real name is Mohammed Jabbateh, and he had been a resident of Philadelphia for nearly twenty years after arriving from Liberia and claiming asylum in 1998. He was among thousands of Liberians fleeing the wars and resettling in Pennsylvania. But in the life he left in Liberia, Jungle Jabbah served as a commander of the United Liberation Movement of Liberia for Democracy during that country's first civil war, from 1989 to 1997.

During his "service," Jabbateh and his soldiers wantonly murdered civilian noncombatants, sexually enslaved women, tortured and executed prisoners of war, desecrated corpses and ritually ate their victims. He would have hearts cut from chests and cooked for his soldiers to eat, according to testimony from Jabbateh's 2017 immigration fraud trial in Pennsylvania. In one instance, fighters under his command murdered a villager, removed his heart, and ordered the town chief's wife to cook it, then killed the town chief and forced her to cook his heart.[374]

This was the man who easily lied his way on immigration applications to twenty years of sanctuary as a neighbor to American citizens until ICE Homeland Security Investigations caught up to him and he landed a thirty-year prison sentence—at considerable investigative and prosecutorial time and expense to U.S. taxpayers to root him out.

He "committed acts of such violence and depravity that they are almost beyond belief," U.S. Attorney William M. McSwain said in a 2018 press release announcing the prison sentence for immigration fraud. "This man is responsible for atrocities that will ripple for generations in Liberia."

Tactics of "Unimaginable Brutality"

Moses Slanger Wright of Philadelphia wasn't one of Liberia's persecuted civilian victims either. His past caught up to him only in June 2022, when federal prosecutors in Philadelphia indicted the sixty-nine-year-old Liberian for lying all over his refugee and immigration applications for years, the most recent being a final citizenship bid. What was he allegedly lying about so successfully for years since the United States granted him asylum in 2000? During Liberia's first civil war, from 1989 to 1997, he served as the "commanding general" in President Charles Taylor's National Patriotic Front of Liberia. His men and victims knew him as "General Moses."

"Wright either personally committed, or ordered Armed Forces of Liberia troops under his command to commit numerous atrocities, including…the persecution, murder, and assault of civilian noncombatant Gio and Mano tribesmen, as well as false arrest and false imprisonment of civilian combatants," the indictment alleged.[375]

Among other Liberians who lied their way into American sanctuary was "General Dragon Master," Laye Sekou Camara, who was among thousands of Liberian civil war refugees who resettled in the Philadelphia region after the western African nation's wars. General Dragon Master got into the country in 2011 on an asylum claim and won a green card in 2012. A May 2022 indictment accuses Camara of lying on various immigration forms to cover up the fact that he led a rebel group called Liberians United for Reconciliation and Democracy, or LURD, which fought against Taylor in Liberia's second civil war from 1999–2003.[376]

"The defendant in this case is alleged to have served as a high-ranking general for a rebel group that fought in the Second Liberian Civil War, all the while employing tactics of unimaginable brutality, including the recruitment of child soldiers," William S. Walker, special agent in charge of the Homeland Security Investigations Philadelphia Field Office.

Jabbateh, Wright, and Camara did not come over the border as complete strangers. But therein lies the problem with border entries. These three entered legally with oversight, applications, and interviews. They easily defeated the system.

No paperwork or interviews stand in the way at Biden's border. Many come in with no identification at all, their documents ending up in my home office grocery bag.

Take the Democratic Republic of Congo, whose citizens are well represented among those crossing the southern border during this crisis. The Congo features a multisided regional conflict with marauders having rampaged for years through villages, going on raping, killing, kidnapping, and looting sprees. Their atrocities and massacres in the eastern part of that country are the stuff of horror films and, hopefully, future international war crimes tribunals in The Hague.

Setting aside militia-backed tribalism, the Islamic State claimed its first attack in the Congo in 2019, killing eight government soldiers on behalf of a self-proclaimed entity it calls the "Central Africa Province of the Caliphate."[377] The Congo Research Group issued a report in November 2018 documenting the increasing spread of Islamist jihadist ideology among some groups and allied militias, particularly in eastern DRC, which seems very much akin to ISIS ideology.[378] Much of this trend seems to have seeding in the Ugandan Allied Democratic Forces, a particularly brutal militia with operations throughout the DRC's east that was rebranding itself as an ISIS franchise and whose members were largely composed of converts to Islam.[379] Thousands of violent militia fighters have been sprung in mass prison breaks in recent years.

Cameroon is another African nation whose citizens are among those crossing the southern border and who likewise defy easy sorting. Warfare between the French-speaking government and the country's separatist English-speaking population in the western part of the country has driven thousands of refugees into neighboring countries like Nigeria.[380]

The U.S.-backed Cameroonian military has been accused of arresting, murdering, torturing, and accosting anyone suspected of working with the English-speaking Anglophone separatists, who run militias with names like the Red Dragon, Tigers, and Ambazonia Defense Forces. Most of the Cameroonians I've met are Anglophones; they speak English. But credible reports have Anglophone militias committing their share of atrocities on Francophone targets.[381]

Millions have died in Congo and Cameroon warfare in successions of violent spasms. But why must U.S. homeland security default to a coin toss when a military-aged man from such countries cross the American border with some totally unverifiable tale of woe? The Biden border crisis ups the odds that some will game the U.S. asylum system to evade war crimes justice or perhaps to even some day commit violent acts in American cities. Both are avoidable and unacceptable.

American hearts naturally go out to people fleeing war-torn states in Africa like Ethiopia.

But few Americans would likely want to see someone like the Ethiopian Mezemr Abebe Belayneh slip into the country and enjoy many years of refuge from the justice he richly deserves. In 2021, federal prosecutors indicted the sixty-five-year-old Ethiopian for covering up his participation as a torturing interrogator during Ethiopia's 1976–1978 "Red Terror" campaign. At that time, he belonged to a Marxist-Leninist group known as the "Derg," which had resorted to unspeakable brutalities to consolidate government power from its rival, the communist Ethiopian People's Revolutionary Party. The Derg was rounding up EPRP supporters and would torture and execute them in makeshift prisons.

Belayneh ran such an operation out of a hotel in the town of Dilla, Ethiopia, from 1977 to 1978, the indictment reads, during which time he "interrogated, severely beat, and ordered others under his control to severely beat members and perceived members of the EPRP who were detained."

He didn't come in over the border as did plenty from Ethiopia and neighboring countries have in recent years—and still are; I have seen their entries in hotel guest books and I've interviewed them in ICE detention. But if anyone should have been found out, it was Belayneh by going through an official vetting system. He won a visa lottery in 2001, then lied on all the government forms and flew in. He eventually achieved citizenship in 2008.

Anyone coming in over the border would go through a fraction of the possible discovery opportunities as people who entered like Belayneh, Jungle Jabba, and "General Moses," which underscores the broader problem of checking personal histories in premodern Africa even in the best of circumstances.

Nothing in the court record indicates that Belayneh and the rest visited their brutal ways on Americans. But that's not the point here. Americans should never have to accept homicidal criminals hiding in their midst or the prospect people predisposed to extreme violence may one day lash out again.

More than anything, these non-border cases underscore the extreme difficulties that American border security and intelligence agencies will eventually have to confront at the land border, when they show up with their totally unverifiable tales of woe and missing identify papers.

Spies and Other Adversaries

Other than countries where Islamic terrorist groups live and breathe, the flooding new multinational river brings potential adversaries who may be well trained to avoid detection.

Many Americans might feel surprised to know that the Border Patrol regularly catches Iranian migrants at the southern border.[382] And when they do cross, Iranians almost always draw a different kind of visitor to the detention center: intelligence officers and FBI agents who—in normal flow times—operate at a higher orbit of thinking about their detained subjects. Could these Iranians be fleeing a brutal theocracy that persecutes gays, Christians, and moderate political opponents?

Or are they infiltrating spies or assassins sent to finally retaliate—as Iran's ruling clerics vowed and swore they would—for the January 2020 U.S. drone-strike assassination of Iran's Islamic Revolutionary Guard Corps Quds Force General Qassem Soleimani?

What about Chinese immigrants who have crossed over the southern border by the thousands for many years? Why wouldn't the Chinese Communist Party send a few spies in among them?

The short answer is that America's homeland security apparatus is not equipped to know for a very long time, if ever, who any of these people really are. That is sometimes known as a "wicked" homeland security problem without a solution other than to simply reduce the gusher to a trickle.

Tens of thousands showed at the border from Ukraine, where organized mafia syndicates have long run black markets in human trafficking, drugs, and vice while ruling over their domains by coercion and murder.[383] Ukrainian syndicates are notorious in their brutality and international reach, and they would love to work their rackets in the United States.

In coming to the United States, they took a pass on rich offers that no other border-crossing immigrant I know of had in hand: invitations to live in any of twenty-seven European Union countries for three years, the wealthiest in the world, with full access to subsidized housing, food, and medical care. We will only learn about the bad apples imported in with them after expensive, time-consuming federal racketeering charges are brought years from now.

Who can forget the 1980 Mariel Boatlift from Cuba that imported the populations of Fidel Castro's prisons and mental health facilities into naively welcoming American arms in Florida and beyond, with criminal impacts so notorious and long-lived that they inspired the Al Pacino movie *Scarface*? Sources and journalist friends who work among the immigrants in Mexico swear that Venezuelan President Nicolas Madura has emptied out his prisons to the United States and that many of them are crossing the southern border with no vetting whatsoever. If this is true on any significant scale, expect newer iterations of the *Scarface* movie over the next decade.

PART IV

SCHIZOPHRENIA

CHAPTER FOURTEEN

"BIDENVILLE"—REVELATIONS FROM THE DEL RIO MIGRANT CAMP CRISIS

One Sunday evening—it was September 11, 2021—a few hundred Haitian immigrant families walked across a shallow Rio Grande and claimed asylum to the Border Patrol under the Del Rio-Acuña International Bridge. It was the standard drill immigrant parents knew would get their families ushered into America.

But the Haitians kept coming. By the thousands.

The next morning, Monday, they numbered 2,000, then 4,000 by nightfall, then 6,000 by the time I showed up Tuesday night. By Wednesday morning, they numbered 10,000. By the end of the week, they were 15,000, some said 17,000. They formed a mammoth, fetid, refugee encampment without modern precedent in America. It reminded me of war refugee camps I'd covered in the Middle East and Bosnia, or seen in the pages of *National Geographic* magazine.

"In my twenty-year career," a CBP officer told me when I showed up, "I have never seen anything this out of control."

In a flash, the area beneath Del Rio's bridge was in the international spotlight. A political nightmare for the White House, this couldn't be ignored like the hundreds of thousands that had poured in for eight months straight; the administration got them off the border fast to make sure they had no time to establish vast unsanitary camps that make for good nightly TV news. But Del Rio was different. It formed so fast and unexpectedly that, before it was all over some twelve days later, it would stand as a consequential fiasco in the broader crisis, a pivot in trajectory at the White House, throughout the borderlands, on the immigrants, and on Mexico's immigration policy and practice.

The Del Rio experience stands as an important laboratory-worthy case study for the lessons it yielded about how mass migration events start in a vacuum of vigilance and comprehension. And especially about what is necessary to end mass migrations fast, with finality, when there is simply the will.

The twelve-day camp forced the White House to openly call up Trump tactics it had condemned and cancelled as inhumane, to quickly end the camp's explosive growth and then liquidate it. Most of all, the Biden administration showed in Del Rio that it can end mass migration whenever it wants to.

Another of the camp episode's revelations was that it exposed an embarrassing degree of diplomatic disrespect by Mexico toward Biden's America. For as I'll exclusively show here, it was Mexico that set the Haitians toward the American border in one volatile mass in violation of agreements with the Biden administration.

To clear streets for a mere holiday party.

Finally, Del Rio is important to understand for one more very good reason. It spurred moderate Democrats inside the White House to rebel against "new theologian" excesses and revealed the presence of a sane faction in the party with whom Republicans could find common cause.

"Bidenville"

Even eight months into the chaos of the Biden border crisis, with record-smashing one million Border Patrol apprehensions to that point, the White House strategy was to pretend nothing amiss was happening at the border; major media only occasionally parachuted in to grudgingly acknowledge that something sort of unusual was happening down there. But none could ignore the dramatic visuals of the Del Rio camp.

At first, the administration chose the news blackout option. CBP officers refused to let media within 200 yards of the Haitians those first few days. When Fox News started flying its drone overhead, the Federal Aviation Administration decided right then was a great time for a new rule: no drones can fly near international bridges. When reporters got up on the bridge and pointed their cameras down on the sea of humanity below, authorities closed the bridge. I heard a National Guard soldier call the camp "Bidenville," with derision.

Luckily, Val Verde County Sheriff Joe Frank Martinez and I had a good relationship from my earlier reporting trips. Some chicken-wire fencing had gone up on the north and east sides of the camp. The sheriff drove me in his squad car through perimeter checkpoints of National Guard by their Humvees and into the heart of insanity.

A sea of men, women, and children enveloped us. They moved in every direction on all four sides of the squad car. The sheriff dared not drive more than a mile an hour or so. Young men roamed in groups of five or six. Women and men hauled young children or pulled them by hand as they strode purposefully here and there. In the shade of an industrial-sized mobile trash dumpster, rows of mothers cleaned diapers.

We cruised past a row of port-o-potties, the stench permeating through the closed squad car windows. Military men in their desert camouflage uniforms stood watch next to Humvees. Border Patrol agents on horseback clopped by my window and on ahead of us, raising dust.

To our right, groups of teens and adults with children sat or lay prone in the shade of a wall of trees and tall carrizo cane, flicking at iPhones. To our left, others slept on pieces of cardboard or dirt. To the front, still others balanced long stacks of carrizo cane stalks on shoulders, cut from thick riverside patches. Under the bridge, frames made of the stalks went up for shelters. Women with babies strapped to backs or carried in slings balanced various items atop their heads. Despite the big dumpster, piles of trash formed pyramids here and there.

"They look like they're all Haitians," I commented to the sheriff. "What's the story with that? Do you know where they're all from?" It was that early in the crisis.

"I don't," the sheriff responded.

With Sheriff Martinez translating Spanish, we rolled down windows to chat. Some said almost everyone in the camp was Haitian, but not all, and could speak Spanish with the sheriff because they had been living long enough in Chile to have learned the language.

One twenty-something Haitian man said in English why he decided to head for the border at this time.

"I wanted to come because I know American people have a good heart. That's why I come."

A man and woman, squeezing river water out of washed socks, said they were Cubans. They came to America now because they heard the border was open and they were going to be let in.

The greatest concentrations of people centered for several hundred yards directly in the shade of the north-south bridge in its shade, right up to the new fencing. Throngs of people also moved east and west, toward or away from the bridge along a white sandy road that paralleled the river for at least a half mile. The sheriff turned west onto the river road, our squad car still surrounded. Carrizo cane and a thick band of trees obstructed our view of the water but we could see some relieve themselves amid the trees. Laundry washed in the Rio Grande drooped from limbs and on rope strung between limbs.

After a time, we came to a large clearing that went down to the river. It was packed with people shoulder to shoulder alongside piles of stinking trash. It was manic down there, like someone had kicked an ant hill. This was the main entrance and exit to the camp. At the bottom of the clearing, a submerged concrete but walkable weir dam over which water spilled stretched about 150 yards across the Rio Grande to the Acuña side in Mexico. Immigrants two and three abreast splashed their way knee deep along the submerged concrete, coming and going both ways with supplies. You could tell the newcomers just entering the camp by the backpacks they carried toward the Del Rio side. Most were hauling in supplies from the Mexican side, jugs of water and bags of food.

Authorities on both sides had to let these illegal entries and exits happen, lest the responsibility for feeding a medium-sized town three square meals a day fall to unprepared governments. To that end, the Border Patrol had parked their vehicles at the Texas-side entry point. Texas National Guard soldiers occupied these, but orders had them standing down. They merely watched the immigrants come and go, as I had seen countless times during this border crisis. I noticed one playing a game on his cell phone.

Method in Mayhem

After the sheriff and I drove around for a while, the outlines of a method in the mayhem began to emerge at this early point in the camp crisis. In this method, I could see that a major humanitarian crisis had just fallen heavily onto the Biden administration's shoulders.

As readers of this book well know by now, rewarding illegal crossings with legalized resettlement always draws in more. That's what was happening. The camp was growing so fast on word of the releases that federal workers processing them into America could not keep up with the lengthening backlog.

This was my first clue that the Biden administration was going to have to act outside political character to close it down. Otherwise, the camp would become a long-lived political liability for the Democrats with midterm elections about a year away. Here's why drastic action was necessary.

Once new arrivals entered camp from the spillway, they were directed to covered mobile shade stations staffed by either Border Patrol agents or National Guard personnel. Over these tables, giant yellow signs read "TICKET." The immigrants got into long lines leading to these tables. When it was their turn, a soldier or Border Patrol agent registered the newcomer and tore a numbered ticket from a big roll, the kind common at any carnival or fairground booth. Elsewhere in the camp, I noticed other long lines. These were for the ticketholders whose numbers had been called. These immigrants would be taken by bus to a Border Patrol station for a day or two of processing, then released into the country with papers granting them temporary permission to remain and stating where and when they should report to ICE.

Math explained all the carrizo cane shelter construction and the Haitian man I saw hauling a full-sized bed mattress back to camp over the river spillway. More were coming in than leaving. The camp and wait times could only grow exponentially unless something drastic reversed this.

Anyone running DHS could see that, sooner or later, the government was going to have to come up with enough food, shelter, medical attention, and whatever else was needed to feed a small city for a very long time, all under the camera spotlight.

But privately, Border Patrol agents and Del Rio city officials saw a scenario even more terrifying. They feared a violent breakout of the sort that these very Haitian immigrants had repeatedly attempted only the week before in Mexico. In the worst of these imagined scenarios, thousands of Haitians would stream forward into Del Rio on foot, in front of television cameras, looting and marauding homes and businesses for food and water as they went.

"We have to be prepared for that," one CBP officer told me. "Because there's nothing that is going to stop them. All it takes is for one person to say, 'You know what, we don't need to be here. We can move.' There's nothing that we can do to hold them back. There's not enough officers or agents in the area to provide coverage for 8,000-plus immigrants."

If violent rioting had just worked in Mexico, it would work in Del Rio.

How a Mexican Holiday Founded a Riverbank Shantytown

Across the river from Del Rio in the Mexican city of Acuña, the central bus station hummed with action. Large commercial buses lumbered slowly through a wide turn from the public street every fifteen minutes and into the bay, for hours on end. Each bus disgorged Haitian men, women, and children until emptied, maybe a stray Mexican or two who lived in Acuña. The parents gathered their belongings from the storage compartment and, with their children, headed out to the streets looking for taxis to the river a mile away. They all knew, from social media, to get to that weir dam spillway and across to Del Rio and that the Americans were going to free them all into America.

When I was in the camp with Sheriff Martinez, I hadn't been able to interview people for longer than a minute. So I went with Auden Cabello, a local photographer and videographer friend who lived in Acuña, and together we made our way to the bus station on my hunch Haitians would be pouring out of buses there. I'd come to have them answer a simple question no one in the media seemed to be asking: Why did this camp form?

What they told me amounted to an outrageous story of diplomatic betrayal and disrespect.

First, recall that even before Biden was inaugurated, his emissaries pressured Mexico to maintain its National Guard soldiers on its southern border and immigration bureaucracy to break up caravans and slow the tens of thousands of Haitians and other immigrants coming in from all over the world.[384] The administration promised $4 billion in various kinds of aid to Mexico, Guatemala, Honduras, and El Salvador, and later large volumes of Covid-19 vaccinations. Thousands would build up behind the bureaucratic dam in Tapachula.

Mexico required the immigrants to wait for months until they could get Mexican asylum or other travel permits as their population built up.

These Haitians, the majority of them families, left Chili in waves starting in July 2021, determined to take advantage of the Biden administration's quick admission of families.[385] By August, an estimated 20,000 Haitians were bottled up. One Haitian named Baya, who was among those I interviewed getting off the bus in Acuña, said every couple of days for more than four months, he would check in at a Mexican immigration office about his papers. Always nothing, Baya said.

As September arrived, he and everyone he knew was feeling angry. During the first week of that September, thousands of Haitians violently demonstrated in Tapachula's streets, demanding to be given their papers now or be set free. Several times the Haitians formed caravans that tried to force through military roadblocks. But Mexican soldiers and riot police prevailed as Mexican President López Obrador vowed to prevent them from advancing.[386] But the violent clashes continued into the second week of September. For days, Mexican government forces battered the attacking caravans, clubbing Haitian men, women, and children back south.[387]

The immigrants could not possibly have known it at the time, but their agitations were threatening a cherished upcoming national Mexican holiday, the weeklong celebration known as El Grito de Independencia. Akin to the American Fourth of July, El Grito is celebrated every year for days starting on September 16 to commemorate a battle cry in the country's 1810 independence uprising against Spanish colonial rule.[388] It is regarded as one of Mexico's most revered holidays, and Haitian unrest was not going to mix well with the planned weeklong parades, parties, fireworks, and family gatherings in Tapachula. So, the Mexicans fixed the problem, notwithstanding agreements with the Biden administration to hold back caravans.

On or about September 10, one day after really violent clashes and with the September 16 El Grito celebration bell about to toll, immigration office officials in Tapachula announced to Baya and everyone else: never mind the in-progress asylum applications. They gave the Haitians a three-day grace period to clear out of Tapachula and provided buses. An exodus of thousands promptly moved northward that day.

"The festivities going in Mexico opened up the opportunity for us to travel," Baya told me. "They said we were free to leave for three days. I went."

Other immigrants told me the same story about how a thick bureaucratic molasses suddenly cleared on about September 10 or 11, for a Mexican holiday, and that they had three days to leave.

"The government allowed us to leave," said another Haitian immigrant who gave his name as Kelson. "A lot of the offices were going to be closing for the holiday."

Another Haitian who wrote his name as Donley Vainqueur said he and his family had been waiting around for months in Tapachula for their "passports" to travel north. Then, one day when he went to check on them at the immigration office, "They [Mexican immigration officials in Tapachula] said, 'Okay, you can cross for three days because of the days of festivities.'"

The move could only have been approved and coordinated by Mexico City; the national guard yielded to 250 buses filled with paperless migrants on their way to Texas, according to a later account in the *Dallas Morning News*.[389] Among them was Haitian Esther Pierre Louie who had come to Tapachula from Brazil and got mired there in southern Mexico with everyone else. Suddenly, around September 12, they were free to escape Tapachula, Louie told the newspaper. She recalled riding on "informal buses" that seemed to be "escorted" around immigration checkpoints by "unknown authorities."

The Mexican government has never confirmed the accounts I took from the immigrants. However, Mexican soldiers stationed at the river in Acuña, as the Haitians filed past them down to the spillway, told me they were under orders not to interfere. State police and national guard soldiers passively observed these thousands of immigrants move back and forth over the river just feet away. Their only duty was to keep order against crime, one State of Coahuila police officer told me. So, to protect a national holiday celebration, Mexico sent thousands of Haitians straight to America despite its agreement not to.

Why Del Rio?

Many months earlier, during a reporting trip to the Mexican area across from Del Rio, I discovered a highly unusual attribute. Here and only here, no Mexican cartel required a large tax to cross into Del Rio or Eagle Pass. The Mexican towns of

Acuña, directly across from Del Rio, and Piedras Negras, fifty-five miles downriver, were in a kind of cartel duty-free zone, and immigrants who came there could cross on their own with no fear of violent reprisal, unlike everywhere else. In a lengthy March 2021 blog post for CIS, I duly reported that intending border-crossers from all over Mexico were fast discovering the area and a crossing fee that couldn't be beat: $0. [390]

During that March trip, many immigrants told me they'd first shopped Mexican crossings to California, Arizona, and West Texas, then discovered the Del Rio magic with its soft-touch cartel. In my March 2021 report, I predicted a rise in traffic into Del Rio as word of its low violence and costs spread.

"According to all my countrymen, Piedras is easier; there's a lot of criminal elements in the other ports—kidnappings, murders…," Honduran Anderson Castaneda told me that spring after describing his shopping tour of crossings. "It's just word of mouth from people I run into."

No one really seems to know for sure why the Del Rio sector is so free and easy. One unproven theory for the cartel's light touch, as explained to me, was that the Mexican towns across from the Border Patrol Del Rio sector are receiving depots for *southbound* drug trafficking cash and weapons for several cartels. All the cartels liked things quiet to give U.S. law enforcement less reason to stack up on the Del Rio side with operations that would find the cash. Another theory was that Mexican federal and state police *were* the cartel and couldn't break their cover using violence and other activity necessary to run human-smuggling operations.

By September, the good word about Del Rio sector's unique attributes had gone viral. So when I got to Del Rio many months later, I immediately understood why all the Haitians Mexico released decided to go there.

So why did the camp form in Del Rio? Mexico freed 15,000-plus violent, rioting Haitians from Tapachula to clear the way for the following week's big fiesta, and free crossings could be had in Del Rio. Why was the camp gone a dozen days later? Because Biden went full Trump on it.

Biden Chooses Trump Over Root Causes

President Biden realized he had a major political catastrophe on his hands in Del Rio that would still be there by the midterm national elections fourteen months later if he did not act decisively. Addressing Haiti's root causes was not a solution, of course. Donald Trump's playbook was.

From what I have pieced together, the administration's initial response to the camp, of slowly admitting Haitians into the country, masked an aggressive plan that was in the works. Secrecy was necessary until it could be implemented because these Haitians were fresh from an orgy of pitched violent confrontations with Mexican police forces in Tapachula. What the administration had in mind for them would surely trigger trouble. Security forces had to be mustered in advance.

The "comprehensive strategy" would finally be announced at a shaded outdoor press conference on Sunday September 19, a quarter mile from the camp. Chief Border Patrol Agent Raul Ortiz—who happened to have been born and raised in Del Rio—explained that DHS had surged in hundreds of federal agent volunteers "to improve control of this area." He would need them for the plan's central element, which he presented next:

"DHS is working to accelerate and increase the frequency and capacity of Title 42 flights to expel individuals *to Haiti* [author's emphasis] and other countries of origin."

So: deportation flights. Not back to comfortable Chile or Brazil where all these Haitians had been living for years. But to the original sin of Haiti itself, which most hadn't seen in half a decade. A rude awakening was coming.

After all, the Haitians had been going through a real process inside the camp; everyone had their carnival tickets to freedom in America. Cell phone selfies were showing friends and relatives from the camp were showing up in American cities of their choice. For several years, Trump's DHS had been flying Haitians back to Haiti. But two weeks after Biden entered office, on February 4, 2021, the administration cancelled those flights "after a night of frantic calls from community activists and congressional staffers to the office of the newly confirmed secretary of homeland security, Alejandro Mayorkas," as a British newspaper reported.[391]

Now all of a sudden, the top Border Patrol chief was saying this:

> I want to reiterate that migrants attempting or considering making the journey to our border should know...that they will *not* be allowed to enter the United States. They *will* be removed and *will* be sent back to their country of origin under our current law. Our partners at the State Department are working to ensure that there is adequate support when they land in Haiti.

Unbeknownst to media or the camp inhabitants, by design, the first flights were already loading up at nearby Laughlin Air Force Base or were in the air to Port-Au-Prince. Secrecy until the last possible moment had held long enough for DHS to move an army of security into place to deter almost certain violence once those planes started to land. DHS had even instructed bus drivers and pilots not to divulge the final Port-au-Prince destination to those first passengers, a bus driver and pilot later told me.

The plan was already in action as Ortiz spoke at the press conference. Local, state, and federal officers, and National Guard soldiers were flooding into the camp to be there when those first flights landed and their passengers sent selfies back. At dusk that night, I was inside the camp, hiking the rows of DPS squad cars hundreds of yards long, a steel cordon. I noticed the entire camp had been militarized compared to when I was in it a few days earlier. Border Patrol horsemen moved on their mounts back and forth, amid greater numbers of Humvees and soldiers than I'd seen earlier. I noticed later from my video that two of the horsemen were the same ones who, a day later, would find themselves at the center of a political storm on false allegations that, out of racist animus, they had used their reins to whip black Haitians. I knew early on that the narrative was as bogus as a subsequent investigation would prove because my friend Auden Cabello's drone had recorded the incident from just overhead.

DHS was quite right to hedge their bets with a population of proven violent predisposition.

Flight, Fight, Hide

It took a while after they were airborne, about the time the plane flew over the Gulf of Mexico, for the Haitian passengers to realize something was amiss. Suspicion pressurized the cabin as the water below turned a familiar Caribbean turquoise blue. Once the hated Port-au-Prince came into view, rage overtook the passengers.

The men began rioting before the flight was down, one of the pilots, whom I met later in McAllen, told me. They ripped every window sun shade from their moorings, bent most overhead luggage compartment doors off their hinges. They tore seat cushions off frames and then ripped out their stuffing, photos on the pilot's personal cell phone showed. The destroyed anything destroyable.

That was the beginning as the power of selfies asserted itself once again.

On the hot tarmac, under a blazing midday sun, dozens of the disembarked Haitians tried to storm back onto the plane, but someone slammed shut the door and a Haitian security officer blocked the stairwell.[392] Then another mob attempted to hijack a second recently arrived flight, this one carrying women and children from Del Rio. Some men assaulted the pilots and demanded to be flown back to the United States while others attacked and bit three resisting ICE agents on the plane.[393] What Chief Ortiz had said at his press conference, about the State Department arranging "adequate security" in Haiti, proved needed now. Haitian security eventually quelled the tarmac violence, but it wasn't easy.

From then on, DHS would load all its flights from Texas with extra security officers. Often, they would have to shackle violence-minded Haitian passengers.

But the trouble was hardly over back in Texas. Those first deportees on the Port-au-Prince tarmac sent selfies of the chaos back to their friends and family who were still in Texas allowing themselves to be loaded onto white government buses. One Haitian in Acuña showed the frantic messages to me:

"Don't get on the white buses! Don't get on the buses, whatever you do! They are taking you to the airport and are going to deport you here!"

Haitians who had already loaded onto Border Patrol buses for the half-hour drive to Laughlin air base and others already inside planes taxiing down the Laughlin Air Force Base runway revolted. They had plenty of signal strength to receive the warnings from Port-au-Prince.

As one plane prepared to taxi onto the Texas air base runway, two Haitian passengers bolted from their seats and attacked ICE agents, demanding the flight be aborted.[394] This delayed the flight. Another insurrection broke out on a second flight. Haitians suddenly began "fighting personnel on that plane," the *Washington Examiner* reported. It too was delayed.

The Haitians "all realized they were going back to Haiti and lost it," a senior federal law enforcement official familiar with the incident explained to the newspaper.

On the highways, Haitian passengers already boarded government buses in the mistaken belief they were driving them to freedom in America also "lost it" when the selfies came in showing a different reality.[395]

Haitians attacked their bus drivers, according to the *Washington Examiner*, forcing their drivers off, then drove some distance away and bailed out. In one event, detainees kicked out a window and twenty-two escaped. In another September 20 incident, the Haitian detainees revolted and seized control of a bus driving them to San Antonio, pulled it over, and ran.[396] ICE search parties eventually recaptured most.[397]

Back in Washington, top DHS officials showed they understood full well the air deportation strategy would work immediate magic.

Appearing at a Senate hearing that same September 20 day, DHS Secretary Mayorkas told lawmakers that the crowd of Haitians under the Del Rio bridge would soon be gone because the administration was continuing to ramp up "the frequency and number" of repatriation flights for the migrants.[398] Indeed, the number of deportation flights went to seven a day, capable of carrying about 950 Haitians each day to Port-au-Prince and Cap-Haitien.

"Expect to see dramatic results within the next 48 to 96 hours," Mayorkas promised.

At that moment, I was with the immigrants on the ground and saw what he meant.

Raw Deterrent Power on Parade

When I returned to the Acuña bus station a mere seventy-two hours after my first visit, when the tide was surging in, the tide was going out hard. Instead of busloads of cheerful *arriving* Haitians taxiing to the weir dam spillway, now the station filled with furious Haitians buying tickets on buses *departing* south. They had fled the air deportations in terror when the first selfies from Port-au-Prince hit their cell phones, they said. They were going to hide deep in Mexico's interior. A clerk at the station told me four buses full of Haitians had just departed Acuña to Mexico City in the last several hours and that he had presold enough tickets to fill seven more buses.

It's worth reiterating that when Washington policies raise the odds that smuggling money investment will pay off with entry and long-term stay, they'll come. Conversely, when policies drive down the odds of investment payoff, they won't. The deportation flights, even if not applied universally in the camp, had just driven down the odds of that money paying off.

"We spent much money to come here. Much, much, much money. And we get nothing now!" a Haitian named Stanley spat fiercely, gesticulating wildly with his hands as he spoke. He had just fled the camp and bought a bus ticket back to Tapachula where he could get Mexican permission to reside there until the flights ended.

The journey from Chile and Brazil had been long, arduous, and expensive. Most had gotten themselves to South America years earlier and sheltered in place through the low-odds Trump policy years. Then, when the Biden administration spiked the odds, they spent thousands to advance on the U.S.

border. This trip involved a days-long guided hike through the Darien Gap. Deportations all the way back to Haiti meant they would have to pay the smuggling fees all over again to repeat the whole nightmare.

The odds of a deportation were far from 100 percent but didn't need to be. DHS was still letting thousands of other Del Rio Haitians stay inside the United States to maybe claim asylum for which few would be eligible. (I have never figured out what criteria DHS was using to determine who stayed and who went.) The specter of air deportations alone was sufficient to staunch all new arrivals but also drive a southward exodus out of the camp. The exodus was far larger than what I saw at the bus station.

Later that evening of September 21, at Acuña's sprawling Braulio Park right across from the camp, I found at least 2,000 Haitians who had just fled it and were settling in for the night. Some showed me the tarmac videos and the text warnings from Haiti as their reason for bailing from the Del Rio camp. They said they'd try again later when Biden lost interest in the flights.

"Our dreams have died," lamented a Haitian who gave his name as Louinoo. "This is very, very sad for us; very, very sad."

In all, only about 2,000 Haitians from the camp were expelled to Haiti on ICE flights, while some 5,000 got to stay inside the United States.[399] Some 8,000 more fled the camp back into Mexico, the Washington Post later reported.[400] For them, the odds just weren't worth risking the investments they'd sunk to get this far.

In fact, the exodus from the deportation flights is credited primarily for having emptied the Del Rio camp as quickly as it did, two DHS officials told the newspaper. "Many of those migrants remain in northern Mexico and still intend to cross into the United States, they acknowledged."

Between American releases of the Haitians into America, repatriation flights, and escapes into Mexico, the camp was empty by the ninety-six hours Mayorkas had promised Congress.

"As of this morning, there are no longer any migrants in the camp underneath the Del Rio international bridge," Mayorkas declared during a September 24 press conference.

The next day, city bulldozers were scraping away the huts and trash. The camp and international media were gone but not the broader crisis that spawned it. Del Rio leaves important lessons behind for that. Among the most important, if not obvious, lessons from Del Rio is that it proved that a White House could end the broader border crisis overnight using existing tools of state power to create real, actual deterrence by threatening the viability of smuggling money return on investment. Del Rio demonstrates that the use of air deportations is an especially impactful tactic. But there are other worthy lessons that are far less obvious.

Mexico's Backstab

Mexico would never have considered unleashing thousands of migrants on America for the sake of El Grito festivities had President Trump been in office with his stick-based diplomacy about the border. Mexico did Trump's bidding on immigration issues in fear of economically ruinous trade tariffs the mercurial American president threatened.

What Del Rio showed was that Mexico regarded Biden's carrots-based approach with naked contempt. Mexico inflicted the camp crisis on Biden for the sake of a holiday party. It was out of this same well of contempt for Biden that Mexico surreptitiously passed a law that emptied its fifty-eight detention facilities of families and triggered the broader mass migration on Biden's Inauguration Day.

Biden's government earned this. It turned the other cheek. There were no repercussions. So Mexico continued sticking it to the Biden administration after Del Rio.

Because it suffered no known consequence for emptying its detention facilities and inflicting Del Rio, Mexico felt free to keep unleashing waves of immigrants on the American border. It just changed strategy to one designed to mask what it was doing from the media and to forestall formations of any other Del Rio–type camps. It continued to release massive waves of immigrants from Tapachula about every three months using a tactic known as "ant operations."

That's a colloquial term for a criminal smuggling tactic of moving large volumes of contraband with small distributed parties or individuals in many single-file lines so as to evade notice.[401]

After Del Rio, Mexico would release 50,000 or 60,000 at a time from Tapachula but arrange that they disperse among a dozen northern Mexican states so that, when they hit the U.S. border at different points, no one would noticed. This perfectly suited the administration since no media covered the movements and they were out of sight and mind in the United States. But inside the White House, the brief Del Rio earthquake had opened a huge rift.

A White House Left vs. Left Rift Opens Wide

The use of Trump air deportations to liquidate Del Rio also exposed ideological rifts between pragmatists and progressives in the White House. Progressives railed over the air deportations. Migrant advocacy groups turned on the administration with ferocity. Democratic lawmakers, such as the Congressional Black Caucus, could not contain their outrage.

"Advocates 'in utter disbelief' after Biden resumes Haitian repatriations," read a headline in *The Hill*.[402] Migrant advocates accused the administration of hypocrisy, immorality, and cruelty as they demanded an immediate halt to the flights.

"That ICE would continue to carry out the mass deportations of our Haitian neighbors—with Haiti in the midst of its worst political, public health, and economic crisis yet—is cruel and callous," Representative Ayanna Pressley (D-MA), a progressive, complained.

"Prolonged administration debates over whether to deport Haitian migrants splintered White House advisers," reported a lengthy investigative *Wall Street Journal* report seven weeks after the camp's liquidation.[403] The fight over the camp proved "especially fractious."

In other words, the Del Rio camp crisis served as a straw-that-broke-the-camel's-back catalyst for what can only be described as an insurrection inside the White House for control of immigration policy.

CHAPTER FIFTEEN

WHITE HOUSE REBELLION

"ICE Air Operations is capable of facilitating the removal of alien nationals from any location in the continental United States to anywhere in the world via commercial airline or charter aircraft, ensuring their safe and humane return to their countries of origin."

—Katrina S. Kane, deputy assistant director for
ICE Air Operations, ICE Air Operations website[404]

At seven one rare rainy morning in December 2021, I parked on a back side street alongside the McAllen International Airport, near a locked rolling gate hung with a red sign that read "Authorized Personnel Only." A chain link fence topped by razor wire followed a row of giant airplane hangars along the street to my right, obscuring all but the tail of a chartered jet.

Right on time, a large 4x4 Toyota Tundra pickup led three large white charter buses past my parked car up to the closed gate and stopped. A GMC pickup pulled up to the side of the second bus. A Ford F-150 brought up the rear behind the third one. I could see through the darkened bus windows that they were full of immigrant women and children, about to be driven onto the tarmac. Soon, the gate rolled open, and the entourage rumbled through and around to an idling silver World Atlantic jet named *Emily*. I knew from earlier internet research that it was contracted to ICE Air.

I leapt from my car and rushed to a fenced gap between hangars and began filming. I knew the pickup drivers were plain-clothed ICE agents and that this was one of hundreds of air deportations of Guatemalan, Honduran, and El Salvadoran women and children—a "chosen" demographic supposedly enjoying Biden's Title 42 reprieve.

Women and children began to step off the buses and up the jet's rear stairwell. The ICE agents sent airport security officers on a golf cart to warn me that I was trespassing. McAllen police showed up a few minutes later as the plane was taking off to Guatemala City, where it was going to deliver the 150 immigrants, then come back for more.

The Biden administration had been secretively deporting them for four months already, somehow escaping all major media notice. The flights were going on even before the fifty-eight Del Rio migrant camp flights to Haiti, stopped amid howls of protest from progressives and migrant advocate supporters who seemed to have no idea of these other ones.[405] By the time I discovered and personally witnessed flights in McAllen, in December 2021, the administration had clandestinely air-deported more than 150,000 supposedly "chosen" immigrants to Central American capital and to two cities in southern Mexico, from which authorities would bus them to their home countries by secret agreement with Biden.[406]

The liberal anti-deportation group Witness at the Border was probably the only entity tracking these "death flights," as the group termed them. The airlift began "mushrooming" in August 2021, wrote retired banking executive Thomas Cartwright, who had worked out a system to tally the air expulsions using public flight tracking databases.[407] The escalation seemed intended to tamp down the highest number of border apprehensions in recorded U.S. history, 213,593 the month before, which had drawn a spate of unwanted national media coverage. The flights doubled, then doubled again over the next year, Cartwright reported.

By the end of Biden's first twelve months, the administration's 1,118 removal flights using five charter carriers (iAero, World Atlantic, GlobalX, Eastern Air, and OMNI) eclipsed Trump's last year of flights by 116, to southern Mexico and sixteen different countries in Latin America, the Caribbean, Africa, and even Vietnam, Cartwright assessed. And *still* kept going at higher rates into 2022 until they surpassed all four Trump years. By the end of July 2022, the ICE Air flights ordered by the Biden administration since inauguration day would hit 1,931, expanding to more countries such as Brazil, Colombia, Haiti once again, and Ecuador, Sierra Leone, Guinea, Liberia, Nigeria, and India.

As when Trump was in office, Biden's DHS would disclose nothing about them (and has never responded to my own requests for details and interviews). But assuming a conservative one hundred deportees per flight (many planes have capacity for 135–150 passengers), they returned, by the end of July 2022, at the very least 195,000 women, children, and single men. The number is likely higher, probably well exceeding 250,000, Cartwright told me in an interview.

The Biden expulsion flights were "incontrovertible" evidence, Cartwright wrote in his June 2022 monthly report, that the airlift was "a significant strategic imperative" of the Biden administration because they worked as "an impactful tool…to deter migration through the threat of immediate return."

As the Biden air expulsion deterrence campaign ground on, advocacy groups, individually and in coalition, railed in public and in private meetings with the administration about "the disastrous impacts of these flights on human rights" but found implacable administration resistance, Cartwright recalled.

"There was a lot of pressure put on politically from advocacy groups regarding those," Cartwright told me. The complaints began "not even a month into those flights, about how horrible they were and how we could possibly be a country that would allow those and that they were certainly not 'restoring the soul' of this country."

To no avail. "They continued for months. I was not told anything" about why, Cartwright said.

Why was something this Trumpian happening on Biden's watch in the face of resounding objection from an important progressive constituency?

The flights campaign was the first evidence that moderate Democrats inside the White House wanted to end the border crisis before it damaged the party in upcoming election cycles. With President Biden's express permission, they went to war against their progressive colleagues to bring the border under control. They owned these expulsion flights and other important deterrence policies to end the Biden border crisis. But could they win?

Insurgency

Special envoy to Haiti, Ambassador Daniel Foote, a career diplomat with twenty-three years in the foreign service that included a decade serving in and around the island nation, was probably the first to fall on his sword as a casualty of the "infighting." His story also enlightens us as to the nature of the Biden administration's rebelling faction and its root motivations.

The Biden administration had appointed Foote in July 2021 right after assassins killed the country's president, Jovenel Moïse, and he was planning to help a commission hold national elections that November 7, 2021, for the first time in years. Moïse's temporary caretaker successor, Dr. Ariel Henry, was to oversee the work of a "provisional Electoral Council" (PEC) that was organizing Haiti's long overdue presidential and parliamentary elections set for November 2021.

Foote had only been in the position for about two months in late September 2021 when ICE Air flights began landing at Port-au-Prince filled with riotous Haitians from the Del Rio migrant camp. On September 22, 2021, the ambassador submitted a resignation manifesto to his boss, Secretary Blinken, and walked away from a position he had just started. [408]

Media outlets homed in only on a line in Foote's letter calling the air deportations "inhumane and counterproductive."[409] The media had it that the deportations had so outraged the ambassador that he felt morally compelled to resign as a protest against them.

But that narrative wasn't true.

In a candid interview with me ten months later, Foote offered a surprising explanation that speaks to the first muscle flexing by an ascendant element of Biden's policy staff that seemed utterly implacable, willing to do anything necessary, for a new cause: preserve Democratic Party power and avoid brand damage before upcoming American elections.

"The biggest reason" he resigned, Foote told me, was that the Biden government anointed Dr. Henry as the assassinated president's de facto replacement in exchange for Henry accepting deportation flights of Haitians from the Del Rio camp so that the administration could quickly liquidate it. By September 27, Henry cancelled the elections and disbanded the PEC, leaving himself as the de facto dictator with no checks on his power.

"They basically anointed the fucking leader of Haiti. I am confident that the chief reason they did that is his [Henry's] malleability and the fact that he agreed that he would take all the deportees that they wanted to send," Foote told me months later, still angry at the memory. "It wasn't long after that that…we started putting them on planes, in some cases in ankle chains, and sending them back to Port-au-Prince."

"Why," I asked, "would the Biden administration feel compelled to cut a deal so damaging to Haiti?"

"I believe they were terrified of immigration as an issue in the mid-terms and beyond," he responded. "I believe that the Biden administration has found many of the Trump-era administration policies to be politically expedient for them. The U.S. carried out a non-democratic transfer of power. We're just kicking the can down the road so that we don't upset the vote moving toward the mid-terms [elections in November 2022]."

The White House communications office never replied to my emailed request for comment.

So in summary: the Biden administration left Haitians with a despised, unelected leader and robbed them of open elections to end international media coverage of the Del Rio camp that might damage the Democratic Party's electoral fortunes.

Foote said he could only speculate about who was behind such a ruthless, self-serving victimization of Haiti; he'd only communicated with senior State Department officials who told him the decision was already in the can.

But subsequent media reporting long after these acts occurred, by the *New York Times, Wall Street Journal*, and *Washington Post*, filled in the blanks. An internal war for control of immigration policy was on. According to this reporting, internal tension rose in the administration's earliest days, when old-school Democratic centrists saw what the progressives had done.

Tensions escalated as border crossings broke all records in the summer of 2021. Taking heat from Republicans and a beating in the polls, Biden and centrist border hawks among his senior advisors agreed that eliminating Trump's policies was responsible and portended Democratic Party losses in upcoming election cycles. The terrible numbers had to be reversed.

According to one *New York Times* account in April 2022, the president's senior aides "channeled" President Biden's stated desire to slow or stop a border crisis that would "potentially sink the party during the 2022 mid-terms."[410] The *Journal* would report that "prolonged administration debates over whether to deport Haitian migrants were especially fractious."

On the one side were senior advisers to the president and career border-enforcement officials pushing tough deterrence strategies, "including ramping up deportations and putting pressure on Mexico to step up enforcement," the *Wall Street Journal* reported in November 2021.[411] They included White House chief of staff Ron Klain, national security advisor Jake Sullivan, homeland security adviser Liz Sherwood-Randall, senior adviser Cedric Richmond, Domestic Policy Council advisor Susan Rice, and White House attorney Jennifer Sokoler. These advisers favored mass deportations on grounds that the spiraling mass migration crisis would damage the president's standing with moderate voters.

"A group of Biden aides more attuned to national security and less sensitive to the activist community has begun asserting control over immigration," the *Washington Post* reported in one of the first stories, in a November 2021 story, citing five current and former administration officials.[412] These advisers viewed the border "almost entirely from a political lens."

On the other side, the *Journal* reported, were officials in immigration policy jobs who helped shape a Biden agenda they liked to call "fair, humane and orderly," a term that signaled open-doors policies. These officials were "members of the Democrats' progressive wing in Congress and immigration advocacy groups influential in the administration and party," the *Journal* reported. Individuals described elsewhere in this book were among their ranks, DHS Secretary Mayorkas, National Security Council advisor Andrea Flores, and Susan Rice's policy council deputies for immigration Tyler Moran and Esther Olavarria.

That record-breaking summer of 2021, Biden authorized Klain and Rice to take action.

Klain called his senior aides together and demanded that they find ways to deter the soaring crossings on grounds that the situation was angering moderate voters, the *New York Times* reported in its April 2022 story.

The moderates scored some deterrence victories that lowered the odds that immigrants could successfully cross the border and stay. Nothing did that better than ICE Air deportation flights. In August 2021, they ordered them ramped up and, after American pressure, the Mexican government's own deportation flights.

The centrist Democrats did not stop there.

The Airport Visa Campaign

From late 2021 on through the fall of 2022, as Border Patrol apprehensions were still breaking new national records week after week, major surges of nationalities were showing up in previously unknown numbers—Ecuadorians, Brazilians, and

Venezuelans. What was different about these nationalities is that they had the money to fly over the Darien Gap passage and land in Mexico City or San Jose, Costa Rica, using easily obtainable visitor's visas. Some binational agreements allowed for visitor visas that could be had for the trouble of a few pesos and minutes online. I often found discarded air tickets among the wet clothes that immigrants abandoned on the Texas banks of the Rio Grande.

The Biden government's border security insurgents saw the air travel on visas as a jugular artery they could pinch closed.

With no fanfare, the insurgents moved to shut down these air travel shortcuts by pressuring Mexico and other governments north of Panama to require visas or implement tough new restrictions that targeted nationalities whose numbers at the border were soaring. The visa restrictions campaign traces to about September 2021 when Mexico suspended its visa waivers for Ecuadorians. This followed a sharp increase of Ecuadorian apprehensions to 60,000 Ecuadorians.[413] Mexico, Belize, Colombia, Costa Rica, Honduras, and Panama adopted onerous new visa restrictions on the nationalities.

In May 2022, a State Department official did publicly acknowledge what the border security faction was up to during testimony before a senate committee and described the visa whack-a-mole game.

"When we notice a trend…of certain nationalities arriving in larger numbers at our border, we will carry that information to countries throughout the region and look for areas of partnership," Emily Mendrala, assistant secretary of state for Western Hemisphere affairs, explained to the Senate Homeland Security and Governmental Affairs Committee. Those countries, she continued, "impose visas on those nationalities that are arriving by air…to make sure those that are arriving by air are not intending migrants to the United States." [414]

When one country slaps on visa restrictions, Mendrala went on, "we are alerting" other neighboring countries to which the flying migrants shift so that those countries also can impose visa restrictions.

The visa whack-a-mole project saw Mexico institute new visa requirements in December 2021 for Brazilians, who started flying in several months earlier when they saw the Biden government was quickly paroling their friends, relatives, and neighbors into America. In February 2022, Costa Rica, Honduras, and Panama, again under Biden administration pressure, put tough new airport entry requirements on Venezuelans, Nicaraguans, Haitians, and Cubans.

One whack-a-mole case in point was the Venezuelans. Many of Venezuela's millions of economic refugees, having fled the country's total economic collapse starting in about 2016, had been living safely and securely in third countries like Argentina, Colombia, Panama, and Chile. They'd been unwilling to risk pricey journeys to a Trump border that was closed. But, of course, tens of thousands headed for the U.S. border when they realized that Biden's DHS was exempting Venezuelan families from Title 42 expulsions and paroling them quickly into America, like the Haitians who'd been waiting out Trump in Chile and Brazil for years.

Venezuelans discovered they had a special advantage, visa waivers between their country and Mexico. They could avoid the Darien Gap trip. They started pouring over the American border in the fall of 2021 to claim asylum because, as one Venezuelan émigré explained, they discovered America was taking them all in.

"Many years ago, the massive exodus was to South America and sometimes to Colombia, Peru, Ecuador, Argentina, Chile," the Venezuelan immigrant Angel Escobar told Noticieros Television in July 2022 while traveling through southern Mexico to the American border.[415] "Well, right now in the United States, with President Joe Biden, everyone who goes to the United States has a condition of not being deported and that, then, is what benefits us. And now, all of us that were in South America and Venezuela and want a better quality of life…we can achieve that."

After some time down on the border, I came to almost appreciate the comical sight of Venezuelans pulling overhead-bin-sized rolling luggage pieces up rocky riverbanks with hardly any trace of trail time on their fashionable clothing, jewelry, makeup, and often the wrong shoes. One colleague reported seeing a Venezuelan woman struggling soaking wet out of the Rio Grande carrying Versace purses, similar to other reports that had Brazilians showing up wearing Gucci brands, also fresh from Mexican airports.[416]

In January 2022, Mexico ended visa waivers for Venezuelans under almost certain U.S. diplomatic pressure once their numbers at the border spiked to nearly 60,000 in just November and December of that fateful first year of the crisis.[417] After the administration's insurgents began deporting Venezuelans by air to Colombia and had Mexico slap on visa restrictions, apprehension rates plummeted to a thousand or two per month.

The faction also proved especially resourceful in undermining a problematic visa waiver deal that Cuba and Nicaragua struck in November 2021.[418]

Overnight, the November 2021 visa waiver deal allowed tens of thousands of Cubans to fly directly to Managua, bypassing the Darien Gap, and to be at the border in days. It became the hottest emigration ticket in Havana. Cubans waited for days on ends in miles-long lines to buy extremely expensive ($3,500) one-way tickets from Havana to Managua, or indirect routes.[419] By March 2022, apprehensions of Cubans at the southern border had quintupled to 32,154, the highest single-month total on record.

The Klain-Price faction clearly targeted the Havana-Managua air routes. Although most American media missed or ignored the story, I've pieced it together from other sources.

Coinciding with a lot of U.S. shuttle diplomacy during the first quarter of 2022, most Central American and Mexican airlines that were flying between Cuba and Nicaragua abruptly started cancelling flights, promising without explanation refunds to angry Cubans.[420] In February 2022, Copa Airlines was the first to cancel flights.[421] Other airlines like Magnibus followed in March, April, and May, providing no public explanation.

Those who tried indirect flights stepped into brand-new visa booby traps, like one in Costa Rica. Hundreds of Cubans who purchased indirect flights to Managua found that Costa Rica suddenly put up a new "transit visa" that demanded a clean criminal bill of health for ten years and proof of economic solvency, Reuters reported.[422] They protested outside Costa Rica's embassy in Havana to no avail. Almost everyone Reuters reporters interviewed insisted, improbably, that they had spent $3,500 on the air ticket, several times the annual salary of most Cubans, so that they could shop as tourists in Nicaragua. One Cuban man did admit that "all Cubans are giving up everything to make this trip."

Foreign media accounts noted that these flight cancellations and visa hurdles for Cubans coincided with American-involved diplomacy about Cubans crossing the American border.

"The cancellation notice was given shortly after a high-level meeting between Cuban and Mexican officials regarding the increase in Cubans arriving at the southern U.S. border," one Mexican media outlet noted in an April 2022 report about how the Mexican airline Viva Aerobus suddenly cancelled flights between Cuba and Nicaragua. "The meeting took place directly before the cancellation notice."[423]

Also coinciding with a U.S. package of diplomatic goodies for Cuba, Nicaragua disappeared from VisaGuide's list of twenty-seven countries where Cubans could travel without a visa.[424] The visa reciprocity between Cuba and Nicaragua ended. Had it been Cuba's plan all along to "weaponize" illegal immigration to secure American concessions? Maybe so. On May 15, 2022, the State Department announced that the United States would resume the cherished Cuban family Reunification Parole Program, increase legal residency permits for which Cubans could apply, and raise remittance money caps that Cubans in America could wire to the island. The cherry on top was a resumption of permission for Cubans living in America to fly to the island and visit relatives.[425]

By June 2022, the numbers of Cubans showing up at the border had fallen by 100 percent to 16,170.

Battlefield Gains

In a sure sign that the air deportation and visa crackdown campaigns were working, eighty-seven human rights and migrant advocacy organizations on June 30, 2022, penned a public outrage letter to the American and Mexican presidents. The groups demanded the countries halt these "enforcement-centric policies" and replace them with "humane migration management," the encrypted catchphrase for open borders. [426]

Deportation flights, visa restrictions, and diplomatic strong-arming to close Cuba-Managua airline flights, the letter's eighty-seven signatories wrote, were "ineffective and unlawful deterrence-based policies and practices that disregard and subvert international refugee and human rights law."

Surely these groups would not have written such a letter protesting "ineffective" measures because, why waste paper? This was reminiscent of Trump's thirty-foot border wall, which though its opponents always insisted it was totally ineffective, drew screeching caterwauling to hurry up and stop construction. The eighty-seven signatories wrote because these measures *were* impactful, while they were in place. An analysis of apprehensions for targeted nationalities shows it. Total Border Patrol apprehensions declined by 30,000 to 50,000 per month from plus-200,000 monthly peaks. The nationalities targeted for air expulsions—certain Central Americans, Haitians, Brazilians, Ecuadorians, and Venezuelans—were the ones that led these declines. But only so long as the expulsions were happening, and they were off and on.

Take the Venezuelans. Their numbers at the border surged from a normal few hundred per month in 2020 to the historic high of 24,950 in December 2021 and another 22,884 in January 2022. After secretively cutting a new deal with Colombia to take Venezuelans back, in mid-December 2021, Biden's DHS began deportation airlifts of Venezuelans from Texas.[427] By February, once word of these spread by cell phone selfies and chat room reporting, apprehensions of Venezuelans plummeted to 3,225 and stayed in a low range for several months until the flights ended, when their numbers skyrocketed again.

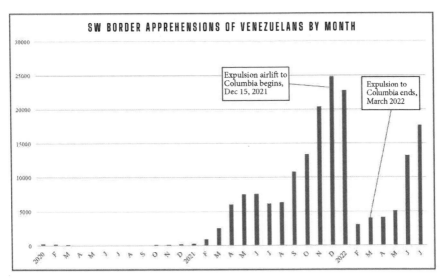

Chart by Ally Thai with permission.

Consider Central American families and adults from Guatemala, Honduras, and El Salvador. Their apprehensions hit stratospheric heights of 94,484 in July 2021 and another 91,925 in August. But after Biden's DHS launched the flights that August, their numbers immediately plummeted to pre-crisis levels of 31,658 in January 2022 and 39,178 in February.

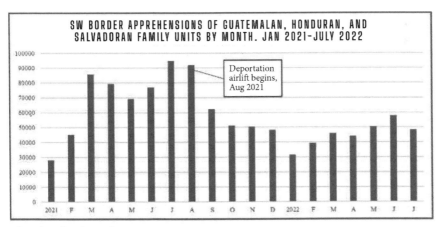

Chart by Ally Thai with permission.

I further confirmed this correlation from the targeted immigrants: fewer were willing to gamble a high smuggling fee and risky travel if the odds of a deportation rose too high. They stayed home or sheltered in place, at least until the threat passed.

In December 2021, for instance, the administration surreptitiously brought back the Haiti deportation flights to tamp down their resurgent crossings, which predictably began soon after the administration cancelled the Del Rio camp flights.

Border Patrol encounters with Haitians fell from 17,638 in September 2021 to 908 in October after the air deportations from Del Rio sector scared them straight. But then the flights ended. By December 2021, the Haitian apprehension numbers climbed sharply sevenfold, to more than 7,000. That's right when the flights were resumed. During another reporting trip I took to Tapachula in January 2022 dozens of Haitians told me they would not dare cross the American border until after the resumed flights ended, even if that meant waiting in Mexico for years.

"Please, tell Joe Biden: Stop! Stop it! Stop the deportations to Haiti!" one Haitian man implored of me in Tapachula that January 2022. "Talk to Joe Biden, please! Stop the deportations. Help us Haitians."

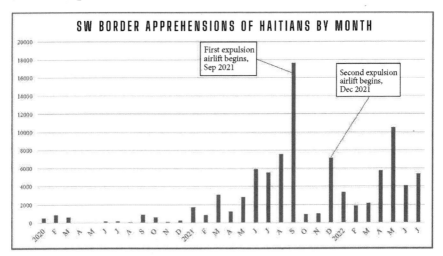

Chart by Ally Thai with permission.

By February, apprehensions had fallen sixfold. Between September 2021 and July 2022, DHS sent about 24,445 Haitians aboard 236 removal flights to Haiti, Witness at the Border reported.[428]

There's no reliable way to really assess deterrence other than by direct testimony and apprehension statistics as they ebb and flow. But by those measures, the flights and visa restrictions turned the tide but only so long as they were consistently applied. They rarely were.

Progressive Casualties of War

The White House insurgents might have considered the resignations of progressive open-borders advocates as achievements too.

Not long into the White House insurgency, "virtually all of the aides who came on board early in the administration have left the White House, frustrated by what they describe as repeated fights with some of the president's most senior advisors over whether to lift Trump-era policies," the *New York Times* would eventually disclose in April 2022.[429]

Next to the air deportations, the tug-of-war over Title 42 qualified as the fiercest. The moderates fought hard to keep it as the last speed bump against the human flow.

"For the immigration advocates working inside the White House, it was all maddening," the *Times* reported. "They had come to work for Mr. Biden to dismantle the worst policies put in place by Mr. Trump. Now they were being asked to make arguments for continuing them."

Harold Koh, a senior adviser and political appointee on the State Department's legal team, became one of the first to resign over the department's use of Title 42 to deport the Haitians. Koh's memo decried the administration's refusal to lift the expulsion measure entirely.

"Our actions and approaches regarding Afghan refugees stand in stark contrast to the continuing use of Title 42 to rebuff the pleas of thousands of Haitians and myriad others arriving at the Southern Border who are fleeing violence, persecution, or torture."[430]

Koh seemed unaware that almost all the Haitians and Venezuelans had been living for years in Chile or Brazil, Argentina or Colombia, where few reported violence, persecution, or torture.

In September 2021, senior DHS adviser David Shahoulian resigned. That December, Tyler Moran resigned. Andrea R. Flores resigned as the NSC's director for border management, telling the *New York Times* that senior aides had disillusioned and frustrated her by "the opportunities I saw them not take. This is an inflection point," she said.

In January 2022, Rice's senior adviser on immigration, Esther Olavarria, resigned. But the one with perhaps the most power and who had the ear of illegal immigration proponents remained, Alejandro Mayorkas.

The Insurgency Is Crushed

In recoiling at the historic metrics of the border crisis their progressive colleagues had wrought, these Democratic centrists—or, if you will, political pragmatists—worked to undermine and eventually replace those radical policies with normal ones to which the Democratic Party was accustomed. Some of the hardline policies the centrist pragmatist faction put into play were impressive in their deterring impacts. The effort was valiant and smart, in line with normal Democratic Party tradition on illegal immigration.

Unfortunately, the insurgency would go down in defeat as the American mid-term elections took place. It failed during this period because the president who ordered it did not understand that suppressive measures had to be applied universally.

Illegal immigration deterrence is an all-or-nothing proposition. And so the closure of a gate or two would never overcome the powerful voodoo of opening side gates, which is what always ended up happening.

The crisis would have ended had these flights been coupled with 100 percent Title 42 expulsions, Remain in Mexico policy, and normal detention and removal operations required by law of all or most illegal entrants. But so long as the administration was still gifting quick entry to the majority of border-crossers and freedom from detention and deportation, net crossings could only ever move higher. Nothing could overcome the narcotic effect of vast admittances when these were coupled with repetitive statements by senior officials that the welcome mat was down.

Also, the progressive faction fought back even after some of its White House foot soldiers fell. For example, when some of the border security moderates pushed to restore Trump's Remain in Mexico asylum policy, the progressives pushed back with fury and prevailed, although later the courts would decide its fate.

When progressives demanded that Biden lift the rest of Title 42 and reopen the asylum system to the entire world's poor, Klain and Rice fought to keep it, fearful of intelligence predictions that its end would bring in between 12,000 and 18,000 illegal immigrants every day. The progressives prevailed; the administration decided to end Title 42. Worse for cross-border flow, the administration publicly set a date: May 23, 2022. Biden's announcement of a particular date lit the whole world of aspiring migrants on fire to come in time for it even after the courts forced the administration to keep it a while longer.

While Title 42 was still set to expire, Mayorkas announced to the world that its way of dealing with the extra onslaught would be to move the most people into America as quickly as possible. His DHS issued a plan called for building cavernous new soft-sided Border Patrol facilities and new camps for unaccompanied minors. The Mayorkas DHS announced a vast expansion of the nonprofits in many other states that Border Patrol could deliver processed migrants to for busing into the country.

Mayorkas and the State Department opened secretive immigration-related talks with Mexico City that, in the spring and summer of 2022, coincided with a new Mexican decision to no longer hold back the migrant tide in Tapachula but to let most through quickly. Mexico immediately began granting travel permits to all immigrants coming in from Guatemala.[431]

Celebratory Mexican media covering successful July 1, 2022, passage of the first caravan to benefit reported that the national guard soldiers that, since Trump, blocked passage north now "limited themselves to observing the transit of the caravan, which celebrated with cries of 'Yes, we can! Yes we can!'"[432] By month's end, Mexican soldiers had allowed sixteen caravans through.[433]

With the new shorter Colombia-to-Panama passage around the Darien Gap, the new Mexico passage amounted to a superhighway for global migration. For unexplainable reasons, the visa restrictions on air travel ended. Thousands of Colombians, for instance, were buying Cancun vacation packages to fly in as tourists and then head for the Texas border in late fall 2022.

Border Patrol apprehension levels soared on news of all these developments, breaking the last freshly broken records from 2021. The continual rewards of allowing entry cancelled out almost everything the rebellious centrists tried, and so did the president's approval of other policies that made the whole endeavor profitable.

DHS, for instance, announced it would provide ID cards to border-crossers for health care and work authorization. The great news just never seemed to end.

This happened for one reason: Biden just didn't get the immigrant decision-making calculus, perhaps was incapable of getting it or, more charitably, wasn't wholly present. He left his warfighters without air support or artillery, like President John F. Kennedy abandoned the Bay of Pigs invaders.

Most debilitating of all was the repetitive public proclamation—followed by action on the ground—that the administration's goal was to create "safe, humane and orderly" pathways rather than obstruction, detention, and deportation. In September 2022, an interviewer asked a Venezuelan migrant who'd been bused to Martha's Vineyard if he believed the border was closed as Vice President Harris had just insisted.

"It's open, not closed. The border is open," the gentleman responded in English. "Everybody believes the border is open. It's open because…we entered! We come in. Free. No problem."

Aftermath

In May 2022, during a check-up visit to Del Rio, I wondered what Ron Klain and Susan Rice might think of the humming industrialized transport machine I found hauling humanity from river to interior America all day seven days a week. I'd gone again to the Val Verde Border Humanitarian Coalition (VVBHC) facility, the little Del Rio nonprofit whose administrators first confirmed to me a seeming lifetime ago in February 2021 that a crisis had begun at the "switch of administrations." All these months later, the machine was bigger, louder, more organized, and moving far more people into the American heartland.

Border Patrol would wheel up its big white buses full of just-processed immigrants to the VVBHC, whose volunteers would put them through some paces to buy tickets on charter buses that also were there. Often the Border Patrol buses would pull up right behind the commercial buses. This went on here in Del Rio but also all along the South Texas border down to Brownsville. The smooth-running machine was moving tens of thousands a day into America now all along the South Texas border down to Brownsville. And in Yuma, Arizona, too.

In the front yard of VVBHC, everyone swilled water against the heat, worked their cell phones, and got ready to board. Texas National Guard soldiers directed the crowds into queues that led into a building and then back out and into buses. There would be no new embarrassing, squalid encampment forming again in Del Rio any time soon, not if DHS could help it.

The immigrants hailed from Cuba, Venezuela, Ecuador, Colombia, Brazil, Nicaragua, and a dozen African countries.

What I saw was almost perfectly emblematic of how contradictory policies work at odds with one another, ever to the net reward of immigrants who had gambled their smuggling money.

Take the Nicaraguans and Cubans I saw boarding buses that day in Del Rio. Diplomatic estrangements prevented the moderate White House faction from air-shipping those nationalities back to either Cuba or Nicaragua. But in April

2022, the faction cut a deal for Mexico to accept American Title 42 expulsions of Cubans and Nicaraguans. Then, Mexico would do the shipping to home countries since those nations still enjoyed normal diplomatic relations.[434]

But then someone in the administration carved out a defeating escape hatch: DHS declared that none would be expelled from the Del Rio sector! The Nicaraguans and Cubans heard about it through the cell phone grapevine and poured in through Del Rio! That's where I found them in significant percentages off the bus lineups as they boarded and went on with their new lives.

The moderate border security Democrats may have felt hope at a last-minute federal court ruling that forestalled Title 42's lifting. But then the administration opened more exemptions from expulsions to more nationalities, ending the flights to Colombia and letting some of the countries renege on the visa restrictions. Mayorkas reduced the expulsion rate from 60 percent, the majority of all border-crossers, to 40 percent by the summer of 2022, CBP statistics show.

With the odds of expulsion so much lower for many nationalities, armies of immigrants, tens of thousands strong, naturally came on that easy new superhighway Mayorkas created from South America through Mexico. Every shelter in northern Mexico filled to capacity.[435]

In Del Rio, a triumphant mood prevailed among immigrants carrying plastic or manila folders full of DHS-stamped papers and travel tip sheets inside with their bus tickets. They smiled and laughed, giddy to have gotten in on this previously unimaginable good fortune. My old acquaintance Tiffany Burrow, the nonprofit center's operations manager, told me the organization was helping immigrants from more than thirty non-Mexican countries make their ways to Florida, New Jersey, New York State, Oregon, Georgia, North Carolina, Kentucky, Ohio, Kansas, Missouri, Nevada, Utah, California, Minnesota, Wyoming, and Colorado.

Burrow was bracing for worse. She said the numbers had prompted American Airlines to triple its capacity at the tiny municipal Del Rio airport starting the first week of June.

"A lot of people are flying out," she said.

After Burrow and her staff helped arrange bus schedules and ticket purchases, I followed one group of 150 as they lined up at an idling charter bus, all smiles. A Cuban named George who illegally swam the Rio Grande two days earlier staked out first place in line. All the others, many still carrying their belongings in plastic bags they got at the Border Patrol processing center, formed behind him three and four abreast in a line stretching half a football field long. Not even the scalding sun overhead could dampen George's ebullience or that of those behind him who giggled, smiled, and took the consequential selfies with the bus as a backdrop. A Texas National Guardsman posed with kids for pictures.

Asked if he was feeling happy to start this last leg of what had been a long journey, George responded in broken English and with a firm thumbs-up, "Yes, very happy, man…because I am in freedom now. *Viva la libertad!*"

Now, George told me he'll move in with his sister in Florida. Asked if he thought America would let him stay in the country forever, George nodded with certainty and a tight-lipped knowing smile: "Yeah, forever. Because it's a very good country, man…really."

That May, Border Patrol smashed through yet another all-time national record: 224,220 apprehensions. The following month, June 2022, would come in big too at 192,418, and another 181,552 in July.

The pragmatists or moderates or centrists—whatever they should be called—may have won battles. They liquidated the Del Rio migrant camp. Perhaps their efforts even alleviated some of the total traffic flow into the nation for a time.

But the crosscurrents were simply too strong and undercutting. The machine I saw pumping foreign nationals into the country was what defeat looked like. The insurgent pragmatists could never apply their ideas consistently and comprehensively across the board as was necessary. By the end of 2022, millions were in and millions more were coming. No one inside the White House or Congress was left to oppose the crisis. But a state was willing to give it a shot: Texas.

CHAPTER SIXTEEN

TEXAS INSURGENCY

Starting at 11 a.m. on April 13, 2022, foot soldiers of Mexico's murderous Gulf Cartel, traveling in two vans on the Mexican highway leading to the Reynosa-Pharr (Texas) International Bridge, doused the first eighteen-wheel cargo truck with gasoline and lit it.[436] The driver fled the furious blaze that engulfed the cab and the attached trailer. Over the next several hours, the prowling arsonists lit up three more trucks, again sending flames leaping, swirling, and lapping at the air twenty feet above them. All morning and well into that spring afternoon, black plumes of smoke rose over the urban Reynosa landscape as a message for all other truckers to see, which was the point of it all.

The craziness in Reynosa that day on the road to the bridge into Texas wasn't over. Next, the cartel arsonists set fire to an empty lot near several "maquiladoras" factories, evidently a warning shot at trade associations that things could get hot for them next if they didn't comply with the cartel's demands. While fires burned, Tamaulipas state police, kitted out like soldiers of the military, spotted four of the cartel arsonists driving away and gave chase. Cornered, the cartel gunmen opened fire, drivers told Mexican press.[437] State police returned fire until they overcame three of the arsonists and took them into custody.

As far as Mexico's ubiquitous cartel violence goes, truck burnings and a gunfight did not even rank on the body count and outrage charts. But this incident scored very high on a different chart; it came as a consequence of an unusual campaign by Texas Governor Greg Abbott to do a federal job, which was to shut down the mass illegal immigration flooding his state.

For more than a year of record-breaking torrents of human traffic over his 1,245-mile border with Mexico, Abbott had been experimenting with a slew of edgy, never-tried ideas to counter what he saw as the White House's comprehensive abdication of its federal duty to enforce basic immigration law. [438]

Stunned by what was happening early in the Biden border crisis, in March 2021 Abbott took national matters into his own hands. He committed to it billions in Texas tax dollars and an indefinite Texas DPS and National Guard air, land, and marine surge known as Operation Lone Star.

This was nothing less than an unarmed insurrection against federal policy. The state under Abbott aimed to find any way it could to end or slow human flow that "continues to escalate because of Biden Administration policies that refuse to secure the border and invite illegal immigration." The state's campaigns also intended to mitigate criminal impacts of the crisis, the Texas governor said in a press release.[439] (Abbott's office did not respond to my written request for an interview.)

The cartel attacks that day in Mexico were a byproduct of Abbott's edgiest and most promising policy experiments yet. On April 6, 2022, he ordered Texas Department of Public Safety vehicle safety inspection officers to shut down normal trade on five of America's busiest international trade bridges.[440]

The idea was to economically pressure senior Mexican officials to slow and deter the immigration on their side. The truck inspections on the Texas side of five bridges from April 6–14 reduced trade between the two countries by 70 percent. It backed up trucks full of perishable goods for up to thirty miles with driver waits that exceeded thirty hours. That hurt because Mexico is by far the top exporter of goods into the

United States, shipping $88.5 billion through Texas land ports in 2020, supporting 910,000 export-supported manufacturing jobs and 29,645 businesses that go on to sell Mexican products overseas.[441] Laredo, for instance, is by far the busiest land port in America for truck traffic, with 2.6 million vehicles crossing in 2021, according to U.S. Bureau of Transportation statistics, with two other Texas land ports among the top ten on the Southwest Border adding 1.4 million more.[442]

Squeals of economic pain came from every quarter. On the third day of inspections, Mexican truckers and manufacturing plant interests could take it no longer. Mexican truckers retaliated with a blockade of Texas trucks crossing southbound to make deliveries inside Mexico, a bid to force Abbott to stop the inspections.[443] But the Mexico-side blockade drew the wrong opponent into the fray, the Gulf Cartel.

Its operatives burned trucks as I described. (A knowledgeable government source later told me the cartel could not tolerate an interruption in diesel fuel shipments it needed from the United States to run its enterprises.) Right after the burnings, the Mexican truckers called the whole thing off and reopened the southbound bridge lanes to Texas trucks entering Mexico.

"They understood that security is a priority," Edgar Zamorano Quintallan, president of the National Chamber of Cargo Transport in Reynosa, told *El Universal*, by way of explanation.

But Abbott kept the pressure on, able to withstand the more civil kind of opposition he drew.

Abbott's Democratic opponent, Robert "Beto" O'Rourke, derided the bridges campaign as a "stunt" that would only exacerbate supply chain problems, product shortages, and consumer price increases. In a back-handed nod to the bridges campaign's intended impact, President Biden's press secretary, Jen Psaki, issued a press statement complaining the "unnecessary and redundant" inspections were causing "significant disruptions to the food and automobile supply chains, delaying manufacturing, impacting jobs, and raising prices for families in Texas and across the country."[444]

Abbott's own natural supporters also whelped in distress.

"This is destroying our business and the reputation of Texas," complained Dante L. Galeazzi, president of the Texas International Produce Association, in an April 8 letter to Abbott. The association complained the blockage at the Pharr international bridge from Reynosa had warehouse staff sitting idle with no trucks to unload, buyers in other parts of the country missing their deliveries, and U.S. trucking companies losing money "as they sit around for days with no loads to haul."[445]

But Abbott held on, perhaps feeling politically secure after just roundly defeating Republican primary challengers to become his party's presumptive nominee for the November 2022 election to a third term as governor. Eight days and 4,100 truck inspections later, he pulled the safety inspectors and restored binational trade to normal.

Left-leaning media crowed, saying Abbott "caved in" to the criticism and suffered a humiliating political defeat.[446]

But the opposite was true.

Abbott did not restore trade because of political miscalculation or constituent complaints but because four Mexican governors of states agreed to conduct counter-immigration operations on their side of the border if Abbott would lift his ruinous safety inspections. This was something different and packed with promise because it opened a way for a mere border state to materially leverage a sovereign country. One by one, the governors of Nuevo León, Coahuila, Tamaulipas, and Chihuahua came to Austin hats in hand to sign "security" agreements with Abbott in exchange for his order to lift the truck safety inspections.[447] Most media did not cover the triumphant signings in Austin, ask hard questions, or follow up on these one-of-a-kind agreements.

In pressing his advantage, Abbott made no pretense of silky diplomatic tact. He let it be known that he would wield that bridges stick like a sword of Damocles. At the first signing ceremony April 12, with Nuevo León Governor Samuel Alejandro Garcia-Sepúlveda, Abbott showcased the agreement as a pain-pleasure proposition to other governors who hadn't yet come forward. All bridges would remain clogged "except for Nuevo León," he said, pointedly. And even Nuevo León was only safe from future clogs, Abbott warned, for "as long as Nuevo León executes this historic agreement."

"Clogged bridges can end only through the collaboration that we are demonstrating today between Texas and Nuevo León," Abbott warned the others, who all showed up and signed over the next couple of days.

Up to that point, nothing that Abbott had tried seemed to meaningfully slow the immigration flows into his state. But Abbott's bridges experiment finally seemed to offer a way to do so by leveraging Mexico into a partnership.

The state-to-state security agreements were short on operational specifics but called on the Mexican governors to work individually and with one another to respond to immigration "hot spots" identified by Texas DPS. The Coahuila agreement, for instance, promised to use preexisting highway checkpoints to roust suspected immigrants from vehicles and return them "to a designated place in Mexico." In Piedras Negras and Acuña, "special teams of personnel and motor equipment" will prevent the crossing of immigrants from those two cities across from the Del Rio sector of Texas.

Because U.S. and Mexican media hated this story of a Texas governor who forced a sovereign nation to do his bidding, no reporters ever pressed to find out if his Mexican counterparts followed through on their side in impactful ways.

But they did follow through. They did deploy. From the day those governments signed on the agreement lines, their state police forces conducted continuous tactical operations all over northern Mexico in close coordination with Texas DPS and the Texas National Guard, working over the so-called "hot spots" as they erupted. Both sides called this joint effort "Operation Mirror," and they went on right up to the day of this writing in September 2022. Consider this episode that was never covered in the American press:

Two months after the agreement signings, the bridges campaign long out of public sight and mind in June 2022, Mexico City suddenly granted transit permits to everyone in a massive caravan of 15,000 immigrants—said to be the largest in Mexican history—to travel from its southern border to the U.S. one. Mexican media reported that almost all of them were heading to Del Rio and Eagle Pass, Texas.[448] Governor Abbott got on the bat phone to Coahuila State Governor Miguel Angel Solis and the other governors. Abbott insisted on Mexican action to stop those who were in the caravan and now streaming across the states toward Texas, in line with the April agreement, a senior State of Texas official with direct knowledge of the operations told me.

"DPS is currently working directly with our counterparts in the four states and the importance of this has been reinforced in subsequent discussions the governor has had with his counterparts about the caravan," the official told me. "You can credit all of it to Abbott, as this was the agreement in exchange for stopping the bridge inspections."

Abbott let the Mexican governors know that he was willing to clog up their bridges again "if it becomes clear they are allowing it to occur and are doing nothing to stop it," the official told me.

No U.S. writer or American outlet reported what happened next in northern Mexico (other than me).[449] But the main body of thousands of Del Rio–bound former caravanners collided with a wide-ranging Nuevo León and Coahuila state police roadblock operation. Mexican state police began preventing migrants from boarding commercial buses in Monterrey and Saltillo to the popular crossings in Piedras Negras and Acuña. The governors decreed that no one in their states could drive the immigrants to the border; they would all have to walk. Coahuila refused to recognize the federal transit papers the migrants were carrying, on supposed grounds that these did not allow their bearers to travel near the northern border, the newspaper *El Siglo de Torreón* reported.[450]

Police units blocking the roads, airports, and bus stations would halt buses, trucks, taxis, and cars. They would pull off migrants carrying the federal transit slips and set some afoot. They would send others back to southern states, flagrantly thwarting Mexican federal government will by refusing to recognize the federal transit permits, according to Mexican media reporting.[451] Others were allowed to walk but might get picked up later and driven back south.

Migrants who thought they were a day or two away from crossing into Texas, where the Biden administration was waiting to admit most of them, were infuriated. They mounted civil disobedience disturbances in Saltillo. They blocked roads. Some sewed lips shut. Others burned tires. Several hundred of the immigrants who were pulled off buses in Saltillo after paying fares staged a days-long sleep-in at the bus station demanding their money back.

Pressure on the Mexican side squeezed immigrants who got as far as the Rio Grande, as several unusual happenings indicated. Authorities had to briefly close the international bridge between Eagle Pass and Piedras Negras when one hundred of the migrants who managed to get through the dragnet hopped a train over, fighting off Mexican police who tried unsuccessfully to stop them. A day later, twenty-five migrants detained by Mexican federal police at the foot of the international bridge in Piedras Negras broke down a door and stormed over the international bridge, some of them barefoot. They got across.[452]

There can be no doubt that Abbott's agreements prompted Mexican action. The important question that defies easy answer is: Did any of this reduce illegal immigration flow over the Texas border? The governors' agreements contained no provisions detailing what success looked like, nor did it measure flows that might hit identified thresholds that would trigger bridge slow-down safety inspections again.

It is inescapable that, in the end, the immigrants kept flowing over the Texas border in even greater numbers, even if a bit more harried by northern Mexico's governors. Apprehensions rose from 40,928 that April 2022 of bridge slow-downs to 44,721 in May and 45,225 in June.

Many can and maybe should argue that the bridges campaign didn't work at all, that Mexican governors and their state police forces are simply too corrupt, cagey, beholden to their violent cartels, and therefore too unreliable as partners to have authentically tried.

I would posit—speculatively, granted—that the numbers likely would have been higher without the Mexican states' operations. Maybe instead of 44,000 or 45,000, the numbers would have been 60,000 or 70,000 had the immigrants seen unobstructed views through Nuevo León and Coahuila to the Rio Grande.

But I also have to admit that it's impossible to measure deterred or diverted trips with certainty, so none of us can really know; it just makes sense that immigrants sent selfies back down the trail of state cops rousting them from buses and setting them afoot, and those down-trail would have gone elsewhere.

Still, I write about the agreements because they rank as a remarkable achievement pregnant with unrealized future potential. An American state used its own police forces to demonstrate that, by disrupting international trade, it could usurp federal responsibility for national diplomacy. Mexican states did conduct operations that would not otherwise have been undertaken. The U.S. federal government did not sue Abbott to stop its binational diplomacy, at least not this time. Mexico's state governments showed themselves to be malleable, or cooperative, if you will, as when President Trump threatened trade tariffs in 2019. But would Abbott, had he continued the bridge clogging for a longer period, have been able to force presidents Biden and Obrador to the table?

I do not know why Abbott never clogged the bridges again as the immigration numbers continued to escalate. As late as September 2022, a senior state government official with whom I talk said Abbott still held out the possibility that he would use the tool.

Experiments

With Biden's election, Texas Republican leadership found itself at the unenviable epicenter of the greatest mass migration crisis in American history. Most of the people were coming through Texas. But states are not statutorily or constitutionally responsible for regulating immigration; the federal government is.

Still, Texas Republican leadership felt obligated to do everything it could to take that federal authority for itself. It was an unarmed insurrection, a classic state-versus-federal power conflict. I recount it here because the Texas insurrection stood side by side with the White House insurrection in creating a possibility of ending the crisis.

As of this writing, the Texas insurrection had not succeeded either.

The bridges campaign was just one of many interesting policy experiments Texas field-tested on its long border with Mexico at considerable expense to itself. Some came off as rank political theater for Abbot's reelection campaign. In 2022, for instance, he provided free busing of immigrant volunteers from Texas to blue liberal sanctuary cities like Washington, DC, New York, and Chicago, which all complained, thus delighting conservatives. He issued an entirely symbolic, meaningless executive order declaring Mexico's cartels as "Foreign Terrorist Organizations" when the state had no authority or practical ability to inflict any new damage on them. Another executive order declared that Texas would round up immigrants and return them to the border, leaving the false impression that he was deporting immigrants when he was just passing them to Border Patrol in a different location. Lacking substance, these were uninteresting sideshows.

But Abbott also tried plenty that was interesting, his bridge-clogging campaign chief among them.

Abbott directed nearly $4 billion to a range of initiatives. That was serious money, even for a wealthy state like Texas with its famous $149 billion "rainy day fund." The state used it to build an initial twenty new miles of Trump-style wall on private ranch lands by the spring of 2022. It laid tens of thousands of yards of raft-deterring razor wire and steel fencing. The state set out hundreds of yards of old shipping containers on its side of the Rio Grande to make those riverbanks unpleasant. The state's Attorney General's Office, meanwhile, federally sued to halt Biden's immigration policies in the conservative Fifth Circuit Court of Appeals and found significant successes.

As the *New York Times* summed up the insurgent state's effort in December 2021: "Texas has been engaged in an effort to repurpose the tools of state law enforcement to stem the sudden increase of people crossing illegally into the country. To do this, Texas officials led by Governor Greg Abbott developed a way around the fact that immigration enforcement is a federal government job." [453]

The still-unfolding Texas story warrants telling for the lessons it offers other states and future leaders.

To Declare an "Invasion"

Deeply frustrated by Abbott's failure to staunch the illegal immigration, Texas and national Republicans on his right demanded that the governor declare an "invasion" and deport illegal immigrants back to Mexico itself.[454] Based on a novel, untested legal theory, the idea was that governors could invoke Article IV, Section 4, and Article I, Section 10, of the U.S. Constitution and declare an invasion. That declaration, the thinking went, would provide governors with extraordinary wartime powers that would allow states to mount their own deportation operations. This idea is worth addressing here because it remained potent and politically possible as of this writing, not only in Texas but in Arizona too, whose attorney general first raised the issue in a written opinion concluding it could be done.[455]

In a practice that has infuriated border security proponents, the extra state police and National Guard that Abbott deployed along his border had always operated under legal orders to quickly turn over illegal immigrants to Border Patrol agents who were under orders to mainline most straight into America or expel them to Mexico under Title 42. Under Operation Lone Star, thousands more state officers and National Guard troops were handing over thousands to Border Patrol for the inevitable releases.

Known as the "guarantee clause," Article IV states, "The United States shall guarantee to every State in this Union a Republican Form of Government, and shall protect each of them from Invasion; and on Application of the Legislature, or of the Executive (when the Legislature cannot be convened) against domestic violence." Article I, meanwhile, provides in part that no state can deploy military assets for war without the permission of Congress "unless actually invaded, or in such imminent Danger as will not admit of delay."[456]

Constitutional law experts have noted that the clauses do not define "invasion," but that the founding authors probably meant an armed, organized military attack by a foreign government, rather than unarmed economic migrants crossing in for jobs.[457] Liberal commentators and migrant advocates panned the notion. The legal basis of the invasion clause idea was "far-fetched," the *Washington Post's* editorial board concluded.[458] But border hawks clung to it in significant numbers as nothing Abbott did seemed to be working.

Abbott's Republican primary challengers framed the invasion clause as a necessary nuclear option, but they never once offered details of how the state would actually deport illegal aliens it caught. Even after Abbott handily beat the pair in the primaries, the invasion clause only gathered urgency, as the Biden administration prepared to lift Title 42. Well into the fall of 2022, eleven Texas counties symbolically declared invasions under the clause to pressure Abbott.[459]

"The solution to our border crisis already exists in the Texas and U.S. constitutions," Kinney County Attorney Brent Smith, whose county covers sixteen miles of border, told The Center Square in May 2022. "The question is whether our elected officials will govern according to the constitution and preserve our state. Texas is running out of time."[460]

One of Arizona's Republican gubernatorial candidates at the time, Kerri Lake, won acclaim and attention from conservatives by vowing to invoke the invasion articles and to seek an "interstate compact" with other border states to form a commission. The commission would create a "dedicated border security force" that would "arrest, detain, and return illegal immigrants back across the border," making sure to let DHS know what was happening "as a courtesy."[461]

Proponents of the idea scoffed at critics who claimed immigration was solely a federal responsibility.

"Statute is clear that the federal government is responsible for enforcing security at our nation's borders," Lake wrote. "But statute does not supersede the Constitution. If Washington refuses to honor its constitutional requirements, states have every recourse and responsibility to take matters into their own hands."

So why hadn't Abbott activated his purported emergency war powers to deal with this "invasion" after eighteen months of crisis?

Abbott's public statements indicate genuine outrage over the crisis but not an appetite to spearhead some big messy state-federal precedent for the invasion declaration. For one, he was in an unexpectedly tight race for the governorship against Democratic nominee Robert "Beto" O'Rourke who was closing in fast in polling and fundraising.[462] And during this period, Abbott was rumored to be interested in a run for the presidency in 2024.[463] Going all in with an invasion clause declaration and state deportation attempts might not play well in a mainstream presidential bid.

But he also didn't believe the theory. At an April 2022 press conference in San Antonio, Abbott questioned whether state law enforcement officers had authority to detain and deport and even worried aloud that, if they tried, the officers could face federal criminal charges.

"There are federal laws that law enforcement officers could be prosecuted under if they were to take someone without authority and immediately return them across the border," Abbott told reporters.[464]

In July 2022, Abbott did finally *seem* to invoke the fabled untested invasion clause with a new executive order that called on DPS troopers and National Guard to apprehend "immigrants who cross the border between ports of entry or commit other violations of federal law, and to return them to ports of entry."[465]

But while this sounded like an order to start deporting, it was more like a fake movie punch. DPS and National Guard soldiers merely started driving immigrants "*to* the border" [author's emphasis], not over it. That meant state police and

National Guard delivered some to Biden's Border Patrol near the Eagle Pass bridge, where most would soon make their way into American cities, just like always. The executive order exercise struck me as silly.

Abbott's reluctance to test-drive the invasion-declaration gambit drove many conservative Texans to outright fury. I could sense a real ugliness under the civility. When I explained a few legal and logistical impediments during a speech I gave to one conservative group in North Texas in late August, some in the audience cried "bullshit!" and at least two suggested that citizens should shoot immigrants in self-defense, an idea I was quick to warn against (and promptly reported to law enforcement intelligence). In late September, police and FBI in Hudspeth County arrested two local residents for allegedly shooting illegal aliens standing by the side of a highway, killing one and critically injuring a second.

In any case, advocates hanging everything on the invasion declaration idea never provided details of how it would be done. There were some real thwarting logistical obstructions to state deportation operations.

For example: armed CBP personnel control the U.S. side of international bridges and answer only to Mayorkas, who could simply order them to block the state officers when they tried to enter the bridge with intended deportees. Game over, at best until the courts decided its legality. At worst, federal-state confrontations might lead to unimaginable armed standoffs.

Many welcomed the legal fight.

For instance, when I spoke of Biden's CBP blocking Texas deportations on *Tucker Carlson Tonight* in April 2022, the broadcaster responded with an idea I'd heard elsewhere after presenting these logistical problems.

"It would be interesting to see who wins that fight, but it would be nice to *have* a fight because the country is disappearing," Carlson replied to me. "Maybe it's worth having, I don't know."[466]

But there was another obvious barrier: Mexico would have to agree to accept deportees and could simply just say no if Biden asked it to.

Texas would be left with some bad options. They could throw women and children back into the river or fire rubber bullets and tear gas at them as iPhone cameras rolled. Most would agree these options would not be politically tenable or go legally unchallenged for long. Immigrants deported to river sandbars would simply try again the next hour somewhere else, as they already did after Title 42 expulsions.

The DPS director, Col. Steven McCraw, pointed out a different problem with state deportations. State and federal intelligence systems do not speak to one another, so the state would be unable to detect convicted and deported criminals or terrorism suspects. They'd be thrown into Mexico where, of course, such subjects would turn right around in Mexico and reenter "with no guarantee that we would detect and detain them a second time," McCraw pointed out.

"So the state would have a program to detect, detain and release everyone into Mexico without knowing their status and spending substantial resources to do so," he said.

In fact, everyone Texas would expel to Mexico would just turn around like they do with the federal Title 42.

"It may look good on TV," McCraw told me. "But it's ineffective as a policy. While we're taking time to put them on the bridge the cartel is exploiting the gaps."

Realities like these came off like excuses for inaction to conservative Texas activists like Sheena Rodriguez, a Dallas-area mom driven to activism after a first border visit who now runs the nonprofit advocacy group Secure the Border. Rodriguez was a fierce advocate of the invasion declaration and state deportations.

Rodriguez had to admit, when I asked her to explain how state troopers would get their deportees past blocking CBP and Mexican bridge officers, that no one in her community of activists ever spoke of those problematic, defeating details. Her frustration turned red at hearing, from me, yet more explanations for why Texas couldn't act.

"People are sick and tired of accepting that 'there's nothing we can do, this is a federal issue,'" she said. "People are tired of hearing that we're securing our borders but…'it's just a federal issue, so throw up the white flag of surrender.'"

Maybe Texas can't logistically deport immigrants, Rodriguez had to concede, but "we have to do whatever it takes to shut this down. We expect our elected state officials to find true, viable solutions to fill the gap the current administration is refusing to address, because it's Texans who are forced to deal with the overwhelming negative consequences."

The frustration is understandable and the desire reasonable when the primary federal government policy goal for the border is to achieve "safe, orderly, and humane" illegal immigration, rather than stopping it as required under congressional statutes. But those elected Texas leaders had been reaching for viable solutions. The problem is that none have appreciably turned back the tide. That is because, as much as frustrated conservatives hate to hear it, slowing illegal immigration is a federal government duty, responsibility, and job.

Jailing Immigrants for Trespassing

Texas found one way to arrest illegal aliens and did so thousands of times hoping it would deter further illegal crossings, at least in certain areas. In June 2021, an innovative state scheme had Texas state police arresting illegal immigrants on criminal trespass charges. A first-offense misdemeanor could land illegal aliens up to six months in jail and potentially problematic criminal record if convicted.

In rolling out this experiment, Abbott and his top lieutenants tapped into the principle that illegal aliens sent influencing messaging back down the trail of bad things that happened to them so that others would stay home.

"The goal is to prevent and deter," DPS Director McCraw told me. "We recognize that arrest and prosecution is a deterrent in itself."

They also understood that aliens who crossed in remote areas and went sneaking about were likelier to be runners with criminal histories, a good demographic to target.

Texas DPS and National Guard set up the operation at first in two counties, Val Verde and McKinney in and around Del Rio and Eagle Pass, and planned to gradually expand to some of the twenty-three other "high priority" regions the agency identified along the border. Huge private ranches touched the Rio Grande in these areas, serving as popular byways for illegal immigrants hoping to evade Border Patrol.

But severe limitations hobbled the program from the start. For one, state troopers could only arrest trespassers on private lands whose owners agreed in writing to serve as complainants, and not all would. That left gaping holes through which smugglers could guide their customers around and through DPS. Only those who didn't know better might stumble into the DPS traps here and there.

Secondly, jail space was in short supply in many of the counties. Operations had to comport with jail capacity, although the state worked hard to convert facilities.

Texas labored under another limitation. DPS would only arrest single adults and not whole families because jail facilities were not equipped for children. So DPS handed off trespassers who were in family groups to the Border Patrol just as they would anywhere else, which as we know, results in their releases into America. With incentive to go through, families kept right on coming through the DPS criminal trespassing traps.

The granddaddy of all undermining limitations: Democratic prosecutors and attorneys in blue counties along the border found a convenient way to happily defeat Republican aims. They would drop the state's charges or recommend no jail time. While some border counties had gone Republican in recent years, plenty still elected Democrats to district attorney and county attorney seats.

"At the end of the day, my office is not enforcing immigration laws," Democratic Val Verde County Attorney David Martinez of Del Rio told me in October 2021, four months into the DPS criminal trespass program. For example, of 231 DPS misdemeanor cases filed in his office during the prior few months, he dismissed or rejected 105 on his judgment that none caused any harm to the complaining landowner.

He said he dismissed some because they planned to file what sounded to Martinez, after listening to their defense attorneys and personal stories, like meritorious asylum claims.

He cut guilty plea deals with 50 others but recommended to the judge that none get jail time beyond what they'd already spent in custody, which was anywhere from fifteen to forty-five days to save taxpayers in a poor county the significant expense.

"As I've considered every aspect in those cases we have dismissed, I'm pretty confident those individuals didn't break anybody's fence, didn't cause destruction, didn't linger, didn't harass anybody in their home," Martinez said. "They're simply crossing what, to them, looks like open rural land. Part of my thought process is to see to it that justice is done and part of that is fairness to taxpayers paying to house these immigrants in jail when they can."

Martinez said he believed the arrests, whatever the outcomes, still deterred down-trail migrants. But I wasn't so sure because of something else Martinez told me.

Biden's DHS had decided that while single adults that Border Patrol found would be expelled under Title 42, any single adult DPS charged would be released into the American interior to pursue asylum claims. Down-trail migrants who saw that outcome would perceive DPS arrest as coming with a reward at the end.

By the end of June 2025, Texas had arrested and charged 4,589 immigrants with criminal trespass. Quite a few were charged with other crimes, such as alien smuggling and drug trafficking, which can be said to always serve a strong public interest. And for that reason alone, it can be argued that the program is worthwhile.

But as for any deterring effect of these arrests on overall illegal immigration through the areas where Texas was filing the charges, escalating apprehension numbers throughout the program indicate little impact. My own travels support my contention. In interviews with immigrants en route, none ever mentioned that they were afraid to cross because DPS might catch them. There are simply too many holes in the net where those caught could go free into interior America.

A Twinkling Lone Star

In an empty parking lot of a deserted downtown Roma, Texas, long after night fell, six members of a Texas DPS "Special Response Team," wearing camouflage military-style uniforms and flak vests, talked smack with each other and traded gossip inside two unmarked Suburbans parked next to each other, the facing windows down. The men chattered in the front and back seats, some fidgeting with their noise-suppressed, fully automatic M4 rifles close at hand while waiting for the "go" from their police radios. The state police agency's SRT members were trained to storm barricaded gunmen and combat with dangerous criminals. Now, they were on the border within sight of the Rio Grande and the notorious cartel drug trafficking town of Miguel Alemán with a different kind of duty.

Night after night like this one in May 2021, the SRT men would silently slip into brushy surveillance spots along the river after dark. They would wait and watch in utter silence through $20,000 white phosphorous night-vision goggles for drug smugglers hiking their loads in from the Mexican side. I was embedded with the team, within eyesight of the Roma-Ciudad Miguel Alemán International Bridge, and we were to hike into the brush to intercept a troop of marijuana smugglers that intelligence reporting indicated would be crossing that night not far away.

Soon, the radio call came in, but it was not the "go" signal. Something had spooked the dope smugglers. They weren't coming that night. The mission was off. While the rest waited in the Suburbans for further orders, one of the SRT agents and I decided to follow a foot path down Roma's fifty-foot bluffs to the Rio Grande just to stretch our legs a little.

Rafts filled with women and children were crossing and landing and had already swamped the few Border Patrol agents and National Guardsmen stationed down there taking down names, snapping photos, and preparing them for transport to a facility where more bureaucracy happened. The Border Patrol agents saw the Texas DPS uniform of my companion— it didn't matter which agency—and gang-pressed him to meet this raft or that raft and bring the passengers over to a lengthening processing line.

The Texas DPS officer moved down the riverbank, guided by a powerful flashlight, to within just feet of one cartel boat smuggler, who had stepped into the ankle-deep Texas water as the mothers and children left the plastic dinghy. The officer would grasp each gently by an arm and point them up the bank with his flashlight to a dirt road.

I asked him as we walked the group back to where the Border Patrol agents were working why he did not tackle and arrest this cartel operative. He replied that there was a good chance the boat pilot might throw a kid in the water to distract an arresting officer, as had recently happened in such a DPS attempt, or pull a hidden gun or knife to resist.

"You gotta think about if you get into a scuffle match there with this guy when there are kids around, innocent bystanders around," he responded. "Or just let him go back and nobody gets hurt. It's one of those deals where you've got to make a decision like, I don't want that to happen."

When it comes to stopping illegal immigration, some plausible set of reasons always got in the way for Texas. Not for lack of trying.

In March 2021, Governor Abbott declared a disaster in sixty-three border counties, which gave him expansive powers to send troops and police. He issued an executive order authorizing Operation Lone Star.[467] It would divert state Highway Patrol troopers, Texas Rangers SWAT and SRT members, intelligence analysts, criminal investigations agents, and pilots, from interior duties to the border to fill what state commanders called untended "high-threat gaps."

In an initial press release, Governor Abbott said he ordered up Operation Lone Star on the grounds that "the crisis at our southern border continues to escalate because of Biden Administration policies that refuse to secure the border and invite illegal immigration."

There was much more value to the operation than merely that.

Border Patrol agents were off the line processing in the families. Drug traffickers and criminal aliens who didn't want to be caught were having a field day.

Operation Lone Star sent well-trained cops to plug many of the holes.

On air, land, and water, the Texas state police were sent first in the highly trammeled Rio Grande Valley, then in the Del Rio sector as the border jumpers with no interest in turning themselves in shifted away from that policing heat and finally in Big Bend country of west Texas. It was never about ending illegal immigration so much as mitigating the effects of the broader collapse the problem caused.

"You have a wide array of state violations. Human smuggling, possession of narcotics, driving while intoxicated, people that are wanted," DPS Regional Commander Victor Escalon told me about the state's vision. "Let's say we see a sex offender wanted for a crime, and they have a lengthy criminal history. They're a felon. They have weapons. And they're also smuggling. So we have all these hooks for plenty of state charges, without a doubt, that are easy to identify, so that's why we're there."

Otherwise, there would be nobody to do those jobs while Border Patrol agents were fetching diapers and baby formula.

Perhaps the most visible elements of Operation Lone Star were the black-and-white Texas Highway Patrol Suburbans at the traffic lights, vacant lots, and store parking areas of border towns like La Gruella, Sullivan City, Roma, Fronton, Harlingen, Brownsville, and McAllen. The surge expanded to other hot regions of the border. DPS vehicles might crunch slowly over rough riverside roads or park under trees out in the brush. They kept a steady pressure on motorists and foot traffic. One day, troopers pulled me over three different times, eyeballing me hard, looking for a sign of jangled nerves and studying the interior of my vehicle.

I once rode with a trooper named "Lupe" for a daytime shift. He explained what the point was.

"Our number one thing is drugs," Lupe explained as we cruised through Rio Grande City. "Most of the time, Border

Patrol is just cutting paper and letting the illegals go. Poor guys…their hands are so tied…. It's hard for them to do anything anymore.

"But when Border Patrol is busy with a hundred illegals like that, we'll work the flanks where the drug smugglers go. They're very strategic, so we're strategic."

Lupe and all DPS troopers were always dialed in to Border Patrol radio. They rushed to and around immigrant apprehensions, chases, and any incident in line with radio traffic, which spikes and ebbs as shifts go on. They were looking for the drug traffickers, who as often as not hit the gas when the lights flash behind them.

Lupe loved the flush-and-chase aspect of the job, quipping that before each shift he "prays to the pursuit gods" to give him some good ones. Lupe started trailing a truck with a back-window "Santa Muerta" symbol on display, the "saint of death" said to be worshipped by drug cartel operatives. But Lupe could find no violation as he ran the license plate through his on-board computer. The driver moved at exactly the speed limit and properly signaled lane changes, and Lupe let the driver eventually disappear from sight.

His pursuit prayers were better answered the week before my arrival, when Lupe flushed a marijuana smuggler he'd tried to pull over. The driver hit the gas pedal instead and careened at high speed down a dirt road to the river. It was a designated flight path. Along the way, the smuggler's well-practiced compatriots, hidden in the brush and obviously in radio contact with the driver, threw a log onto the road. Lupe swerved around it. Then, someone else slammed closed the ranch gates. Lupe had to get out and open them, which bought the driver time to launch his car right into the river. By the time Lupe showed up, the driver and his associates were floating away on a raft with the drugs back to the Mexican side, flipping off Lupe defiantly.

Lupe knew he wasn't stopping the illegal immigration; he was a barrier to drug trafficking. When he and other DPS troopers happened across aliens looking to check in with a uniformed officer for the sure-thing admittances, Lupe said he'd interview them for intelligence about their smugglers and pass the information on to law enforcement. But otherwise, he was under orders to deliver them to Border Patrol as fast as possible—he regarded them as a nuisance—and returned to the field to light up drug smugglers. Through July 29, 2022, DPS passed along 287,000 immigrants to Border Patrol.

In the National Interest

Of all the state's initiatives, Operation Lone Star probably served America's national interests most. The operation led to thousands of drug seizures, arrests, and prosecutions that would otherwise never have happened. The statistics, albeit disputed by liberal media outlets, outline general contours of the contribution during its first sixteen months: 17,730 criminal arrests, 15,110 felony charges, and $10,698,05 in currency seizures through July 2022.

DPS agents assisted in the seizure of drugs that would almost certainly would have gotten through: 20,553 pounds of marijuana, 2,983 pounds of cocaine, 10,942 pounds of methamphetamine, 243 pounds of fentanyl, 325 million lethal doses of fentanyl, Abbott's office claimed.

Without DPS, most of the drugs and criminals would have gotten through. When ranchers felt threatened and wanted to report incursions, they called troopers rather than Border Patrol voice mail. The operation was expensive and drew plenty of detractors and lawsuits. Conservatives were angry that it couldn't stop the illegal immigration, and liberals seemed to take delight in pointing out that it didn't stop illegal immigration.

Staking such state jurisdiction claims on traditionally federal responsibilities is unusual; none of the other border states—New Mexico, Arizona, or California—similarly stepped up with such a major commitment of manpower and tax dollars. None of the others tried like Texas.

DPS was in the air with extra helicopters and fixed-wing aircraft, with a goal of having state officers up at least twenty-two hours per day trying to spot illegal immigrants and smugglers and to lead ground forces to them.

Others state troopers were neither flying nor driving. They were on the river in DPS gunboats. The black-and-white cigarette boats, with their 900-horsepower banks of four engines each, have been churning up a forty-mile stretch of the Rio Grande for years already to deter drug smugglers and occupy that busy smuggler's lane as best as possible. The shifts increased for Operation Lone Star. The crews included trained trackers who could work out foot traffic sign on the Texas bank. Officers man each of four .30-caliber fully automatic machine guns mounted on the boats.

At the height of the Biden border crisis in fall 2022, Texas leadership was refusing to put an end date or spending cap on this $4 billion-and-counting deployment. The last time DPS similarly invested in border security like this was during the Obama administration years with an initiative called "Operation Strong Safety," ordered up by then-Governor Rick Perry. That one went on for four years at a cost of some $800 million. Operation Lone Star will cost billions.

But at its heart, this is a Republican effort. Liberal Democrats are gunning for control of Texas. When I worked for DPS, I often heard it said around our headquarters campus in Austin that "Texas security is national security" and "as Texas goes, so goes the country." It was as true then as it is now. The 1,254-mile Texas border is the biggest gateway for illicit narcotics, as well as foreign strangers who pose national security threats, violent criminals, and huge impoverished foreign populations to reach interior America.

For that reason, much is at stake in the next few state and national elections, chiefly the trajectory of ills that can harm the country. Progressive liberal Democrats are gunning for Republican control of Texas. They hate everything that Abbott has done with his border policy. They deny there is a problem. If Democrats can break a nearly three-decade Republican Party lock on Texas government, they would seek the dismantlement of it all, even an operation of value such as Operation Lone Star.

Early Takeaways

The story of what Texas did during the first two years of the Biden border crisis holds wisdom for other states and Washington to excavate. At some point, the state's Republican governor may find the elusive elixir necessary to make an impact on illegal immigration in addition to drug trafficking and the rest. But that hadn't happened by the end of 2022.

One important takeaway should be that, while Abbott's Texas border insurgency against the White House probably enhanced broader American public safety in significant ways, it appeared increasingly obvious that only the executive branch of the U.S. government can ever effectively impact illegal immigration flow along the entire border, even with congressional legislative action. The executive branch has proven willing to ignore congressional mandates such as detention and deportation.

On their own, individual states can contribute to the national interest when they impact drug trafficking, human smuggling crime, and other border crime but seem unable to appreciably reduce illegal immigration, their limited span of authorities insufficient to that task.

But the most visible and impactful of the Texas initiatives two years in, I would argue, was Abbott's mobilization of 10,000 National Guard troops and surge of Texas DPS state troopers for Operation Lone Star, despite criticism otherwise. Its most meaningful achievement was not that it stopped or slowed economic migration—it didn't—but that it plugged holes in the nation's line of defense on other problems after its abandonment by Border Patrol to family-processing duties.

Liberal media outlets have raised questions about the state's claimed statistics.[468] But there can be no doubt that Texas caught drug traffickers, seized drug payloads, rescued people, busted cartel smugglers, discovered deportable criminal aliens, and brought state criminal charges against criminals who victimized or exploited the immigrants and Texas residents. All that can only portend a net good for the whole nation's interior. Most importantly, Texas soldiers and state troopers held anarchy at bay from overwhelmed communities for hundreds of miles in their own state. Texas reinforced local sheriffs whose entire staffs were gang-pressed into dealing with illegal immigrants day and night for months on end.

None of that negates the fact that, some two years into Joe Biden's "safe, orderly and humane" vision, Texas had not found the remedy from it by itself. Future Texas leaders, if they are Republican, no doubt will continue mixing political and legal chemicals like mad scientists, hoping to stumble onto just the right potion. The law, politics, progressive litigation, courts, Democratic oppositionists, and federal policy all stack against such a discovery, but the American Way is that they should keep trying.

CHAPTER SEVENTEEN

FOREVER IMPACTS

"The originals" of Liberty County, Texas—the self-descriptor of lifelong Anglo residents like Jimmy Rollins, who trace their lineage to early settler families—have mostly fled what they regard as ruinous, irredeemable change.

Settlement in the county wilderness some forty miles northeast of Houston dates to the 1830s and 1840s and boomed a bit when an oil field was discovered there in 1925 but still didn't much change the cherished small-town closeness, long lonely country lanes through uninterrupted timberland, the hunting and fishing subsistence lifestyle, and tiny high school graduating classes.

Until very recently, the loggers, train mechanics, ranchers, and state prison workers made their homes in and around Liberty County's quaint old townships carved out of dense pine forests with names like Plum Grove, Cleveland, Dayton, and Splendora. They raised each other's barns and dug one another's wells.

Now seventy-two and among a much-dwindled number of "originals," Rollins was still farming and ranching acreage near Dayton when I met him in May 2022. Just like his father, who was born and lived until he was buried at age ninety-five in Plum Grove, Rollins recalled riding a horse every Sunday to church and to school as a kid, "barefoot until junior high," and he raised his own family much the same way, by farming and following a rural country code of life.

"It was all country people. We got our meat out of them woods there. They was behind in time, but everybody pretty much knew everybody," Rollins recalled. "I enjoyed living here."

Not anymore.

A vast jumble of single- and double-wide trailers on low stilts, hand-hewn shacks made of leftover construction material, double- and single-wide mobile homes, and parked motor homes has quickly overtaken tens of thousands of Liberty County acres and eradicated its rural way of life. The community is named "Colony Ridge." It sprawls over some thirty-five square miles of unincorporated former timber company lands all around the outskirts of the towns, nary a group of trees in sight now.

Upwards of 50,000 mostly Spanish-speaking Latinos, maybe more—nobody knows, really—are living on some 30,000 homestead lots they purchased in recent years from "Houston Terrenos," the land development company started by an "original" named William Henry "Trey" and brother John Harris a decade earlier.

From just 2019 through 2022, Colony Ridge more than doubled in size to almost 20,000 acres.[469] Another 20,000 lots under development in 2022 surrounded Rollins's 192-acre farm out near Dayton. Rollins and the originals experienced all this in stunned disbelief.

"They clear-cut everything. Everything!" Rollins lamented. "The deer's moved. I don't see hog here anymore. Where they went I don't know. They want to call it progress, and I guess it is, but to me it's not the right kind of progress.

They're just taking over there, and that's fine if they do it legally," he continued. "Hell, I don't like it but ain't nothing I can do about it. I don't mind if they do it right and make 'em all legal. That's my biggest problem with it. They need to pay to the society just like we do, and they don't, and there's no way to keep up with it."

The Harris brothers come from an "original" family out of Cut 'n' Shoot, Texas, with some interesting history; both Trey and an uncle were accomplished professional boxers before the family went into real estate development. The uncle, Ray Harris, once fought world heavyweight champion Floyd Patterson in 1958 and Sonny Liston in 1960.[470]

A significant portion of the new population that bought Terrenos lots are illegally present, according to the settlers themselves, local police, school officials, teachers, and other residents. No one really knows how many, but no one denies that a great many are; I saw flags of foreign nations fly here and there over dwellings representing El Salvador, Cuba, Nicaragua, and Mexico.

The population of Latinos drawn to Liberty County ballooned after 2017 into the 40,000 and 50,000 range when Houston Terrenos acquired vast new tracts of timber company land and, on Spanish-language media platforms with international reach, began marketing lot purchases with its unique "owner-to-owner method."[471] The method held a powerful appeal for illegal immigrants who heard it (and anyone with low income and bad credit scores): they could buy land with less than $1,000 down directly from Terrenos, skipping traditional bank mortgage requirements that borrowers prove a history of legal income and financial stability.

Of course, interest charged on the owner loans might range to 13 percent or reportedly even higher, and the company would foreclose after just a few missed payments. But obviously, plenty of buyers believed the Terrenos Houston website promise that buying a quarter or three-quarter acre here, and then a do-it-yourself dwelling is "the perfect solution for you to become the owner of your own land in the United States...."[472]

I explore the case of Liberty County and its booming Colony Ridge development in this book because it makes for an apt emblematic harbinger of the kind of change that sudden explosive growth in illegal alien population can portend for citizens and residents already living in receiving communities. Liberty County may stand as a rather extreme example of this kind of explosive growth, mainly because of the unique real estate opportunities that catered to and drew illegal immigrants only here. In 2020, analyst Chuck DeVore of the Austin-based Texas Public Policy Foundation think tank dubbed Colony Ridge "the fastest-growing Hispanic population in the United States and one of the fastest growing school districts." When the massive development is fully built out, DeVore figured, the population of these communities is projected to reach as high as a quarter million people, a significant percentage of them not legally present in the country.[473]

But therein is the value. To varying degrees up to the extreme case of Liberty County, a great many other preexisting communities in America already are seeing very significant sudden growth in illegal alien populations from the Biden border crisis. It's too early in the Biden border crisis to fully calculate the fast-moving impacts until the growth slows or stops. But not in Liberty County. Most of those who bought in and live in Liberty County did not come in the great Biden border crisis of 2021–present, but in the five or ten years past. So the area is there for ready examination as to what some secondary impacts may look and feel like after sudden high growth of illegal immigrant settlement. Americans can expect to feel the change in qualify-of-life metrics as Liberty County certainly has, and I'll take readers into some of that.

But probably the very first area of civic life where most Americans will experience the impact of the Biden border crisis will be in the public schools.

Canaries in the Coal Mine: America's Public Schools

"Teachers don't come back from Christmas."

—a former teacher of the Cleveland Independent
School District in Texas

Local schools face the most immediately visible impacts because a main feature of the Biden border crisis, and also of the earlier Trump swell (2018–2019), was children in family groups coming to exploit the Flores loophole. It's impossible to determine from available public records exactly how many children came in among roughly two million people in family groups that Border Patrol apprehended and likely stayed from 2018 through 2022. But these events probably added close to 2 million to the nation's 49.5 million students who attend American public schools.[474]

Border Patrol counts family groups as small as one parent and one child, but I've seen a great many single parents come in with two, three, or more children, or both parents show up with four or five, or just one, plus a family pet. Short of any other reasonable way to estimate, let's presume for analytical purposes a reasonable middle-ground supposition that all two million people that CBP statistics counted as family groups consisted of two parents and one child and also that two parents brought in two children. That would mean, conservatively, that somewhere between 666,000 and 1.2 million children entered during those few years.

Add to that some 800,000 "unaccompanied minors" we do definitively know from government reporting crossed without a parent or guardian from 2018 through mid-2022.[475] Tallying those 800,000 with the family group children, it becomes reasonable to assume that up to 2 million kids who entered the U.S. through the southern border in those few years.

A 1982 Supreme Court ruling required enrollment regardless of immigration status, so school districts must take any kid who shows up no matter their numbers, costs, and hardships.[476]

What might those be? Enrollments, long-term costs, and hardships are extremely hard to assess because local media outlets often report "spiking enrollments," bond elections, and English as a second language (ESL) teacher shortages but then, bizarrely, take elaborate pains to thread their way around reporting who the new children are or why they suddenly came in huge numbers.

Immigrant children influxes are almost always treated in local media as a sensitive Thanksgiving dinner subject to avoid and therefore hard to track if media reporting is a starting point.

"That's something that can be thrust on a school district very, very quickly," said Tony Kinnett, former science director for Indianapolis Public Schools and cofounder of *Chalkboard Review*, a publication that covers education. "Schools simply don't have the infrastructure to educate kids who aren't in the language bracket of fluency and sub-fluency."

The public will not easily learn when it happens because schools in wide swaths of the country are not required to publish detailed budgets that would reveal the presence of illegal immigrant enrollments in the nation's Midwest, Northeast, East Coast, or South, Kinnett said. Only budgets showing staffing, construction, and general curriculum have to be published, he said.

Districts can build departments full of dedicated ESL instructors that can "leach" funding from other needy program areas as it expands, Kinnett said, but "you can sweep a lot of stuff under those three subjects."

(Hint: Internet news browser searches of "portable classrooms" or "bond elections" will indicate which districts may be laboring already under immigrant children influxes and, with some digging, can lead an enterprising researcher to learn where it is happening.)

The National Center for Education Statistics did provide some general indication of where it was happening during and after Trump's 2019 immigrant family crisis but had not updated its reporting in 2022.[477] The center tracked English learner (EL) enrollments from 2010 through the fall of 2019, by which time the bulk of nearly one million family members that included kids had already crossed the border that crisis year were in the country. The report found that the number of EL students grew by 600,000, to 5.1 million students, nationally. Texas (19.6 percent), California (18.6 percent), and New Mexico (16.5 percent) led the way in EL students among twelve states where EL kids reached more than 10 percent. EL students gravitated to big cities at an average of 14.8 percent of total public school enrollments, 10 percent in suburban areas, 7 percent in towns, and 4.4 percent in rural America.

But public schools will be the first place most Americans see, feel, and suffer from the Biden border crisis. For what that may look like, parents whose children attend public schools across the United States need look no farther than Cleveland Independent School District (CISD), which encompasses 60,000 people of Colony Ridge and some of the old towns within its 143 square miles.[478]

The ills there take the form of classroom and school overcrowding that require portable classroom farms, sharp spending increases to hire new teachers and bus drivers, continual requests for voters to approve bonds to build new schools, fallouts from language barriers and uneven education levels, less individualized teacher time per student, poorer academic performances for all, and public safety concerns.

Opening the Book on Education in "Hyper-Growth" Texas District

Those afflictions started to hit CISD when student population exploded during the 2016–2017 school year. Hurricane Harvey had devastated wide swaths of the nearby Houston metropolitan area, creating an enduring demand for illegal alien reconstruction labor.[479] Terrenos Houston stepped up land acquisition and sales to catch that wind in the sail. Escalating enrollments changed this school district forever just like it will change many others. In 2019, the Texas Education Agency labeled CISD as a "hyper-growth" district.[480]

"This was always known as a quiet little country town. I mean, it really was," Superintendent Stephen McCanless told me during a long candid interview at CISD administration headquarters in Cleveland. "This was a pass-through on the way north to Livingston to go camping, or on the way north to Lufkin. You stopped here to get gas and eat, but it's always been a quiet, blue-collar community."

In the few years since Hurricane Harvey, the quaint country CISD of four K-12 schools has morphed into an almost unrecognizable beast of twelve schools, some of which had to be doubled in size, plans for twenty more schools and ever-expanding farms of portable classrooms.

"Is it all because of immigration?" McCanless asked rhetorically. "I'm not going to sit here and say that we have other students moving in as well. Those *are* our highest percentage of enrollments."

Data reflecting those enrollments remove all doubt as to how torrential that growth was. For the 2011–2012 school year, a year now regarded fondly as the good old days when a local Dairy Queen was sufficient to serve as the main high school hangout, CISD enrolled 3,693 students from kindergarten through twelfth grade. About 40 percent were Hispanic, 45 percent white, and 12 percent black.

Fast-forward a decade to 2021–2022. Total enrollments had nearly tripled to 10,875, of which 9,275 were Hispanic, pushing 90 percent, district records show.

The trajectory's end is nowhere in sight for CISD and, to varying degrees, for districts across America. CISD is projecting yet another doubling in size by 2026, which would bring the student body from the current 10,875 students to more than 20,000.

It projects having to spend $1.2 billion to build the twenty new schools over ten years.

McCandless had to admit that "there are days in my office that I'm, uh, it's difficult." New students were pouring in every day through mid-2022: 100, 200, 300 every month. After one Christmas break, school reopened to 1,200 new students, McCandless recalled.

"Every day, our teachers see another student and you know, it's 'here's Johnny,'" he said. "And, 'welcome to class, Johnny, we're so glad to have you. I don't have a desk for you. But here's a chair.' So we've been dealing with a lot of *that*."

Most of the new students could not speak English, according to district data reflecting English as a second language curriculum and as limited English proficient. The percentage who couldn't speak English proficiently rose from 20 percent in the 2011–2012 school year to nearly 55 percent in 2021–2022.

That's "extremely high," McCandless conceded and so was the district's need for bilingual teachers to staff a dual language program and special education programs where large numbers of the kids are taught half a day in English and half a day in Spanish. A nationwide shortage of bilingual teachers drove CISD to unusual lengths. It started hiring foreign-born teachers from Colombia, Venezuela, and even Italy and importing them to Texas on H1-B specialist worker visas the school district has to sponsor.

Recruiting them proved so difficult the district pays $4,000 annual stipends to help keep them around when money could not be tighter. Red tape at the State Department to acquire and keep them requires a full-time attorney.

"But we need them, so we work hard," the superintendent told me.

ESL made up more than half of all school curricula too. Almost the entire teaching staff is required to obtain state ESL certification or an equivalent one. The training for that is expensive and time consuming and requires constant management.

A majority of the parents speak limited English too, if at all.

"They don't engage with us a lot at our meetings and activities," which is a state requirement, McCanless said. The reason? Some fear that school officials will report them to ICE, he explained.

"That's one reason they want to stay away. They're afraid, but that's not what Cleveland ISD is about. We're here to educate children and build school-to-home community relationships."

Shoehorning a Fit

A teacher who used to work in the CISD and now works for another one in East Texas, speaking on condition that she not be identified, told me she realized one-room schoolhouse life was for sure over when, on the eve of a big basketball game between rival schools, the district installed metal detectors at the doors.

"That was totally new to me," I was like, what? What! I'd never seen anything like that," the teacher told me. "I was like, 'what are y'all doing? Someone was thinking, there's this big rivalry, so…guns or knives."

Many of the newcomers came in not fitting well in a school. One girl told the teacher she had reached a strictly transactional agreement to marry a U.S. citizen boy so she could get permanent immigration status and go to college after graduation. Others were disciplinary cases kicked out of Houston schools.

"We had our *entrepreneurs* on campus," the teacher said, explaining that this was a euphemism for drug dealer. "When a kid is coming in eighteen years old and has four or five credits, why would they come back to high school and not just get their GED? The registrar would tell us, 'this kid's coming in for business. I mean, if your income is school-based, then… you know.'"

Superintendent McCandless acknowledged problems like that but insisted they were isolated and did not constitute organized gang activity in his view.

"Now, do we have some little groups that want to cause some trouble and do some behavior that I consider criminal? Yes, we've had them. And we have dealt with them," he said. "And I have expelled them. And I told the parents you can find an education somewhere but it won't be here."

There'd be sixteen-, seventeen-and eighteen-year-olds who spoke no English, hadn't been to school in years, and had to start from Dick-and-Jane scratch, the teacher recalled. McCandless told me students like this were categorized as "newcomers."

There is already evidence elsewhere that such newcomers were reaching other districts. In May 2022, New York City education officials grappling with older illiterate teen immigrants who have gone years without formal education agreed to launch a pilot program that would all 400 "newcomers" fan out to identified high schools where they can learn English.[481]

"Texas Education Agency says they have a right to a free public education," McCanless said. "And I can't put a fourteen-year-old in a second-grade class, so we put them in an age-appropriate grade level and we give them all the supports we can, and then you're like, 'how do we teach a fourteen-year-old how to read!? I mean, that should have been learned in first or second grade. But we have to do it. We're doing it. We have some now. And then the state tells us they're expected to take the state test!"

"How are they doing on the tests?" I asked.

"How do *you* think?" McCanless replied.

Perhaps there are not enough Anglo "originals" even in the schools anymore. I couldn't readily find any to interview, and some of the old-timers in Plum Grove told me many turned to home-schooling or moved away. The percentage of white students in CISD fell from 45 percent a decade earlier to less than 10 percent in 2021–2022.

But newcomers who are not legally present appreciate the opportunity, even with the traffic and overcrowding. It handily beats anything they had in their home countries.

Like a restaurant worker I met in Dayton named Benjamin. He admitted he was an illegal alien from Mexico who crossed the border some years earlier and decided to stay in Liberty County when he saw he could easily buy a Terrenos lot and home for his wife and two young daughters, also all illegal.

He said he understood the ire of old-line Liberty County native families over the traffic and crime and noise; he didn't like any of that either. But Benjamin just shrugged and said he had his own family to worry over. The Houston Terrenos promise of owning land in the United States spoke to Benjamin because illegals can't readily rent apartments without U.S. residency, which unscrupulous landlords exploit as opportunity to overcharge. Even with the high interest rates Terrenos charged on its loans, Benjamin's monthly mortgage payment still came out to less than when he had to rent a house on the black market.

"Nowhere else will it be that easy to buy land without a Social Security card," Benjamin said of Colony Ridge and Terrenos.

He put $500 down plus a few hundred dollars in fees on a three-quarter acre lot Terrenos sold him on a $65,000 loan at 12.9 percent interest, according to loan agreement papers he showed me. He took out another loan for $55,000 using the name of a brother, who had U.S. residency, and bought a double-wide mobile home to put on the property, eventually hooking it up to sewer and water lines Terrenos ran to it as part of the deal. Terrenos will foreclose if he misses any four payments over the life of the loan.

Provisions like that no doubt pushed Liberty County to among the highest home foreclosure rates in the nation by mid-2020, according to property data provider Attom Data Solutions, the twenty-fourth highest of more than 1,700 counties.[482]

But it's all worth it for as long as he can possibly do it because of the schools.

Benjamin said he worked at the restaurant more or less constantly to keep it all together so that his older daughter can attend the local Cleveland Independent School District elementary school. This school, he said, far surpasses those back home in Zacatecas, Mexico, academically and in every other way. The girl has shown early promise as a saxophonist, using a school-supplied instrument she can take home.

"We are illegal, but I know this country has done a lot for me," Benjamin told me as we sat together in the mobile home after his restaurant shift. "How do I pay it back? By being nice to everybody." And, he added with no hint of irony, "by being a good citizen."

Out of Space

Some rarefied media reporting does point to signs that many other American school districts are feeling the uncomfortable pressure of illegal immigrant student growth like CISD, with varying degrees of consequence. There will be many more as the Biden border crisis goes on.

For instance, in and around New York City, a significant surge of 5,000 immigrant children flooded into four counties in a single eleven-month span through August 2021, posing a $139 million additional burden on New York taxpayers to educate them. The arrivals of mostly teenage boys "is creating a classroom crisis that is strapping educational resources, costing taxpayers millions in un-budgeted dollars, and aiding gang-recruiting efforts," the *New York Post* reported.[483]

In Austin Independent School District, teachers protested in April 2022 about a 400-student influx of immigrant teenagers from Central America at its International High School and Eastside Early College High School campus. Teachers complained they were left to give instruction in hallways and conference rooms.[484]

CISD has handled the new enrollments in the usual ways that many Americans should already be seeing in their own systems. This district has bought acres of portable classrooms using general operation funds, the first nine in 2016, records show. By 2022, the district had spent nearly $10 million for more than sixty portables containing more than 250 classrooms spread among the schools.

That stop-gap measure wasn't close to sufficient. The CISD had to mount a parallel strategy of calling bond elections to build schools. In May 2017, district voters passed a first bond election for $85 million to build two new elementary schools and to double the size of Cleveland High School. Two years later, administrators went back to voters hat in hand asking for another one. That failed in May 2019, but one for $198 million passed that November. By November 2021, with the Biden border crisis raging beyond all known bounds, voters apparently had had enough. They rejected a third bond for $150 million, some voters feeling fed up with the Colony Ridge population boom, according to public posts on social media.

"This country needs to uphold its laws and provide for its own," voter Regina Ott wrote on the CISD Facebook page where the district conceded defeat.[485] "I am all for legal immigration, and I don't blame anyone for wanting a better life for their family. The U.S.A. is overwhelmed right now and needs a break to regroup and review our situation. We are fast becoming a third world country ourselves. We cannot save the world. I apologize if this offends anyone. It is not meant to. It's just the truth."

Wrote Kristy Morales, "How about not worrying about making more schools, but get immigration out here kicking out all the illegals who are taking up space and trashing the area."

As for the 2021 bond election defeat, McCandless blamed voter misunderstanding that the recent years of tax increases were tied to rising home value appraisals, not any extra burden put on by past bonds.

"It's all part of marketing and messaging. What we wanted them to know is we're not raising the tax rate. It's zero," he said. "The messaging didn't sink in. They're afraid of taxes, period."

McCanless and his school board were already busy planning the next bond election for the November 2022 ballot, this one for $115 million. There was no choice. The monthly crush of new kids and enrollment projections put unremitting pressure on the district for space.[486]

Most American families in school districts that experience immigrant child influxes will end up picking up big new tax tabs for them. CISD is an exception to the rule because, whereas parents in other overwhelmed school districts will end up paying more in school taxes to support illegal immigrant education, most of the CISD newcomers, like Benjamin, actually support the costs because *they* own the property from which school taxes are automatically assessed and paid through county governments.

The number of rooftops paying those school taxes into CISD has expanded so much and so rapidly that rates actually have declined per capita during the years of growth, my analysis of tax rates shows. In other words, Colony Ridge's new legal and illegal immigrants are almost all homeowners who seem to be supporting CISD for their own children rather than burdening longer-term residents who had lived there before the population boom. But that won't be the case elsewhere. But this circumstance is rare.

In other overwhelmed American school districts, far fewer illegal immigrants have the opportunity to buy land like they do from Terrenos in Liberty County.

Those already there will pay for the newcomers.

Costs and Consequences

If CISD can serve as a harbinger, those other American school districts also will pay in other ways. The district has to get creative to schedule security when 2,000 kids fill the hallways during class changes. Maintenance staff is always short to clean bathrooms, classrooms, cafeterias, hallways, and outside grounds. Bus rides of just a few miles to and from Colony Ridge homesteads can take more than an hour with the new traffic. When schools let out one day, I saw miles-long lines of private vehicles waiting their turns to pick up children.

But more seriously, a broad language barrier plagues CISD schools and can only suppress academic achievement, although McCandless denies this. Texas caps the number of students per teacher at twenty-two in grade school, to ensure teachers can tend each child enough, but schools are freer to break the cap in higher grades. At CISD, some student-teacher ratios range into the upper thirties per teacher for certain core classes.

"That's crowd control, not education," the teacher who used to work in the district told me.

She recalled having to sit kids on the floors, up against walls. Academic abilities and experience range so widely that teachers can be forced to provide instruction that caters to the lowest common denominator that would exist if all students had come up through a common system with universal standards. The unspoken truth about teaching foreign kids of wide proficiency ranges and years in the classroom is that "you teach to the middle," meaning high-performance students in those classrooms will not be challenged.

"When you double a teacher's class load, you're not just doubling the kids in the room, it's the accommodations, the data you have to collect, adaptations…and how to make sure Johnny is not touching Suzy when they're all on top of each other in class."

"Teachers don't come back from Christmas."

Involving parents in improving academic performance requires punching through a language barrier, she said. "Having to contact parents when the parents don't speak English…you can't even send them a letter. Anything you send out on social media, you have to send out in Spanish."

State accountability ratings of CISD and its individual campuses have fared about as well as anyone might expect of a student body that is made up almost entirely of foreigners from developing nations.

The last available school academic performance reports I could find in mid-2022, which are based on state testing, show scores significantly below state average percentages for meeting grade level. Tracking academic performance from before the enrollment boom to 2022 was hobbled by introduction of a new scoring system in 2018 and the cancellation of standardized tests in 2020 and 2021 due to the Covid pandemic. In the 2018–2019 school year, the first year of an A-to-F grading system and the last year of scoring, CISD overall and Cleveland High School's state accountability ratings came in at a "C."

The grade for Cleveland High came with an alarming statistic: 49.8 percent of its students were considered to be at risk of dropping out of high school. Cleveland Middle School came in at a "D" with 55.8 percent of its 2,238 students considered at risk of dropping out.[487]

It should come as no surprise if performance scores don't improve in coming years because these students are taking standardized tests in a language they barely know. The teacher I interviewed said the state can issue standardized-test waivers to monolingual students if they complete a special project. This teacher regards the whole system as a "a little sketchy." McCanless insists that academic performance has remained at an even keel, rarely affected by the onslaught of immigrants.

Many families of kids who were there first and found themselves overwhelmed by these changes have simply fled if their families could, said Plum Grove's combative former mayor, Lee Ann Walker. Many switched to home-schooling. Others enrolled in charter schools that are opening up. Still others have moved with their families to school districts as far away from CISD has they can get.

There should be little doubt, whether anyone ever wants to admit it, that this "originals-out-border-children-in exchange" will transform American public education if the border flood of families and unaccompanied minors continues unabated at this rate.

Quality of Life in Liberty County

As a former Plum Grove mayor, city council woman, and apartment real estate developer and proud original, Walker has waged an unremitting legal and political "war" to contain the ongoing Terrenos Houston development. She refers to this enemy she refers to as "the Kraken," a multiarmed Octopus-like sea monster of Scandinavian sailing mythology that would drag ships to the bottom. I met with Walker in a downtown Plum Grove coffee shop that also sells local arts and crafts to a dwindling Anglo customer base.

"I was born and raised by the forest, by the most salt-of-the-Earth people you could meet, by an original," she told me. "My father was an original. His mother was an original. We're all on the same land. We are called the originals of Plum Grove."

Walker's grievances and stories of battle with "the Kraken" are far too long to recount here, such as whether the rapid pace of development floods the towns during hard rains and allegedly poisoned rivers and the Gulf of Mexico with raw human waste.

But at the root of her many disputed claims—that Terrenos has broken federal environmental protection laws and every possible standard development practice and regulation—is that the clear-cutting, traffic, and crime have driven a majority of the original families to flight while more broadly harming America by luring illegal immigrants.

"It's the traffic! And there's no trees. That's what killed it all," she told me. "The suffering I have seen on the Americans, the veterans, the elderly...They were old, veterans...World War II, Vietnam, Korea. If you're older people like them and you need an ambulance, they can't get to you. About 70 percent of them are gone. There's about 28 percent of us still hanging in there."

Almost as offensive to the originals than the clear-cutting, traffic jams, and floods they blame on the ever-sprawling Colony Ridge is that the newcomers also make for bad neighbors.

"The amount of gunfire that is out there would blow your mind. I have a video you can listen to on New Year's Eve. It sounded like Falluja," she recounted, moving on to, "The loud Mexican music they play from Thursday night to Sunday. They all put their music on the same fucking station and turn it up. Our homes at one o'clock in the morning doing this…," Walker said, using her hand to thump the table like a drum. "And that's why the originals all left."

But Walker refuses to leave. She wants to shut down the settlement and see the illegal immigrants cleared out in a roll-back that will make other illegals never want to buy.

"When you're running, it's going to grow," she said of Colony Ridge. "If you stand and fight, you hold it where it is."

While we were talking, a friend of Walker's walked up to our table to say hello, another original who works in the residential real estate business.

"It is gut-wrenching," the woman said. "It breaks my entire heart, growing up out there and seeing what it is now, and every one of my family out there, except for my aunt—and I'm trying to sell her house now—is gone. Everybody's gone. They can't deal with it anymore."

The tide of battle did not seem to be favoring Walker and Liberty County's remaining originals when I visited in May 2022.

Driving Colony Ridge and talking to its residents reminded me of Juarez or Matamoros, with the housing mashups as far as the eye could see, business signs in Spanish, and the ubiquitous traffic jams. Gas station convenience store clerks did not speak English. Large signs on store windows informed passing traffic on a jam-packed street that "We Accept Lone Star," in reference to state welfare debit cards.

I drove my 4x4 pickup slowly for miles over new mud and dirt roads just hewn through plundered forest.

Bulldozers and heavy earth-moving equipment ground noisily at the earth on a vast physical scale, their stacks belching black smoke, as they scraped thousands of new lots for sale. The men and machinery had piled logs and brush into ten-foot-tall pyres stretching to the dust-filled horizon. The iron shovels and scoops dug miles-long drainage ditches through the old forest floor to prevent easy flooding of dwellings that would soon start to pop up. They covered over ponds with dirt fill. Other work crews were building steel towers that would carry electricity lines in to power it all.

The development has swallowed up all the land around Jimmy Rollins's place far outside of Dayton. Worse than the loss of forest and familiar faces for originals like Rollins and Walker was that basic infrastructure like sewage disposal, concrete roads, and fresh water have never been able to keep up with the population in the unincorporated or de-annexed lands outside the towns. Daily traffic jams turned twenty-minute country drives of recent memory into two-hour nightmares.

Mexican Cartels Come to Town

Extreme violent crime of new sorts really frightened not just local old-timers like Rollins but also their grown children who also wanted to live in Liberty County. The Rollins's two grown children sold out in 2020 and fled with their own young families as part of an exodus of originals chasing the quiet to just about anywhere else "because of the traffic, the people, the shooting, the wrecks, and the thieving," Rollins said.

"They got scared," he said of the kids. "They wasn't raised in all that."

In 2020, for instance, an illegal alien from Mexico who settled in Colony Ridge chained two house cleaners to a bed and sexually assaulted them as part of a blackmail scheme in which he took nude photos.[488] The nightmare ended when one of the women attempted an escape in her vehicle but didn't make it; her assailant managed to shoot her to death and set her car on fire with her inside before fleeing back to Mexico. Border Patrol caught him trying to cross again in California a short time later.

In 2016, owners of a Colony Ridge lot who were clearing it of brush discovered the decomposing remains of a single mother of five children named Esmeralda Pargas-Nunez, forty-two, who'd been reported missing a month earlier. It took two years but homicide detectives tracked down her alleged killer to Houston in 2018, another woman named Sabrina Olarosa Garcia, and charged her with murder.[489] This was evidently part of a kidnapping scheme in Houston where the alleged murderer first lured her victim to a meeting.

In September 2022, passersby in Colony Ridge found a dead sixteen-year-old girl shot to death in a ditch.[490]

Before all the change, crime mostly consisted of a few white country meth-heads, two local police investigators who work in the area told me privately. But now the crime is *very* different. The Gulf and Sinaloa Cartels invested in Colony Ridge from its earliest inception, they said, financing lots for local operatives to run safe houses through which they move smuggled drugs and people from the border to interior America. They were using them still to smuggle people coming in under Biden.

Evidence of cartel involvement dates to at least 2013, when federal, state, and local investigators raided a Mexican drug cartel's marijuana grow operation on 300 acres in Liberty County, finding explosives, 6,000 marijuana plants, worker bunk houses, and guard towers. Local police at the time called it the "largest and most sophisticated marijuana-growing operation" in the county's history.[491] During a recent trip, a police investigator drove around several town neighborhoods pointing out high-end brick homes where cartel management figures have lived.

In July 2021, the DEA broke that dubious record with the new biggest drug bust in Liberty County history with a raid that broke up a multimillion-dollar methamphetamine manufacturing lab operating inside one of the Colony Ridge dwellings.[492]

This kind of criminality grew so problematic by 2021 that the fearful town leaders of Plum Grove established a first police department that works in concert with two county-paid bilingual constables that Liberty County funded to exclusively patrol Colony Ridge. But all this amounts to a drop in the ocean, one officer from the region told me. Drive-by shootings, stealing, and drug trafficking are rampant, victimizing mostly the new community.

"It's a cluster fuck over there and it's only getting worse," said the officer, who was not authorized to speak publicly. "It's its own closed community out there, and the Salvadorans, Ecuadorans, South Americans…they really clique up."

Indeed, a five-month-long gang and narcotics investigation by the Liberty County Sheriff's Office came to a dramatic end in December 2021 with the arrest of two fifteen-year-old boys and a seventeen-year-old boy who were part of a violent drug-trafficking racket in Colony Ridge.[493] After three or four months where the boys would engage in gun battle with drug buyers who wouldn't pay on time, local police had to investigate. When the day came to make arrests, the armed seventeen-year-old rammed a police car during a pell-mell car chase near Plum Grove, fled home, and barricaded himself in his house until a SWAT unit had to extract him and a girlfriend inside, who also was arrested amid drugs that were found.

If those who committed these crimes were in the country illegally, none of this should have happened. In that vein, Liberty County also is a microcosm of a vast scale of unnecessary crime that is already here with much more on the way.

The Great Unnecessary Crime Wave

For years, advocates of a borderless United States have asked Americans to shed all concern that some portion of illegal aliens will commit crimes after their crossings and not insist that they be blocked and deported. These advocates often point to academic-seeming "studies" that compare illegal alien criminality to American citizen criminality and then conclude that Americans commit more than the illegal immigrants.[494] Its progenitors then cite the comparison to nullify concerns about illegal immigrant crime.

They use it to argue that the American people should leave the illegal immigrants alone and more properly tend to American citizen criminals. While America is busy with that ostensibly more real problem, the nation's leaders should let the illegal immigrant flow continue unimpeded since that population is so much less worrisome.

The comparison-based argument has found surprising purchase with mainstream media reporters and commentators who uncritically spread the idea that Americans need not concern themselves with slowing the illegal immigrant flow over the border since those coming in are less dangerous, per capita, than themselves.

For instance: "The social-science research on immigration and crime is clear: Undocumented immigrants are considerably less likely to commit crime than native-born citizens..." trilled *Washington Post* reporter Christopher Ingraham in a 2018 news column titled "Two charts demolish the notion that immigrants here illegally commit more crime."[495]

It's not clear who first came up with the idea that these two groups should be compared. But the "research" that continually flows from it, diverting attention from illegal immigrant crime, constitutes one of the greatest academic and intellectual frauds in the annals of immigration studies. The notion that these two groups should be compared is intellectual misconduct of the highest order, a sham campaign that almost surely has extended the unnecessary carnage against American citizens and lawful residents.[496] The comparison studies factory is a sham because illegal immigrants, and especially those with knowable criminal histories, are uniquely subject to government deportation and detention, which does not exist for American citizens and lawful residents. So, unlike every crime committed by American citizens, *every* crime committed by illegally present immigrants with criminal histories was avoidable.

Because illegal immigrants are constantly subject to entry blockage and removal, all of their crimes must be counted as a 100 percent net-gain increase of a social ill that hurts real people in the worst imaginable ways on a consistent, long-term basis.

Conversely, American citizens and lawful residents, obviously, are *not* subject to a national government apparatus in place to block and remove them from American territory so that they are not present to commit crime. America is stuck with its criminal citizens before, during, and after every crime they commit. The DHS detention and removal machine cannot and will not ever prevent a single crime by an American citizen.

That is a Grand Canyon–sized difference between the two groups disqualifying them for comparison in crime or anything else, like how often both use public assistance. Immigration enforcement will always eliminate or reduce the presence of illegal immigrants who commit crimes but never American residents. Americans have no choice but to suffer every single American citizen–committed crime but should never have to suffer one single illegal immigrant–committed crime.

Those who created and purvey the obviously false citizen-illegal immigrant crime rate comparison should, in addition to feeling great shame, stop doing it because they become partly culpable for the argument used to defray solutions. Meanwhile, those who oppose illegal immigration should never again confer legitimacy on the comparison ruse by engaging in any debate about it, as this only satisfies the nefarious political purpose of its construction, which is to neutralize urgency to blunt illegal immigration that criminally victimizes people who legally live here.

Graves That Need Never Have Been Dug

Illegal immigrant crime is notoriously difficult to measure. But in addition to sudden painful public school enrollments, most Americans will suffer more crime committed by more illegal immigrants. Most U.S. states do not keep track of crime committed by illegal immigrants, and neither does the federal government.

But the bogus comparison "studies" were useful in one important regard; they surfaced one rare data source that establishes what any reasonable person would agree is an unacceptable level of unnecessary illegal immigrant crime: Texas. Only Texas tracks much of its crime by noncitizenship. It is too early as of this writing to guess the extent to which alien crime that will result from the Biden border crisis. But if the past is any indicator of the future and the Texas numbers can indicate problem scope, America is in for a sustained unnecessary crime wave of preventable murder, rape, child abuse, burglary, felony theft, drug trafficking, alien smuggling, and drunken driving manslaughter on a higher permanent scale.

The Texas DPS learns the immigration status of suspects booked into local jails through a program that submits fingerprints to the FBI for criminal history and warrant checks, and to DHS, which returns immigration status information on those whose fingerprints were already on file (which is not all of them).[497] The glimpse is limited and not a reflection of much almost certain higher totals, but it is telling about the trend line ahead across America.

Between June 1, 2011, and July 31, 2022, these 259,000 illegal aliens were charged with more than 433,000 unnecessary, preventable criminal offenses.

Those included 800 homicide charges (resulting in 374 convictions as of July 2022), 822 kidnapping charges (resulting in 265 convictions), 5,470 sexual assault charges (resulting in 2,593 convictions), 6,485 sexual offense charges (resulting in 3,065 sexual offense convictions), and 4,945 weapons charges (resulting in 1,723 weapons convictions).

What the Texas data show is that hundreds of dead people should be alive, thousands of sexual assault and sexual offense victims should never have suffered the trauma, and tens of thousands of assault charges involving victims would not have been hurt. The Texas data also shows that criminal aliens took up police time and clogged up the American justice system that could have been more dedicated to American criminals. Thousands of drug, burglary, robbery, and weapons charges need not have jammed the Texas criminal justice systems at taxpayer cost. The Texas program found that another 10,590 illegal aliens were identified while they were in Texas state prisons over the past decade.

Among them were prisoners serving time for 119 more unnecessary homicides.

The graves of all their dozens of dead victims are real. One of the unnecessarily murdered was twenty-year-old San Antonio college student Jared Vargas, an aspiring cybersecurity student at Northwest Vista College who had never been in trouble and was beloved by a large circle of friends.[498]

Firefighters found Jared strangled and charred inside his burning apartment they were called to put out on June, 18, 2018. His murderer taped Jared's mouth and nose, wrapped his head in plastic, then strangled him, slit his throat, and stabbed him repeatedly before hiding the body in a closet for two days before deciding to set the apartment on fire. The illegal immigrant who did this after crossing the border illegally from Mexico is Ernesto Esquivel-Garcia. He had a long criminal history and could have been deported several times in the weeks and months before he murdered Jared, I discovered while spending time with Jared's grieving family.[499]

Esquivel-Garcia had been in front of immigration judges repeatedly after drunken driving convictions and criminal mischief charges related to one instance when he tried to run over the parents of a girlfriend who scorned him. But the system would not deport Esquivel-Garcia. In one round, just weeks before the murder, an immigration judge in liberal San Antonio granted Esquivel-Garcia the chance to voluntarily leave the country, a so-called "voluntary departure" that most simply ignore, like Esquivel-Garcia did. That decision killed Jared, his aunt, Christen Vargas, told me the family believes.

"When we talk about that there's this thing called 'voluntary departure,' people are completely and utterly shocked," Vargas told me. "The concept of voluntary departure is alarming."

Stories of tragedies that deportation would have prevented abound nationwide. Often enough, the preventable violence is exceptionally brutal, scenes from the most extreme horror movies. There are far too many to recount here, although some simply demand that faces be put to the increasing numbers of them.

In Alabama one August 2022 day, police hunted down and arrested a Mexican illegal immigrant who tied up a twelve-year-old girl and held her captive in the family mobile home amid the bloody dismembered remains of her mother, her under-fourteen brother, and a twenty-nine-year-old woman. The child ruined her braces gnawing through her binds and escaped the rape and carnage.[500]

Police said the suspect, thirty-seven-year-old Jose Paulino Pascual-Reyes, had been in a boyfriend-girlfriend relationship with the children's mother. He'd been deported to Mexico in 2014 but returned recently and began living in the mobile home with the family in February 2022, most likely amid the chaos of the Biden border. The brutalized family was in the U.S. pending an asylum claim. Investigators believe Pascual-Reyes smothered the girl's mother with a pillow, then beat and kicked her brother to death. He cut the bodies up into small pieces at the joints to hide the evidence, according to a police complaint.[501]

Pascual-Reyes saved the girl for sex abuse, tying her by the arms and legs to bedposts for nearly a week.

In March 2022, a Haitian border-crosser who ended up in Daytona Beach, Florida, is alleged to have randomly selected a young couple riding their bicycles home from a bar near their home and murdered them. Police accused Jean R. Macean of slashing their throats with a knife, leaving them in pools of blood.[502]

Harris County, Texas, Precinct 5 Constable Charles Galloway would be alive today had El Salvadoran national Jose Oscar Rosales been blocked at the southern border or captured beforehand. On January 29, 2022, the lawman died when he flashed down the illegally present Rosales in his vehicle and the suspect came out shooting. Rosales fled over the Rio Grande from Del Rio to escape arrest but was caught and extradited to face murder charges. Meanwhile, his wife and brother-in-law in Houston were facing charges too because they got caught wiping down his vehicle after the killing.[503]

Eventually, many children of immigrants may well become net contributors to the American economy. But six or ten million largely poor, uneducated, and needy people—many whose short-term legality will run out and leave them to live marginally in the shadows—will impact the American criminal justice system in permanent burdensome ways. Many of these impacts are not calculable as the human torrent continues. But as millions of illegal immigrants push the U.S. population into new record territory at extraordinary rates, the nation should expect to see unplanned-for demands on public welfare and assistance programs, health care systems, Social Security, housing, labor markets, playgrounds, and homeless encampments.

THERE IS HOPE

The question I am most often asked by interviewers, congressional staffers, and audiences is: what can *we* do to stop this? My answer is usually not very gratifying, I'm afraid. The puppet strings for the important control of illegal immigration all lead into the White House and, to a limited extent, Congress. Short of any appreciable congressional action, the White House becomes the default location where a mass migration is started and stopped. As we now know from the failed Texas and internal White House insurgencies to stop this crisis, moderate Democrats and Republicans interested in border security must sweep away the New Theologian extremists from halls of power.

I offer several overarching suggestions for what their reasonable replacements can do to alleviate this mass illegal immigration event and future ones.

For starters, as I hope to have proven beyond all reasonable doubt in these pages, Democrats and Republicans who do not want mass illegal immigration must run every proposal through this analytical litmus test: Will this or that elevate—or lower—the odds that an aspiring immigrant's smuggling fee investment pays off with successful entry over the border and long-term legal or illegal stay inside America?

If the policy will increase an immigrant's entry-and-stay odds high enough, it is the wrong one and should be rejected in any form. Conversely, if the policy will *reduce* the entry-and-stay odds, it is the right one and should be accepted in any form.

This simple calculus, though it may seem obvious, should no longer be allowed to defy broad absorption. If immigrants are telling us that they run this basic calculus through *their* skein when deciding to stay or go, so too should American leaders.

Hear the immigrants.

I offer several recommendations guided by the immigrants' calculus that are pivotal to permanently ending unwanted mass migrations.

Tear Down and Rebuild the American Asylum System

The United States must withdraw from the United Nations Convention Relating to the Status of Refugees treaty that President Lyndon Johnson signed in 1968 and rebuild the U.S. asylum system that treaty obliged after Congress incorporated its provisions in the Refugee Act of 1980.

As this book has amply demonstrated in my chapter "Insane Asylum," no other enticement exerts a greater gravitational pull on illegal immigration than does the easy ability to defraud the American asylum law as it now stands to achieve long-term entry. The asylum system must be torn down and rebuilt because it directly nullifies most congressionally approved immigration statutes that should, if actually executed faithfully, staunch mass illegal immigration.

Center for Immigration Studies Executive Director Mark Krikorian, a prominent proponent of this unconventional idea, calls the treaty an outdated anachronism of the Cold War era that has morphed into a wedge that immigrants and their advocates now mainly use to decide whether they will come in and stay.

"While it is national governments that decide whom to resettle from abroad, foreign intruders are the ones deciding to make an asylum claim, a claim we are bound by treaty to consider and that is subject to litigation in our courts," Krikorian wrote once in the *National Review Online*. "Asylum therefore represents a profound surrender of sovereignty, a limitation of the American people's ability to decide which foreigners get to come here from abroad."[504]

The time has arrived for this idea to enter into mainstream policy discussion because laws that work at cross-purposes with other laws, as does asylum, constitute an unnecessary tangle that democratic nation-states are not well suited to easily unravel. Nations are allowed to rethink international or binational agreements with other countries. None are permanent marriages where divorce is illegal or too immoral to contemplate. This divorce is necessary.

Until that happens, the threat and probability of mass illegal immigrations will persist. But it may not happen right away; divisions in government may prevent the legislative activity necessary to achieve the outcome even after a UN treaty withdrawal. In the meantime, leadership should feel obliged to reconstitute Trump-era stop-gap policies that, collectively, neutralized the narcotic draw of the asylum system by denying seekers the main motivating benefit: that a claim gets them in to stay permanently win, lose, or abandon. The measures were impactful but not permanent fixes and, as we have seen, reversible by the next White House occupant. While those Band-Aids were better than nothing, the permanent fix to this problem is to eliminate and rebirth an appropriate asylum law.

End the Gold Rush Loopholes

Second only to the asylum law, broad global discovery of the Flores Settlement loophole and the William Wilberforce Trafficking Victims Protection Reauthorization Act of 2008 (TVPRA) draws in millions of unaccompanied minors and families with children lured by a DHS requirement to quickly release them from detention. Congress needs to sew up both.

As I've described at length in this book, TVPRA required the quick release of immigrant kids if they are from noncontiguous countries but quick deportations of Mexicans, so untold thousands of non-Mexicans naturally came when the wider world discovered the law's almost magical properties in 2014, when Obama was president. Likewise, the Flores loophole as amended in 2015 requires DHS to release children from detention within twenty-one days and allows their parents to go forth with them.

The Trump administration came up with the fix required by the liberal Ninth Circuit Court of Appeals. The court rejected Trump's proposed fix one week prior to his leaving office, and his DOJ ran out of time to appeal it to the U.S. Supreme Court. When Biden came into office a week later, his DOJ chose not to appeal, and so Flores, in conjunction with the asylum law, stands as one of the most powerful draws on illegal immigration by families.

Republicans and Democrats have good reason to join together for these fixes and a logical place to start: the bipartisan Homeland Security Advisory Council's *CBP Families and Children Care Panel Final Report*, page two.[505]

In their section on "Interim Emergency Recommendations," appointees from both parties urged lawmakers to amend the TVPRA to require the same treatment of non-Mexican kids as for Mexican kids, which would then allow for the expedited removal and turn the tractor beam off.

"It is time for Congress to address this issue head on…," the authors concluded.

As for the Flores loophole, the panel recommended a legislative fix that would lift the twenty-one-day detention limit "to remove any uncertainty and make clear that the Flores restriction on the number of days a [family unit] may be detained has been lifted. Twenty days is insufficient in most cases…." The panel emphasized that it was not recommending indefinite detentions but "believes that DHS and the immigration courts need more flexibility and time to process the unauthorized arrivals than what is currently permitted."

In the alternative, say a gridlocked Congress, the regulation that Trump wrote is written and waiting. It could be resurrected and put back through the court system until the Supreme Court ultimately upholds it.

A Solution to the Multinational Immigrant Flow and to Protect National Security

As detailed in Part III of this book, the greatest proportion of multinational immigrants in contemporary U.S. history is carrying into the country suspected terrorists and potential war criminals and the spies of adversarial governments. A great many must pass from South America, through Colombia, and into Central America through Panama and Costa Rica. As I reported, all three of those U.S.-allied nations move the migrants northward as a matter of government policy called "Controlled Flow." This policy has facilitated the movement of migrants out of their territories and into American territory.

The United States should demand that these countries end their controlled flow policies and, in their place, install a U.S.-funded infrastructure in each that would fly all immigrants to origin countries anywhere in the world, on national security grounds.

I've demonstrated the awesome deterring power of air-repatriation flights, in chapter fourteen's revelations about the Del Rio migrant camp crisis and in chapter fifteen about the White House insurgency. Panama and Costa Rica happen to be geographically well suited for maximum impact of air-repatriation operations such as these. Panama and Costa Rica are trail-route bottlenecks with oceans on two sides. A series of air operations in these countries should prove especially impactful on downstream motivation to move through the Darien Gap and then toward Mexico. If immigrants slip past the Colombia air-repatriation operation, they would know they faced another one in Panama and then yet another one in Costa Rica. The U.S. should consider the option of an additional air-repatriation operation in southern Mexico, although this would likely prove unnecessary as the total flow by Mexico would be vastly diminished.

No one should expect these countries to fund an American national interest out of their treasuries. So the U.S. would need to fund detention facilities, legal processing infrastructure, and especially air transport to origin countries. DHS and ICE are already well familiar with international air-repatriation flights and operate a fleet of chartered aircraft that already range from Texas and Arizona as far as Africa and India.

As a final note, both polling and my own reporting detailing the failed White House rebellion by moderate Democrat advisors demonstrate that this border crisis presents a rare opportunity for both parties to find common ground and equal willingness to fix an obvious homeland security problem. If partisans will divide on just about every other issue, a mass migration emergency of this historic magnitude should stand as one of the few that ought to draw an authentic bipartisan response.

The White House rebellion and the polls demonstrate that most Democrats are not in favor of mass migration crises, not the ones that were smaller and shorter in duration and certainly not this one. Looking back from years hence, it would be gratifying to see that Democrats realized that a fanatical few managed for only a brief time to escape the closet but were quickly rounded up and put back in under sturdy lock and key.

Enforce Existing Immigration Law Universally and Consistently

Once the asylum law is scrapped and rebuilt and loopholes closed, the laws already on the books are sufficient to end mass illegal immigration if merely enforced to their letter, with consistency over time across the entirety of the border. Because the system was otherwise never "broken" beyond the asylum law and loopholes that allow foreign nationals to bypass congressional law, "comprehensive immigration reform" beyond those two problems was never necessary. Only when the end-runs are pinched closed and the remaining sensible laws enforced with universal consistency will the vast numbers of foreign nationals finally stop coming—and dying on the way.

ENDNOTES

1   "Obama Says Haitian Migrants' Plight Is 'Heartbreaking,' but Biden Knows System Is Broken," ABC Audio Digital Syndication, September 28, 2021, https://digital.abcaudio.com/news/obama-says-haitian-migrants-plight-heartbreaking-biden-knows-system-broken.

2   Mike Dash, "Uncovering the Truth Behind the Myth of Pancho Villa, Movie Star," *Smithsonian Magazine*, November 6, 2012, https://www.smithsonianmag.com/history/uncovering-the-truth-behind-the-myth-of-pancho-villa-movie-star-110349996/.

3   Tom K. Wong, Gabriel De Roche, and Jesus Rojas Venzor, "The Migrant 'Surge' at the U.S. Southern Border Is Actually a Predictable Pattern, Evidence Reveals the Usual Seasonable Bump—Plus Some of the People Who Waited during the Pandemic," *Washington Post*, March 25, 2021, https://www.washingtonpost.com/politics/2021/03/23/theres-no-migrant-surge-us-southern-border-heres-data/.

4   Todd Bensman, "U.S.-Bound Migrants Gambling on Trump Defeat in November," Center for Immigration Studies, January 17, 2020, https://cis.org/Bensman/Migrants-Hope-Trump-Loses-Election.

5   World Poverty Map, the World Data Lab, https://worldpoverty.io/map.

6   "2021 Global Multidimensional Poverty Index," United Nations Development Programme, https://hdr.undp.org/en/2021-MPI.

7   "Road to the White House 2008, Biden Campaign Event," C-Span video, starting minute 33, August 12, 2007, https://www.c-span.org/video/?200403-1/biden-campaign-event.

8   Todd Bensman, "Interview of Migrants outside Roma, Texas," May 2021, Rumble, https://rumble.com/v1k37h9-september-14-2022.html.

9   Ursula Perano, "Biden Calls Border Situation Normal: 'It Happens Every Single Solitary Year,'" Axios, March 25, 2021, https://www.axios.com/2021/03/25/biden-border-immigration-child-migrants-press-conference.

10 Tim Hains, "Obama DHS Secretary: 'We Are Truly in a Crisis' at Border," MSNBC interview with former DHS Secretary Jeh Johnson, March

29, 2019, https://www.realclearpolitics.com/video/2019/03/29/obama_dhs_secretary_jeh_johnson_we_are_truly_in_a_crisis_on_southern_border.html.

11   "Defendants' Monthly Report for June 2022," *State of Texas, State of Missouri v. Joseph R. Biden, Jr., et al.*, Civil Action No. 2:21-cv-00067-Z, U.S. District Court of the Northern District of Texas, Amarillo Division, Document 143 filed July 15, 2022, https://storage.courtlistener.com/recap/gov.uscourts.txnd.346680/gov.uscourts.txnd.346680.143.0.pdf; Case No. 2:21-cv-00067, U.S. District Court of the Northern District of Texas, April 13, 2021, https://www.courtlistener.com/docket/59815977/state-of-texas-v-joseph-r-biden/.

12   Andrew R. Arthur, "Nearly 1.06 Million CBP Encounters at Southwest Border Thus Far in FY 2022: And Biden Illegal Migrant Releases Now Exceed 836,000—Does the President Have a Plan?" Center for Immigration Studies, April 19, 2022, https://cis.org/Arthur/Nearly-106-Million-CBP-Encounters-Southwest-Border-Thus-Far-FY-2022; Andrew R. Arthur, "Under Biden DHS Has Released More Than 756,000 Southwest Border Migrants," Center for Immigration Studies," April 14, 2022, https://cis.org/Arthur/Under-Biden-DHS-Has-Released-More-756000-Southwest-Border-Migrants.

13   Olafimihan Oshin, "DHS Preparing for as Many as 18,000 Migrants Per Day After Lifting of Title 42, Mayorkas Says," *The Hill*, May 1, 2022, https://thehill.com/homenews/sunday-talk-shows/3472980-dhs-preparing-for-as-many-as-18000-migrants-per-day-after-lifting-of-title-42-mayorkas-says/.

14   Ellis Island," History.com, https://www.history.com/news/immigrants-ellis-island-short-processing-time#:~:text=More%20than%2012%20million%20immigrants,United%20States%20in%201907%20alone.

15   "Number of Noncitizens ICE Sought to Remove Who Were Allowed to Remain in U.S. through February 2022," Syracuse University School of Law Transactional Records Access Clearinghouse, https://trac.syr.edu/phptools/immigration/court_backlog/apprep_outcome_stay.php.

16   Jessica M. Vaughan, "ICE Records Confirm Steep Decline in Deportations: In 2021, ICE Removals Fell Nearly 70 percent," Center for Immigration Studies, May 17, 2022, https://cis.org/Vaughan/ICE-Records-Confirm-Steep-Decline-Deportations.

17   Fernanda Echavarri, "Biden Vastly Expands 'Protected Areas' Where ICE Can't Arrest Immigrants," *Mother Jones*, October 28, 2021, https://www.motherjones.com/politics/2021/10/biden-vastly-expands-protected-areas-where-ice-cant-arrest-immigrants/.

18   *United States of America v. Sebastian Tovar, et al.*, Case No. 2:21-cr-00546, U.S. District Court for the Western District of Texas, Document 1,

March 17, 2021, https://www.pacermonitor.com/public/case/39861971/USA_v_Sealed.

19   Jon Feere, "Insiders Leak ICE Enforcement Data Covered Up by Biden Administration," Center for Immigration Studies, March 17, 2022, https://cis.org/Feere/Insiders-Leak-ICE-Enforcement-Data-Covered-Biden-Administration.

20   Stephen Dinan, "Secret ICE Data Shows Drop in Arrests of Criminals, Surge in Arrest of Non-Criminals," *Washington Times*, March 16, 2022, https://www.washingtontimes.com/news/2022/mar/16/exclusive-secret-ice-data-shows-drop-arrests-crimi/.

21   McHugh, Patrick. "Interior Immigration Enforcement Decline under Biden: State and Local Statistics." *CIS.org*, 8 Dec. 2022, https://cis.org/Report/Interior-Immigration-Enforcement-Decline-Under-Biden-State-and-Local-Statistics.

22   "Drug Cartels May Be 'Making More Money from Human Smuggling' Than Drugs: Ken Cuccinelli," Fox News, April 16, 2022, https://www.foxnews.com/media/drug-cartels-making-money-human-smuggling-drugs-ken-cuccinelli.

23   Salvador Rizzo, "Do Mexican Drug Cartels Make $500 Billion a Year?" *Washington Post* Fact-Checker, June 24, 2019, https://www.washingtonpost.com/politics/2019/06/24/do-mexican-drug-cartels-make-billion-year/.

24   Miriam Jordan, "Smuggling Migrants at the Border Now a Billion-Dollar Business," *New York Times*, July 25, 2022, https://www.nytimes.com/2022/07/25/us/migrant-smuggling-evolution.html.

25   Stephen Dinan, "DHS: Cartels Earn Up to $6 Billion a Year from Smuggling Migrants," *Washington Times*, August 4, 2021, https://www.washingtontimes.com/news/2021/aug/4/dhs-cartels-earn-6-billion-year-smuggling-illegal-/.

26   Stephen Dinan, "DHS Cancels Deportation Request for Hit-and-Run Killer," *Washington Times*, January 30, 2022, https://www.washingtontimes.com/news/2022/jan/30/dhs-cancels-deportation-request-hit-and-run-killer/.

27   "Mayorkas Says DHS Has 'Effectively Managed' the Border," *Fox News Sunday*, May 1, 2022, https://www.youtube.com/watch?v=QgRDVyynC-NE.

28   Gabriel Stargardter, "Decline in Migration under Trump Could Quickly Reverse, History Shows," Reuters, March 10, 2017, https://www.reuters.com/article/us-usa-immigration-centralamerica/decline-in-migration-under-trump-could-quickly-reverse-history-shows-idUSKBN16I025.

29   Jeff Salamon, "The Trump Effect on Immigration," *Texas Monthly*, February 2018, https://www.texasmonthly.com/news-politics/trump-effect-immigration/.

30 Ashley Parker, "Donald Trump Gets Earful in Spanish as Latino Outlets Air Disdain," *New York Times*, August 26, 2015, https://www.nytimes.com/2015/08/27/us/politics/latino-news-media-offended-by-donald-trump-shows-it-in-broadcasts.html.

31 CNN Press Room, "CNN Worldwide Fact Sheet," https://cnnpressroom.blogs.cnn.com/cnn-fact-sheet/.

32 Priscilla Alvarez, "Can Univision Swing the 2016 Election?" *The Atlantic*, July 19, 2016, https://www.theatlantic.com/politics/archive/2016/07/univision-2016-election/491903/.

33 Benjy Sarlin and Alex Seitz-Wald, "Donald Trump and Hillary Clinton Are Universes Apart on Immigration," ABC News, September 2, 2016, https://www.nbcnews.com/politics/2016-election/donald-trump-hillary-clinton-are-universes-apart-immigration-n641686.

34 Mark Hoekstra and Sandra Orozco-Aleman, "Illegal Immigration: The Trump Effect" (working paper 28909), National Bureau of Economic Research Working Paper Series, June 2021, https://www.nber.org/system/files/working_papers/w28909/w28909.pdf.

35 "The Department of Homeland Security's 'Metering' Policy: Legal Issues," Congressional Research Service, updated October 15, 2021, https://sgp.fas.org/crs/homesec/LSB10295.pdf; Todd Bensman, "Encampment of International Migrants in Mexico Reminds That Homeland Security Must Vet as Ever More Arrive," Center for Immigration Studies, August 23, 2019, https://cis.org/Bensman/Encampment-International-Migrants-Mexico-Reminds-Homeland-Security-Must-Vet-Ever-More.

36 Todd Bensman, "A United Nations of Mass Illegal Immigration, Part 3: The Bogus Narrative of Haitian 'Asylum-Seekers' Crossing the Southern Border," July 6, 2021, https://cis.org/Bensman/United-Nations-Mass-Illegal-Immigration-Part-3.

37 Maria Sacchetti, "Biden Sees Obama's Mass Deportations as a 'Big Mistake,' Plans to Pause Expulsions," *Washington Post*, December 2, 2020, https://www.washingtonpost.com/politics/2020/12/02/biden-deportations-ice-immigration-enforcement/.

38 Jørgen Carling and Cathrine Talleraas, *Root Causes and Drivers of Migration: Implications for Humanitarian Efforts and Development Cooperation*, Peace Research Institute Oslo, 2016, https://ethz.ch/content/dam/ethz/special-interest/gess/cis/center-for-securities-studies/resources/docs/PRIO-%20Root%20Causes%20and%20Drivers%20of%20Migration.pdf; Patryk Kugiel, Henriette U. Erstad, Mortn Boas, and Jolanta Szymanska, "Can Aid Solve the Root Causes of Migration? A Framework for Future Research on the Development-Migration Nexus," Policy Paper for The Polish Institute of International Affairs, no. 1 (March 2020): 176, https://nupi.brage.unit.no/nupi-xmlui/bitstream/handle/11250/2647594/PISMPolicyPaperno1%2528176%2529%2bP.%2b-

Kugiel%252C%2bH.%2bU.%2bErstad%252C%2bM.%2bB%25C3%25B
8%25C3%25A5s%252C%2bJ.%2bSzyma%25C5%2584ska%2b-%2bCan-
%2bAid%2bSolve%2bthe%2bRoot%2bCauses%2bof%2bMigration....
pdf?sequence=1&isAllowed=y.

39   Adam Shaw, "Kamala Harris Emphasizes 'Root Causes' of Border Surge,
Says Problem Is 'Complex,'" Fox News, April 22, 2021, https://www.fox-
news.com/politics/kamala-harris-root-causes-border-surge.

40   Peter J. Meyer, "Central American Migration: Root Causes and U.S. Policy," Congressional Research Service, updated March 31, 2022, https://
sgp.fas.org/crs/row/IF11151.pdf.

41   Melissa Siegel, "Throwing Development Money at the 'Migration
Problem'—Is It Completely Misguided?" MIGNEX Insights. Oslo:
Peace Research Institute Oslo, November 15, 2019, available at https://
www.mignex.org/publications/throwing-development-money-migra-
tion-problem-it-completely-misguided.

42   Hein De Haas, "Turning the Tide? Why Development Will Not Stop
Migration," *Development and Change* 38, no. 5 (September 2007): 819–
841 (published on behalf of International Institute of Social Studies,
The Hague), https://onlinelibrary.wiley.com/doi/pdf/10.1111/j.1467-
7660.2007.00435.x.

43   Jennifer Rigby and James Crisp, "Fortress Europe," *Daily Telegraph*, https://
www.telegraph.co.uk/global-health/fortress-europe-borders-wall-fence-
controls-eu-countries-migrants-crisis/.

44   Stuart Anderson, "All the President's Immigration Lawsuits," *Forbes
Online*, November 5, 2019, https://www.forbes.com/sites/stuartander-
son/2019/11/05/all-the-presidents-immigration-lawsuits/?sh=57fbae-
c97d8e.

45   Stargardter, "Decline in Migration under Trump."

46   David Nakamura," "Influx of Minors across Texas Border Driven by Belief That They Will Be Allowed to Stay in U.S.," *Washington Post*, June
13, 2014, https://www.washingtonpost.com/politics/influx-of-minors-
across-texas-border-driven-by-belief-that-they-will-be-allowed-to-
stay-in-us/2014/06/13/5406355e-f276-11e3-9ebc-2ee6f81ed217_story.
html?utm_term=.a5e9f8455d34&itid=lk_inline_manual_21.

47   "Remarks by the President on Immigration," White House, Office of the
Press Secretary, press release, June 15, 2012, https://obamawhitehouse.
archives.gov/the-press-office/2012/06/15/remarks-president-immigra-
tion.

48   "An Open Letter to the Parents of Children Crossing Our Southwest
Border," DHS Press Office, press release (translation), June 23, 2014,
https://www.dhs.gov/news/2014/06/23/open-letter-parents-children-
crossing-our-southwest-border.

49   Carl Hulse, "Immigrant Surge Rooted in Law to Curb Child Trafficking,"
      New York Times, July 7, 2014, https://www.nytimes.com/2014/07/08/us/
      immigrant-surge-rooted-in-law-to-curb-child-trafficking.html; Public
      Law No. 110-457 William Wilberforce Trafficking Victims Protection Re-
      authorization Act of 2008, H.R.7311, 110th Congress (2007–2008), https://
      www.congress.gov/bill/110th-congress/house-bill/7311?q=%7B%-
      22search%22%3A%5B%22William+Wilberforce+Trafficking+Vic-
      tims+Protection+Reauthorization+Act+of+2008%22%5D%7D&r=1.

50   Diana Villiers Negroponte, "The Surge in Unaccompanied Children
      from Central America: A Humanitarian Crisis at Our Border," The
      Brookings Institute, July 2, 2014, https://www.brookings.edu/blog/up-
      front/2014/07/02/the-surge-in-unaccompanied-children-from-cen-
      tral-america-a-humanitarian-crisis-at-our-border/.

51   Zeke J. Miller, "Obama: Migrant Children without Humanitarian Claims
      Will Be Sent Back," *Time*, July 25, 2014, https://time.com/3037414/
      barack-obama-migrant-children-humanitarian-claims/.

52   Jerry Markon and Joshua Partlow, "Unaccompanied Children Cross-
      ing Southern Border in Greater Numbers Again, Raising Fears of New
      Migrant Crisis," *Washington Post*, December 16, 2015, https://www.
      washingtonpost.com/news/federal-eye/wp/2015/12/16/unaccompa-
      nied-children-crossing-southern-border-in-greater-numbers-again-
      raising-fears-of-new-migrant-crisis/.

53   "The History of the Flores Settlement," Center for Immigration Studies,
      February 11, 2019, https://cis.org/Report/History-Flores-Settlement.

54   Julia Preston, "Judge Orders Release of Immigrant Children De-
      tained by U.S.," *New York Times*, July 25, 2015, https://www.nytimes.
      com/2015/07/26/us/detained-immigrant-children-judge-dolly-gee-rul-
      ing.html.

55   Miriam Jordan, "Swift Frontier Justice for Migrants Brought to Fed-
      eral Courts," *New York Times*, July 19, 2018, https://www.nytimes.
      com/2018/06/19/us/border-immigration-courts.html.

56   Kung Li, "Operation Streamline," American Civil Liberties Union, Au-
      gust 5, 2013, https://www.aclu.org/blog/immigrants-rights/ice-and-bor-
      der-patrol-abuses/operation-streamline.

57   *Review of the Department of Justice's Planning and Implementation of
      Its Zero Tolerance Policy and Its Coordination with the Departments of
      Homeland Security and Health and Human Services*, Department of Jus-
      tice Office of the Inspector General Report 21-028, January 2021, https://
      oig.justice.gov/sites/default/files/reports/21-028_0.pdf.

58   Dylan Matthews, "Polls: Trump's Family Separation Policy Is Very Un-
      popular—Except among Republicans," Vox Media, June 18, 2018, https://
      www.vox.com/policy-and-politics/2018/6/18/17475740/family-separa-
      tion-poll-polling-border-trump-children-immigrant-families-parents.

59 *CBP Families and Children Care Panel Final Report*, Homeland Security Advisory Council, November 14, 2019, chaired by Administrator (Ret.) Karen Tandy, Drug Enforcement Administration and Vice Chair Jayson Ahern, principal and head of Security Services, The Chertoff Group, https://www.dhs.gov/sites/default/files/publications/fccp_final_report_1.pdf.

60 Maya Averbuch and Elisabeth Malkin, "Migrants in Tijuana Run to U.S. Border, but Fall Back in Face of Tear Gas," *New York Times*, November 25, 2018, https://www.nytimes.com/2018/11/25/world/americas/tijuana-mexico-border.html.

61 Jugal K. Patel and Troy Griggs, "Three Places Where Migrants Tried to Cross the Border, Facing Tear Gas and Barbed Wire," *New York Times*, November 26, 2018, https://www.nytimes.com/interactive/2018/11/26/us/migrant-border-crossing-map.html.

62 Nina Lakhani and agencies, "'Yes, We Can' Caravan of 1,600 Honduran Migrants Crosses Guatemala Border," *The Guardian*, October 15, 2018, https://www.theguardian.com/world/2018/oct/15/guatemala-caravan-honduras-migrants-border-reject.

63 Adolfo Flores and Karla Zabludovsky, "The US Has Fired Tear Gas and Closed the Largest Border Crossing with Mexico After Migrants Marched to the Border," BuzzFeed News, November 25, 2018, https://www.buzzfeednews.com/article/adolfoflores/migrant-caravan-tear-gas-border-san-ysidro.

64 Associated Press, "US Authorities Fire Teargas across Border to Repel Central Americans," *The Guardian*, January 2, 2019, https://www.theguardian.com/us-news/2019/jan/01/us-mexico-border-migrant-caravan-tijuana-tear-gas.

65 Rafael Carranza and Daniel Gonzalez, "Here's What Happened to the Migrant Caravan That Arrived in Tijuana Last Year," *El Paso Times*, February 11, 2019, https://www.elpasotimes.com/story/news/2019/02/11/what-happened-last-years-migrant-caravan-tijuana/2831764002/.

66 Elliot Spagat and Delmer Martinez, "Last Year's Central American Caravan Dwindles, New One Forms," Associated Press, January 16, 2019, https://apnews.com/article/midterm-elections-north-america-donald-trump-caribbean-immigration-be98c131631d49f0943e1f7ac6a4993b.

67 Charlie Lapastora and Charlie Watson, "El Paso Sector Border Patrol Sees Jump in Apprehensions as Large Migrant Groups Cross into US," Fox News, February 13, 2019, https://www.foxnews.com/us/el-paso-border-patrol-jump-apprehensions-large-migrant-groups-cross.

68 Patrick J. McDonnell, "Thousands of Migrants at Mexico's Southern Border Seeking New Humanitarian Visas," *Los Angeles Times*, January

23, 2019, https://www.latimes.com/world/mexico-americas/la-fg-mexi-co-visa-20190123-story.html.

69   Mary Beth Sheridan and Sarah Kinosian, "More Than 10,000 Migrants Request Visas as Caravan Hits Mexico," *Washington Post*, January 23, 2019, https://www.washingtonpost.com/world/the_americas/more-than-10000-migrants-request-visas-as-caravan-hits-mexico/2019/01/23/340169b8-1f2b-11e9-a759-2b8541bbbe20_story.html.

70   Todd Bensman, "Mexico's Dispersal of Latest Caravan Simply Frees Migrants to Cross the U.S. Border Less Visibly," Center for Immigration Studies blog post report, February 18, 2019, https://cis.org/Bensman/Mexicos-Dispersal-Latest-Caravan-Simply-Frees-Migrants-Cross-US-Border-Less-Visibly.

71   Domenico Montanaro, "7 Takeaways from President Trump's Oval Office Address," National Public Radio, January 9, 2019, https://www.npr.org/2019/01/09/683474397/7-takeaways-from-president-trumps-oval-office-address.

72   David A. Graham, "What Was the Point of Trump's Oval Office Address?" *The Atlantic*, January 8, 2019, https://www.theatlantic.com/politics/archive/2019/01/president-trumps-speech-shutdown-and-wall/579844/.

73   Ibid.; *CBP Families and Children Care Panel Final Report*, p. 14, https://www.dhs.gov/sites/default/files/publications/fccp_final_report_1.pdf.

74   Ibid.

75   "Read Trump's First Oval Office Address," NBC News, January 8, 2019, https://www.nbcnews.com/politics/donald-trump/read-trump-s-first-oval-office-address-n956516.

76   Mica Rosenberg, Kristina Cooke, and Daniel Trotta, "Thousands of Central American Migrants Take Free Rides Home Courtesy of U.S. Government," Reuters, August 21, 2019, https://www.reuters.com/article/us-usa-immigration-returns/thousands-of-central-american-migrants-take-free-rides-home-courtesy-of-u-s-government-idUSKCN1VB0ZJ.

77   "Obama's 2005 Remarks Reflect Strong Stance on Controlling Immigration," Associated Press, November 2, 2018, https://apnews.com/article/archive-fact-checking-2477111077.

78   Brittany Bernstein, "Bill Clinton: 'There Is a Limit' to How Many Migrants U.S. Can Take," National Review Online September 29, 2022.

79   "Who Are Antifa?" Anti-Defamation League website, accessed June 8, 2022, https://www.adl.org/antifa.

80   Josh Meyer, "FBI, Homeland Security Warn of More 'Antifa' Attacks," *Politico*, September 1, 2017, https://www.politico.com/story/2017/09/01/antifa-charlottesville-violence-fbi-242235.

81   Ibid.

82   Jose A. Del Real, "Trump Critics Clash with Police at California Rally," *Washington Post*, April 29, 2016, https://www.washingtonpost.com/news/post-politics/wp/2016/04/29/protests-outside-trump-rally-turn-violent/.

83   Sean Sullivan and Michael E. Miller, "Ugly, Bloody Scenes in San Jose as Protesters Attack Trump Supporters outside Rally," *Washington Post*, June 3, 2016, https://www.washingtonpost.com/news/morning-mix/wp/2016/06/03/ugly-bloody-scenes-in-san-jose-as-protesters-attack-trump-supporters-outside-rally/.

84   Kayla Epstein and Katie Mettler, "Anti-Trump Protesters at Trump Rally Throw Rocks, Bottles at Albuquerque Police," *Washington Post*, May 25, 2016, https://www.washingtonpost.com/news/morning-mix/wp/2016/05/25/protesters-at-trump-rally-throw-rocks-bottles-at-albuquerque-police/.

85   Lee Stranahan, "Dallas Anti-Trump Protestors Are Entitled, Vile and Stupid," Breitbart News, June 17, 2016, https://www.breitbart.com/border/2016/06/17/dallas-anti-trump-protesters-entitled-vile-stupid/).

86   Manny Fernandez, Richard Pérez-Peña, and Jonah Engel Bromwich, "Five Dallas Officers Were Killed as Payback, Police Chief Says," *New York Times*, July 8, 2016, https://www.nytimes.com/2016/07/09/us/dallas-police-shooting.html).

87   "Baton Rouge Protests Turned Tense and Dangerous," CBS News, July 10, 2016, https://www.youtube.com/watch?v=j49dIz6Kh9k.

88   Gavin Long manifesto and suicide note as published by *The Advocate*, https://bloximages.newyork1.vip.townnews.com/theadvocate.com/content/tncms/assets/v3/editorial/e/b8/eb8a5584-5daa-11e7-b31c-4b9625b33ad8/595671da54de3.pdf.pdf.

89   Camila Domonoske, "Anti-Trump Protest in Portland, Ore., Turns Destructive, Declared a Riot," National Public Radio, November 11, 2016, https://www.npr.org/sections/thetwo-way/2016/11/11/501685976/anti-trump-protest-in-portland-ore-turns-destructive-declared-a-riot; Melanie Eversley, Aamer Madhani, and Rick Jervis, "Anti-Trump Protests, Some Violent, Erupt for 3rd Night Nationwide," November 11, 2016, *USA Today*, https://www.usatoday.com/story/news/nation/2016/11/11/anti-trump-protesters-pepper-sprayed-demonstrations-erupt-across-us/93633154/; Jonathan Landay and Scott Malone, "Violence Flares in Washington during Trump Inauguration," Reuters, January 20, 2017, https://www.reuters.com/article/us-usa-trump-inauguration-protests/violence-flares-in-washington-during-trump-inauguration-idUSKBN1540J7; Katie Utehs, "Fires Erupt, Vandalism Reported at Anti-Trump Protest in Oakland," November 10, 2016, ABC7 News, https://abc7news.com/donald-trump-protest-oakland-protests/1599421/; J. J. Gallagher, David Caplan, and Stephanie Ebbs, "Tens of Thousands Protest Trump

Election Victory, 124 Arrested," November 10, 2016, ABC News, https://abcnews.go.com/Politics/thousands-us-protest-president-elect-donald-trump/story?id=43427653; Kyle Swenson, "Black-Clad Antifa Members Attack Peaceful Right-Wing Demonstrators in Berkeley," August 28, 2017, *Washington Post*, https://www.washingtonpost.com/news/morning-mix/wp/2017/08/28/black-clad-antifa-attack-right-wing-demonstrators-in-berkeley/.

90   Matthew Watkins, "Watch Texas DPS Troopers in Riot Gear Separate Dueling Protests at the Capitol," *Texas Tribune*, November 19, 2016, https://www.texastribune.org/2016/11/19/watch-dps-troopers-riot-gear-separate-dueling-prot/; "8 Arrests as Rival Protesters Clash Near Texas State Capitol," Associated Press, November 19, 2016, https://www.gosanangelo.com/story/news/local/texas/2016/11/19/8-arrests-rival-protesters-clash-near-texas-state-capitol/94152368/.

91   David Laconangelo, "Cesar Chavez Legacy: From 'Wet Lines' to an 'Illegals Campaign,' a Dark Side in Latino Icon's Opposition to Undocumented Immigrants," *Latin Times*, March 30, 2015, https://www.latintimes.com/cesar-chavez-legacy-wet-lines-illegals-campaign-dark-side-latino-icons-opposition-162528.

92   Ibid.; Eladio Bobadilla, "Chavez, the UFW and the 'Wetback' Problem," Duke Human Rights Center at the Franklin Humanities Institute," June 13, 2014, https://humanrights.fhi.duke.edu/chavez-ufw-and-wetback-problem/.

93   Miriam Pawel, *The Crusades of Cesar Chavez: A Biography* (London, UK: Bloomsbury Press, 2014).

94   "Cesar Chavez—Lost Interview—Illegal workers," YouTube, April 10, 2020.

95   Letter from Coretta Scott King and seven co-signatories of the Black Leadership Forum to The Honorable Orrin G. Hatch, U.S. Senate, July 9, 1991, https://cis.org/sites/cis.org/files/king-letter.pdf.

96   *Becoming an American: Immigration and Immigrant Policy*, 1997 Report to Congress, U.S. Commission on Immigration Reform, September 1997, https://www.numbersusa.com/sites/default/files/public/from_drupal5/JordanCommissionfull-report.pdf.

97   Ezra Klein, "Bernie Sanders, The Vox Conversation," Vox, July 28, 2015, https://www.vox.com/2015/7/28/9014491/bernie-sanders-vox-conversation.

98   Ibid.

99   "Illegal Immigration Reform and Immigrant Responsibility Act (1996)," Immigration History, https://immigrationhistory.org/item/1996-illegal-immigration-reform-and-immigrant-responsibility-act/.

100 "Bill Clinton on Illegal Immigration at 1995 State of the Union," YouTube, posted on January 18, 2019, by Congressman French Hill, https://www.youtube.com/watch?v=1IrDrBs13oA.

101 Roll Call Vote 109th Congress—2nd Session, https://www.senate.gov/legislative/LIS/roll_call_votes/vote1092/vote_109_2_00262.htm; Roll Call 446, Bill Number: H.R. 6061, September 14, 2006, https://clerk.house.gov/Votes/2006446.

102 Muzaffar Chishti, Sarah Pierce, and Jessica Bolter, "The Obama Record on Deportations: Deporter in Chief or Not?" Migration Policy Institute, January 26, 2017, https://www.migrationpolicy.org/article/obama-record-deportations-deporter-chief-or-not.

103 Dan Roberts, "Obama Confronts Hecklers during Immigration Speech," *The Guardian*, November 25, 2013, https://www.theguardian.com/world/2013/nov/25/obama-hecklers-confront-immigraiton-speech.

104 "Transcript: President Obama's Interview with Univision," ABC News, January 31, 2013, https://abcnews.go.com/ABC_Univision/Politics/transcript-president-barack-obama-interview-univisions-maria-elena/story?id=18365068.

105 Brian Contreras and Paige Cornwell, "Armed Man Attacking Tacoma's ICE Detention Center Killed in Officer-Involved Shooting," *Seattle Times*, July 13, 2019, updated July 14, 2019, https://www.seattletimes.com/seattle-news/law-justice/tacoma-police-armed-man-throwing-incendiary-devices-shot-outside-ice-detention-center/.

106 Travis Fedschun, "Washington ICE Detention Center Attacker Willem Van Spronsen Wrote 'I Am Antifa' Manifesto before Assault," Fox News, July 15, 2019, https://www.foxnews.com/us/washington-man-killed-at-ice-detention-center-manifesto.

107 The manifesto of Willem Van Spronsen, https://mediaweb.kirotv.com/document_dev/2019/07/15/Manifesto_15897725_ver1.0.pdf; "Emma Goldman, American Anarchist," *Encyclopedia Britannica*, https://www.britannica.com/biography/Emma-Goldman.

108 Seth G. Jones and Catrina Doxsee, "Examining Extremism: Antifa," The Center for Strategic & International Studies, June 24, 2021, https://www.csis.org/blogs/examining-extremism/examining-extremism-antifa.

109 Hannah Allam and Jim Urquhart, "'I Am Antifa': One Activist's Violent Death Became a symbol for the Right and Left," National Public Radio, July 23, 2020, https://www.npr.org/2020/07/23/893533916/i-am-antifa-one-activist-s-violent-death-became-a-symbol-for-the-right-and-left.

110 "John Brown Gun Club," The Counter Extremism Project, https://www.counterextremism.com/supremacy/john-brown-gun-club.

111 Ibid.

112 Marisa Iati and Hannah Knowles, "ICE Detention-Center Attacker Killed by Police Was an Avowed Anarchist, Authorities Say," *Washington Post*,

July 19, 2019, https://www.washingtonpost.com/nation/2019/07/19/ice-detention-center-attacker-killed-by-police-was-an-avowed-anarchist-authorities-say/.

113   Adam Gabbatt, "The Growing Occupy ICE Movement: 'We're Here for the Long Haul,'" *The Guardian*, July 6, 2018, https://www.theguardian.com/us-news/2018/jul/06/occupy-ice-movement-new-york-louis-ville-portland.

114   Abigail Hauslohner and Nick Miroff, "As Immigrant Families Wait in Dread, No Sign of Large-Scale Enforcement Raids," *Washington Post*, July 14, 2019, https://www.washingtonpost.com/immigration/as-im-migrant-families-wait-in-dread-no-sign-of-large-scale-enforcement-raids/2019/07/14/ff29326a-a644-11e9-86dd-d7f0e60391e9_story.html.

115   Lucy Diavolo, "ICE Protests Draw Thousands as Immigration Detention Facilities Face More Militant Direct Actions," *Teen Vogue*, July 15, 2019, https://www.teenvogue.com/story/ice-protest-draw-thousands-immi-graiton-detention-facilities-militant-direct-actions.

116   Susan Riemer, "Tacoma Police Provide Further Information on Fatal Shooting," *Vashon-Maury Island Beachcomber*, July 24, 2019, https://www.vashonbeachcomber.com/news/tacoma-police-provide-fur-ther-information-on-fatal-shooting/.

117   *Texas Domestic Terrorism Threat Assessment*, Texas Department of Public Safety, January 2020, starting page 25, https://www.dps.texas.gov/sites/default/files/documents/director_staff/media_and_communica-tions/2020/txterrorthreatassessment.pdf.

118   James N. Gregory, "Remapping the American Left: A History of Radical Discontinuity," Labor and Working-Class History Association, Duke University Press, May 2020, https://depts.washington.edu/moves/pdf/Gregory_Remapping_the_American_Left_LABOR_May2020.pdf.

119   Paul Starr, "Center-Left Liberalism," *The Oxford Companion to American Politics*, 2012, https://www.princeton.edu/~starr/articles/articles12/Starr_Center-left-liberalism.html.

120   Jonathan Haidt, *The Righteous Mind: Why Good People Are Divided by Politics and Religion* (New York: Pantheon Books, 2012), 316–317.

121   "Who Are Antifa?"

122   Anonymous, "We Are the Fire That Will Melt ICE—Rest in Power, Will Van Spronsen [Olympia, WA]," Puget Sound Anarchists, July 13, 2019, https://pugetsoundanarchists.org/we-are-the-fire-that-will-melt-ice-rest-in-power-will-van-spronsen-olympia-wa/.

123   Nathaniel Flaken, "ICE versus the Gestapo: A Comparison," Left Voice News, July 15, 2019, https://www.leftvoice.org/ice-vs-the-gesta-po-a-comparison/; Brett Wilkins, "A Brief History of U.S. Concentration Camps," *CounterPunch*, June 21, 2019, https://www.counterpunch.org/2019/06/21/a-brief-history-of-us-concentration-camps/;   Eric

Levitz, "With Trump's Migrant Camps, the History We Should Fear Repeating Is Our Own," *New York Magazine*'s Intelligencer, June 30, 2019, https://nymag.com/intelligencer/2019/06/aoc-holocaust-why-migrant-detention-centers-are-concentration-camps-explained.html.

124 Witness at the Border organization website, https://witnessattheborder.org.

125 Willem Van Spronsen "What Follows Is the Written Manifesto of Willem Van Spronsen," https://mediaweb.kirotv.com/document_dev/2019/07/15/Manifesto_15897725_ver1.0.pdf.

126 Peter Beinart, "The Rise of the Violent Left," *The Atlantic*, September 2017, https://www.theatlantic.com/magazine/archive/2017/09/the-rise-of-the-violent-left/534192/.

127 Kim Voss, Fabiana Silva, and Irene Bloemraad, "The Limits of Rights: Claims-Making on Behalf of Immigrants," *Journal of Ethnic and Migration Studies* 46, no. 4 (January 28, 2019): 791–819, https://csls.berkeley.edu/sites/default/files/voss-silva-bloemraad-limits-of-rights-jems-online-2019_0.pdf.

128 Guillermo Contreras, "San Antonio Student Activist under Investigation by FBI Now in Detention Facing Deportation," *San Antonio Express-News*, August 6, 2018, updated August 7, 2018, https://www.mysanantonio.com/news/local/article/San-Antonio-student-activist-under-investigation-13136448.php#photo-15914422.

129 "It's Going Down" podcast, minute 47:43, https://itsgoingdown.org/?powerpress_pinw=157114-podcast.

130 Antonia Noori Farzan, "He Offered $500 on Twitter to Anyone Who Killed an ICE Agent; He Was Only Joking, a Jury Ruled," *Washington Post*, December 9, 2019, https://www.washingtonpost.com/nation/2019/12/09/brandon-ziobrowski-ice-agent-twitter-threat/.

131 Erich Wagner, "Homeland Security Warns of Increased Threats to Employees," GovExec, June 25, 2018, https://www.govexec.com/management/2018/06/homeland-security-warns-increased-threats-employees/149257/.

132 Ibid.; Molly Hensley-Clancy and Lissandra Villa, "Kamala Harris Wants You to Know She's Definitely Not Calling for Abolishing ICE," BuzzFeed News, July 3, 2018, https://www.buzzfeednews.com/article/mollyhensleyclancy/kamala-harris-abolish-ice.

133 Matthew Impelli, "What Kamala Harris Has Said about Immigration Before Leading White House Border Response," *Newsweek*, March 24, 2021, https://www.newsweek.com/what-kamala-harris-has-said-about-immigration-before-leading-white-house-border-response-1578550.

134 Lissandra Villa, "Calls to Abolish ICE Are Splintering the Democratic Party," BuzzFeed News, July 2, 2018, https://www.buzzfeednews.com/article/lissandravilla/abolish-ice-democrats-congress#.clLy3WX6E.

135 Eric Bradner, Gregory Krieg, and Caroline Kenny, "2020 Insights: Dem Prospects Call for Abolishing ICE; Harris 'Not Ruling It Out'; Warren Sounds Like a Candidate," CNN, July 1, 2018, https://www.cnn.com/2018/06/30/politics/2020-insight-democrats-abolish-ice/index.html.

136 Dave Quinn, "Cynthia Nixon Calls ICE a 'Terrorist Organization' as She Calls for Its Abolishment," *People,* June 22, 2018, https://people.com/politics/cynthia-nixon-ice-terrorist-organization-abolishment/.

137 Nick Givas, "Most Dems Vow to Decriminalize Illegal Immigration during Night 2 Debate," Fox News, June 27, 2019, https://www.foxnews.com/politics/democratic-candidates-vow-to-decriminalize-illegal-immigration-during-debate?utm_source=feedburner&utm_medium=-feed&utm_campaign=Feed%3A%20foxnews%2Fpolitics%20%28Internal%20-%20Politics%20-%20Text%29.

138 "The Biden Plan for Strengthening America's Commitment to Justice," Biden-Harris Campaign, https://joebiden.com/justice/ ; https://joebiden.com/immigration/.

139 "The Biden Plan for Securing Our Values as a Nation of Immigrants," Biden-Harris campaign website, https://joebiden.com/immigration/.

140 Matt Stevens, "Beto O'Rourke Proposes Immigration Overhaul That Would Undo Trump Policies," *New York Times*, May 29, 2019, https://www.nytimes.com/2019/05/29/us/politics/beto-orourke-immigration.html?action=click&module=RelatedLinks&pgtype=Article.

141 Alexander Bolton, "All Candidates Raise Hands on Giving Health Care to Undocumented Immigrants," *The Hill*, June 27, 2019, https://thehill.com/homenews/campaign/450797-all-candidates-raise-hands-on-giving-health-care-to-undocumented-immigrants/.

142 Alex Samuels, "Julián Castro Shifted the Democratic Conversation about Immigration Reform. Can It Help His Bid?" *Texas Tribune*, August 29, 2019, https://www.texastribune.org/2019/08/29/julian-castro-immigration-reform-2020-presidential-candidacy/.

143 "A Fair and Welcoming Immigration System," Elizabeth Warren campaign website, https://elizabethwarren.com/plans/immigration.

144 Voss, Silva, and Bloemraad, "The Limits of Rights."

145 "No Human Is Illegal," Immigration Law Center of Minnesota Fact Sheet, May 23, 2019, https://www.ilcm.org/latest-news/no-human-is-illegal/.

146 "Creating a 21st Century Immigration System," Democratic National Committee Where We Stand Platform, https://democrats.org/where-we-stand/party-platform/creating-a-21st-century-immigration-system/.

147 Jerry Kammer, *Losing Control: How a Left-Right Coalition Blocked Immigration Reform and Provoked the Backlash That Elected Trump*, pp. 109–

122, Center for Immigration Studies, 2020, "Immigration Policy and the Politics of Bernie Sanders," Center for Immigration Studies, April 19, 2016, https://cis.org/Report/Immigration-Policy-and-Politics-Bernie-Sanders.

148   Ibid.; Beinart, *The Atlantic*.

149   "Bernie Sanders—On the Issues," a document by the Bernie 2016 campaign, http://www.reinhardhaase.de/Bernie_Sanders_2016_Program_On-the-Issues_L_download_16-02-28.pdf.

150   Priscilla Alvarez, "No One Knows How Latinos Will Vote in 2016," *The Atlantic*, June 11, 2016, https://www.theatlantic.com/politics/archive/2016/06/polling-hispanics-hillary-clinton-donald-trump/486650/.

151   Jeff Stein, "Bernie Sanders Moved Democrats to the Left. The Platform Is Proof," Vox, July 25, 2016, https://www.vox.com/2016/7/25/12281022/the-democratic-party-platform.

152   Alex Samuels, "How Democrats Became Stuck on Immigration," FiveThirtyEight, March 30, 2021, https://fivethirtyeight.com/features/how-democrats-became-stuck-on-immigration/.

153   Weiyi Cai and Ford Fessenden, "Immigrant Neighborhoods Shifted Red as the Country Chose Blue," *New York Times*, December 20, 2020, https://www.nytimes.com/interactive/2020/12/20/us/politics/election-hispanics-asians-voting.html.

154   "Beyond Red vs. Blue: The Political Typology," Pew Research Center, November 9, 2021, https://www.pewresearch.org/politics/2021/11/09/the-democratic-coalition/#the-2020-democratic-primary-through-the-lens-of-the-typology-groups.

155   "A Welcoming and Safe America for All," Bernie Sanders 2020 immigration platform, https://berniesanders.com/issues/welcoming-and-safe-america-all/.

156   Zolan Kanno-Youngs, Michael D. Shear, and Eileen Sullivan, "Disagreement and Delay: How Infighting over the Border Divided the White House," *New York Times*, April 9, 2022, https://www.nytimes.com/2022/04/09/us/politics/biden-border-immigration.html?searchResultPosition=1.

157   Todd Bensman, "Alejandro Mayorkas: A Portrait of the Intended Nominee for DHS Secretary," Center for Immigration Studies, November 30, 2020, https://cis.org/Bensman/Alejandro-Mayorkas-Portrait-Intended-Nominee-DHS-Secretary.

158   Letter of findings to DHS Secretary Janet Napolitano from the office of Sen. Chuck Grassley, October 14, 2010, https://cis.org/sites/cis.org/files/articles/2010/sen-grassley-letter-oct-14.pdf.

159   "HIAS Congratulates Board Member Alejandro Mayorkas on DHS Nomination," HIAS website, November 23, 2020, https://www.hias.org/

news/press-releases/hias-congratulates-board-member-alejandro-may-orkas-dhs-nomination; "AILA Welcomes Nomination of Alejandro Mayorkas to Lead DHS for the Biden Administration," American Immigration Lawyers Association, November 23, 2020, https://www.aila.org/advo-media/press-releases/2020/aila-welcomes-nomination-of-alejandro-mayorkas.

160   Fred Lucas, "Exclusive: Pro-Amnesty Groups Supplied These 5 Players on Biden's Immigration Team," The Daily Signal, August 15, 2021, https://www.dailysignal.com/2021/08/15/pro-amnesty-nonprofits-supplied-these-5-players-on-bidens-immigration-team/.

161   FWD.US website, www.fwd.us.

162   America's Voice website, https://americasvoice.org/blog/title42/

163   "Tyler Moran: "We're Taking a More Comprehensive Approach to the Border and to Immigration Itself," MSNBC, June 12, 2021, https://www.msnbc.com/american-voices/watch/tyler-moran-we-re-taking-a-more-comprehensive-approach-to-the-border-and-to-immigration-itself-114717765934.

164   National Immigration Law Center website, "What We Do," https://www.nilc.org/about-us/what_we_do/.

165   Immigration Hub website, "About Us," https://theimmigrationhub.org/about-us.

166   "Interview with Esther Olavarria," Edward M. Kennedy Institute for the United States Senate, 2016, https://www.emkinstitute.org/resources/esther-olavarria.

167   "Center for American Progress," Influence Watch, https://www.influencewatch.org/non-profit/center-for-american-progress-cap/.

168   Michael D. Shear, Natalie Kitroeff, Zolan Kanno-Youngs, and Eileen Sullivan, "Biden Pushes Deterrent Border Policy After Promising 'Humane' Approach," New York Times, September 22, 2021, https://www.nytimes.com/2021/09/22/us/politics/biden-immigration-border-haitians.html.

169   Anita Kumar, "Biden Taps Lawyer to Help Rescind Trump Immigration Policy," Politico, August 2, 2021, https://www.politico.com/news/2021/08/02/biden-immigration-lawyer-502190.

170   American Civil Liberties Union website, https://www.aclu.org/news/by/lucas-guttentag/.

171   Lucas Guttentag and Sharon Driscoll, "Crisis at the Border? An Update on Immigration Policy with Stanford's Lucas Guttentag," Stanford Law School Blogs, April 22, 2019, https://law.stanford.edu/2019/04/22/crisis-at-the-border-an-update-on-immigration-policy-with-stanfords-lucas-guttentag/.

172   Amy Pope, "To Truly Improve Border Security, the US Must Deal with the Drivers of Migration," Chatham House, April 2, 2019, https://

www.chathamhouse.org/2019/04/truly-improve-border-securi-ty-us-must-deal-drivers-migration.

173 Maria Sacchetti, "Biden Administration's Contradictions on Immigration Overshadow His Achievements," *Washington Post*, January 19, 2022, https://www.washingtonpost.com/national-security/biden-border-policy/2022/01/19/8b75ccf2-7932-11ec-83e1-eaef0fe4b8c9_story.html.

174 "Actions Needed to Strengthen USCIS's Oversight and Data Quality of Credible and Reasonable Fear Screenings," Government Accountability Office, February 2020 (Why GAO Did This Study section), https://www.gao.gov/assets/gao-20-250.pdf.

175 "Fact Sheet: Asylum Fraud and Immigration Court Absentia Rates," National Immigration Forum, October 8 , 2021, https://immigrationforum.org/article/fact-sheet-asylum-fraud-and-immigration-court-absentia-rates/.

176 "8-Year-Old Migrant Boy Who Died in U.S. Custody Laid to Rest in Guatemala," CBS News, January 27, 2019, https://www.cbsnews.com/news/yalambojoch-guatemala-felipe-gomez-alonzo-migrant-boy-dead-us-custody-funeral-today-2019-01-27/.

177 Adolfo Flores, "A Guatemalan Boy Who Died in US Custody Told His Father, 'I'm Going to Die,'" BuzzFeed News, April 15, 2020, https://www.buzzfeednews.com/article/adolfoflores/guatemalan-immigrant-boy-death-border-patrol-report.

178 Nina Strochlic, "How This Quiet Region in Guatemala Became the Epicenter of Migration: A Child's Death at the U.S. Border Put a Spotlight on the Peaceful Highlands, Where More People Than Ever Are Fleeing for the United States," July 26, 2019, *National Geographic*, https://www.nationalgeographic.com/culture/article/how-quiet-guatemala-region-became-migration-epicenter#:~:text=This%20has%20given%20Guatemala%20a,interests%20often%20with%20government%20backing.

179 Maura Hohman, "Family of 8-year-old Immigrant Boy Who Died in U.S. Custody Speaks Out: He 'Always Wanted a Bicycle,'" *People*, December 28, 2018, https://people.com/politics/felipe-alonzo-gomez-family-after-he-died-custody/.

180 Maria Sacchetti, "Official: Guatemalan Boy Who Died in U.S. Custody Tested Positive for Influenza B, Final Cause of Death Remains under Investigation," *Washington Post*, December 28, 2018, https://www.washingtonpost.com/local/immigration/father-whose-son-died-in-custody-knew-bringing-him-would-ease-entry-into-us/2018/12/27/4c210bfc-0a1d-11e9-85b6-41c0fe0c5b8f_story.html.

181 Ibid.

182 Hohman, "Family of 8-year-old Immigrant Boy Who Died in U.S. Custody Speaks Out."

183 "9 World Poverty Statistics That Everyone Should Know," Life-water, January 28, 2020, https://lifewater.org/blog/9-world-poverty-statistics-to-know-today/?gclid=Cj0KCQjw6J-SBhCrARIsAH0yMZj9PLYZZqGUl4B8C3ZtPfEHR6Om-k4FpfAKdluXIcYgKLW4p2WG688aAp9XEALw_wcB.

184 *Women on the Run: First-Hand Accounts of Refugees Fleeing El Salvador, Guatemala, Honduras and Mexico,* United Nations High Commission on Refugee, date unknown, https://www.unhcr.org/5630f24c6.html; Stephanie Leutert, "Why Are So Many Migrants Leaving Guatemala? A Crisis in the Coffee Industry Is One Reason," *Time,* July 27, 2018; https://time.com/5346110/guatemala-coffee-escape-migration/.

185 "USCCP Migration Chairman and CRS President Issue Statement Supporting Texas-Mexico Border Bishops' Statement on Recent U.S. Government Asylum Policy," United States Conference of Catholic Bishops, Public Affairs Office, March 13, 2019, https://www.usccb.org/news/2019/usccb-migration-chairman-and-crs-president-issue-statement-supporting-texas-mexico-border.

186 "New Asylum Restrictions a Death Sentence for Central Americans Fleeing Violence," Medecins Sans Fronieres/Doctors Without Borders, June 12, 2018, https://www.doctorswithoutborders.org/latest/new-asylum-restrictions-death-sentence central-americans-fleeing-violence.

187 Scott Bixby, "House Plans Probe of Migrant Boy's Death as Homeland Security Points Fingers," The Daily Beast, December 26, 2018, updated December 27, 2018, https://www.thedailybeast.com/homeland-security-blames-everyone-but-itself-for-8-year-old-migrant-felipe-alonzo-gomezs-death.

188 "Guatemala Village Mourns Child Who Died in U.S. Border Patrol Custody," *PBS NewsHour,* December 31, 2018, https://www.pbs.org/newshour/world/guatemala-village-mourns-child-who-died-in-u-s-border-patrol-custody.

189 Andrew Selee, Luis Argueta, and Juan José Hurtado Paz y Paz, "Migration from Huehuetenango in Guatemala's Western Highlands: Policy Development Responses," Migration Policy Institute and Asociación Pop No'j, March 2022, https://www.migrationpolicy.org/sites/default/files/publications/mpi-huehuetenango-report-eng_final.pdf.

190 Executive Office for Immigration Review Adjudication Statistics, Credible Fear and Asylum Process: Fiscal Year 2008–FY2019, https://www.justice.gov/eoir/file/1216991/download.

191 "Actions Needed to Strengthen USCIS's Oversight and Data Quality of Credible and Reasonable Fear Screenings," Government Accountability Office, February 2020, Table 20, https://www.gao.gov/assets/gao-20-250.pdf.

192   Ryan Baugh *Refugees and Asylees: 2019, Annual Flow Report*, Depart-
       ment of Homeland Security, September 2020, https://www.dhs.gov/
       sites/default/files/publications/immigration-statistics/yearbook/2019/
       refugee_and_asylee_2019.pdf.

193   Executive Office for Immigration Review Adjudication Statistics, "Cred-
       ible Fear and Asylum Process—Guatemala: Fiscal Year (FY) 2019,"
       https://www.justice.gov/eoir/page/file/1218201/download.

194   "Immigration Court Backlog Tool," Syracuse University Transactional
       Records Clearinghouse Access, https://trac.syr.edu/phptools/immigra-
       tion/court_backlog/.

195   Luis Noe-Bustamante, Antonio Flores, and Sono Shah, "Facts on His-
       panics of Guatemalan Origin in the United States, 2017," Pew Research
       Center, September 16, 2019, https://www.pewresearch.org/hispanic/
       fact-sheet/u-s-hispanics-facts-on-guatemalan-origin-latinos/.

196   Sarah Lynn Lopez, *The Remittance Landscape: Spaces of Migration in Ru-
       ral Mexico and Urban USA* (Chicago: University of Chicago Press, 2015).

197   "U.S. Border Patrol Nationwide Apprehensions by Citizenship and Sec-
       tor, FY2007–FY2019," U.S. Customs and Border Protection, https://www.
       cbp.gov/sites/default/files/assets/documents/2020-Jan/U.S.%20Bor-
       der%20Patrol%20Nationwide%20Apprehensions%20by%20Citizen-
       ship%20and%20Sector%20%28FY2007%20-%20FY%202019%29_1.
       pdf; Sydney Hernandez, "Border Patrol Sees 'Significant' Increase in
       Chinese Nationals Illegally Crossing U.S.," Valley Central News, No-
       vember 21, 2019, https://www.valleycentral.com/news/local-news/
       border-patrol-sees-significant-increase-in-chinese-nationals-illegal-
       ly-crossing-us/; Tatiana Sanchez, "California Sees Surge in Chinese Il-
       legally Crossing Border from Mexico," *Los Angeles Times*, June 7, 2016,
       https://www.latimes.com/local/lanow/la-me-ln-chinese-border-califor-
       nia-20160607-snap-story.html.

198   Peter Orsi and Amy Guthrie, Associated Press, "A Grim Border Drown-
       ing Underlines Peril Facing Many Migrants," ABC News, June 26, 2019,
       https://abcnews.go.com/International/wireStory/father-daughter-bor-
       der-drownings-highlight-migrants-perils-63939729.

199   The laws governing asylum protection were first established in statute
       with the passage of the Refugee Act of 1980, Pub. L. No. 96-212, tit. II, §
       201, 94 Stat. 102, 102-06 (1980) (codified at 8 U.S.C. §§ 1101(a)(42), 1157-
       1159), https://www.flickr.com/photos/usnationalarchives/22755449997/
       in/album-72157661462319371/.

200   "8 U.S. Code 1225—Inspection by Immigration Officers; Expedited Re-
       moval of Inadmissible Arriving Aliens; Referral for a Hearing," Legal In-
       formation Institute, https://www.law.cornell.edu/uscode/text/8/1225.

201   Andrew R. Arthur, "DHS/DOJ: Raise Credible Fear Standard for Stat-
       utory Withholding and CAT," Center for Immigration Studies, June

25, 2020, https://cis.org/Arthur/DHSDOJ-Raise-Credible-Fear-Standard-Statutory-Withholding-and-CAT.

202   *Department of Homeland Security v. Thuraissigiam*, United States Supreme Court, No. 19-161, June 25, 2020, https://casetext.com/case/department-of-homeland-security-v-thuraissigiam.

203   Ibid.; "Actions Needed to Strengthen USCIS's Oversight and Data Quality of Credible and Reasonable Fear Screenings," Government Accountability Office, February 2020, https://www.gao.gov/assets/gao-20-250.pdf.
"Fact Sheet: Asylum Fraud and Immigration Court Absentia Rates," National Immigration Forum, October 8, 2021, https://immigrationforum.org/article/fact-sheet-asylum-fraud-and-immigration-court-absentia-rates/.

204   "Immigration Policy on Expedited Removal of Aliens," Congressional Research Service, updated January 30, 2009, https://crsreports.congress.gov/product/pdf/RL/RL33109/8.

205   Robert Barnes, "Supreme Court Rules against Detained Immigrants Facing Deportation," *Washington Post*, June 13, 2022, https://www.washingtonpost.com/politics/2022/06/13/supreme-court-immigrants-bond-hearings/.

206   "A Mounting Asylum Backlog and Growing Wait Times," Syracuse University Transactional Records Access Clearinghouse, https://trac.syr.edu/immigration/reports/672/.

207   "ACLU Condemns Biden Administration's Deplorable Treatment of Haitian Migrants and Reiterates Call to Immediately End Title 42 and Overhaul CBP," ACLU, press release, September 22, 2021, https://www.aclu.org/press-releases/aclu-condemns-biden-administrations-deplorable-treatment-haitian-migrants-and.

208   Verónica Reyes, "Government Reveals Latest Number of Migrants: Largest Communities Are Venezuelan, Peruvian, and Haitian," biobiochile.cl, March 14, 2020, https://www.biobiochile.cl/noticias/nacional/chile/2020/03/14/gobierno-revela-ultima-cifra-de-migrante-mayores-comunidades-son-venezolanas-peruanas-y-haitianas.shtml; "Chile Economic Overview," *Central Intelligence Agency World Fact Book*, https://www.cia.gov/the-world-factbook/countries/chile/#economy; Caitlyn Yates, "Haitian Migration through the Americas: A Decade in the Making," Migration Policy Institute, September 30, 2021, https://www.migrationpolicy.org/article/haitian-migration-through-americas.

209   Reyes, "Government Reveals Latest Number of Migrants"; "Chile Economic Overview"; Yates, "Haitian Migration through the Americas."

210   "Brazil and Haiti: Employment Situation of Haitians in Brazil, Including Treatment in the Workplace; Whether Haitians Face Discrimination in Hiring," Electronic Country of Origin database, Research Directorate,

Immigration and Refugee Board of Canada, 2018–June 2019, https://www.ecoi.net/en/document/2017565.html.

211 "Brazil Economic Snapshot," Organization of Economic Co-operation and Development, December 2021, https://www.oecd.org/economy/brazil-economic-snapshot/.

212 Maria Sacchetti, "ICE to Avoid Detaining Pregnant, Nursing and Postpartum Women," *Washington Post*, July 9, 2021, https://www.washingtonpost.com/immigration/ice-pregnant-immigrants/2021/07/09/882be75a-e000-11eb-9f54-7eee10b5fcd2_story.html.

213 David J. Ley, "Forget Me Not: The Persistent Myth of Repressed Memories," *Psychology Today*, October 6, 2019, https://www.psychologytoday.com/us/blog/women-who-stray/201910/forget-me-not-the-persistent-myth-repressed-memories.

214 Jeffrey S. Passel and D'Vera Cohn, "Birth Regions and Nations," Pew Research Center, September 2016, https://www.pewresearch.org/hispanic/2016/09/20/1-birth-regions-and-nations/.

215 "U.S. Border Patrol Nationwide Apprehensions by Citizenship and Sector, 2007–2019" (last available year), U.S. Border Patrol, https://www.cbp.gov/sites/default/files/assets/documents/2020-Jan/U.S.%20Border%20Patrol%20Nationwide%20Apprehensions%20by%20Citizenship%20and%20Sector%20%28FY2007%20-%20FY%202019%29_1.pdf.

216 "Mexico Deports 311 Indian Migrants to New Delhi," Aljazeera, October 18, 2019, https://www.aljazeera.com/news/2019/10/18/mexico-deports-311-indian-migrants-to-new-delhi/; "Immigration: 'Recalcitrant' Countries and the Use of Visa Sanctions to Encourage Cooperation with Alien Removals," Congressional Research Service, updated January 23, 2020, https://sgp.fas.org/crs/homesec/IF11025.pdf; "Recalcitrant Countries: Denying Visas to Countries That Refuse to Take Back Their Deported Nationals," Hearing before the Committee on Oversight and Government Reform, House of Representatives, 114th Congress, July 14, 2016, https://www.govinfo.gov/content/pkg/CHRG-114hhrg25546/pdf/CHRG-114hhrg25546.pdf.

217 Lauren Frayer, "The Long, Perilous Route Thousands of Indians Have Risked for a Shot at Life in U.S.," National Public Radio, July 9, 2020, https://www.npr.org/2020/07/09/814957398/the-long-perilous-route-thousands-of-indians-have-risked-for-a-shot-at-life-in-us.

218 *United States of America v. Elvis Harold Reyes*, Case 8:20-cr-VMC-AAS, United States District Court Middle District of Florida, Tampa Division, filed March 5, 2020, https://casetext.com/case/united-states-v-reyes-510.

219 "Phony Immigration Attorney Who Filed Hundreds of Fraudulent Asylum Applications Sentenced to More Than 20 years in Federal Prison," U.S. Department of Justice, press release, April 12, 2021, https://www.

justice.gov/usao-mdfl/pr/phony-immigration-attorney-who-filed-hun-
dreds-fraudulent-asylum-applications-sentenced.

220   Katie Shepherd, "Florida Man Promised Immigrants Licenses, Work
Permits. Instead, He Stole Their Money and Got Them Deported,"
Washington Post, April 13, 2021, https://www.washingtonpost.com/na-
tion/2021/04/13/florida-elvis-reyes-immigration-fraud/.

221   George Fishman, "The Pernicious Perversion of Parole: A 70-Year Battle
between Congress and the President," Center for Immigration Studies
Backgrounder Paper, Center for Immigration Studies, February 2022,
https://cis.org/sites/default/files/2022-02/fishman-parole_0.pdf.

222   Ibid.

223   Nick Miroff and Maria Sacchetti, "Biden Officials Bracing for Unprecedented Strains at Mexico Border if Pandemic Restrictions Lifted," *Washington Post*, March 29, 2022, https://www.washingtonpost.com/nation-
al-security/2022/03/29/border-pandemic-title-42-immigration/.

224   "Tell Biden's White House: Immediately Undo All Trump-Era Inhumane Immigration Policies," The Refugee and Immigrant Center for Education and Legal Service, https://www.raicestexas.
org/2022/03/01/tell-bidens-white-house-undo-all-trump-era-
immigration-policies-tweet-now/?ms=em20220303_launch_
tweet_soturesponse&sourceid=1009638&emci=a767659a-2e9b-
ec11-a22a-281878b85110&emdi=88734fad-4e9b-ec11-a22a-
281878b85110&ceid=161953.

225   "Justice Department and DHS Public Notice of Proposed Rulemaking to
Make Asylum Process More Efficient and Ensure Fairness," Department
of Justice, Office of Public Affairs, press release, August 18, 2021, https://
www.justice.gov/opa/pr/justice-department-and-dhs-publish-notice-
proposed-rulemaking-make-asylum-process-more.

226   Michael D. Shear and Miriam Jordan, "Biden Is Hoping Small Changes
Go a Long Way on Immigration," *New York Times*, September 27, 2022,
https://www.nytimes.com/2022/09/27/us/politics/biden-immigra-
tion-asylum.html.

227   Eileen Sullivan, "Biden Administration Prepares Sweeping Change to
Asylum Process," *New York Times*, March 24, 2022, https://www.ny-
times.com/2022/03/24/us/politics/us-asylum-changes.html.

228   Andrew R. Arthur, "Biden Administration Finalizes Plan to Rubber-Stamp Asylum Grants," Center for Immigration Studies, March 24,
2022, https://cis.org/Arthur/Biden-Administration-Finalizes-Plan-Rub-
berStamp-Asylum-Grants.

229   Ibid.; Sullivan, "Biden Administration Prepares Sweeping Change."

230   Salvador Castro, "Migrants Protest on the Paso del Norte Bridge," *Journal of Juarez*, December 29, 2020, https://diario.mx/juarez/protestan-
migrantes-en-el-puente-paso-del-norte-20201229-1746432.html.

231 Rocio Gallegos, "Protest of Cuban Asylum Seekers Falls on Deaf Ears," *Havana Times*, January 1, 2021, https://havanatimes.org/features/protest-of-cuban-asylum-seekers-falls-on-deaf-ears/.

232 Daniel Borunda, "Paso del Norte Bridge Blocked After More Than 100 Cuban Migrants Show Up at El Paso Border," *El Paso Times*, December 30, 2020, https://www.elpasotimes.com/story/news/immigration/2020/12/30/cuban-migrant-surge-blocks-el-paso-paso-del-norte-border-bridge/4087083001/.

233 Paola Gamboa, "Cuban Migrants Are Tricked into Crossing into the US," *El Sol de Parral* (Mexico), December 31, 2020, https://www.elsoldeparral.com.mx/local/migrantes-cubanos-son-enganados-para-cruzar-a-eeuu-frontera-paso-del-norte-sueno-americano-mejor-vida-aduana-noticias-de-parral-chihuahua-6192123.html.

234 "Quarantine Halts Migrants in Panama," United Nations Department of Global Communications, https://www.un.org/en/coronavirus/quarantine-halts-migrants-panam%C3%A1.

235 Lauren Villagran, "'All I Want Is a Tranquil Life': Asylum Claims Skyrocket in Mexico as Haitians Flee to U.S. Border," *El Paso Times*, April 16, 2020, updated April 28, 2020, https://www.elpasotimes.com/in-depth/news/2020/04/16/asylum-us-mexico-border-migrants-refugee-trump/5108171002/; Kate Morrissey, "Mexico Still Accepting Asylum Applications as U.S. Asylum System Grinds to Halt," *San Diego Union-Tribune*, April 1. 2020, https://www.sandiegouniontribune.com/news/immigration/story/2020-04-01/mexico-still-accepting-asylum-applications-as-u-s-asylum-system-grinds-to-halt.

236 "Desperation and Violence in Panama Migrant Camp," *Tico Times* (Costa Rica), August 12, 2020, https://ticotimes.net/2020/08/12/desperation-and-violence-in-panama-migrant-camp.

237 Glenda Boza Ibarra (*El Toque*), "The Fate of the Cuban Migrant Caravan in Suriname," *Havana Times*, December 31, 2020, https://havanatimes.org/features/the-fate-of-the-cuban-migrant-caravan-in-suriname/.

238 Jose Cabezas, "Migrant Caravan Sets Off to U.S. from Honduras, Risking New Tensions," Reuters, December 9, 2020, https://www.usnews.com/news/world/articles/2020-12-09/migrant-caravan-sets-off-to-us-from-honduras-risking-new-tensions.

239 Kevin Sieff and Nick Miroff, "Migrant Caravans Could Be Early Test for Biden and Post-Trump Relations with Mexico," *Washington Post*, December 2, 2020, https://www.washingtonpost.com/politics/2020/12/02/biden-migrant-caravans/.

240 Miriam Jordan, "As Biden Prepares to Take Office, a New Rush at the Border," *New York Times*, December 13, 2020, https://www.nytimes.com/2020/12/13/us/border-crossing-migrants-biden.html?referringSource=articleShare.

241 Trevor Hunnicutt, "Biden Transition Official Honing Migration Policy with Mexico: Aide," Reuters, January 6, 2021, https://www.reuters.com/article/us-usa-biden-mexico/biden-transition-official-honing-migration-policy-with-mexico-aide-idUSKBN29B2TP; "Press Release—Readout of Biden-Harris Transition Team Conversation with Mexican Government Officials," The American Presidency Project, January 14, 2021, https://www.presidency.ucsb.edu/documents/press-release-readout-biden-harris-transition-team-conversation-with-mexican-government.

242 Laura Gottesdiener, Frank Jack Daniel, and Ted Hesson, "Insight: U.S. Continues Plan to Keep Central American Migrants at Bay," Reuters, February 12, 2021, https://www.reuters.com/article/usa-immigration-military-idINKBN2AC199.

243 Sonny Figueroa and Claudio Escalon, "Guatemala Tries Blocking Caravan of 9,000 Honduran Migrants," Associated Press, January 17, 2021, https://apnews.com/article/honduras-health-immigration-coronavirus-pandemic-guatemala-2768cc6d691ef9c84719e3462666e564; Mark Stevenson, Rob Gillies, and Aamer Madhani, "Mexican Leader Says Biden Offers $4B for Central America," Associated Press, January 23, 2021, https://apnews.com/article/joe-biden-north-america-mexico-justin-trudeau-coronavirus-pandemic-070159520dd892ad0f-4233cfec7e2827.

244 Marcel Osorto, "Biden Administration Seeks to Avoid Deportation of More Than One Million Migrants, Including Hondurans," El Heraldo (Colombia), December 21, 2020, https://www.elheraldo.hn/hondurenosenelmundo/biden-busca-evitar-deportacion-de-hondurenos-guatemaltecos-LBEH1430957.

245 Miriam Jordan and Zolan Kanno-Youngs, "Biden Says He Cannot Quickly Undo Trump Border Policies," New York Times, December 22, 2020, https://www.nytimes.com/2020/12/22/us/biden-border-asylum.html.

246 Maria Verza, Associated Press, "First Caravan of 2021 of Honduran Migrants to the United States Begins," Aldia Dallas, January 14, 2021, https://www.dallasnews.com/espanol/al-dia/inmigracion/2021/01/14/inicia-primera-caravana-de-2021-de-migrantes-hondurenos-hacia-estados-unidos/.

247 Jorge Ramos, "More Immigrants Will Come to the U.S. under President Biden. That's a Good Thing," New York Times, January 8, 2021, https://www.nytimes.com/2021/01/08/opinion/international-world/ramos-biden-immigration.html.

248 AFP, "Honduran Hopes Biden Will Let Him into the United States," La Prensa, January 13, 2021, https://www.laprensa.hn/premium/es-

peciales/hondureno-espera-biden-estados-unidos-migrar-carava-na-CCLP1435373.

249   "Migrant Caravan: The Violent Repression in Guatemala against Groups Walking to the US," *BBC News World*, January 17, 2021, https://www.bbc.com/mundo/noticias-america-latina-55698861.

250   Aileen B. Flores, "A Community, and Its Holy Ground at Stake," *El Paso Times/USA Today* Network, https://www.usatoday.com/border-wall/story/a-city-and-its-holy-ground-at-stake/573659001/.

251   Silvia Foster-Frau, Arelis R. Hernández, Kevin Sieff, and Nick Miroff, "Biden Faces Border Challenge as Migrant Families Arrive in Greater Numbers and Large Groups," *Washington Post*, February 7, 2021, https://www.washingtonpost.com/national/migrant-families-us-border-biden/2021/02/07/1bf05212-6970-11eb-9ed1-73d434b5147f_story.html.

252   Val Verde Border Humanitarian Coalition web site, "Who We Are," https://vvbhcoalition.com/.

253   Magda Guardiola, "40 Haitians Mobilize U.S. and Mexican Authorities as They Try to Cross the Rio Grande into the U.S.," El Financiero, January 31, 2021, https://www.elfinanciero.com.mx/estados/40-haitianos-movi-lizan-a-autoridades-de-eu-y-mexico-al-intentar-cruzar-por-el-rio-bra-vo-hacia-eu/.

254   Todd Bensman, "'Catch and Release' Resumes on Texas Border in the Face of Rising Migrant Numbers," Center for Immigration Studies, February 3, 2021, https://cis.org/Bensman/Catch-and-Release-Resumes-Texas-Border-Face-Rising-Migrant-Numbers.

255   Lomi Kriel, "How Inconsistent Policies and Enforcement Have Created False Hope for Migrants at the Border," *Texas Tribune* and ProPublica, May 13, 2021, https://www.texastribune.org/2021/05/13/biden-bor-der-policy-migrants/.

256   Poder Ejecutivo Secretaria De Governacion, November 11, 2020, http://www.diputados.gob.mx/LeyesBiblio/ref/lmigra/LMigra_ref11_11n-ov20.pdf; Diario Oficial de la Federación, SEGOB, November 11, 2020, https://www.dof.gob.mx/nota_detalle.php?codigo=5604705&fe-cha=11/11/2020.

257   "Entry into Force of the Reforms in Favor of Migrant Children and Adolescents, Asylum Seekers and Refugees: 'Historic Progress in Terms of Rights,'" UNICEF Mexico, press release, November 12, 2020, https://www.unicef.org/mexico/comunicados-prensa/entrada-en-vigor-de-las-reformas-favor-de-la-ni%C3%B1ez-y-adolescencia-migrante.

258   "Implementation of the Mexican Legal Reforms That Prohibit Detention of Accompanied and Unaccompanied Migrant Children," Institute for Women in Migration, March 2021, https://imumi.org/wp-content/up-loads/2021/03/Asylum-migrant-children-march-2021.pdf.

259   Foster-Frau, Hernandez, Sieff, and Miroff, "Biden Faces Border Challenge."

260   Alan Rappeport and Katie Rogers, "Trump's Embrace of Sanctions Irks Allies and Prompts Efforts to Evade Measures," *New York Times*, November 15, 2019, https://www.nytimes.com/2019/11/15/us/politics/trump-iran-sanctions.html; "Canada Slaps Retaliatory Tariffs on US Aluminum Goods," BBC World News, August 7, 2020, https://www.bbc.com/news/world-us-canada-53683569; Ryan Browne, "Trump Administration to Cut Its Financial Contribution to NATO," CNN, November 28, 2019, https://www.cnn.com/2019/11/27/politics/trump-nato-contribution-nato/index.html.

261   Ibid. Kriel.

262   "ICE Directive 11032.4: Identification and Monitoring of Pregnant, Postpartum, or Nursing Individuals," July 1, 2021 issue date, https://www.ice.gov/doclib/detention/11032.4_IdentificationMonitoringPregnant-PostpartumNursingIndividuals.pdf; Camilo Montoya-Galvez, "Biden Administration Bars ICE from Detaining Pregnant or Nursing Women," CBS News, July 9, 2021, https://www.cbsnews.com/news/biden-administration-bars-ice-from-detaining-pregnant-or-nursing-women/.

263   "Pregnant Woman, Baby Die After Migrants Abandoned in Truck in Mexico," CBS News DFW, March 6, 2022, https://www.cbsnews.com/dfw/news/woman-fetus-die-after-migrants-abandoned-in-truck-in-mexico/.

264   Stephen Dinan, "Pregnant Woman Dies from Apparent Fall from Border Wall," *Washington Times*, March 30, 2022, https://www.washingtontimes.com/news/2022/mar/30/pregnant-woman-dies-apparent-fall-border-wall/.

265   Brian Naylor and Tamara Keith, "Kamala Harris Tells Guatemalans Not to Migrate to the United States," National Public Radio, updated June 7, 2021, https://www.npr.org/2021/06/07/1004074139/harris-tells-guatemalans-not-to-migrate-to-the-united-states.

266   *United States of America v. Kevin Joel Perdomo-Cardona*, Case 2:20-cr-01625-AM, Document 22, Stipulation of Facts, U.S. District Court Western District of Texas Del Rio Division, June 24, 2021, https://www.pacermonitor.com/public/case/36732833/USA_v_PerdomoCardona.

267   *United States of America v. Belkin Idania Martinez-Parada and Marvin David Castaneda-Guardado*, Case 2:21-cr-00050-AM, Document 1 Criminal Complaint, November 24, 2020, U.S. District Court for the Western District of Texas, Del Rio, https://www.pacermonitor.com/public/case/37944236/USA_v_MartinezParada_et_al.

268   "CBP Officials Implemented Rapid DNA Testing to Verify Claimed Parent-Child Relationships," DHS Office of Inspector General, Report

22-27, February 8, 2022, https://www.oig.dhs.gov/sites/default/files/assets/2022-02/OIG-22-27-Feb22.pdf.

269   Anna Giaritelli, "DNA Tests Reveal 30% of Suspected Fraudulent Migrant Families Were Unrelated," *Washington Examiner*, May 18, 2019, https://www.washingtonexaminer.com/policy/defense-national-security/dna-tests-reveal-30-of-suspected-fraudulent-migrant-families-were-unrelated.

270   Anna Giaritelli, "Border Agents Performing Fewer DNA Tests to Catch Fake Families under Biden," *Washington Examiner*, April 15, 2021, https://www.washingtonexaminer.com/news/border-agents-performing-fewer-dna-tests-fake-families-biden.

271   Luciana Magalhaes, Samantha Pearson, and Michelle Hackman, "Desperate to Cross into the U.S., Some Brazilians Create Phony Families," *Wall Street Journal*, May 8, 2022, https://www.wsj.com/articles/desperate-to-cross-into-the-u-s-some-brazilians-create-phony-families-11652025729?st=jpur7tzx5x30dl6&reflink=article_imessage_share.

272   Ibid.

273   "Agents Identify Fraudulent Family Units in Two Different Cases," Customs and Border Protection, press release, April 13, 2021, https://www.cbp.gov/newsroom/local-media-release/agents-identify-fraudulent-family-units-two-different-cases.

274   Camilo Montoya-Galvez, "12,212 Migrant Children Reentered U.S. Border Custody Alone in 2021 After Being Expelled," CBS News, May 20, 2022, https://www.cbsnews.com/news/immigration-migrant-children-us-border-custody-unaccompanied-minors-2021/.

275   Hamed Aleaziz, "Biden Is Dropping Trump's Policy of Immediately Expelling Unaccompanied Immigrant Children at the Border," BuzzFeed News, February 2, 2021, https://www.buzzfeednews.com/article/hamedaleaziz/biden-unaccompanied-immigrant-children-border.

276   Ibid.

277   Tim Hains, "DHS Secretary Mayorkas to 'Loving' Parents Abroad: 'We Will Not Expel' Your Child if Sent Here Alone through Mexico," RealClear Politics, March 18, 2021, https://www.realclearpolitics.com/video/2021/03/18/dhs_secretary_mayorkas_to_parents_abroad_we_will_not_expel_your_child_if_sent_here_alone.html.

278   Ben Gittleson, "Biden Tells Migrants 'Don't Come Over' in ABC News Exclusive Interview," ABC News, March 16, 2021, https://abcnews.go.com/Politics/biden-tells-migrants-dont-abc-news-exclusive-interview/story?id=76490159.

279   Dara Lind, "The 2014 Central American Migrant Crisis," Vox News, October 10, 2014, https://www.vox.com/2014/10/10/18088638/child-migrant-crisis-unaccompanied-alien-children-rio-grande-valley-obama-immigration.

280 Nick Miroff, "Biden Officials Fall Behind in Race to Add More Shelter Space for Migrant Teens and Children," *Washington Post*, March 12, 2021, https://www.texastribune.org/2021/03/12/border-immigration-shelters-migrant-children/.

281 Nick Miroff, "Biden Administration Spending $60 Million Per Week to Shelter Unaccompanied Minors," *Washington Post*, April 8, 2021, https://www.washingtonpost.com/national/border-shelters-cost/2021/04/08/c54eec3a-97bd-11eb-8e42-3906c09073f9_story.html.

282 "Operation Artemis Senior Leader Brief," document provided as acquired by *New York Times*, May 6, 2021, https://int.nyt.com/data/documenttools/migrant-children/1c763659c2e28826/full.pdf.

283 Eileen Sullivan, Zolan Kanno-Youngs, and Luke Broadwater, "Overcrowded Border Jails Give Way to Packed Migrant Child Shelters," *New York Times*, May 7, 2021, https://www.nytimes.com/2021/05/07/us/politics/migrant-children-shelters.html.

284 Dara Lind, "'No Good Choices': HHS Is Cutting Safety Corners to Move Migrant Kids Out of Overcrowded Facilities," ProPublica, April 1, 2021, https://www.propublica.org/article/no-good-choices-hhs-is-cutting-safety-corners-to-move-migrant-kids-out-of-overcrowded-facilities.

285 "Operation Artemis Senior Leader Brief."

286 Ibid.; Miroff, "Biden Officials Fall Behind in Race to Add More Shelter Space for Migrant Teens and Children."

287 Ibid.; Sullivan, Kanno-Youngs, and Broadwater, "Overcrowded Border Jails Give Way to Packed Migrant Child Shelters."

288 Camilo Montoya-Galvez, "U.S. Closing 6 Makeshift Housing Sites for Unaccompanied Migrant Children," CBS News, June 30, 2021, https://www.cbsnews.com/news/immigration-us-closing-makeshift-shelters-unaccompanied-migrant-children/.

289 Miranda Devine, Jack Morphet, Kevin Sheehan, Christopher Sadowski, and Bruce Golding, "Biden Secretly Flying Underage Migrants into NY in Dead of Night," *New York Post*, October 18, 2021, https://nypost.com/2021/10/18/biden-secretly-flying-underage-migrants-into-ny-in-dead-of-night/.

290 Miranda Devine, "Still More Secret Migrant Flights, Why Is Biden Keeping This off the Books?" *New York Post*, April 20, 2022, https://nypost.com/2022/04/20/still-more-secret-migrant-flights-why-is-biden-keeping-this-off-the-books/.

291 Glenn Kessler, "Claims of 'Ghost Flights' of 'Illegal Immigrants' Don't Add Up," *Washington Post Fact Checker*, February 4, 2022, https://www.washingtonpost.com/politics/2022/02/04/claims-ghost-flights-illegal-immigrants-dont-add-up/.

292 "Press Briefing by Press Secretary Jen Psaki," White House Briefing Room, October 19, 2021, https://www.whitehouse.gov/briefing-room/

press-briefings/2021/10/19/press-briefing-by-press-secretary-jen-psa-ki-october-19-2021/.

293   Letter from Representatives Elise M. Stefanik and Lee Zeldin of New York State to President Joe Biden, January 31, 2022, https://stefanik.house.gov/_cache/files/2/d/2d4f5dfa-1880-4cfb-ba17-8d3646a5838c/DD0DDE368E9CAA5F7F982AC1BC0B8F37.immigrant-flights-letter.pdf.

294   Kessler, "Claims of 'Ghost Flights' of 'Illegal Immigrants' Don't Add Up."

295   "Joint Operation Nets 24 Transnational Gang Members, 475 Total Arrests under Operation Matador," U.S. Immigration and Customs Enforcement, press release, March 29, 2018, https://www.ice.gov/news/releases/joint-operation-nets-24-transnational-gang-members-475-total-arrests-under-operation#:~:text=Operation%20Matador%20results%20since%20May,street%20gang%20with%2015%20arrests; Stephen Dinan, "MS-13's Wave of Murder Fueled by Illegal Immigrants," *Washington Times*, October 22, 2020, https://www.washingtontimes.com/news/2020/oct/22/ms-13s-wave-murder-fueled-illegal-immigrants/.

296   Christopher Hutton, "Illegal Immigrant Charged with Murder After Posing as a Minor to Cross Border," *Washington Examiner*, November 4, 2021, https://www.washingtonexaminer.com/news/illegal-immigrant-charged-murder-posing-minor-border.

297   Stephen Dinan, "'Family Loophole' Lies Damn Immigrant Children to Hellish Homes," *Washington Times*, August 21, 2022, https://m.washingtontimes.com/news/2022/aug/21/illegal-immigrant-girls-used-sex-forced-labor-spon/.

298   Joshua Schneyer, Mica Rosenberg, and Kristina Cooke, "Exclusive: Hyundai Subsidiary Has Used Child Labor at Alabama Factory," Reuters, July 22, 2022, https://www.reuters.com/world/us/exclusive-hyundai-subsidiary-has-used-child-labor-alabama-factory-2022-07-22/.

299   Joshua Schneyer, Mica Rosenberg, and Kristina Cooke, "Teen Risked All to Flee Guatemala. Her Payoff: Grueling Job in U.S. Chicken Plant," Reuters, February 7, 2022, https://www.reuters.com/investigates/special-report/usa-immigration-alabama/.

300   "Fact Sheet: President Biden Outlines Steps to Reform Our Immigration System by Keeping Families Together, Addressing the Root Causes of Irregular Migration, and Streamlining the Legal Immigration System," White House Briefing Room, February 2, 2021, https://www.whitehouse.gov/briefing-room/statements-releases/2021/02/02/fact-sheet-president-biden-outlines-steps-to-reform-our-immigration-system-by-keeping-families-together-addressing-the-root-causes-of-irregular-migration-and-streamlining-the-legal-immigration-syst/.

301 "DHS Statement on the Suspension of New Enrollments in the Migrant Protection Protocols Program," Department of Homeland Security, January 20, 2021, https://www.dhs.gov/news/2021/01/20/dhs-statement-suspension-new-enrollments-migrant-protection-protocols-program.

302 "The US Citizenship Act of 2021: What's Inside and Who Could Be Eligible for Immigration Relief," Center for Migration Studies Explainer, March 11, 2021, https://cmsny.org/citizenship-act-2021-explainer/.

303 Nick Miroff and Arelis R. Hernández, "Biden Orders a 'Pause' on Border Wall Construction, Bringing Crews to a Halt," *Washington Post*, January 20, 2021, https://www.washingtonpost.com/national/biden-border-wall-executive-order/2021/01/20/5f472456-5b32-11eb-aaad-93988621dd28_story.html.

304 "The Biden Plan for Securing Our Values as a Nation of Immigrants," Biden-Harris campaign website, https://joebiden.com/immigration/.

305 Barbara Sprunt, "Biden Would End Border Wall Construction, but Wouldn't Tear Down Trump's Additions," National Public Radio, August 5, 2020, https://www.npr.org/2020/08/05/899266045/biden-would-end-border-wall-construction-but-wont-tear-down-trump-s-additions.

306 Stuart Anderson, "Trump Spent $15 Billion on Border Wall but Skimped on Vaccines," *Forbes*, December 9, 2020, https://www.forbes.com/sites/stuartanderson/2020/12/09/trump-spent-15-billion-on-border-wall-but-skimped-on-vaccines/?sh=68d2e17e6a9d.

307 Kenneth Maxwell, review of *Operation Gatekeeper: The Rise of the 'Illegal Alien' and the Remaking of the U.S.-Mexico Boundary*, by Joseph Nevins, *Foreign Affairs*, March/April 2003, https://www.foreignaffairs.com/reviews/capsule-review/2003-03-01/operation-gatekeeper-rise-illegal-alien-and-remaking-us-mexico.

308 "The Obama-Biden Administration Built More Than 100 miles of Border Wall. The Biden-Harris Administration Should Tear Walls Down," Southern Border Communities Coalition, https://www.southernborder.org/the_obama_biden_administration_built_more_than_100_miles_of_border_wall_the_biden_harris_administration_should_tear_walls_down.

309 Nick Miroff, "The Border Wall Trump Called Unclimbable Is Taking a Grim Toll," *Washington Post*, April 29, 2022, https://www.washingtonpost.com/national-security/2022/04/29/trump-border-wall-injuries-deaths/.

310 Ibid.

311 Nick Miroff, "Trump's Border Wall Has Been Breached More Than 3,000 Times by Smugglers, CBP Records Show," *Washington Post*, March 2, 2022, https://www.washingtonpost.com/national-security/2022/03/02/trump-border-wall-breached/.

312   Julian Resendiz, "Sheriff: Migrant Surge, Border Agents' Reassignment Leads to 60,000 'Get-Aways,'" Border Report, May 12, 2021, https://www.borderreport.com/regions/arizona/sheriff-migrant-surge-border-agents-reassignment-leads-to-60000-get-aways/.

313   Nick Miroff, "Where Trump's Border Wall Left Deep Scars and Open Gaps, Biden Plans Repair Job," *Washington Post*, February 19, 2022, https://www.washingtonpost.com/national-security/2022/02/19/trump-biden-border-wall/.

314   "Road to the White House 2008: Biden Campaign Event," C-Span video, starting minute 36, August 12, 2007, https://www.c-span.org/video/?200403-1/biden-campaign-event.

315   Elaine Duke, "Homeland Security Secretary: Border Walls Work. Yuma Sector Proves It," *USA Today*, August 22, 2017, updated August 23, 2017, https://www.usatoday.com/story/opinion/2017/08/22/homeland-security-secretary-border-walls-work-yuma-sector-proves-it-elaine-duke-column/586853001/.

316   Salvador Rivera, "Migrants Streaming into U.S. through Little-Known Pathway Where Arizona, Mexico and California Meet," Border Report, December 9, 2021, https://www.borderreport.com/regions/arizona/migrants-streaming-into-u-s-through-little-known-pathway-where-arizona-mexico-and-california-meet/; Andrew R. Arthur, "Illegal Migrants Surge through the 'Yuma Gap,'" Center for Immigration Studies, March 1, 2022, https://cis.org/Arthur/Illegal-Migrants-Surge-through-Yuma-Gap.

317   "DHS to Address Life, Safety, and Operational Requirements in the U.S. Border Patrol's Yuma Sector," DHS, press release, July 28, 2022, https://www.dhs.gov/news/2022/07/28/dhs-address-life-safety-and-operational-requirements-us-border-patrols-yuma-sector.

318   Ibid.

319   *United States of America v. Sebastian Tovar*, Superseding Indictment, Case No. 2:21-cr-00546-AM, Document 97, September 15, 2021.

320   Jerry Clayton, "High-Speed Chases Endanger Lives of Migrants and Area Residents in South Texas," Texas Public Radio, August 6, 2022, https://www.tpr.org/news/2022-08-06/high-speed-chases-endanger-lives-of-migrants-and-area-residents-in-kinney-county.

321   Charlotte Culberson, "High-Speed Chases, Smuggling Crashes Take Toll on Small Border Town," *Epoch Times*, February 24, 2022, https://www.theepochtimes.com/high-speed-chases-smuggling-crashes-take-toll-on-small-border-town_4297541.html.

322   Shaley Sanders, "KOLD Investigates: Cartel Hiring Arizona Teens to Smuggle Undocumented Immigrants, New Law Aims to Close Legal Loopholes," KOLD News 13, June 27, 2022, https://www.kold.

com/2022/06/28/kold-investigates-cartel-hiring-arizona-teens-smuggle-undocumented-immigrants-new-law-aims-close-legal-loopholes/.

323   Julian Resendiz, "Far West Texas County Deals with Huge Spike in Migrants Smuggling," Fox59, March 9, 2021, https://fox59.com/news/far-west-texas-county-deals-with-huge-spike-in-migrant-smuggling/.

324   Sachi McClendon, "High-Speed Chase Cuts through Marfa, Fort Davis," *Big Bend Sentinel*, April 21, 2021, https://bigbendsentinel.com/2021/04/21/high-speed-chase-cuts-through-marfa-fort-davis/.

325   Title 6 United States Code 223: Border Security Metrics, Definitions (3) Got away, https://uscode.house.gov/view.xhtml?req=(title:6%20section:223%20edition:prelim).

326   Nick Miroff, "Border Officials Say More People Are Sneaking Past Them as Crossings Soar and Agents Are Overwhelmed," *Washington Post*, April 2, 2021, https://www.washingtonpost.com/national/got-aways-border/2021/04/01/14258a1e-9302-11eb-9af7-fd0822ae4398_story.html.

327   "Review of and Interim Revision to Civil Immigration Enforcement and Removal Policies and Priorities," Secretary of Department of Homeland Security memorandum to Troy Miller, Tae Johnson, Tracey Renaud, Karen Olick, and David Pekoske, January 20, 2021, https://www.dhs.gov/sites/default/files/publications/21_0120_enforcement-memo_signed.pdf.

328   "FAQs: Protected Areas and Courthouse Arrests," U.S. Immigration and Customs Enforcement website, accessed September 1, 2022, https://www.ice.gov/about-ice/ero/protected-areas.

329   "Interim Guidance: Civil Immigration Enforcement and Removal Priorities," memorandum for All ICE Employees from Activing ICE Director Tae D. Johnson, February 18, 2021, https://www.ice.gov/doclib/news/releases/2021/021821_civil-immigration-enforcement_interim-guidance.pdf; Nick Miroff and Maria Sacchetti, "Biden Memo for ICE Officers Points to Fewer Deportations and Strict Oversight," *Washington Post*, February 18, 2021, https://www.washingtonpost.com/national/biden-memo-for-ice-officers-points-to-fewer-deportations/2021/02/18/1d-6ca98e-71fd-11eb-a4eb-44012a612cf9_story.html.

330   Maria Sacchetti, "DHS Issues New Arrest and Deportation Guidelines to Immigration Agents," *Washington Post*, September 30, 2021, https://www.washingtonpost.com/immigration/ice-deportations-migrants-guidelines/2021/09/30/8c110eec-21ee-11ec-8200-5e3fd4c49f5e_story.html.

331   "Guidelines for the Enforcement of Civil Immigration Law," DHS memorandum from Secretary Alejandro N. Mayorkas to Troy Miller, Ur Jaddou, Robert Silvers, Katherine Culliton-González, and Lynn Parker

Dupree, September 30, 2021, https://www.ice.gov/doclib/news/guide-lines-civilimmigrationlaw.pdf.

332   Stephen Dinan, "Exclusive: Secret ICE Data Shows Drop in Arrests of Criminals, Surge in Arrests of Non-Criminals," *Washington Times*, March 16, 2022, https://www.washingtontimes.com/news/2022/mar/16/exclusive-secret-ice-data-shows-drop-arrests-crimi/; Stephen Dinan, "Federal Sanctuary: Marshals Service to Stop Holding Illegal Immigrants for ICE," *Washington Times*, August 17, 2022, https://www.washingtontimes.com/news/2022/aug/17/federal-sanctuary-marshals-service-stop-holding-il/.

333   Jessica M. Vaughan, "ICE Records Confirm Steep Decline in Deportations," Center for Immigration Studies, May 17, 2022, https://cis.org/Vaughan/ICE-Records-Confirm-Steep-Decline-Deportations.

334   "Criminal Noncitizen Statistics Fiscal Year 2022," U.S. Customs and Border Protection website, https://www.cbp.gov/newsroom/stats/cbp-enforcement-statistics/criminal-noncitizen-statistics.

335   "Calexico Agents Arrest Documented Gang Member," Customs and Border Protection, press release, March 10, 2022, https://www.cbp.gov/newsroom/local-media-release/calexico-agents-arrest-documented-gang-member?language_content_entity=en; "RGV Agents Arrest Sex Offenders and Gang Members," CBP, press release, June 15, 2022, https://www.cbp.gov/newsroom/local-media-release/rgv-agents-arrest-sex-offenders-and-gang-members; "Del Rio Sector Border Patrol Agents Arrest Four Sex Offenders," CBP, press release, June 15, 2022, https://www.cbp.gov/newsroom/local-media-release/del-rio-sector-border-patrol-agents-arrest-four-sex-offenders; "RGV Agents Continue to Stop Criminals at the US Border," CBP, press release, June 10, 2022, https://www.cbp.gov/newsroom/local-media-release/rgv-agents-continue-stop-criminals-us-border; "Border Patrol Agents Arrest Man Convicted of Manslaughter," CBP, press release, June 8, 2022, https://www.cbp.gov/newsroom/local-media-release/border-patrol-agents-arrest-man-convicted-manslaughter-0; "RGV Agents Continue to Make Significant Arrests," CBP, press release, June 8, 2022, https://www.cbp.gov/newsroom/local-media-release/rgv-agents-continue-make-significant-arrests.

336   "RGV Agents Arrest Dangerous Migrants," CBP, press release, August 12, 2022, https://www.cbp.gov/newsroom/local-media-release/rgv-agents-arrest-dangerous-migrants.

337   Ibid.

338   Adam Shaw, "Border Patrol Agents See 3,166% Increase in Convicted Sex Offender Arrests in Del Rio Sector," Fox News, May 27, 2021, https://www.foxnews.com/politics/border-patrol-agents-increase-convicted-sex-offender-arrests-del-rio.

339   Shaley Sanders, "KOLD Investigates: Cochise College's Douglas Campus Beefs Up Security as Border Activity Increases," KOLD 13 News, June 17, 2022, https://www.kold.com/2022/06/17/kold-investigates-cochise-colleges-douglas-campus-beefs-up-security-border-activity-increases/.

340   Morgan Phillips, "Border Patrol Deploying Hundreds of Agents from Canada, Coastal Areas to Southern Border," Fox News, February 26, 2021, https://www.foxnews.com/politics/border-patrol-deploying-hundred-agents-northern-border-coast-southern-border.

341   Todd Bensman, "Panama and Costa Rica Doing Smugglers' Work with 'Controlled Flow' Policy," Center for Immigration Studies, December 27, 2018, https://cis.org/Bensman/Panama-and-Costa-Rica-Doing-Smugglers-Work-Controlled-Flow-Policy.

342   Sibylla Brodzinsky, "Refugees and Migrants Brave Jungle Wilderness in Search of Safety," United Nations Refugee Agency, March 22, 2022, https://www.unhcr.org/en-us/news/   stories/2022/3/6242ff434/refugees-migrants-brave-jungle-wilderness-search-safety.html.

343   "How the Darien Gap Is Reshaping MIgrant Journeys," The New York Times,   https://www.nytimes.com/2022/11/09/world/americas/migrants-darien-gap.html.

344   "Record Number of Children Crossing the Darien Gap towards the US This Year." UNICEF, https://www.unicef.org/lac/en/press-releases/record-number-of-children-crossing-darien-gap-towards-us-this-years

345   "Total Encounters by Fiscal Year (Oct. 1st through Sept. 30th)," U.S. Customs and Border Patrol, https://www.cbp.gov/sites/default/files/assets/documents/2021-Aug/U.S.%20Border%20Patrol%20Apprehensions%20From%20Mexico%20and%20Other%20Than%20Mexico%20%28FY%202000%20-%20FY%202020%29.pdf.

346   "U.S. Border Patrol Nationwide Apprehensions by Citizenship and Sector, 2009–2019," U.S. Border Patrol, https://www.cbp.gov/sites/default/files/assets/documents/2020-Jan/U.S.%20Border%20Patrol%20Nationwide%20Apprehensions%20by%20Citizenship%20and%20Sector%20%28FY2007%20-%20FY%202019%29_1.pdf.

347   Alexandra Mendoza and Kate Morrissey, "Dozens of Ukrainians Stuck in Tijuana After U.S. Policy Change," San Diego Union-Tribune, April 26, 2022, https://www.sandiegouniontribune.com/news/immigration/story/2022-04-26/ukrainians-stuck-tijuana.

348   "Risking It All: Migrants Brave Darien Gap in Pursuit of the American Dream," The Guardian, April 28, 2022, https://www.theguardian.com/global-development/2022/apr/28/risking-it-all-migrants-brave-darien-gap-in-pursuit-of-the-american-dream.

349   Julie Turkewitz, Natalie Kitroeff, and Sofia Villamil, "Perilous, Roadless Jungle Becomes a Path of Desperate Hope," New York Times, October

2, 2021, https://www.nytimes.com/2021/10/02/world/americas/haitian-migrants-mexican-border.html.

350 "Though Fewer People Are Making the Crossing to Panama, the Darien Gap Is as Dangerous as Ever," Reliefweb International, May 6, 2022, https://reliefweb.int/report/panama/though-fewer-people-are-making-crossing-panama-dari-n-gap-dangerous-ever; "Mixed Movements through Darien in 2021," United Nations High Commission for Refugees, n.d., https://reporting.unhcr.org/document/1801.

351 "The United States and Panama Advance Migration Cooperation," Antony J. Blinken, Secretary of State, U.S. Department of State, press statement, April 19, 2022, https://www.state.gov/the-united-states-and-panama-advance-migration-cooperation/.

352 Claire Savage, "Misleading Claim about UN Aid for Migrants in Mexico Spreads Online," AFP Fact Check, December 8, 2021, https://factcheck.afp.com/http%253A%252F%252Fdoc.afp.com%252F9U77HR-1.

353 Todd Bensman, "In Mexico's Deep South, the United Nations Explains Handing Cash to U.S.-Bound Migrants," Center for Immigration Studies, January 20, 2022, https://cis.org/Bensman/Mexicos-Deep-South-United-Nations-Explains-Handing-Cash-USBound-Migrants.

354 Todd Bensman, "United Nations Grantee Uses U.S. Tax Dollars to Fund Illegal Immigration," The Federalist, December 16, 2021, https://thefederalist.com/2021/12/16/united-nations-grantee-uses-u-s-tax-dollars-to-fund-illegal-immigration/.

355 Chuck Holton, "Report from the Migrant Trail in South America," Center for Immigration Studies, February 3, 2022, https://cis.org/Holton/Report-Migrant-Trail-South-America.

356 Todd Bensman, "Inside a Most Unusual Mexican Migrant Camp," Center for Immigration Studies, November 22, 2021, https://cis.org/Bensman/Inside-Most-Unusual-Mexican-Migrant-Camp.

357 Henry Rodgers, "Exclusive: Republicans Vying to Prevent United Nations from Giving Money to Migrants Illegally Entering US," Daily Caller, December 7, 2021, https://dailycaller.com/2021/12/07/lance-gooden-republicans-bill-united-nations-money-illegal-immigration/.

358 IOM Cash-Based Interventions Annual Report and Case Studies 2020, International Organization of Migration Publications Platform, https://publications.iom.int/books/iom-cash-based-interventions-annual-report-and-case-studies-2020.

359 The Grand Bargain (official website), accessed August 30, 2022, https://interagencystandingcommittee.org/grand-bargain.

360 "Increase the Use and Coordination of Cash-Based Programming," Inter-Agency Standing Committee, website accessed August 30, 2022, https://interagencystandingcommittee.org/increase-the-use-and-coordination-of-cash-based-programming.

361 "CBP Enforcement Statistics Fiscal Year 2022," CBP, website accessed August 30, 2022, https://www.cbp.gov/newsroom/stats/cbp-enforcement-statistics.

362 "Two Yemeni Men Arrested by Border Patrol Identified on the FBI's Terrorism Watch List," CPB, press release, April 5, 2021, accessed August 30, 2022 via Wayback Machine Archive, http://web.archive.org/web/20210405193826/https:/www.cbp.gov/newsroom/local-media-release/two-yemeni-men-arrested-border-patrol-identified-fbi-s-terrorism-0

363 Adry Torres, "Saudi Arabia Terrorist Is Busted Illegally Crossing the Border into the US from Mexico," *Daily Mail*, December 21, 2021, https://www.dailymail.co.uk/news/article-10333305/Arizona-border-patrol-agents-arrest-Saudi-terror-suspect-illegally-crossed-Mexico.html.

364 "House Homeland Security Committee Holds Hearing with Mayorkas on Immigration," *PBS NewsHour*, March 17, 2021, minute 1:48, YouTube, https://www.youtube.com/watch?v=wWiIfkDbRX4.

365 Charlie Leduff, "Is This Venezuelan in Metro Detroit an Asylum Seeker or Suspected Terrorist?" Deadline Detroit, January 27, 2022, https://www.deadlinedetroit.com/articles/29777/leduff_is_this_venezuelan_in_dearborn_an_asylum_seeker_or_suspected_terrorist.

366 "Terrorism-Related Inadmissibility Grounds (TRIG)," U.S. Citizenship and Immigration Services website, https://www.uscis.gov/laws-and-policy/other-resources/terrorism-related-inadmissibility-grounds-trig.

367 Nick Miroff, "U.S. Sends Venezuelan Migrants to Colombia under Biden's New Border Plan," *Washington Post*, January 31, 2022, https://www.washingtonpost.com/national-security/2022/01/31/biden-border-venezuelan-migrants-colombia/.

368 Bill Melugin and Adam Sabes, "Border Patrol Released Suspected Terrorist Who Crossed into U.S. Illegally, ICE Took Weeks to Rearrest Him," Fox News, May 23, 2022, https://www.foxnews.com/us/border-patrol-released-suspected-terrorist-ice-rearrest-weeks.

369 "FBI Foiled Terror Plot to Kill George W. Bush," BBC News, May 24, 2022, https://www.bbc.com/news/world-us-canada-61569650.

370 "Department of State Offers Reward for Information to Bring Pakistani Human Smuggler to Justice," U.S. Department of State, Bureau of International Narcotics and Law Enforcement Affairs, press statement, October 14, 2021, https://www.state.gov/department-of-state-offers-reward-for-information-to-bring-pakistani-human-smuggler-to-justice/.

371 "Specially Designated Nationals List Update," U.S. Department of the Treasury, April 7, 2021, https://home.treasury.gov/policy-issues/financial-sanctions/recent-actions/20210407.

372 Ibid.

373   "Evaluation of the Screening of Displaced Persons from Afghanistan (DODIG-2022-065)," Department of Defense, Office of Inspector General, February 17, 2022, https://www.dodig.mil/reports.html/Article/2938359/evaluation-of-the-screening-of-displaced-persons-from-afghanistan-dodig-2022-065/.

374   "Former Liberian War Lord Known as 'Jungle Jabbah' Sentenced to 30 Years in Prison for Immigration Fraud and Perjury," Department of Justice, U.S. Attorney's Office, Eastern District of Pennsylvania, press release, April 19, 2019, https://www.justice.gov/usao-edpa/pr/former-liberian-war-lord-known-jungle-jabbah-sentenced-30-years-prison-immigration.

375   "Former Armed Forces of Liberia Commanding General Charged with Immigration Fraud, Perjury Following HSI Philadelphia Investigation," ICE, press release, June 24, 2022, https://www.ice.gov/news/releases/former-armed-forces-liberia-commanding-general-charged-immigration-fraud-perjury.

376   "Former Liberian Rebel General Charged with Immigration Fraud," Department of Justice, U.S. Attorney's Office, Eastern District of Pennsylvania, press release, May 5, 2022, https://www.justice.gov/usao-edpa/pr/former-liberian-rebel-general-charged-immigration-fraud.

377   Steve Wembi and Joseph Goldstein, "ISIS Claims First Attack in the Democratic Republic of Congo," *New York Times*, April 19, 2019, https://www.nytimes.com/2019/04/19/world/africa/isis-congo-attack.html.

378   "Inside the ADF Rebellion: A Glimpse into the Life and Operations of a Secretive Jihadi Armed Group," Congo Research Group, Center on International Cooperation, New York University, November 2018, https://insidetheadf.org/wp-content/uploads/2018/11/Inside-the-ADF-Rebellion-14Nov18.pdf.

379   Robert Postings, "The Tentative Ties between the Allied Democratic Forces and ISIS," *The Defense Post*, December 4, 2018, https://www.thedefensepost.com/2018/12/04/tentative-ties-allied-democratic-forces-isis-dr-congo/.

380   Dionne Searcey, "Cameroon on Brink of Civil War as English Speakers Recount 'Unbearable' Horrors," *New York Times*, October 6, 2018, https://www.nytimes.com/2018/10/06/world/africa/cameroon-election-biya-ambazonia.html.

381   Farouk Chothia, "Cameroon's Anglophone Crisis: Red Dragons and Tigers—the Rebels Fighting for Independence," BBC News, October 4, 2018, https://www.bbc.com/news/world-africa-45723211; Moki Edwin Kindzeka, "Cameroon French Towns Create, Train Militias to Fight English-Speaking Separatists," Voice of America, October 19, 2021, https://www.voanews.com/a/cameroon-french-towns-create-train-militias-to-fight-english-speaking-separatists/6276820.html.

382 "Del Rio Sector Border Patrol Agents Encounters [*sic*]Three Large Groups of Migrants," U.S. Customs and Border Protection, news release, July 1, 2022, https://www.cbp.gov/newsroom/local-media-release/del-rio-sector-border-patrol-agents-encounters-three-large-groups; "Yuma Sector BP Agents Arrest Group of Iranians," U.S. Customs and Border Protection, news release, February 3, 2021, https://www.cbp.gov/newsroom/local-media-release/yuma-sector-bp-agents-arrest-group-iranians.

383 Anna Giaritelli, "20,000 Ukrainians Reached the US Southern Border in April After Fleeing War," *Washington Examiner*, May 17, 2022, https://www.washingtonexaminer.com/policy/20-000-ukrainians-reached-us-southern-border-in-april-after-fleeing-war; Associated Press, "Migrant Border Entries Rise in April, Boosted by Ukrainians," Voice of America, May 17, 2022, https://www.voanews.com/a/6577451.html; "Ukraine," Organized Crime Index profile, https://ocindex.net/country/ukraine.

384 Nick Miroff, Karen DeYoung, and Kevin Sieff, "Biden Will Send Mexico Surplus Vaccine, as U.S. Seeks Help on Immigration Enforcement," *Washington Post*, March 18, 2021, https://www.washingtonpost.com/national-security/biden-mexico-immigration-coronavirus-vaccine/2021/03/18/a63a3426-8791-11eb-8a67-f314e5fcf88d_story.html; Mary Beth Sheridan and Gabriela Martínez, "In Mexico, Biden Team Asks for More Help Stopping Irregular Migration," *Washington Post*, March 23, 2021, https://www.washingtonpost.com/world/the_americas/mexico-biden-immigration-surge-border/2021/03/23/2b993ec8-8bde-11eb-9423-04079921c915_story.html; Rodrigo Cervantes, "Mexico Intensifies Immigration Security Measures," Fronteras Desk, March 22, 2021, https://fronterasdesk.org/content/1668800/mexico-intensifies-immigration-security-measures; "Top US Diplomat 'Visits' Mexico, Canada on Virtual Trip," Voice of America, February 26, 2021, https://www.voanews.com/a/usa_top-us-diplomat-visits-mexico-canada-virtual-trip/6202614.html.

385 "New Wave of Haitian Migrants in Tapachula; 2,000 Applied Monday for Asylum," *Mexico News Daily*, July 16, 2021, https://mexiconewsdaily.com/news/new-wave-of-haitian-migrants-in-tapachula-2000-applied-monday-for-asylum/.

386 Marco Ugarte, "Migrant Caravan Broken Up Again in Southern Mexico," Associated Press, September 5, 2021, https://apnews.com/article/mexico-caribbean-immigration-f5ec13f73e502f3ae9c09242cd00f2af.

387 Felicia J. Persaud, "Haitian Migrants Are Being Met with Force by Mexican Immigration Agents," *New York Amsterdam News*, September 9, 2021, https://amsterdamnews.com/news/2021/09/09/haitian-migrants-are-being-met-force-mexican-immig/.

388 Ciara Rouege and Michelle Homer, "'El Grito'—Mexico's Independence Day on Sept. 16 Celebrates Freedom Much Like Our 4th of July," KHOU 11 News, September 15, 2021, updated September 16, 2021, https://www.khou.com/article/life/people/our-story-our-history/mexican-independence-day-celebration-of-freedom-culture/285-c705bdf1-2dfb-4600-95e5-813fe78b9580.

389 Alfredo Corchado, "How Could the Mass Migration of Haitians to the U.S. Border Have Been a Surprise?" *Dallas Morning News*, October 9, 2021, https://www.dallasnews.com/news/immigration/2021/10/09/how-could-the-mass-migration-of-haitians-to-the-us-border-have-been-a-surprise/.

390 Todd Bensman and Bryan Griffith, "Border Sector Shopping: Migrants Probe for Security Weaknesses," Center for Immigration Studies, March 25, 2021, https://cis.org/Video/Border-Sector-Shopping.

391 Julian Borger, "US Suspends Haiti Deportation Flights as Biden Administration Tries to Control ICE," *The Guardian*, February 5, 2021, https://www.theguardian.com/us-news/2021/feb/05/us-haiti-deportation-flights-suspended-ice-immigration.

392 Keith Griffith and Rachel Sharp, "Haitian Deportees Bite ICE Agents and Assault Pilots on Deportation Flights Back to Port-au-Prince," *Daily Mail*, September 22, 2021, https://www.dailymail.co.uk/news/article-10017749/Haitian-deportees-assault-pilots-ICE-agents-deported-Port-au-Prince.html.

393 Julia Ainsley, "Haitian Deportees Assaulted U.S. Pilots, Injured Three ICE Officers," NBC News, September 21, 2021, https://www.nbcnews.com/politics/immigration/haitian-deportees-assaulted-u-s-pilots-injured-three-ice-officers-n1279775.

394 Anna Giaritelli, "Two Haitian Migrants Bite ICE Officers on Deportation Flight," *Washington Examiner*, September 22, 2021, https://www.washingtonexaminer.com/news/haitian-migrants-bite-ice-officers-deportation-flight.

395 Anna Giaritelli, "Haitian Migrants in Custody Have 'Hijacked' Multiple Buses," *Washington Examiner*, September 22, 2021, https://www.yahoo.com/video/haitian-migrants-custody-hijacked-multiple-155100481.html.

396 Anna Giaritelli, "Haitian Migrants Revolt in Custody and Seize Control of Privately Contracted Bus," *Washington Examiner*, September 21, 2021, https://www.yahoo.com/video/haitian-migrants-revolt-custody-seize-154100629.html.

397 Sydney Hernandez, "Several Migrants Attempt to Flee ICE Transport Bus, Back in Custody," Valley Central News, September 20, 2021, https://www.valleycentral.com/news/local-news/several-migrants-attempt-to-flee-ice-transport-bus-back-in-custody/.

398   Nick Niedzwiadek, "Mayorkas Vows 'Dramatic Results' in Coming Days on Haitian Migrants," *Politico*, September 21, 2021, https://www.politico.com/news/2021/09/21/mayorkas-haitian-migrants-dramatic-results-513439.

399   Felicia Sonmez, "All Migrants Have Been Cleared from Encampment in Del Rio, Homeland Security Secretary Says," *Washington Post*, September 24, 2021, https://www.texastribune.org/2021/09/24/texas-border-migrants-camp-del-rio-haitians/.

400   Nick Miroff, "Most of the Migrants in Del Rio, Tex., Camp Have Been Sent to Haiti or Turned Back to Mexico, DHS Figures Show," *Washington Post*, October 1, 2021, https://www.washingtonpost.com/national/haitians-border-deportations/2021/10/01/bfa38852-222a-11ec-8fd4-57a5d9bf4b47_story.html.

401   "'Operation Ant' Invades the North of Coahuila," K911 Noticias, November 22, 2021, https://k911noticias-com.translate.goog/operacion-hormiga-invade-el-norte-de-coahuila/?_x_tr_sl=es&_x_tr_tl=en&_x_tr_hl=en&_x_tr_pto=sc; Carolina Gómez Mena, "We Sneak among the Pilgrims," *La Jornada* (Mexico), December 13, 2021, https://www-jornada-com-mx.translate.goog/2021/12/13/politica/003n2pol?_x_tr_sl=es&_x_tr_tl=en&_x_tr_hl=en&_x_tr_pto=sc.

402   Rafael Bernal, "Advocates in 'Utter Disbelief' After Biden Resumes Haitian Repatriations," *The Hill*, September 16, 2021, https://thehill.com/latino/572588-advocates-in-utter-disbelief-after-biden-resumes-haitian-repatriations/.

403   Michelle Hackman and Tarini Parti, "Biden Immigration Policy Marred by Internal Rifts: 'A Recipe for Disaster,'" *Wall Street Journal*, November 18, 2021, https://www.wsj.com/articles/biden-trump-immigration-southern-border-mexico-11637256075.

404   "ICE Air Operations Prioritizes Safety and Security for Its Passengers," ICE Air website, accessed July 14, 2022, https://www.ice.gov/features/ICE-Air.

405   Alicia A. Caldwell, Michelle Hackman, and Juan Montes, "U.S. Flies Haitian Migrants Home in Bid to Manage Del Rio Border Crisis," *Wall Street Journal*, September 20, 2021, https://www.wsj.com/articles/u-s-flies-haitian-migrants-home-in-bid-to-manage-del-rio-border-crisis-11632167064?mod=article_inline.

406   "Mexico Likely Deportation Flights on Magnicharters to Northern Triangle Countries, 1 May–31 August 2021," Witness at the Border, https://static1.squarespace.com/static/5e221cacff87ba2d2833cf54/t/61343685093fa65431b5ebd3/1630811781731/MX_TO_NOTRI_PDF.pdf.

407   "ICE Air Flights, August 2021and Last 12 Months," Witness at the Border, August 2021, https://static1.squarespace.com/static/5e221cacff-

87ba2d2833cf54/t/61491fb5a35ffc26df69ddab/1632182197564/
ICE+Air+Aug+2021+PDFv2.pdf.

408   "Read: Resignation Letter from U.S. Special Envoy for Haiti, Daniel
       Foote," *Washington Post*, September 22, 2022, https://www.washington-
       post.com/context/read-resignation-letter-from-u-s-special-envoy-for-
       haiti-daniel-foote/3136ae0e-96e5-448e-9d12-0e0cabfb3c0b/.

409   Chandelis Duster and Etant Dupain, "Special Envoy for Haiti Resigns Cit-
       ing 'Inhumane' US Decision to Deport Thousands of Haitians from US
       Border," CNN, September 23, 2021, https://www.cnn.com/2021/09/23/
       politics/daniel-foote-haiti/index.html.

410   Zolan Kanno-Youngs, Michael D. Shear, and Eileen Sullivan, "Dis-
       agreement and Delay: How Infighting over the Border Divided the
       White House," *New York Times*, April 9, 2022, https://www.nytimes.
       com/2022/04/09/us/politics/biden-border-immigration.html.

411   Hackman and Parti, "Biden Administration Marred by Internal Rifts."

412   Nick Miroff and Sean Sullivan, "Biden's Border Woes Expose White
       House Divisions as Centrists Assert More Control," *Washington
       Post*, November 8, 2021, https://www.washingtonpost.com/national/
       biden-border-divisions/2021/11/07/e87c8630-3b24-11ec-a67c-d7c-
       2182dac83_story.html.

413   "Mexico Temporarily Suspends Visa Exemption for Citizens of Ecua-
       dor," Government of Mexico, press release, August 20, 2021, https://
       www.gob.mx/sre/prensa/mexico-temporarily-suspends-visa-exemp-
       tion-for-citizens-of-ecuador?idiom=en; Vincent Ricci, "More Ecuador-
       ians Leaving for US amid 'Burst in Migration,'" Aljazeera, September
       23, 2021, https://www.aljazeera.com/news/2021/9/23/more-ecuador-
       ians-leaving-for-us-amid-burst-in-migration#:~:text=Thousands%20
       leaving&text=In%20a%20speech%20on%20September,the%20first%20
       half%20of%202021.

414   "Securing and Ensuring Order on the Southwest Border," U.S. Senate
       Committee on Homeland Security and Governmental Affairs, May 5,
       2022, starting minute 1:24, https://www.hsgac.senate.gov/hearings/se-
       curing-and-ensuring-order-on-the-southwest-border.

415   Karina Andrew Herrera, "Migration in Tapachula Has a New Face, Mas-
       sive Phenomenon Is Now of Venezuelans," Noticieros Television, July 23,
       2022, https://noticieros.televisa.com/ultimas-noticias/migracion-tapa-
       chula-nuevo-rostro-fenomeno-masivo-venezolanos/.

416   Eugene Scott, "Graham Says Tens of Thousands of Brazilian Immigrants
       'Wearing Designer Clothes and Gucci Bags' Are Headed for Connecti-
       cut," *Washington Post*, October 13, 2021, https://www.washingtonpost.
       com/politics/graham-immigration-brazil/2021/10/13/2abe389e-2c49-1
       1ec-985d-3150f7e106b2_story.html.

417 "Mexico to Impose Visa Requirement on Venezuelans to Stem Migration," Reuters, December 17, 2021, https://www.reuters.com/world/americas/mexico-impose-visa-requirements-venezuelans-2021-12-17/.

418 "The Road to Nicaragua," *OnCuba*, November 29, 2021, https://oncubanews-com.translate.goog/cuba/el-camino-de-nicaragua-nueva-ruta-para-los-cubanos/?_x_tr_sl=es&_x_tr_tl=en&_x_tr_hl=en&_x_tr_pto=sc.

419 Lioman Lima, "'It's a Silent Mariel': The Thousands of Cubans Who Use Nicaragua as a Route to Reach the Untied States," BBC World News, March 22, 2022, https://www-bbc-com.translate.goog/mundo/noticias-america-latina-60788280?_x_tr_sl=es&_x_tr_tl=en&_x_tr_hl=en&_x_tr_pto=sc.

420 "No More Flights between Cuba and Nicaragua with the Airline Viva Aerobus," Havana Live, April 11, 2022, https://havana-live.com/no-more-flights-between-cuba-and-nicaragua-with-the-airline-viva-aerobus/.

421 "Copa Airlines Cancels Flights from Cuba to Nicaragua," CubaNet, February 22, 2022, https://www.cubanet.org/english/copa-airlines-cancels-flights-from-cuba-to-nicaragua/?print=pdf.

422 Nelson Gonzalez and Nelson Acosta, "Cubans Protest in Havana as Costa Rica Tightens Visa Restrictions," Reuters, February 21, 2022, https://www.reuters.com/world/americas/cubans-protest-havana-costa-rica-tightens-visa-requirements-2022-02-22/.

423 "Cuba to Managua Routes Grounded by Mexican Airline," *Nica-Biz*, April 12, 2022, https://nica-biz.com/2022/04/12/cuba-to-managua-routes-grounded-by-mexican-airline/.

424 "Visa Free Countries for Cubans in 2022," VisaGuide.World, last accessed August 1, 2022, https://visaguide.world/visa-free-countries/cuban-passport/.

425 Mariakarla Nodarse Venancio, "The Biden Administration Takes Constructive First Steps on Cuba Relations," Washington Office on Latin America (WOLA), May 19, 2022, https://www.wola.org/analysis/biden-administration-takes-positive-steps-on-cuba/; Ned Price, "Biden Administration Expands Support to the Cuban People," U.S. State Department, press statement, May 16, 2022, https://www.state.gov/biden-administration-expands-support-to-the-cuban-people/.

426 "Letter from Human Rights Groups to Presidents Andrés Manuel López Obrador and Joe Biden," Human Rights Watch website, June 30, 2022, https://www.hrw.org/news/2022/07/11/letter-human-rights-groups-presidents-andres-manuel-lopez-obrador-and-joe-biden.

427 Nick Miroff, "U.S. Sends Venezuelan Migrants to Colombia under Biden's New Border Plan," *Washington Post*, January 31, 2022, https://

www.washingtonpost.com/national-security/2022/01/31/biden-bor-der-venezuelan-migrants-colombia/.

428 Thomas H. Cartwright, "ICE Air Flights July 2022 and Last 12 Months," Witness at the Border, August 3, 2022, https://static1.squarespace.com/static/5e221cacff87ba2d2833cf54/t/62e9e7084a5c497562af-f8a6/1659496205550/ICE+Air+Jul+2022+v1THCPDF.pdf.

429 Ibid.; Kanno-Youngs, Shear, and Sullivan, "Disagreement and Delay: How Infighting Over the Border Divided the White House."

430 Harold Koh, memo of resignation: "Re: Ending Title 42 return flights to countries of origin, particularly Haiti," October 2, 2021, as obtained by *Politico*, https://www.politico.com/f/?id=0000017c-4c4a-dddc-a77e-4ddbf3ae0000.

431 "Mexico Granted Transit Visas to New Migrant Caravans," El Pitazo (Venezuela), June 28, 2022, https://elpitazo.net/migracion/mexico-otor-go-visas-de-transito-a-una-nueva-caravana-de-migrantes/; "Mexi-co Dissolves Migrant Caravan, Distributes 3,000 Permits," Associated Press, June 26, 2022, https://quepasamedia.com/noticias/mundo/mexi-co/mexico-disuelve-caravana-migrante-otorga-3-000-permisos/.

432 "Migrant Caravan Leaves Southern Mexico in Fear After Texas Trage-dy," Qué Pasa, July 1, 2022, https://quepasamedia.com/noticias/inmigra-cion/caravana-migrante-parte-del-sur-de-mexico-con-temor-tras-tra-gedia-en-texas-2/.

433 "A New Migrant Caravan Is Formed," *El Siglo* (Panama), July 26, 2022, https://www.elsiglodedurango.com.mx/noticia/2022/se-for-ma-una-nueva-caravana-migrante.html.

434 Nick Miroff and Kevin Sieff, "Mexico Will Take Back More Nicaraguans and Cubans Expelled by the U.S.," *Washington Post*, May 4, 2022, https://www.washingtonpost.com/national-security/2022/05/04/us-bor-der-mexico-cubans-nicaraguans/.

435 John Salazar, "Haitians Lining Up by the Thousands in Anticipation of Lifting of Title 42," Spectrum News, May 17, 2022, https://spectrum-localnews.com/tx/south-texas-el-paso/news/2022/05/18/haitians-lin-ing-up-by-thousands-anticipating-termination-of-title-42; Joe Khalil and J. Scott Wilson, "Biden Fights to End Title 42, Border Packed in Anticipation," NewsNation, *Morning in America*, May 2, 2022, https://www.newsnationnow.com/morninginamerica/biden-fights-to-end-ti-tle-42-border-packed-in-anticipation/.

436 "Cartel Gets Involved in Truckers' Border Protest; Sets Trucks on Fire," *Mexico News Daily*, April 14, 2022, https://mexiconewsdaily.com/news/cartel-truckers-border-protest/.

437 Sandra Tovar, "After Burning Units, Carriers Remove Blockade on Reynosa-Pharr International Bridge," *El Universal* (Mexico), April 13, 2022, https://www.eluniversal.com.mx/estados/tras-incendio-de-uni-

dades-transportistas-retiran-bloqueo-en-puente-internacional-reyno-sa-pharr.

438   "Governor Abbott, DPS Launch 'Operation Lone Star' to Address Crisis at Southern Border," Office of the Texas Governor, Greg Abbott, press release, March 6, 2021, https://gov.texas.gov/news/post/governor-abbott-dps-launch-operation-lone-star-to-address-crisis-at-southern-border.

439   Ibid.

440   "Governor Abbott Takes Aggressive Action to Secure the Border as President Biden Ends Title 42 Expulsions," Office of the Texas Governor, Greg Abbott, press release, April 6, 2022, https://gov.texas.gov/news/post/governor-abbott-takes-aggressive-action-to-secure-the-border-as-president-biden-ends-title-42-expulsions.

441   "Texas: Trade Statistics," Global Edge, 2020 data, https://globaledge.msu.edu/states/texas/tradestats.

442   "Border Crossing Entry Data/All 2021 Ranking," U.S. Department of Transportation, https://explore.dot.gov/views/BorderCrossingData/CrossingRank?%3AisGuestRedirectFromVizportal=y&%3Aembed=y.

443   "Organized Crime Sets Fire to Three Trailers for Blocking Motor Transport Drivers," *Excélsior* (Mexico), April 13, 2022, https://www.excelsior.com.mx/nacional/crimen-organizado-incendia-tres-trailers-por-blo-queo-de-choferes-de-autotransporte/1509711.

444   "Statement by Press Secretary Jen Psaki on the Impact of Texas Border Delays," White House Briefing Room, April 13, 2022, https://www.whitehouse.gov/briefing-room/statements-releases/2022/04/13/state-ment-by-press-secretary-jen-psaki-on-the-impact-of-texas-border-de-lays/.

445   Steve Taylor, "Fresh Produce Companies: Abbott's Border Truck Inspections Are Destroying Our Business," *Rio Grande Guardian*, April 10, 2022, https://riograndeguardian.com/fresh-produce-companies-ab-botts-border-truck-inspections-are-destroying-our-business/.

446   Alyssa Guzman, "Governor Greg Abbott Caves on Beefed-Up Truck Inspections at Texas-Mexico Border After Psaki Blamed His 'Unnecessary' Measures for Fueling Inflation by Holding Up an Already Beleaguered Supply Chain," *Daily Mail*, April 13, 2022, updated April 14, 2022, https://www.dailymail.co.uk/news/article-10716667/Abbott-caves-truck-inspections-TX-border-Psaki-blames-measures-price-increases.html.

447   "Governor Abbott Signs Border Security Memoranda of Understanding in Austin with Chihuahua Governor Campos, Coahuila Governor Riquelme," Office of Texas Governor, Greg Abbott, press release, April 14, 2022, https://gov.texas.gov/news/post/governor-abbott-signs-bor-der-security-memoranda-of-understanding-in-austin-with-chihua-hua-governor-campos-coahulia-governor-solis; "Memorandum of Un-

derstanding between the State of Texas and the Free and Sovereign State of Chihuahua," https://gov.texas.gov/uploads/files/press/Texas_MOU.pdf; Memorandum of Understanding between the State of Texas and the Free and Sovereign State of Coahuila de Zaragoza, https://gov.texas.gov/uploads/files/press/Texas_MOU_(2).pdf; Todd Bensman, "Texas Governor's Unprecedented Trade Disruption Strategy Yields First Fruit," Center for Immigration Studies, April 14, 2022, https://cis.org/Bensman/Texas-Governors-Unprecedented-Trade-Disruption-Strategy-Yields-First-Fruit.

448 Jose Torres and Lizbeth Diaz, "Migrant Caravan in Mexico Heads for U.S. Border as Americas Summit Starts," Reuters, June 7, 2022, https://www.reuters.com/world/us/migrant-caravan-mexico-heads-us-border-americas-summit-starts-2022-06-06/; "Mexico Disbands Migrant Caravan That Set Out for U.S. during Americas Summit," Reuters, June 11, 2022, https://www.reuters.com/world/americas/mexico-disbands-migrant-caravan-that-set-out-us-during-americas-summit-2022-06-11/.

449 Todd Bensman, "Migrant Caravan Runs Face-First into Texas Governor Greg Abbott," Center for Immigration Studies, June 15, 2022, https://cis.org/Bensman/Migrant-Caravan-Runs-FaceFirst-Texas-Governor-Greg-Abbott.

450 Ibid.; René Arellano, "They Contain the Arrival of Migrants to Piedras Negras and Acuña," El Siglo de Torreón (Mexico), June 14, 2022, https://www.elsiglodetorreon.com.mx/noticia/2022/contienen-arribo-de-migrantes-a-piedras-negras-y-acuna.html; Sergio A. Rodríguez, "Migrants Pass Walking to Monclova," El Siglo de Torreón, June 14, 2022, https://www.elsiglodetorreon.com.mx/noticia/2022/pasan-migrantes-caminando-a-monclova.html.

451 Arellano, "They Contain the Arrival of Migrants to Piedras Negras and Acuña"; Rolando Chacon, "Topa en Coahuila la Caravan Migrante," Reforma (Mexico), June 12, 2022, https://www.reforma.com/aplicacioneslibre/preacceso/articulo/default.aspx?__rval=1&urlredirect=/topa-en-coahuila-la-caravana-migrante/ar2418949#cxrecs_s.

452 René Arellano, "Flight of Migrants Blocks the Way to the United States," El Siglo de Torreón, June 15, 2022, https://www.elsiglodetorreon.com.mx/noticia/2022/fuga-de-migrantes-cierra-paso-a-estados-unidos.html.

453 J. David Goodman, "Helicopters and High-Speed Chases: Inside Texas' Push to Arrest Migrants," New York Times, December 11, 2021, updated December 15, 2021, https://www.nytimes.com/2021/12/11/us/texas-migrant-arrests-police.html.

454 Ken Cuccinelli, "Policy Brief: How States Can Secure the Border," Center for Renewing America," October 26, 2021, https://americarenewing.com/issues/policy-brief-how-states-can-secure-the-border/.

455 Adam Shaw, "Arizona AG Brnovich Issues Legal Opinion Declaring Border Crisis 'Invasion' under Constitution," Fox News, February 7, 2022, https://www.foxnews.com/politics/arizona-ag-brnovich-legal-opinion-declaring-border-crisis-invasion-constitution; "2.7 Brnovich Opinion on Border Crisis," State of Arizona, Office of the Attorney General, No. 122-001 (R21-015), February 7, 2022, accessed at Scribd, https://www.scribd.com/document/557489409/2-7-Brnovich-Opinion-on-Border-Crisis.

456 "The Constitution of the United States: A Transcription," National Archives, America's Founding Documents, https://www.archives.gov/founding-docs/constitution-transcript.

457 Jonathan J. Cooper, "Arizona Lawmakers Urge Ducey to Use War Power at Border," Associated Press, January 12, 2022, https://apnews.com/article/immigration-joe-biden-phoenix-doug-ducey-constitutions-a8e57c51e7bc2bc1dabca98fe8dcb309.

458 Editorial Board, "Opinion: In a Close Race, Texas's Gov. Abbott Talks War—Against Migrants," Washington Post, July 15, 2022, https://www.washingtonpost.com/opinions/2022/07/15/greg-abbott-texas-reelection-immigration/.

459 Bethany Blankley, "Ninth Texas County Declares Invasion at the Southern Border," The Center Square," August 9, 2022, https://starlocalmedia.com/news/state/ninth-texas-county-declares-invasion-at-southern-border/article_6199f969-7bd9-5dd5-8fd6-84c64d0b94c6.html.

460 Bethany Blankley, "Conservatives Urge Paxton, Abbott to Declare Border Crisis an 'Invasion,'" The Center Square, May 2, 2022, https://www.thecentersquare.com/texas/conservatives-urge-paxton-abbott-to-declare-border-crisis-an-invasion/article_e45b1f48-c955-11ec-89be-2f0d6f713810.html.

461 "Official Policy Release Immigration and Border Security," Kari Lake for Governor website, accessed August 17, 2022, https://www.karilake.com/border.

462 Julia Mueller, "Abbott Lead over O'Rourke Steady in New Texas Poll," The Hill, August 14, 2022, https://thehill.com/homenews/statewatch/3601981-abbott-lead-over-orourke-steady-in-new-texas-poll/.

463 Jack Buckby, "Will Texas Governor Greg Abbott Run for President (And Anger Donald Trump)?" 19fortyfive.com, February 9, 2022, https://www.19fortyfive.com/2022/02/will-texas-governor-greg-abbott-run-for-president-and-anger-donald-trump/.

464 Hayden Sparks, "Though Skeptical, Abbott Mulls Calling Illegal Immigration 'Invasion' under U.S. Constitution," The Texan, April 22, 2022, https://thetexan.news/though-skeptical-abbott-mulls-calling-illegal-immigration-invasion-under-u-s-constitution/.

465 James Barragán and Patrick Svitek, "Gov. Greg Abbott Empowers State Authorities to Return Migrants to Border Crossings," *Texas Tribune*, July 7, 2022, https://www.texastribune.org/2022/07/07/texas-greg-abbott-state-police-border/.

466 "Texas Is Using Their 'Muscle' to Force Mexico to Clean Up Their Side of the Border: Todd Bensman," Fox News, *Tucker Carlson Tonight*, April 13, 2022, https://www.foxnews.com/media/texas-using-muscle-force-mexico-clean-up-side-border.

467 Andrew Schnitker, "Gov. Abbott, DPS Launch 'Operation Lone Star' to Address Security at the Border," Border Report, March 7, 2021, https://www.borderreport.com/immigration/border-crime/gov-abbott-launches-operation-lone-star-to-address-security-at-the-texas-border/.

468 Lomi Kriel and Perla Trevizo, "Reality Check: 7 Times Texas Leaders Misled the Public about Operation Lone Star," The Marshall Project and ProPublica, April 27, 2022, https://www.themarshallproject.org/2022/04/27/reality-check-seven-times-texas-leaders-misled-the-public-about-operation-lone-star?gclid=Cj0KCQjwkOqZBhDNARIsAACsbfLkIweFObS-cVkYPDWfFvnl4ot3f-2bDYfrqfwNrGbzX1nr4555v-SEaArUuEALw_wcB.

469 "Controversial Colony Ridge Development Doubles in Size," Reduce Flooding Now website, https://reduceflooding.com/2022/07/26/controversial-colony-ridge-development-doubles-in-size/?fbclid=IwAR0n-2j_7c6QEsHYHXg9RcAaE9PHRvljO5doDtm79bRaihhhtXk0Om9tf2_.

470 Kimberly Stauffer, "Boxing Legend Recalls Title Bout 50 Years Ago," *Houston Chronicle*, August 26, 2008, https://www.shsu.edu/dept/office-of-alumni-relations/clubs/military-science/msac-profiles/1956_Harris_Roy_Profile.pdf.

471 Terrenos Houston website, accessed August 20, 2022, https://terrenoshouston.com/en/home-english/.

472 Ibid.

473 Ken Oliver, "Illegal Immigration Mars Massive Texas Housing Development," Texas Public Policy Foundation (originally published in the *Houston Courant*, June 9, 2020), https://www.texaspolicy.com/illegal-immigration-mars-massive-texas-housing-development/.

474 "Back-to-School Statistics," National Center for Education Statistics, https://nces.ed.gov/fastfacts/display.asp?id=372#:~:text=Preliminary%20data%20for%20fall%202021,students%20(source%2C%20source).

475 Anna Flagg and Andrew Rodriguez Calderón, "500,000 Kids, 30 Million Hours: Trump's Vast Expansion of Child Detention," The Marshall Project, October 30, 2020, https://www.themarshallproject.org/2020/10/30/500-000-kids-30-million-hours-trump-s-vast-expansion-of-child-detention.

476 "Student Immigration Issues in Texas Public Schools," Texas Association of School Boards, December 2018 publication, https://www.tasb.org/services/legal-services/tasb-school-law-esource/students/documents/student_immigration_issues.aspx#:~:text=Since%201982%2C%20the%20United%20States,regardless%20of%20their%20immigration%20status.

477 "English Learners in Public Schools," National Center for Education Statistics, May 2022, https://nces.ed.gov/programs/coe/indicator/cgf/english-learners.

478 "Fitch Affirms Cleveland ISD, TX's ULT Bonds and IDR at 'AA-'; Outlook Stable," Fitch Ratings, July 2, 2022, https://www.fitchratings.com/research/us-public-finance/fitch-affirms-cleveland-isd-tx-ult-bonds-idr-at-aa-outlook-stable-07-07-2022.

479 Sarah Stillman, "The Migrant Workers Who Follow Climate Disasters," *New Yorker*, November 1, 2021, https://www.newyorker.com/magazine/2021/11/08/the-migrant-workers-who-follow-climate-disasters; Arelis R. Hernández and Aaron C. Davis, "'If They Deport All of Us, Who Will Rebuild?' Undocumented Workers Could Be Key to Texas Recovery," *Washington Post*, September 4, 2017, https://www.washingtonpost.com/national/if-they-deport-all-of-us-who-will-rebuild-day-laborers-seen-as-key-to-texas-recovery/2017/09/04/53a22acc-914d-11e7-89fa-bb822a46da5b_story.html; Ramon Taylor, "Despite Health Risks, Undocumented Immigrants Clean Up Houston," Voice of America, November 16, 2017, https://www.voanews.com/a/despite-health-risks-undocumented-immigrants-clean-up-houston/4119725.html.

480 "District Improvement Plan 2021–2022," Cleveland Independent School District, January 11, 2022, https://resources.finalsite.net/images/v1641917222/clevelandisdorg/pjko9hhjfvdup4zvppto/DistrictPlan13.pdf.

481 Reema Amin, "NYC to Expand Transfer High Schools to Help English Language Learners," Chalkbeat, May 11, 2022, https://ny.chalkbeat.org/2022/5/11/23067687/nyc-newcomer-immigrants-transfer-schools-expansion.

482 Samuel Stebbins, "Liberty County, Texas Has One of the Highest Foreclosure Rates in the Nation," 24/7 Wall St., https://247wallst.com/city/liberty-county-texas-has-one-of-the-highest-foreclosure-rates-in-the-nation/.

483 Kerry J. Byrne, "Border Crisis Hits Classrooms as Unaccompanied Minors Flood NY Schools," *New York Post*, October 30, 2021, https://nypost.com/2021/10/30/border-crisis-hits-classrooms-as-unaccompanied-minors-flood-ny-schoolsborder-crisis-hits-classrooms-as-unaccompanied-minors-flood-ny-schools/.

484 Natalie Haddad, "Austin ISD Confirms One Campus Is Overcrowded, Not All Students Are in Classrooms," KVUE ABC News, April 29, 2022,

https://www.kvue.com/article/news/education/austin-isd-campus-overcrowded/269-855e40b4-f0cd-4e96-90df-3758aa5659fe.

485 Cleveland Independent School District Facebook page, November 2, 2021, accessed August 22, 2022, https://m.facebook.com/story.php?story_fbid=4533252660103485&id=884093178352803.

486 "Bond Elections," CISD website, accessed August 23, 2022, https://www.clevelandisd.org/about-us/bond-elections.

487 "Cleveland High School," *Texas Tribune* Public Schools Explorer, https://schools.texastribune.org/districts/cleveland-isd/cleveland-high-school/.

488 Dorian Geiger, "Man Who Allegedly Killed Woman and Sexually Assaulted Another He'd Chained to a Bed Arrested by Border Patrol," Oxygen True Crime, November 25, 2020, https://www.oxygen.com/crime-news/jose-soriano-caught-on-mexican-border-after-allegedly-murdering-maid#:~:text=Man%20Who%20Allegedly%20Killed%20Woman,blackmail%20them%20using%20lewd%20photos.

489 Nicole Hensley, "Houston Woman Arrested for Murder in 2016 Cold Case," *Houston Chronicle*, September 18, 2018, updated September 20, 2018, https://www.chron.com/news/houston-texas/houston/article/Houston-woman-arrested-for-murder-in-2016-cold-13240265.php.

490 "Updated: Homicide Investigation Underway in Colony Ridge Community," *Bluebonnet News*, September 4, 2022, https://bluebonnet-news.com/2022/09/04/homicide-investigation-underway-in-colony-ridge-community/.

491 "Drug Cartel Linked to Multi-Million-Dollar Pot Bust in Liberty County," KHOU TV Houston, November 9, 2013, https://www.khou.com/article/news/drug-cartel-linked-to-multi-million-dollar-pot-bust-in-liberty-county/285-320664013#:~:text=News-,Drug%20cartel%20linked%20to%20multi%2Dmillion%2Ddollar%20pot%20bust%20in-,6%2C000%20fully%20mature%20pot%20plants.

492 Aaron Drawhorn, "DEA Fighting on the Frontlines: Biggest Drug Bust in Liberty County's History," KFDM 6, July 14, 2021, https://kfdm.com/news/local/dea-fighting-on-the-frontlines-biggest-drug-bust-in-liberty-countys-history.

493 "LCSO Deputies, Pct. 6 Constable's Office Arrest Suspects in Plum Grove Area for Alleged Gang Activity," *Bluebonnet News*, December 9, 2021, https://bluebonnetnews.com/2021/12/09/lcso-deputies-pct-6-constables-office-arrest-suspects-in-plum-grove-area-for-alleged-gang-activity/.

494 Michael T. Light, Jingying He, and Jason P. Robey, "Comparing Crime Rates between Undocumented Immigrants, Legal Immigrants, and Native-Born US Citizens in Texas," *Proceedings of the National Academy of Sciences of the United States of America* 117, no. 51 (December 7, 2020), https://www.pnas.org/doi/10.1073/pnas.2014704117.

495 Christopher Ingraham, "Two Charts Demolish the Notion That Immigrants Here Illegally Commit More Crime," *Washington Post*, June 19, 2018, https://www.washingtonpost.com/news/wonk/wp/2018/06/19/two-charts-demolish-the-notion-that-immigrants-here-illegally-commit-more-crime/.

496 Alex Nowrasteh, Andrew C. Forrester, and Michelangelo Landgrave, "Illegal Immigration and Crime in Texas," Cato Working Paper No. 60, Cato Institute, October 13, 2020, https://www.cato.org/sites/cato.org/files/2020-10/working-paper-60.pdf.

497 "Texas Criminal Illegal Alien Data," Texas DPS website, accessed August 26, 2022, https://www.dps.texas.gov/section/crime-records/texas-criminal-illegal-alien-data.

498 Elizabeth Zavala, "Undocumented Immigrant Sentenced to Life in Slaying, Burning of S.A. College Student," *San Antonio Express-News*, October 11, 2019, https://www.expressnews.com/news/local/article/Undocumented-immigrant-sentenced-to-life-in-14515185.php?fbclid=IwAR2bl8lmOMUbxhu6CxARY8qmuBHEvnUqm27cfHyf-2heq7IDrPOJENpijNMI#photo-18420516.

499 Todd Bensman, "Facts about How a Deportable Criminal Alien Was Left Free to Kill Are Excluded from Murder Trial," Center for Immigration Studies, October 15, 2019, https://cis.org/Bensman/Facts-About-How-Deportable-Criminal-Alien-Was-Left-Free-Kill-Are-Excluded-Murder-Trial.

500 "Girl Was Held Captive by Illegal Immigrant in Alabama with Dismembered Remains of Her Mother, Brother, Police Say," Alabama Now, August 4, 2022, https://www.alabamanow.com/2022/08/04/girl-was-held-captive-by-illegal-immigrant-in-alabama-home-with-her-mother-brothers-dismembered-remains-police-say-1/.

501 "Horrific Details Revealed about Victims After Abducted Girl's Dramatic Escape Leads to Discovery of 2 Bodies," CBS News, August 4, 2022, https://www.cbsnews.com/news/alabama-abducted-girl-chews-through-restraints-escape-victims-dientified-jose-paulino-pascual-reyes-charged/.

502 Adam Poulisse, "'A Monster': Man Arrested in Connection with Deadly Stabbing of Daytona Beach Couple," WFTV 9, March 10, 2022, https://www.wftv.com/news/local/chief-man-arrested-connection-with-fatal-stabbing-daytona-beach-couple/ZP273NI2U5G7NDJS3VK-VD25AFQ/.

503 Chris Elliot, "Is the Media Burying the Truth? ICE Confirms Accused Texas Cop Killer Is an Illegal Immigrant," Law Enforcement Today, January 29, 2022, https://www.lawenforcementtoday.com/ice-confirms-accused-texas-cop-killer-is-an-illegal-immigrant/.

504   Mark Krikorian, "Time to Withdraw from the U.N. Refugee Treaty,"
       National Review Online, July 28, 2021, https://www.nationalreview.
       com/2021/07/time-to-withdraw-from-the-u-n-refugee-treaty/.

505   *Homeland Security Advisory Council CBP Families and Children Care
       Panel Final Report*, U.S. Department of Homeland Security, November
       14, 2019, https://www.dhs.gov/sites/default/files/publications/fccp_fi-
       nal_report_1.pdf.

ACKNOWLEDGMENTS

The writing of a nonfiction, journalistic book requires a bifurcated effort. There is the field reporting, interviewing, and research. Then comes production and writing. I could not have accomplished either half of the whole without my wife's high tolerances for so much of my absence from a working household. She has my recognition and enduring gratitude for keeping it all going.

I direct a goodly share of appreciation to Mark Krikorian, executive director for the Center for Immigration Studies (CIS), for clearing well-supported decks, flashing only the green light, and dishing encyclopedic immigration knowledge on a speed-dial basis. At the top of the list of speed-dial-able experts who deserve a public thank-you for the reporting and research part of this affair is CIS fellow Andrew R. Arthur, who picked up no matter that he was always in the "middle of something" and gave me access to the valuable library in his head.

A special thank-you for the "intel" and cartel fact checks goes to my former captain at Texas Department of Public Safety intelligence division, Jaeson Jones, who still spends much time down in the brush. It is also good for all of humanity that retired Captain Jones wages maximum fight against Mexico's drug cartels.

For high-value research assistance, Adam Morys deserves gratitude for doing everything so well.

Thank you also Ally Thai, who did too.

I incurred a debt of gratitude for Michael Taylor, one of the very best editors and friends out there, for volunteering that precious skill.

Thanks to Alex Conway for bulletproofing citations.

Texas DPS Lieutenant Brian Nichols earns my appreciation for the field work assistance that one week on his own time.

For their street savvy, reportorial prowess, and fellowship with me out there in the wilds, further thanks go to international correspondents Michael Yon and Chuck Holton, as well as the fearless Auden Cabello of Acuña.

I could not have done a lot without Tony and Cathy Castaneda of Quemado.

Finally, I bow to the selfless dedication of all who serve the U.S. Customs and Border Patrol, especially those mounted agents, ICE, HSI, Texas DPS, and the National Guard. Believe me when I say that far more are with you than not.

Todd Bensman currently serves as the Texas-based Senior National Security Fellow for the Center for Immigration Studies (CIS), a Washington, D.C. policy institute for which he writes, speaks, and grants media interviews about the nexus between immigration and national security. For nearly a decade prior to joining CIS in August 2018, Bensman led counterterrorism intelligence for the Texas Department of Public Safety's Intelligence and Counterterrorism Division and its multi-agency fusion center. Before his homeland security service, Bensman was a journalist for twenty-three years, covering national security after 9/11 as a staff writer for major newspapers. He earned accolades—such as two National Press Club awards—for his border reporting. Bensman holds an MA in security studies from the Naval Post-graduate School, Center for Homeland Defense and Security (2015, Outstanding Thesis designee). He also holds an MA in journalism from the University of Missouri School of Jour-nalism (2009) and an undergraduate degree in journalism with honors from Northern Arizona University.

Made in the USA
Columbia, SC
20 October 2024